Between Woman and Nation

BETWEEN WOMAN AND NATION

Nationalisms, Transnational Feminisms, and the State

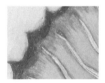

Edited by Caren Kaplan,
Norma Alarcón, and Minoo Moallem

Duke University Press   Durham and London, 1999

© 1999 Duke University Press
All rights reserved
Printed in the United States of America on acid-free paper ∞
Designed by Rebecca Filene
Typeset in Trump Mediaeval by Tseng Information Systems, Inc.
Library of Congress Cataloging-in-Publication Data
appear on the last printed page of this book.

Contents

Acknowledgments   vii

Norma Alarcón, Caren Kaplan, and Minoo Moallem
Introduction: Between Woman and Nation   1

I. Whose Imagined Community?

Laura Elisa Pérez
El desorden, Nationalism, and Chicana/o Aesthetics   19

Elspeth Probyn
Bloody Metaphors and Other Allegories of the Ordinary   47

Norma Alarcón
Chicana Feminism: In the Tracks of "The" Native Woman   63

Rosa Linda Fregoso
Re-Imagining Chicana Urban Identities in the Public Sphere,
Cool Chuca Style   72

Mary N. Layoun
A Guest at the Wedding: Honor, Memory, and (National) Desire
in Michel Khleife's *Wedding in Galilee*   92

II. The Production of Nationness: Reading Regulatory Practices

Saidiya Hartman
Seduction and the Ruses of Power   111

Danielle Juteau
From Nation-Church to Nation-State: Evolving Sex-Gender
Relations in Québec Society   142

Suad Joseph
Women Between Nation and State in Lebanon   162

Daiva K. Stasiulis
Relational Positionalities of Nationalisms, Racisms, and
Feminisms   182

Emma Pérez
Feminism-in-Nationalism: The Gendered Subaltern at the Yucatán
Feminist Congresses of 1916   219

**III. Transnational Subjects of Feminism: Critical Interventions
in an Era of Globalization**

Minoo Moallem and Iain A. Boal
Multicultural Nationalism and the Poetics of Inauguration   243

Angie Chabram-Dernersesian
"Chicana! Rican? No, Chicana Riqueña!" Refashioning the
Transnational Connection   264

Dorinne Kondo
Fabricating Masculinity: Gender, Race, and Nation in a
Transnational Frame   296

Minoo Moallem
Transnationalism, Feminism, and Fundamentalism   320

Caren Kaplan and Inderpal Grewal
Transnational Feminist Cultural Studies: Beyond the Marxism/
Poststructuralism/Feminism Divides   349

Works Cited   365

Index   397

Contributors   405

Acknowledgments

This volume was inspired by a conference held at the University of California at Berkeley in the spring of 1993 sponsored by the Beatrice Bain Research Group, The Townsend Center for the Humanities, and the Department of Women's Studies. The stimulating debates and discussions across social sciences and humanities fields prompted us to pursue additional pieces to complement the original presentations. We would like to thank all of the contributors for their hard work, patience, and good humor. During the production of this manuscript across the years, the editors were greatly supported by the administrative assistants at the Beatrice Bain Research Group at the University of California, Berkeley: Eli Coppola, Agy Lejman, Phoebe Southwood, and Gee Gee Lang. For their dedicated efforts in the final stages of manuscript preparation, we extend appreciative thanks to Gee Gee and Phoebe in particular. At Duke University Press, the editors wish to thank Ken Wissoker for his enthusiastic support and excellent guidance. Also at Duke, we would like to thank Katie Courtland and Kay Robin Alexander, as well as all the people involved in production. Three anonymous reviewers gave us rigorous readings and we have appreciated their suggestions. Many thanks to Kris Peterson for help with the index.

Many thanks as well to our *compañeros* and *compañeras*, especially Eric Smoodin, who pitched in with typing and proofreading. In the process of compiling and editing this book, we have come to enjoy each other's intellectual companionship as well as culinary arts. There is something comforting about discussing work over pistachio nuts, *ash reshteh*, salsa, pomegranates, hummus, onion-dill bread, olives, and other delights, such is the material grounding of our feminist practice and theory!

We thank the publishers for permission to republish the following essays, which appeared previously as follows: Elspeth Probyn, "Bloody Metaphors and Other Allegories of the Ordinary," *Continuum: The*

Australian Journal of Media and Culture 11, no. 2 (1997): 113–25; Norma Alarcón, "Chicana Feminism: In the Tracks of 'The' Native Woman," *Cultural Studies* 4, no. 3 (October 1990): 248–56; Saidiya Hartman, "Seduction and the Ruses of Power," in *Scenes of Subjection: Terror, Slavery, and Self-Making in 19th-Century America,* © 1997, reprinted by permission of Oxford University Press; Emma Pérez, "Feminism-in-Nationalism: Third Space Feminism at the Yucatan Feminist Congresses of 1916," in *The Decolonial Imaginary: Writing Chicanas into History,* © 1999, reprinted by permission of Indiana University Press; Angie Chabram-Dernersesian, "'Chicana! Rican? No, Chicana-Riqueña!' Refashioning the Transnational Connection," in *Multiculturalism: A Critical Reader,* ed. David Theo Goldberg, © 1994 by Basil Blackwell Press, reprinted by permission of Basil Blackwell Press; Dorinne Kondo, "Fabricating Masculinity: Gender, Race and Nation in a Transnational Frame," in *About Face: Performing Race in Fashion and Theatre,* © 1997, reprinted by permission of Routledge; Caren Kaplan and Inderpal Grewal, "Transnational Feminist Cultural Studies: Beyond the Marxism/Poststructuralism/Feminism Divides," *positions: east asia cultures critique* 2, no. 2 (fall 1994): 430–45. The following artwork is reprinted by permission of the artists: *Libertad,* © 1976, *La Virgen de Guadalupe Defendiendolos Derechos de los Xicanos,* © 1975, *La Ofrenda/The Offering I,* © 1990, by Ester Hernandez; *Portrait of the Artist as the Virgin of Guadalupe, Margaret F. Stewart: Our Lady of Guadalupe, Victoria F. Franco: Our Lady of Guadalupe,* by Yolanda M. Lopez.

Introduction: Between Woman and Nation

Norma Alarcón, Caren Kaplan, and Minoo Moallem

It is a commonplace of our time to note that nation-state formations are influenced, underpinned, and even founded by ideas rooted in the Enlightenment and liberalism of the West. These twin pillars of political philosophy, together with or in opposition to Marxism and capital, generate what we in the West have become accustomed to name "modernity." Thus, while the socioeconomic processes of modernization are "uneven," ragged, and brutal across their globalization, the practices that fuel the making of new "civilizations," even "postcolonial" ones, starting with the Americas at the end of the eighteenth century and the beginning of the nineteenth, are imbricated in notions of "The Rights of Man" and "Rights of the Citizen" in "the modern dialectic of equality and freedom" (Balibar 1994, 39). From its very inception, then, as excentric subjects, women have had a problematic relationship to the modern nation-state and its construction of subjectivity.

As the central site of "hegemonic masculinity" (Connell 1987), or what Luce Irigaray calls "hom(m)o-sexuality" as social mediation, the nation-state sharpens the defining lines of citizenship for women, racialized ethnicities, and sexualities in the construction of a socially stratified society (Irigaray 1985, 171). Etienne Balibar has argued that the fissures in the "modern political community" emerge from the "practical and ideological *sexism* [sic] as a structure of interior exclusion of women generalized to the whole society" (1994, 57). If we add race to Balibar's analysis, we can view the modern political community as the "unstable equilibrium of the denial and universalization" of sexual (and racial) difference (Balibar 1994, 58; Anthias and Yuvall-Davis 1992; Omi and Winant 1994). Though, in their historical effects, these distinctions are not necessarily equivalent, "the affirmation of (these) difference(s) as a political force becomes the most sensitive point of the crisis of the community (or of the communal identity crisis)" (Balibar 1994, 58). Moreover, at the core of the modern nation-state, a contradiction is set in motion insofar as there is denial of sexual or racial difference or both, and simultaneous universalization of difference. An *aporia*, a spatial-temporal indeterminacy where *différance* as "interminable experience" comes into being, is not a "dialectizable contradiction in the Hegelian or Marxist sense" and is constitutive of a double bind that cannot be overcome except through an epistemological metanarrative, which in turn denies the marginalization of difference qua difference and the suffering that construction entails (Derrida 1993, 16). The leap to the metanarrative erases the nondialectical character of the double binds generated through aporias and reinstalls universalized identity (Adorno 1973; Bateson 1972; Fanon 1967a).

This deeply contradictory position, virtually foundational of the modern nation-state, underpins institutional, political, and cultural practices for the "good of the people." This basic contradiction and paradox, so caught up with notions of equality and liberty, property, and individual self-possession, has become the complex crucial crisis of the "modern political community" today. Sometimes referred to as "postmodernity," this crisis is characterized by critiques of modernity's gendered and raced failures and excesses (Grewal and Kaplan 1994; Huyssen 1986). Wahneema Lubiano describes certain aspects of this "crisis" as the "spectacle of men out of control," arguing that those in dominant positions articulate their sense of destabilization and disequilibrium as they begin to experience gendered and racial constraints themselves (1991, 152). Alice Jardine has termed this crisis "loss of legitimation, loss of authority, loss of seduction, loss of genius—*loss*" (1985, 68). Yet this destabilization and legitimation crisis, so prevalent since the late 1960s and early 1970s according to both Fredric Jameson and David Harvey, is unevenly experienced and very much contained within the contradictory logic of modernity (Habermas 1973; Jameson 1991; Harvey 1989; Massey 1994). Thus, we cannot speak of postmodernity succeeding modernity, but rather we have to analyze their entwinement or, if you will, their disunified totality and aporetic quality, in which, as Balibar puts it, we must deal simultaneously with the state, class struggles, and "anthropological difference" (Balibar 1994, 59).

The Nation-State and the Rhetoric of Borders

It is this second contradictory and paradoxical character of both totality and disunification in modernity that must be accounted for in any analysis of globalization with its concomitant production and heterogeneous localities and transnational affiliations and corporate practices, and which is closely tied to the simultaneous denial *and* universalization of difference. If the latter is constitutive of the modern nation-state, the former obscures this in its claim to political and analytical urgency in the face of socioeconomic crisis for "the people." Thus, the marxist call to "totalize" in opposition to "globalization" ignores the implications for many subjects vis-à-vis the (dis)array of localities and differences that have been produced through the material effects of discursive practices *and* the discursive effects of material practices.

For example, Arif Dirlik's critique of postcolonial intellectuals and their impressive production of a theoretical and critical discourse takes a "kill the messenger" approach. Basing his critique primarily on one essay by Gyan Prakash, Dirlik is distressed at the displacement of such terms as margin and periphery, structure and totality, and what he thinks is the repudiation of capitalism as a foundational category in critical theory. Though he is aware that "borders and boundaries have been confounded" and concedes that "the globe has become jumbled up spatially as the ideology of progress has temporally" (1994, 352), as well as the fact that the critical discourse of postcoloniality "addresses [these situations] of crisis that elude understanding in terms of older conceptualizations" (353), he still prefers to blame the "postcolonial intelligentsia" for obfuscating our contemporary world. In this way, allying himself implicitly with Aijaz Ahmad's (1992) critique of deviations from marxist methodologies pure and simple, he scapegoats this imaginary group for not "formulating practices of resistance" (Dirlik 1994, 356). Yet Dirlik himself is at a loss to provide such a critical practice precisely because he depends on the older conceptualizations that took as their point of departure the nation-state whose deployment of capital had a recognizable national structure that was clearly articulated within colonized areas. The breakup of the colonial world, like the breakup of the Soviet Union, proliferated the creation of new nation-states. Recently, the creation of these new states coincides with a moment when global capital has adhered less and less to national ties even as it has depended increasingly on the proletarianization of female labor (Spivak 1996; Morley and Robins 1995; Harvey 1996; Ong 1987; Bonacich 1994; Zavella 1984; Morokvasic 1983).

That a "postcolonial intelligentsia" can so brilliantly diagnose, without, as Dirlik claims, eschewing history or the functions of capital, the condition of our contemporary world is to be commended rather than berated. However, Dirlik has trouble interfacing or articulating postcolonial theoretical discourse to the "emergence of global capitalism" (1994, 352) or the creation of new consumer and citizen subjects. For if one can posit that, historically, the postcolonial is an aftermath of colonialism in its older, modern capitalist guise and in a sense sets up the new conditions for capital's innovative maneuvers in conjunction with new technologies, one can't agree to "kill the messengers" (Shohat 1992; McClintock 1992; Frankenberg and Mani 1993). Dirlik's failure to articulate what he can perceive as new formations of capitalism in relation to postcolonial theoretical and critical discourse is symptomatic of the intellectual crisis in the academy itself, wherein intellectuals turn on each other over the failure to formulate vanguard practices of resistance. Such practices might be better formulated by neozapatistas in Chiapas, Mexico, and by other intellectuals and activists around the globe. This is not to foreclose radical intellectual practices but to argue for closer attention to local institutional politics in our academies and associations as well as to transnational conditions of knowledge production and consumption.

The divide between theory and practice, speculation and fact, and abstraction and substance has a peculiar history in modernity that clearly resonates throughout discourses of vanguard criticism, especially in its masculine variants that querulously deplore the loss of more structuralist typologies (Miyoshi 1993; Harvey 1989). Yet, that divide has to be continuously destabilized and made historically specific. Viewing the world as constituted only through margins and centers, for example, as Wallerstein and others would have us understand the processes of advanced capitalism, leaves us within the discursive cosmos of colonial power relations, helpless to recognize the complex and nuanced manifestations of transnational circulations of peoples, goods, and information in the present moment (Wallerstein 1974, 1980, 1988; Balibar 1991). Thus, the nostalgic longing for substance and presence through nationalist activism over and against such academic practices as "postcolonial criticism" or "cultural studies" misrecognizes the social relations of academic life globally. It is not that there is a better vanguard politics that academics can "practice" through adherence to socialist, nationalist methods of political economy. Rather, our tasks as critics must revolve around a constant critique of the construction of all methods and disciplines as ideological constructions within the context of the relationship between transnational capitalism, corporate cultures, and the state (Rouse 1995).

If in the U.S. academy the rhetoric of margins and centers was an initial phase of the postcolonial theory of modernity, the effects of globalization, of NAFTA and GATT, for example, have produced the rhetoric of borders and hybridities. For in an era of "global reach," the totalization of capital still gives us boundaries. Yet the idea of the nation-state as a totalizable possibility is disrupted by political resistance as well as transgressive and incoherent acts within capitalism. While the nation-state continues to have value as the administrative and ideological unit through which nationalist discourses seek to impose what Frederick Buell calls the "Janus-faced" nature of the state, that inner/outer dichotomy that R. Radhakrishnan puts forth as a crucial aspect of the narrative of identity in the modern nation works against that valuation and against hegemony (Buell 1994; Radhakrishnan 1992). The concept of inner/outer constructs an edge, or a border, that helps us apprehend the double movements of the nation-state, its plural logic of doubleness and aporias (Derrida 1993; Trinh 1989). This doubleness serves to speak simultaneously in the name of the people "inside" and those who are outside. In attempting to consolidate its nationalist power for the well-being of the people, the nation-state often overlooks the effects its decisions and consequent events may have on diverse populations whose difference, often marked through concepts such as sexuality, gender, race, ethnicity, and class, may situate them adversely to a "center."

Consequently, the notion of borders refers to two heterogeneous boundaries and not to a single "line." As Derrida argues, one type of border "passes among *contents* [sic] (things, objects, referents: territories, countries, states, nations, cultures, languages, etc.). The other type of borderly limit would pass between a *concept* and an other, according to the bar of an oppositional logic" (1993, 17–18). At stake is the "double concept of the border" (18) as contents and concepts that generate contradictions and aporias as "interminable experiences." Thus the "impossible unity" of the nation as a symbolic force that Bhabha argues is always transitional, hybrid, and inalterably social (1990a, 1). Doubleness or multiplicity? The emergence of these theories of the boundaries of identity and community signal the discontinuous particularity of these zones (Anzaldúa 1987; Arteaga 1994). As borders become "confused" (Bhabha 1994, 9) the subject that would be contained has to be perceived as an interstitial deconstruction, whether through doubling or through scattered hybridity. Theorizing the deconstruction of center and periphery promotes the articulation of "impossible" unities, subjects, and practices, including the possibility of gendered subjectivities. As Elspeth Probyn argues in her essay in this collection, the retrospective activity of nation-building in modernity is always predicated upon Woman as trope, displacing historical women, consolidating hybridity into totality, and erasing the doubled border into a single sign.

Thus, in the universal crisis of the modern political community, the moment we would term postmodernity, the woman/feminine signifier continues to serve as an alibi or figure of resistance in the fraternal struggles for control of the nation-state and the national project (Masiello 1992, 22; McClintock 1992; Alarcón 1989). It becomes necessary to "read" the signifiers' maneuverability in their historical and contingent deployment, for the national project appears interminable. Thus, we have the neverending experience of nation making, through which the vulnerability of certain citizens, some of whom are often in question, can be mapped. Often these subjects stand on the edge of contradictory boundaries—equality and liberty, property and individual self-possession, and citizenship itself—that the modern nation-state cannot resolve. In this sense of the process of nation making, we can agree with Benedict Anderson's (1983) notion of the "imagined community" as an unstable fiction whose desire must be continually posed and questioned. It is the utopia and dystopia of the nation-state and the people.

Whose Imagined Community? Inventing Nation, Consuming Modernity

"Between woman and nation" refers to a particular situated space of the performative and performativity where women and nation intersect in specific ways, giving rise to the interval of *différance*. Following Derrida, "this interval is what might be called *spacing*, the becoming-space of time or the becoming-time of space (temporization)" (1982, 13). It is a "constitution of the present" through the analysis of (non)representation of that *différance* in the production of the critical and social text situated in that interval (13). Bhabha theorizes, through Derrida, this "interval" as a spatiotemporal performative that interrupts the "pedagogy" of the nation-state, in a sense, implicitly agreeing with Butler's position that "performance presumes a subject" (Butler 1990, 33). For Bhabha, the performing subject is key to a political imaginary that displaces the "pedagogy of the nation," that is, its efforts to produce citizen-subjects who mirror its political desire. Butler sees performativity as "that aspect of discourse that has the capacity to produce what it names through repetition and recitation" inasmuch as the notion may be aligned to a degree with Bhabha's notion of pedagogy (although the latter is more appropriate to the nation-state's probable intentions—to produce subjects it can subject) (Butler 1993, 33; Lowe 1996).

Bhabha argues that the counternarratives of the nation evoke and disturb those ideological maneuvers through which "imagined communities" are given essentialist identities. We propose that it is through racialization, sexualization, and genderization that the nation is able to transcend modernities and to become a timeless and homogenized entity. In this sense, woman as a monolithic category—represented either in the particularistic discourses of nationalism or in the universalizing discourse of "global feminism"—is problematized and put in crisis not only because of their inability to bring into view the instability of a national or an international order that transcends itself to the level of "essence," but also because they guarantee agency to some while at the same time turning others into a spectacle (Moallem, this volume). In her essay in this volume, Norma Alarcón examines the centrality of the figure of the "native woman" in the work of Chicana scholars across a wide spectrum of disciplines to investigate the implication of the name "Chicana" on the one hand, and its validity to cultural nationalist movements on the other. Within the context of new transnational economies, Alarcón queries the construction of identities and subjects as contested sites of feminist and nationalist signifying practices.

Thus, Partha Chatterjee's important question—"Whose imagined community?"—reminds us that some nations and cultures are situated as "consumers of modernity," choosing certain " 'modular' forms already made available to them by Europe and the Americas" (1993, 5). As a product of Europe and the Americas, nationalisms are always already implicated in modernity. Yet, as Chatterjee points out, Anderson's account of such hegemonic formations does not allow for the evidence of local "difference" as the "modular" forms of national society are interpellated by specific sites and social relations (5). Constitutive of those sites of "difference," both in metropolitan "centers" as well as in the so-called peripheries, are raced and gendered relations. As Laura Elisa Pérez argues in her essay in this collection, through artistic imagination Chicana feminists destabilize "nations" of ordered unities into disordered borders. From this vantage point, it becomes clearer that the rhetoric of margins and centers is complicitous in the production of inner and outer boundaries in a complex web of multiple logics of power that may be better tracked through the rhetoric of the "double concept of the border." It appears, at this juncture, that the margin/center opposition serves only too well the hegemonization of masculinities.

Anderson's imagined community is indeed a continuous or, as we remarked earlier, an interminable project of production and reproduction within the bureaucratized spaces of modern nation-states where the intersection of power and knowledge becomes the very condition of belonging. Unlike Chatterjee, however, we share Homi Bhabha's concern around temporality of nationness as a form of textual, cultural, and social affiliation, "the complex strategies of cultural identification and discursive address that function in the name of 'the people' or 'the nation' and make them the immanent subjects of a range of social and literary narratives" (1994, 140). Thus, we discover that the space of the modern nation-state is crosscut by a "temporality of representation that moves between cultural formations and social processes without a centered causal logic" (141). As Masiello argues, the crosscutting of space and temporality in the interminable nationalist project leads to the observation that the nation-state manipulates the logic of margin/center to its advantage (1992, 3). Thus, to speak from the margin is to be already complicit with the discourse of the nation-state, which, moreover, appears to be unavoidable in contemporary political life.

Judith Butler, for example, has noted that Foucault, in *The History of Sexuality,* "points out that juridical systems of power *produce* the subjects they subsequently come to represent. [As such] the feminist subject turns out to be discursively constituted by the very political system that is supposed to facilitate its emancipation" (1990, 2). Thus, the subject of sexual difference is also constitutive of a strong complicity with discourses of power. Yet, as Spivak notes, " 'politics as such' [are] the prohibition of marginality implicit in the production of any explanation" (1987, 113). She argues that the choice and deployment "of particular binary oppositions" are "the condition of possibility for centralization"

(113). Such centralizing, on the one hand, in its theorization generates a politics that prohibits the marginalized from engagement, and on the other, produces the conditions of their existence through discourse and practice. In her elaboration of this passage in Spivak's work, Butler comments that Spivak "locates politics in the production of knowledge that creates and censors the margins that constitute, through exclusion, the contingent intelligibility of that subject's given knowledge-regime" (1990, 153). Consequently, a double bind is constructed a priori for the marginalized, which prompts us to question the sufficient explanatory capacity of the theoretical rhetoric of margins, even though it is constitutive of the "subject on the margins" who unwittingly succumbs to an oppositional logic and whose initial contestation is often necessarily complicit with the discourse of systems of power in the nation-state.

In both aspects, international and national, that logic must be displaced by the more complex rhetoric of the double concept of borders insofar as the former keeps woman/women sequestered "inside" the nation in the face of transnational movements or turns them into "boundary subjects" (Kristeva 1993, 35; Anzaldúa 1987). Yet, as Mary Layoun argues in her essay in this collection, while national desire is erected in the absence and longing for possession and control of Woman (in the case of Palestine, linked to "land–as–national fulfillment"), certain representational practices challenge the putative naturalness of discourses of nation that require such territorialization. Today, in the face of the construction of an "outer" zone or space whose artificiality is left unquestioned, those movements are even more acutely uneven than at the variable "inception" of modernity. Moreover, the nation-state's Janus-faced movements belie the nonporosity implied by the structural concepts of margin/center or inner/outer. In her essay in this collection, Rosa Linda Fregoso rereads the discourses of passivity and domesticity to argue that for some emerging subjects (the pachuca, for example), the line between public and private is always already disturbed, thereby constituting family solidarity and female sexuality in the spaces of both "street" and "home." Tracking the changes in the status of boundaries reflects the trajectories of spatiotemporal change.

Thus, while we agree with Bhabha about the ambivalence of the "nation" as a narrative strategy, we question the continuous repetition of gender and sexuality and their symbolic power both in the historicity and temporality of the nation, as well as in the repetition of raced ethnicities as powerful signifiers whose counternarratives and counterperformances disrupt the nation's tendency to totalize its pedagogy for the people. As Kum-Kum Sangari, Sudesh Vaid, Gayatri Spivak, Ella Shohat, Rey Chow, Norma Alarcón, and Anne McClintock, among others, have argued, the "essential woman" (raced or not) becomes the national iconic signifier for the material, the passive, and the corporeal, to be worshipped, protected, and controlled by those with the power to remember and to forget, to guard, to define, and redefine (Sangari and Vaid 1990; Spivak 1987; Shohat 1991; Chow 1993a, 1991; Alarcón 1989; McClintock 1995).

The Production of Nationness: Reading Regulatory Practices

"Nationness" in the context of modernity is based on a normativity achieved through the consolidation of the nation-state. The regulatory processes of the nation-state are located at various institutional sites and are practiced in multiple ways, including a double process of subordination and contestation. For example, both consent and coercion are intrinsic to the practices of a racialized and gendered citizenry. The institutionalization of national body politics involves the (hetero)-sexualization of women via their vulnerability to sexual assault and criminalization in Western masculinist legal practices. In her essay in this volume, Saidiya Hartman argues that for African American slave women the official repression or "effacement" of rape depended on blurred boundaries between consent and coercion, situating slave women as both powerless objects of property and powerful agents of resistance against domination through the actual fear or threat of violent retribution. Drawing on the case of a slave woman who murdered her master after his repeated sexual assaults, Hartman points to the legal construction of a discourse of seduction that posited *both* "perfect submission" and "alluring agency." Here state power within a local patriarchal practice of white supremacy invalidates slave marriages, negates kinship, and disavows rape in the service of the construction of black "criminality," yet the same practices indicate consistent and concerted resistance to such patriarchal and white supremacist domination.

   The regulatory practices of the nation-state, founded upon a timeless notion of the people and the compulsory state, are by no means static and fixed. Rather, they change over time to sanction access to the nation-state's resources. For example, specific versions of sex-gender systems are essential in the distribution, redistribution, and regulation of property rights and cultural resources. In her essay in this volume, Danielle Juteau maps the transformation of church-dominated Québec into a state-dominated system within the context of shifts in the condition of women. Under the domination of the church, women in Québec were discursively situated as mothers or nuns, signaling a collective appropriation of labor power as both reproductive and productive. In the last third of the twentieth century, a secular transformation has displaced nuns from their high administrative positions in health, education, and social services, leading to greater "freedom" yet instigating a certain crisis in the caretaking and emotional work of the nation. Thus, sex-gender systems, or *sexage,* create historically specific practices of appropriation, private and public, that constitute specific practices of femininity (Guillaumin 1978b).

National and political citizenships are also sites of contradictory regulatory practices. "Nation" and "state" can be contested through women's local networks and feminist interventions with and between dominant male discourses. The normalized spaces of "woman," "nation," and "state" are often based on the suppression or neglect of specific histories of women's struggles, especially under colonial regimes, by masculinist nationalist narratives and accounts (Enloe 1989; Hélie-Lucas 1987). In her essay in this collection, Emma Pérez explores the historical instance of Yucatecan feminism as a kind of mimicry of nationalist hegemonic discourse. Drawing on Bhabha's well-known argument, Pérez traces this form of feminist rhetoric of repetition and doubling that comes to constitute a crucial "difference," at least in retrospect. However, as she notes, it is difference that is subsumed (*sous rature*) in order to facilitate the universalization that repetition and doubling make possible.

As Christine Delphy (1984) has observed, the feminist doubling of nationalism as ideal model or rival position is productive of contradictions. In her contribution to this volume, Daiva Stasiulis examines the contradictory positioning of feminism vis-à-vis nationalist discursive and political practices in contemporary Canada. Stasiulis problematizes the notion of "three nations" that include Anglophone and Francophone Québec and the First Nations in order to question the existing power relations between groups with conflicting nationalist claims (settler vs. native). Within this context of a hegemonic nation with contesting minorities, Stasiulis notes that feminist organizations such as the National Action Committee on the Status of Women are compelled increasingly to consider women's attachments to ethnic communities, and any effort toward "inclusion" in a feminist polity expresses a pluralistic model of multiple nations within a state, submerging and suppressing contending nationalisms.

Modern nation-states participate in the institutionalization of women's subordination by means of regulatory processes, the discursive formations that construct and discipline citizen-subjects. Yet, the quotidian practices that regulate women, nation, and state can be subverted by local community networks and relations out of which emerge a civil arena to counter masculinist nationalist agendas. Drawing on several decades of research in working-class neighborhoods in Beirut, Suad Joseph discusses the many ways in which local conditions can structure citizenship, especially for women. Although the sectarian state in Lebanon is organized around religious fragmentation that consolidates patriarchal tendencies, women can be seen to maneuver creatively to cross boundaries and position themselves as members of diverse rather than singular communities. Joseph argues that in resituating themselves across religious divisions as they are played out in neighborhood borders and zones, many women in Lebanon are creating a civil arena of counterpractices to the nationalist dictates of a postindependence masculinist elite. Thus, it is in practicing citizenship that women create social spaces for contestation and resistance.

Transnational Subjects of Feminism:
Critical Interventions in an Era of Globalization

Women are both of and not of the nation. Between woman and nation is, perhaps, the space or zone where we can deconstruct these monoliths and render them more historically nuanced and accountable to politics. The figure of "woman" participates in the imaginary of the nation-state beyond the purview of patriarchies. For example, modernity has produced numerous feminist practices that support and bolster the international as well as the national. The discourses of "international" or "global" feminism rely on political and economic as well as cultural concepts of discrete nations who can be placed into comparative or relational status, always maintaining the West as the center. Chandra Mohanty (1987) has critiqued the liberal underpinnings of such a "global feminism" and the cult of transparent "experience" as part of the project of the nation in the aftermath of European imperialism.

Thus, although a supposedly "international" movement—as an "international" movement—it relies on and reinforces the discrete nature of the nation, reifying and mystifying the historical phenomenon of the modern state. "Global feminism" makes nations look "natural," mystifying the humanism inherent to representations of world alliances among sovereign nations (Berlant 1991). The related notion of "global sisterhood" constructs an essentialized category of woman through the invention and reinvention of a globalized woman's body, leaving the nation undisturbed. Refusing "global feminism" requires questioning the dominance of the nation-state's mythic narrativization or representation of itself. Only then can we begin to grasp, as Inderpal Grewal has argued, that universalizing feminist discourses that have structured themselves only in relation to men can be understood to be structured through relations among women of other classes, races, and nationalities (1996, 11). Critically reading the spaces between woman and nation as not only structured by patriarchy, we can begin to grasp the supra- and transnational aspects of cultures of identity, what Mohanty has referred to as "imagined communities of women" with "divergent histories and social locations, woven together by the *political* threads of opposition to forms of domination that are not only pervasive but also systemic" (1991, 4).

The essays in *Between Woman and Nation* critique the naturalization and essentialization of nation and woman in modernity. For example, the discursive processes of racing, gendering, and sexualizing the nation, through both narratives of romance that eroticize what Lauren Berlant calls the "maternal-beloved feminine imagery" and its "bloody metaphors," find their expression in the rape of the landscape, a usurped beloved, an aborted fetus, and so on (Berlant 1991; Probyn this volume). These discursive formations normalize authorities that render ordinary, natural, and even compulsory the relationship between woman and nation. It becomes, in Foucauldian terms, a site of "biopower," negating what is historical and contingent about both woman and nation (1978, 140–44). In her essay in this collection, Angie Chabram-Dernersesian insists upon the historical contingency of identity, refashioning the nationalism of "Chicano" movements not simply to include the feminine but to embrace the fulsome multiplicity of Latino/a communities under conditions of migration and settlement. Such an intervention into oppositional representational politics proposes a new practice of multiculturalism that "decolonizes representation" in terms of "power relations between communities" and within communities (Shohat and Stam 1994, 5).

In this respect, notions such as country, homeland, region, locality, and ethnicity and their construction through racialization, sexualization, and genderization of female corporeality become crucial sites of inquiry and investigation. The essays in this volume consider the significance of spatiality, nationalism, belonging, and locational identities in the perpetuation of race-gender-sex relations in the context of modernities, analyzing a series of dichotomies—material and ideal, reason and emotion, body and mind, public and private, production and reproduction, male and female, West and non-West, white and nonwhite—challenging the very conditions of belonging and becoming as they are constructed through the discursive racializing, genderizing, and sexualizing signifiers. These metaphorical pairs not only have resonance with each other but also generate that space which is neither/nor, neither inner nor outer but a common zone—this encounter with the nation taking place through interaction and performative events—between women and nation. This betweenness not only refuses two temporally ordered entities of woman and the nation, but also refuses a moment of reversal of women for nation, as in the discourse of global feminism, or nation for woman, as in the nationalist discourse. "Between" refers to a peculiar form of temporality, a "suspended moment," a moment of simultaneity and mutual inclusiveness or the spatiotemporal interval of *différance* essayed by Derrida (1982). Nation and woman include a political economy that is related to the production, distribution, consumption, and circulation of discourses and practices dividing time and space between bodies who are the occupants of metaphoric and national homelands.

Nationalism, or even what Sau-ling Wong (1995) has termed "denationalization," cannot bring us to this site of betweenness that allows us to query those productions of modernity. How to imagine or retheorize this space of betweenness or relationality that structures the sexual politics and geopolitics of postmodernity? In their essay in this collection, Minoo Moallem and Iain Boal deconstruct the mythologies of what they term "multicultural nationalism," an emerging liberal discourse that recuperates the originary narrative of diversity without questioning the "very process by which 'othering' is fabricated in American society." If global and international feminisms can be seen to be imbricated in the liberal nation-state and its doubled articulations of citizenship, notions of gendered transnational practices may provide critical avenues of analysis (Grewal and Kaplan 1994). As Armand Mattelart (1983) and others have pointed out, the "struggle for culture" is staged in national as well as regional and transnational arenas. If modernity displays gendered emblems of nationalist identity, postmodernity expresses its social relations in a gendered manner as well, drawing upon national and transnational icons and discourses as needed.

The transnational corporation appears to understand the power of local idioms, strategies, and identities as a critical component of any larger or postnational activity (Mattelart 1983). The fragmentation of mass markets and the targeting of specific audiences or sets of consumers has a double edge; the recognition or hailing of the transnational subject of feminism, for example, can occur in just such corporate contexts even as any celebration of such appropriations and utilizations of cultural identities is always already suspect in the analytical framework of resistance (Morley and Robins 1995; Schein 1994; Kaplan 1995). In her essay in this collection, Dorinne Kondo explores the construction of masculinity in the context of a Japanese fashion powerhouse, Comme des Garçons, positioning the national culture of a non-Western corporation in the field of European and U.S. elite clothing industries. In this instance, the production and marketing of the "men's suit" in Japan produces numerous meanings in the midst of globalized mass culture.

Thus, in an era of globalization, it is appropriate to ask how postmodernity produces feminist practices that can be seen as part of the transnational circulation of cultures and politics as well as material goods. The essays in this collection pose systematic connections among nationalism as it is related to spatiality (territoriality/deterritorialization), temporality (time of national culture, timelessness of the nation), nationalist body politics (national body, body as landscape, landscape as feminized body, national hero as masculinized body), and nationalist heterosexual and kinship metaphors of state fatherhood and motherhood. Minoo Moallem, in her essay in this collection, examines the complex positioning of Muslim fundamentalism in contemporary geopolitical reception in relation to the differently inflected practices of feminism in a transnational moment. Moallem deconstructs the dichotomization of feminism and fundamentalism, linking their emergence to specific manifestations of modernity and their continued linkage in postmodernity. Thus, as Spivak has argued, it is imperative to "negotiate between the national, the global, and the historical, as well as the contemporary diasporic" if we are to comprehend the critical possibilities of feminist alliances across discrepant and distinct material conditions (1993, 278). As Caren Kaplan and Inderpal Grewal argue in their essay in this collection, Spivak's practice of "negotiation" bypasses "conventional binary divisions between positive and negative judgments in order to articulate a relationship between the subject and the world." The "worlding" of subjects and the processes of the production of new subjects of history as they enter the "contact zones" (Pratt 1992) of conquest, enslavement, and colonizations in modern(ist) nation making are the purview of this collection.

Our collection aims to pursue what Butler calls the "tradition of immanent critique" (1997, 1) in the in-between spaces of the temporality of the nation-state's telos. The essays in this collection formulate a reciprocity between the cultural critic and theorist and the subjects of history as they are generated by the "aporetic borders" of contents and concepts, margins and peripheries, Man and Woman, universalization and the denial of difference, which together give rise to the contemporary "crises of legitimation." As Sophie tells Velma in *The Salt Eaters* by Toni Cade Bambara, "Find meaning where you're put, Vee." Immanent critique is precisely about that practice; however, the cultural critic may also find little or no meaning, as such, except the desire to make home and *familia* from scratch for a postcontemporary worlding.

I

Whose Imagined Community?

El desorden, Nationalism, and Chicana/o Aesthetics

Laura Elisa Pérez

O Te Aclimatas, O Te Aclimueres[1]

Chicana/o cultural practices have operated in disordering, profoundly disturbing ways with respect to dominant social and cultural, spatial and ideological topographies of the "proper" in the United States. Cultural practices that code themselves as "Chicana/o" function as paradoxes within the ordering logic of dominant U.S. discourse, for as they bear the identifying graffiti of a tenacious, socially and economically overdetermined biculturality, so do they operate bidiscursively, articulated both within and without the oppressive ideological territories of "Occupied America."[2] Practices articulating themselves through Chicana/o identity construct themselves through, and in turn shape, both Chicana/o nationalist discourse and the collectively imagined Chicana/o "nation," Aztlán. Constructed through the willful acts of a collective Chicana/o imagination, Aztlán exists as an invisible nation within the engulfing "imagined community"[3] of dominant U.S. discourse. The day-to-day practices in this invisible collective zone are disordering to the dominant culture's *migra*,[4] for they embody that which is meant to be disembodied within the dominating symbolic order. Aztlán's "existence" as a nation goes against "reason"; unauthorized, its discourse[5] has the status of fiction. Both Chicana/o nation and discourse are denied within the ordering reason of dominant culture. But, for Chicana/os, "nation" is made to signify differently, and symbolic language is made to course through alternative venues than the ones imagined, colonized, legitimized by the order that denies oppressed peoples access to its centers of articulation. The Chicana/o nation and its cultural practices are *rasquache*, fly-by-night productions.[6] They are cheap, economical, and thus they are doable.

Aztlán came into being during the United States' first massive national identity crisis, the 1960s, when visible sectors of the population refused to continue imagining, that is, producing the nation as usual. Unlike nations born and operative through discourses of "order and progress," the Chicana/o nation's motto remains "disorder and progress." In practice, Chicana/o discourse strips parts from "nation," "nationalism," and "identity" as if they were unattended vehicles on the street. Components are recycled, transformed, and recirculated through the crevices of the symbolic and social order. Cannibalized material, cultural, and ideological products defined as waste are melded with or simply sutured to castoff vestiges of U.S. and Mexican dominant cultures, that is, with the *indígena,* the rural, the working class. And thus, to recycle Tomás Ybarra-Frausto's observations on the Chicana/o aesthetics of the rasquache, the resulting cultural practices of the Chicana/o (not necessarily of the Mexican American), are "vulgar," "tacky," "lower class"—on both sides of the U.S.-Mexico cultural, political borders. Mongrel products pilfered from dominant cultures illegally, without sanction, are redeployed back into national discourse as agents of ideological disorder, of cultural aperture. More than the disturbances of the return of the repressed, that is, as the negative, inverted terms within the dominant symbolic order, cultural practices articulated through Chicana/o discourse are the disordering embodiment of the radically *abject* in U.S. dominant cultural logic.[7]

The practices of which I speak, those that emerged after the mid-1960s to the present through a Chicana/o discourse, were/are heterogeneous and conflictive, *with respect to both Chicana/o and dominant U.S. culture.* They are the products of a social, economic, ideological *spectrum* of "politically conscious" Mexican Americans scattered throughout the United States.[8] Dwelling illicitly within the abandoned or uncolonized spaces of the dominant symbolic order squats a mutant, part like and part unlike the colonizing host. Thus, the cultural practices of Chicana/o discourse may indeed "pass"—into the ever refurbished dominant discourse, but they are not fully translatable: they are not fully digestible, and it is precisely their ideological unpalatability that is again recycled, again injected, like endless fishbones: slowly, steadily wounding the consuming body. It is the master's waste, his or her partial, painful digestion that betrays the ruse of total mastery.

Aztlán, or, Disordering the Nation(s)

Mexicans were incorporated into the body of the nation in a disorderly and ultimately disordering manner, a method that produced a separate/d Mexican American community. Mexican Americans were first etched into U.S. national discourse in 1848 as mute, incomprehensible glyphs upon the massive territories—almost half of Mexico—that the United States' colonialist desire seized through the U.S.-Mexico War (1846–48). The new house that the Fourteenth Colony family moved into in 1848 was built upon the subjugation—the binding beneath—of the Mexican American as nationally abject.

The figures of indeed slouching, brawling, disorderly half-breeds cast their disturbing shadows upon the continually whitewashed walls of the dominating nation. A shared experience of Mexican American individual and collective identity was simultaneously constructed in histories of oppression and opposition. The history of Mexican American opposition includes armed struggle and legal contestations and, on more mundane levels, ubiquitous resistances effected through tenacious bicultural and bilingual practices. It is from this remembered fund of both dispersed and constant resistance that Mexican Americans in the 1960s drew to collectively articulate at a national level imaginings of a different, disordered nation.

As the organizing signifier of a guerrilla discourse of outnumbered and severely disempowered national subject(ed)s, Aztlán's invisibility as a constructed discursive space in the minds and actions of a socially and politically abject people has, ironically, been its advantage in a grossly unbalanced—unequal *and* thus seemingly insane—war of the Chicana/o subject and collectivity against the dominant geographic, political, economic, social, and cultural ordering of the United States. Perhaps the most exemplary and powerful disordering *movidas* with respect to U.S. dominant national discourse were precisely the imagining and production of Aztlán, Chicana/o identity, and Chicana/o nationalism. These three axes organized a politics aimed, in some of its manifestations, at dismembering the dominant nation through political secession of the territories that had once belonged to Mexico, and more generally at the disarticulation of its discourse of ordered unity.

Chicana/o productions of knowledge, art, and the very media in which to circulate the former in the second half of the 1960s through the 1970s played crucial roles in constructing the idea of Aztlán and Chicana/o identity, and ovulating it into found spaces in U.S. national identity discourse. Aztlán was thus a shape changer: the Chicana/o nation, like those Anderson discusses, was decisively produced in its organs of circulation throughout Mexican American communities in the United States. As a productive, and in many ways self-reproducing community, Aztlán grew through the political and aesthetic movable parts it produced in its printed media, on public spaces (as in murals), in the foundation of community political and arts centers, and so on. Built of both paved and dirt venues, these types of erratic and largely unstable thoroughfares, by virtue of their relative and long-term invisibility to dominant culture, ironically allowed for the seizing of large amounts of freedom in which to craft a collective identity politics and from which to deploy its subversive practices. Excluded from "white" American media, Chicana/os created their own presses, journals, newspapers, galleries, *talleres, teatros,* films, television, and radio programs —and, crucially, their own ideological and aesthetic norms—from material and discursive resources culled in large part from the dominant culture. Chicana/os of all stripes were able to nationally and locally analyze their oppression and collectively produce oppositional tactics that could then be deployed repeatedly in diverse, specific contexts.

Chicana feminist and feminist lesbian practices have been the most profoundly disordering in their struggle to reshape Chicana/o discourse, and in so doing, to render Aztlán as a collective fund of resistance that in turn is more effectively disturbing of the U.S. national discourse into which it leaks. They have done so through a variety of media, some of which I will examine in the pages that follow. I first turn to the emergence of early Chicana feminist discourse through journalistic, academic, and creative forms of writing that early on theorized, contested, and otherwise shaped Chicana/o discourses of identity and notions of nation, and then I will turn to some visual arts practices of the 1970s and 1980s.

A feminist politics emerges at the beginning of the Chicana/o movement, during the founding, collective imagining of Aztlán in the late 1960s and early 1970s, bidding throughout the numerous movements of the movement to construct the Chicana/o nation as a community of practiced, coexisting differences. I am not suggesting that Chicanos promptly signed up for gender deprogramming workshops as a result of their encounters with a spectrum of Chicana feminist practices.

However, Chicana feminist discourse does appear to have had a significant amount of mobility and access to effective circulation and central
media within the movement. What sorts of activities embodied Chicana
feminist practice? How did/do these negotiate nation, gender, sexuality,
identity? What effects did/do these operate upon Chicana/o and U.S.
national discourses? These are some of the questions that guide the
partial inquiries in the remainder of this essay.

It was in Denver, in 1969, that the diverse cultural and political movements and practices (which mushroomed after the FLOC/United Farm
Worker's struggle burst onto the scene in 1965) were collectively imagined as the discursive body of Chicana/o nationalism, Aztlán. Read
before a Chicana/o assembly of youth, "El Plan Espiritual de Aztlán"
declared "the independence of our mestizo nation. . . . Before the world,
before all of North America, before all our brothers in the brown continent, we are a union of free pueblos, we are *Aztlán*."[9] The National
Chicano Youth Liberation Conference, however, shaped the nation in
another fundamental way, galvanizing the conscious elaboration of Chicana feminism, for it was here that the Chicana Caucus perhaps unwittingly revealed its impossible positioning between patriarchal nationalism and Chicana feminism in its declaration in the name of Chicana/o
political unity that "It was the consensus of the group that the Chicana
woman does not want to be liberated."[10] Throughout the 1970s, Chicana feminist intellectuals returned to that troubling moment in 1969,
arguing for the tactical alliance of Chicana/o feminist and national liberation struggles. In 1971, for example, shortly after the Denver conference, Francisca Flores, the founding editor of an important Los Angeles–
based political-cultural Chicana/o magazine, *Regeneración*, seized the
opportunity to, in turn, issue a feminist declaration on its editorial page
to the incipient Chicana/o nation: "The issue of equality, freedom and
self-determination of the Chicana—like the right of self-determination,
equality and liberation of the Mexican community *is not negotiable.*
Anyone opposing the right of women to organize into their own form
of organization has no place in the leadership of the movement. . . . the
Chicana feminist movement is not anti men [*sic*]! . . . They [Chicanas]
want the opportunity to assume organization, political leadership and
responsibility in the movement of La Causa" (Flores 1971b).[11]

Flores's demands for feminist space and the eradication of sexism
within the movement were widely shared by other Chicanas, many of
whom set upon theorizing the specificity and function of Chicana femi-

nism. Reporting on the "Conferencia de Mujeres por la Raza" held in Houston in May 1971, for example, Elizabeth Olivárez wrote that "[t]he Mexican American women . . . clearly indicated that they too wanted liberation and equal opportunity but that their manner of liberation could not and would not be like their Anglo counterparts. The obvious reasons given were the cultural considerations and the political ties to the Mexican American movement, but also some women felt that the Anglo women's liberation groups in the main had their origin in the leisure time that comes with the luxury of being fashionable, middle-class, materialistic and competitive" (Olivárez 1975, 40).

The analysis of the difference of interests and social positioning between Chicana and "Anglo" or Euroamerican-dominated mainstream feminist agendas expressed in Houston was historically contextualized by Gracia Molina de Pick (1972, 1975). Molina de Pick aimed to contest ahistorical and Eurocentric representations of the Chicana and mainstream feminist movements as unprecedented vanguards in their respective struggles for Mexican American and U.S. feminist social empowerment. She characterized the contemporary mainstream women's movement, unlike that of Chicanas, as a recent "replanteamiento del movimiento feminista en los Estados Unidos después de un largo suspenso, suspenso que las mujeres de la raza no hemos conocido ya que nuestro esfuerzo por lograr igualdad y justicia para nuestra gente nunca se ha detenido."[12] Implicit in Molina de Pick's (1972, 1975) analysis, once again, was the crucial difference in social positioning between the two simultaneous movements. She concluded that powerful and insightful text by warning that: "hoy en día es peligroso desconocer nuestra historia como mujeres de la raza que nos muestra NO QUE SOMOS *causa y víctimas* del nombrado "machismo" que otros han inventado y con el que nos quieren caracterizar y dividir los verdaderos bandidos de las películas del oeste . . . sino que hable de una tradición ininterrumpida de participación en todos los niveles. . . ." (1975, 33–34).[13]

The texts I have quoted are striking in that they represent the foundation of Aztlán as simultaneously constructed by Chicana/o nationalism and Chicana feminism. Chicana feminists refused to atomize their multiple struggles, and already in the early 1970s, they criticized the narrowness of mainstream feminism's hierarchical privileging of gender analysis as bourgeois and racist, as merely reformist of the capitalist and colonizing ideology that oppressed Chicana/os and other communities of color. Prominent Chicana feminists were politically marginalized and silenced in the discursive construction of the Euroamerican-dominated mainstream feminist movement in the United States; however, they were able to seize spaces of their own in the Chicana/o movement, and to negotiate decisively within it.[14] Thus, Chicana feminists were heavily invested in struggling within the Chicana/o movement that already positioned itself in radical opposition to dominant U.S. ideology. In "Chicanas and El Movimiento," for example, which appeared as the first article in the spring/fall 1974 issue of *Aztlán*, Adaliza Sosa Riddell argued the tactical importance for the Chicana/o nation, with respect to the dominant culture, of eliminating gender inequalities within the movement: "La Chicana is not only placed in a status below the Chicano (male), but in a category apart vis-à-vis the dominant society. That division is manipulated and exploited to further control Chicanos. To end the division by including Chicanas as an integral, not subordinate, part of the group we call Chicanos, is also to diminish the ability of outside groups to manipulate and exploit us. This should be one of the goals of the Chicano Movimiento" (1974, 163). Sosa Riddell's intervention constituted an important challenge to the patriarchal underpinnings of the movement expressed five years earlier in Denver—a challenge that has crucial implications for the general disordering effects of the Chicana/o movement. "El Plan Espiritual de Aztlán" reproduced the theoretical paradigm of the division and hierarchical ranking of simultaneous struggles below one principal contradiction—cultural/"racial" oppression. The rest, class and gender, for example, was presumably to be attended to after resolution of the key struggle.

A crucial front of Chicana feminist struggle—with respect to the reshaping of both Aztlán and the United States—was disordering the content of patriarchal and Eurocentric notions of subject, family, community, and nation. Alternative conceptual models of these bodies, culled from Native American cultures of both Mexico and the United States, were, however, reclaimed in Chicana/o *mestizo* identities early on, often in contradictory ways that reinforced patriarchal ideologies. Aztec culture, which dominated a Mesoamerican empire from the fourteenth century until the Conquest, was idealized in Aztlán early on, but finally submitted to critical reexamination in the Chicana feminist struggle as patriarchal and imperialist, as contradictory to Chicana/o ideals culled from other Native American models of community. So, for example, in the discourse of the late 1960s and early 1970s, Chicana/o *mestizo* identity was constructed through ideals of the interdependency of individual practices and collective consciousness, powerfully allowing for the imagining of Aztlán, and its production through isolated and individual practices. But further, notions of subjectivity and community rooted in Native American philosophies allowed for a radical critique of the "Anglo" dominant culture's compartmentalized ordering of individual, family, and nation as colonializing, capitalist strategies.

Even so, founding Chicana/o conceptions of subject, family, and nation were a field of contradictions, as was, of course, Chicana feminism. Thus, for example, early theorists like Bernice Rincón and Evangelina Longauez y Vásquez responded to Chicana/o heterosexist and homophobic reactions to feminism in the movement (e.g., feminism is "white," "lesbian," a "colonizing tool of divide and conquer through destruction of the *familia*") by retrenching traditional notions of *familia* as the model for Chicana/o unity.[15] To a large degree, the Chicana/o movement was and is shaped by the struggle over imagining "family" that is willfully other than that of received/imposed European, Mexican, Native American, and Mexican American patriarchal traditions.

Rendering the Nation a S/he

The most profound challenges to patriarchal ideologies of the subject, family, and nation, as well as deeply disordering alternative models of these social bodies, made/are making their way more visibly into Chicana/o discourse and U.S. dominant culture venues through artistic cultural practices, particularly those of literary and visual art production. In this section, I discuss a few of these kinds of early movement literary and visual art texts among a relatively large corpus of Chicana feminist art production from the late 1960s through the 1980s.

In "Woman to Woman," in Sylvia Alicia González's self-published 1974 collection of feminist prose and poetry, we can read a subtle challenge to patriarchal and heterosexist notions of family and sisterhood. The last strophe of the poem ambiguously reads as follows:

Fear finds nourishment in solitude
You no longer are alone.
Take shelter in your sister's arms
And while she comforts you

Linger there awhile,
Soothing each other's fears
In discovery of each other.

A woman-identified poem, it closes by opening to the possible reading of finding not only care in the arms of a "sister," but perhaps also sexual pleasure and love. Similarly, *Capirotada* (1977), a University of Texas at El Paso Chicana feminist literary and art magazine, stated in its first and only issue that it "arose from the needs of the mind, the spirit, and the body of la mujer Chicana"[16] (Meléndez Hayes 1977, 3). Among several texts of similar politics, Blanca R. Sandoval's poem, "Eres Mujer Chicana," from which the following final verses are taken, is quite clear in laying claim to both a Chicana identity and lesbian desire:

Eres mi madre,
Eres mi hermana,
Eres mi amor,
Eres Mujer Chicana (*Capirotada:* 5)[17]

A radical, and somewhat humorous critique of the family is made in Clara Gloria Castrellón's article, "Love and Revolution" (*Capirotada,* 7), where she argues that love and the revolutionary struggle are antithetical, and that the institution of marriage is counterrevolutionary, but that "the most insidious group of counter-revolutionary agents" are children, who especially monopolize the female revolutionary's time. While a brief and moving narrative of the emergence of Chicana lesbian identity is poetically traced by Leona Ruth Chacón in "Nací mujer," Chacón criticizes both the heterosexism of the Chicana/o movement and the racism of (white) lesbians:

Pero por ser lesbiana esta cultura mía me rechasó y de su seno me expulsó. Me refugié con mis hermanas lesbianas y por ser Chicana— de piel morena, lengua y costumbres raras—el hablar se me negó. Y a otras de mis hermanas Chicanas, su iniciativa propia les arrancaron dejándonos así como muertas levantando banderas de vida . . . sin voluntad.
Espero ansiosa el despertar de nuestro espirito [*sic*]—espirito [*sic*] tantas veces pisoteado—para empezar a engrandecer nuetra cultura Chicana y enseñar a nuestro pueblo, nuestra fuerza e integridad de mujeres: Madres, Lesbianas, Chicanas. Como Mujeres. (13)[18]

In its one issue, *Capirotada* created one of the most open spaces in a predominantly heterosexist Aztlán for Chicana lesbian feminism to articulate itself and to disorder patriarchal and heterosexist attempts to dominate a heterogeneity of Chicana/o identity and politics. Through their circulation in Chicana/o communication organs, the *many* Chicana lesbian texts, of 1974 through 1977, such as Sylvia Alicia Gonzáles's, Blanca Sandoval's, and Leona Ruth Chacón's, were part of the *foundational* struggle over how to *undefine* Aztlán, how to imagine and attempt to produce a utopic model of the homeland in that no-place that is everywhere embodied in discursive and other cultural practices. These concerns are echoed in the writings of Cherríe Moraga, Gloria Anzaldúa, and other Chicana lesbian writing and art practices of the 1980s, to which I will turn shortly. For the moment, I would like to consider Chicana feminist visual art practices that uniquely struggled to shape early Chicana feminism and Chicana/o discourse.

Two images that are especially emblematic of the Mexican American community's struggles for social justice and cultural freedom in the various movements of the Chicana/o movement emerged from the United Farm Worker's labor rights struggles: the stylized, Aztec thunderbird and the Virgen de Guadalupe. Both became shared, potent symbols of Mexican American cultural specificity and Chicana/o resistance to oppression in the United States. The image of the Virgen de Guadalupe, upon which I focus, became a site of feminist struggle within the movement, contested as a trope (i.e., a tricky carrier) for the gendering and neocolonization of the nation.

Ester Hernández and Yolanda López are two of the numerous female artists who in the 1970s and 1980s reappropriated female images central to patriarchal and culturally colonizing national discourses, and who rearticulated from the ruins of these, powerful models of womanhood, central to the construction of new kinds of community and nation.[19]

Through an irreverent, scavenging aesthetic that disturbed racist and classist demarcations between the fields of the (Eurocentric) sacred/elite and the (Chicana/o) ordinary/popular, Hernández's black-and-white etching, *La Virgen de Guadalupe Defendiendo los Derechos de los Xicanos/The Virgin of Guadalupe Defending the Rights of the Xicanos*,[20] transmuted a revered "feminine" ideal into a feminist model (figure 1). In this representation, the central image of the Virgin (along with the metonymic chain of her attendant "virtues" central to the reproduction of patriarchy and colonialism) is displaced by that of a Chicana warrior in karateka garb. The mark of the sacred, the enveloping aureola, is appropriated and transgressed in one gesture, for the new female image is marked as a new ideal through its familiar signs of venerability, while its received construction is pierced, as by a warrior's side kick.

In a related piece, *Libertad/Liberty* (1976),[21] Hernández redresses U.S. and Chicana/o dominant cultural practices in the nation(s), chiseling out the figure of a new national discourse that *does* embody freedom for both Chicanas and Chicanos (figure 2). From the body of the familiar edifice, a woman artist carves out an older, pre-Columbian, Mayan-style female image whose left hand serves as a scaffold for the artist's body and feminist labors. By being shown contiguous with rather than completely displacing the Statue of Liberty, Hernández's image interrogates the ideal of freedom which the statue symbolizes, but that is denied to oppressed "minority" groups that have consequently been made to carve out nations, like Aztlán, within the nation. *Libertad* can also be read as insisting upon the connection between liberty and female bodies which the French Independence gift first suggested, albeit within patriarchal conceptions of the nation. By inscribing "Aztlán" at the base of the visibly fused statues, Hernández's drawing suggests that the nation itself, and not just the ideal of liberty, can be, and might have been, female-centered. The right hand of the pre-Columbian female figure, held up near its full, bare breasts in a gesture reminiscent of traditional African sculptures that with breast cupped in hand offer a nurturing welcome to those who enter the space they preside over, reinforce a reading of the nation as a "she" that truly welcomes, protects, and nurtures all.[22] Like the Statue of Liberty, *Libertad* is a symbolic representation of the nation, of community, but one that insists upon the fulfillment of the United States' democratic ideals. Hernández's etching is perhaps the first symbolic representation of Aztlán and the United States as spaces of potential female empowerment, and among the first to represent the hybrid ethnic origins and identity of the nation(s).

"The Guadalupe Series" (1978)[23] by Yolanda López also refigured the relations of gender, nation, and cultural identities. Through this cross-generational triptych of portraits, López explores the specificity of these relations for the Chicana/self, the Mexican American woman/mother, and the *mexicana*/grandmother with respect to their particular historical insertion within the United States and Mexico and within the respective dominant cultures of both nations.[24] In *Portrait of the Artist as the Virgen de Guadalupe*, López depicts herself as a beaming young

Figure 1. Ester Hernández, *La Virgen de Guadalupe Defendiendo los Derechos de los Xicanos/ The Virgin of Guadalupe Defending the Rights of the Xicanos,* 1975. Etching, 9 × 12 inches. (Collection of the artist)

Figure 2. Ester Hernández, *Libertad/Liberty*, 1976. Etching, 9 × 12 inches. (Collection of the artist)

Figure 3. Yolanda López, *Portrait of the Artist as the Virgen de Guadalupe,*
1978. Oil pastel on paper, 32 × 24 inches. (Collection of the artist)

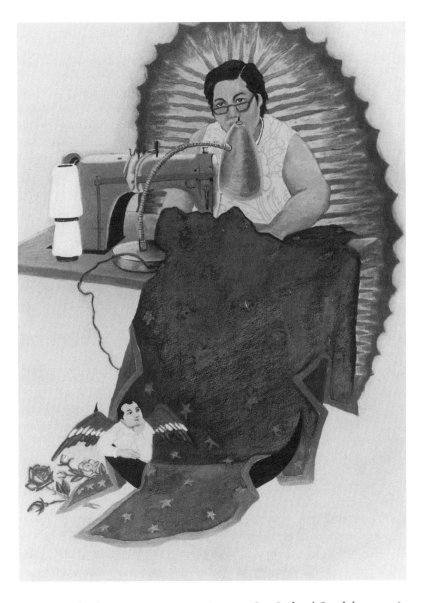

Figure 4. Yolanda López, *Margaret F. Stewart: Our Lady of Guadalupe,* 1978.
Oil pastel on paper, 32 × 24 inches. (Collection of the artist)

woman, running powerfully forward, and away from the framing of patriarchal and colonizing feminine ideals (figure 3). The Chicana artist carries with her symbols of self-affirmation, woman-centered knowledge, and power salvaged from the traditional Virgen de Guadalupe iconography. Retaining the celestial fabric of the original's clothing, this modernly attired "Guadalupe" grasps the serpent of knowledge in one hand and a super-heroine-like cape in the other. Her relation to the United States, Mexican, and Mexican American cultures is suggested in her running over the brown cherub's red, white, and blue-green wings, whose coloring invoke both national flags. Symbol of the Father's omnipresence, the angels in traditional Virgen de Guadalupe iconography can be read not only as holding the Virgin up, but perhaps also as holding her in place. In the triptych series as a whole, López portrays these creatures as brown and male, thus loading them as signifiers for the patriarchal and melting-pot politics of Mexican American (again, vs. Chicana/o) and U.S. dominant cultures. Like Hernandez's pieces discussed above, this visual text deploys a rasquache aesthetic, scavenging from the very images and discourses it destroys. Siphoning the power of familiar symbols of the ideal and the feminine, the artist alters them—like Chicana/o slang—in order to project them back into the everyday world under the guise of the familiar, but functioning to introduce the unfamiliar, and the normally marginalized or unspeakable.

In the portrait of her mother, *Margaret F. Stewart: Our Lady of Guadalupe,* López maneuvers differently with the received iconography (figure 4). For here it is the subject's own, apparently untroubled/untroubling relationship to the traditional power relations embodied in the Virgin that determines their treatment within the portrait. The trace of a subversive Chicana feminist tampering nonetheless renders an empowering image of womanhood: the mantle that the Mexican American mother works on is visually continuous with the traditional aureola that surrounds her. The painting thus suggests that she labors to create by her own mundane efforts a space of dignity, respect, and the sacred. At her feet, a brown (balding, no less) cherub attired in Mexican-flag (red, white, and green) wings rather unindustriously, if placidly, gazes up, perhaps at her. Read cynically, the Father/Nation's demeanor may indeed be relaxed when women, specifically Mexican American and other oppressed "minority" women, are "held in place" through domestic or low-wage employments symbolized in the sewing machine.

Victoria F. Franco: Virgen de Guadalupe, brings to mind Esperanza

Vásquez's 1977 film, *Agueda Martínez: Our People, Our Country,* in its subtle contest to renarrate the Chicana/o nation through an optic that privileges a female legacy recovered through the valorization of Mexican–Native American women's everyday practices (figure 5).[25] In this portrait of the mexicana–Native American grandmother, it is her own dignity and simplicity that most powerfully define the portrait. Thus, she sits upon the mantle, bears the lunar crescent (which the Virgin traditionally stands upon) in a small pin upon her chest, and calmly holds a skinned snake between her hands, one of which still holds a blade, upon her lap. This portrait subverts Guadalupe iconography very subtly, for the symbols that appear in the Virgin's traditional image are clearly replaced by visually similar ones, but whose significance, drawn from pre-Columbian and pagan female cultures, is quite different from the patriarchal Catholic Church's. Whereas the serpent beneath the Virgin's feet in the traditional representation symbolizes evil forbidden knowledge and the material world over which the Virgin stands in victory, the skinned snake in López's rendition invokes Native American and other "pagan" symbols representing womanhood itself and the natural cycle of death and rebirth, experienced in women's bodies uniquely through menstruation and childbirth. The snake thus represents women's power specifically. Like Ester Hernández's *Libertad,* this piece interrogates the history of discursive and visual nation building as patriarchal and Eurocentric, and directs our gaze to the marginalized meanings of everyday symbols that narrate radically other, seemingly more liberating models of nation rooted in female empowerment.

The politics of López's and Hernández's aesthetics negotiate multiple cultural histories as they radically displace the patriarchal and colonialist underpinnings of the Mexican, Mexican American, and dominant U.S. cultures that have shaped the Chicana in complex, gendered ways. The rasquache aesthetic of these artists is an ironic one that appropriates and redefines crucial signifiers, thus destabilizing their function within Mexican, Mexican American, and U.S. dominant discourses. The delimitation of the possible meanings of "nation" is disordered, and revealed as an ideologically invested, disempowering space for women. Particularly for Chicana women, disordering the rules of the patriarchal and racist nation is the tactic that enables other ways to imagine and practice community.

La Ofrenda I/The Offering I (1988)[26]—a final, more recent piece in

Figure 5. Yolanda López, *Victoria F. Franco: Our Lady of Guadalupe*, 1978. Oil pastel on paper, 32 × 24 inches. (Collection of the artist)

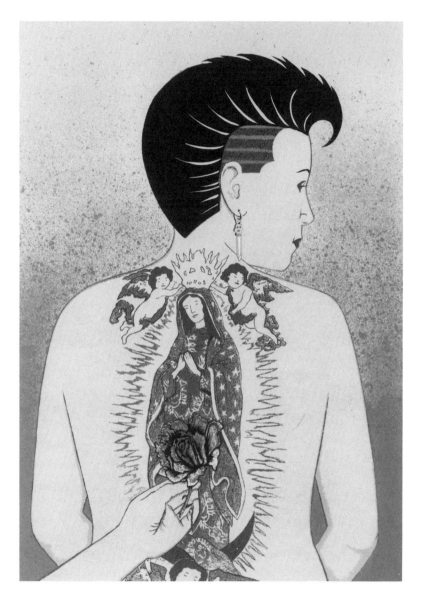

Figure 6. Ester Hernández, *La Ofrenda I/The Offering I*, 1988. Serigraph, 37$\frac{1}{2}$ × 25$\frac{1}{8}$ inches. (Collection of the artist)

the disordering of nation through Guadalupe iconography—depicts the somewhat somber profile and nude back of a gender-bending, Mohawked figure that appears to be female (figure 6).[27] Recalling *This Bridge Called My Back* (Moraga and Anzaldúa 1981), tattooed on the young woman's back is an image of a clearly mestiza Virgen de Guadalupe. Two angels crown her with an object that bears a resemblance to the skull and lavender quartz earring hanging from the young woman's visible ear. She is held up and in place by another angel, in the traditional fashion. The wings of these angels are the colors of the Mexican flag. Attention is called to the ambiguity of their "sex" by a red cloth that runs through the legs of the two cherubs, whose lower torsos are visible, covering their possible genitalia, and by their longish, fluffy hair. An arm that also appears to be a woman's reaches into the picture, offering a blooming, pink rose before the image of the Virgin and to the body bearing its inscription upon her back. Torso and arm float within a deep blue backdrop in which tumble, needle-like shapes that evoke psychological pain. While *La Ofrenda* might be read as depicting a peace offering (the rose/the silkscreen) from a friend or lover, it may perhaps also be seen in its representation of gender ambiguity to suggest, like Gloria Anzaldúa's *Borderlands/La frontera: The New Mestiza*, the heroic role of Chicana lesbians in calling for an "accounting" from all the many "nations" they simultaneously inhabit. "So, don't give me your tenets and laws. Don't give me your lukewarm gods. What I want is an accounting with all three cultures—white, Mexican, Indian. I want the freedom to carve and chisel my own face, to staunch the bleeding with ashes, to fashion my own gods out of my entrails. And if going home is denied me then I will have to stand and claim my space, making a new culture—*una cultura mestiza*—with my own lumber, my own bricks and mortar and my own feminist architecture" (Anzaldúa 1987, 22).

Ester Hernández's piece/*pieza* ("weapon"), like Anzaldúa's "Coatlicue state" aesthetic, creates "a third perspective—something more than mere duality or a synthesis of duality" (Anzaldúa 1987, 46). Thus, in the serigraph, the image of the Virgin is indeed the image of the woman who does not have sexual "knowledge" of man and her mestizaje is of gender as well as "race." Inserting her piece into the long tradition of national discourse articulated through Virgen de Guadalupe iconography, the artist might be seen to join Anzaldúa in saying "People, listen to what your *jotería* is saying" (85). The ordered state is so because it does not forget that without force and rules, it loses its artificial borders.

The Spirit of Disorder

American *locos*, several screws clearly loose, we Chicana/os have tenaciously dedicated ourselves, like other marginalized folk, to conversing with images that "sane" folk don't see. Our rasquache productions— garbled and annoying as Spanish to the racist's ear—still produce a knowledge whose ragged discursive edges scrape at the delicate skins of the dominating culture's claims to normality, authority, and universalism. "I know things older than Freud, older than gender," mocks Anzaldúa (1987, 26). We scrape from both inside and out.

We occupy a nation that does and doesn't exist. We practice a nationalism that we do and don't believe in. We produce art and thought from the useful scraps of norms we mock. We can converse in English Only to say: "Opposition is not necessarily the negative of the Master's positive dyad." "The Father's presence is not necessarily ubiquitous." "There are uncolonized spaces within the imposed symbolic orders where the imagination can transform meaning." *I/We remember.* Our social psychological, and spiritual well-being continues to depend upon the discursive disordering of "power's" collectively imposed imaginings. The kinds of cultural practices I have discussed follow discursively and visually symbolic insane logics, with respect to various dominant cultures' "orders."

To reoccupy Aztlán, the oppressed hallucinate—and that practice has no borders.

Notes

This *pieza* is for the *colegas* of Azatlán and allied nations, and those who trip up the master's "racings."

This paper was first presented at the Susan B. Anthony Center for Women's Studies Critical Colloquium, 3 February 1993, under the auspices of a Susan B. Anthony Center for Women's Studies Fellowship at the University of Rochester, Rochester, New York. It was also presented at the University of California, Berkeley, 16 February 1993, and at Cornell University, 5 April 1993. Shorter versions were presented at the National Association

for Chicano Studies, San Jose, California, March 1993, and at the Modern
Languages Association, Toronto, December 1993.

1   A Mexican *dicho* ("saying") that translates as "Either you acclimate, or you
acli-die." In Spanish, there is a further degree of irony in the pun which
is lost in translation: *Te aclimatas* literally reads as "to acli-kill-yourself."
Thus, whether you acclimate or not, the choice is between killing yourself
or dying. I borrow the cleverness from Iris Blanco and Rosalía Solórzano,
who titled their article included in the Mexican feminist magazine *fem's*
first issue devoted to Chicanas, "*O te aclimatas o te aclimueres. La mujer
invisible: aspectos de la emigración en la frontera con California.*"

2   I am, of course, making reference to the Chicana/o euphemism for the territories that the United States seized from Mexico in 1848, at the conclusion
of the spurious U.S.-Mexico War, and which Rodolfo Acuña (1981) incorporated as the title of his landmark critique and revision of dominant culture
U.S. historiography, inserting into the national narrative a politically oppositional Mexican American history of economic, social, political, and cultural presence.

3   "In an anthropological spirit, then, I propose the following definition of the
nation: it is an imagined political community—and imagined as both inherently limited and sovereign. . . . It is *imagined* because the members of
even the smallest nation will never know most of their fellow-members,
meet them, or even hear of them, yet in the minds of each lives the image of
their communion" (Anderson 1983, 15). Anderson's usage of nation refers to
nation-states, though the passage cited serves to describe the construction
of the Chicana/o Nation. Aztlán, as a feat of the collective imagination of an
oppressed Chicana/o minority, is willfully embodied through oppositional
cultural practices as a nation-within-a-nation, and pushes even Anderson's
subversive thinking beyond the imagined limits of what is "properly" defined as a nation. What the *appearance* and *persistence* of Aztlán, the Black
Nation, and the Queer Nation indicate, as do the survival of the Native
American nations, is that military, political, economic, and social control
of demarcated geographical territories by dominant groups or groupings in
the United States have not been as successful in reproducing their particular and interested imaginings of what the national community is or
should be. Thus, what is at issue in the inclusion or exclusion of oppositional "minority" nations such as the Chicana/o in "serious" discussions
of "real" nations is nothing less than the politics of who and what constitutes nation, and how and why this is so. The insistent appropriation of the
term "nation" by politically disempowered and oppressed peoples (who may
very well be grouped diasporically rather than in geographically contiguous ways) to collectively represent and organize themselves in consciously
and collectively imagined ways is particularly significant precisely because

of the "realness" of its effects. While the struggles continue, the collective power claimed by the Native American, the Chicana/o, the African American, and the Queer defining themselves as nothing less than nations has produced the real effects of greater cultural and physical survival of these oppressed and "minoritized" groups, while transforming the nation into a more democratic one. These alternatively imagined and lived nations have transformed our understanding and experience of what the nation means.

4   *Migra* is Mexican and Chicana/o slang for the Immigration and Naturalization Services, that is, border patrol agents.

5   The distinction no longer refers essentially to the traditional binomial set of "theory" and "practice," specified by a further distinction between "speculation" aimed at deciphering the book of the cosmos and concrete "applications"; rather the distinction concerns two different *operations*, the one discursive (in and through language) and the other without discourse. Since the sixteenth century, the idea of *method* has progressively overturned the relation between knowing and doing: on a base of legal and rhetorical practices, changed little by little into discursive "actions" executed on diversified terrains and thus into techniques for the transformation of a milieu, is imposed the fundamental schema of a *discourse* organizing the way of *thinking* as a way of operating, as a rational management of production and as a regulated operation on appropriate fields. That is "method," the seed of modern science. Ultimately, it systematizes the *art* that Plato had already placed under the sign of activity. But it orders a know-how (savoir-faire) by means of discourse. The frontier thus no longer separates two hierarchized bodies of knowledge, the one speculative, the other linked to particulars, the one concerned with reading the order of the world and the other coming to terms with the details of things within the framework set up for it by the first; rather it sets off practices articulated by discourse from those that are not (yet) articulated by it. (Certeau 1984, 65)

Chicana/o cultural practices are mobile, scattered, tactical gestures that erode the dominant discourse of power (as Certeau describes immigrant and minority gestures), *but*, I have been arguing, they are constructed through a symbolic order that is as hybrid as they are, a collective language constructed both inside and outside of the imperatives of dominant culture. Chicana/o cultural practices construct themselves bidiscursively and not merely as reactions, flashes, or perruques within the system.

6   I am indebted to *el maestro* Tomás Ybarra-Frausto's insights on the rasquache, morsels of which I would like to inscribe here:

One is never rasquache, it is always someone else, someone of a lower status, who is judged to be outside the demarcators of approved taste and decorum. Propriety and keeping up appearances—el qué dirán—are the codes shattered by the attitude of rasquachismo. This outsider view-point stems from a funky, irreverent stance that debunks convention and spoofs protocol. To be rasquache is to posit a bawdy, spunky conscious-ness, to seek to subvert and turn ruling paradigms upside down. It is a witty, irreverent, and impertinent posture that recodes and moves out-side established boundaries.

Rasquachismo is rooted in Chicano structures of thinking, feeling, and aesthetic choice. It is one form of a Chicano vernacular, the verbal-visual codes we use to speak to each other among ourselves. Chicanos theorize about their creations and their lives through vernacular idioms like ras-quachismo that encode a comprehensive worldview. (1990, 155)

7   My thanks to Ondine Chavoya for referring me to Julia Kristeva's fertile ex-cretions on the abject:

The abject has only one quality of the object—that of being opposed to *I*. If the object, however, through its opposition, settles me within the frag-ile texture of a desire for meaning, which, as a matter of fact, makes me ceaselessly and infinitely homologous to it, what is *abject*, on the con-trary, the jettisoned object, is radically excluded and draws me toward the place where meaning collapses. A certain "ego" that merged with its mas-ter, a superego, has flatly driven it away. It lies outside, beyond the set, and does not seem to agree with the latter's rules of the game. And yet, from its place of banishment, the abject does not cease challenging its master. Without a sign (for him), it beseeches a discharge, a convulsion, a crying out. To each ego its object, to each superego its abject. . . . On the edge of nonexistence and hallucination, of a reality that, if I acknowl-edge it, annihilates me. There, abject and abjection are my safeguards. The primers of my culture. (1982a, 1–2)

8   The Chicana/o movement of the 1960s and 1970s was never a homogeniz-ing one that imagined itself as some kind of flat totality. Research into the documents of the period leave little doubt that the movement was per-ceived, characterized, imagined from the start, as a field of competing, shift-ing, often heterogeneous interests that nevertheless linked into a network of crucial common interests, tactics, politics. "El Plan Espiritual de Aztlán," a founding document of the Chicano Nation, for example, declared Aztlán "a union of free pueblos" and thus tactically deployed "[n]ationalism as the key to organization [that] transcends all religious, political, class, and eco-nomic factions or boundaries. Nationalism is the common denominator that all members of La Raza can agree upon." Or consider another very early theorization of the Chicana/o nation and its practices which appeared in the first issue of a central organ of Chicana/o thought, *Aztlán. Journal of the Social Sciences and the Arts:*

Chicano (or Mexican American) activities in all social spheres are a practical set of directed behavior patterns in terms of a heterogeneous ethnic satellite system with thrust and objectives emerging from, revolving around, and converging at a collective focal point: LA RAZA.

Chicano or Mexican American activities include all forms of social phenomena identifiable with Chicano or Mexican American individuals or groups. The social spheres of activity encompass cultural, social, economic, political and all other areas of social action and interaction. The practical set of directed behavior patterns is conceived to mean the concrete stimulus and response manifestations as opposed to abstract conceptions of action; these manifestations are directed in the sense that they are motivated by some common factor or factors (in this instance La Raza and the attainment of La Raza self-determination). By a heterogeneous ethnic satellite system is meant an ethnically or culturally distinguishable group's diverse components (diverse for example in terms of social class, age groups, regional idiosyncrasies, political, philosophical and ideological orientation) functioning toward seemingly shared goals, but with a variety of modes of operation, as opposed to a system with components operating in a uniform pseudo-non-conflicting fashion. La Raza is understood to include all individuals of Mexican ancestry in contrast to Spanish-speaking individuals in general. La Raza is distinguished from La Raza Bronce which includes all peoples of the Brown Race or all of the peoples originating in that portion of the American continent south of the North American United States. (Hernández 1970, 13–14)

9   The first three paragraphs of "El Plan" were reprinted in the founding issue of UCLA Chicano Studies Center's *Aztlán. Chicano Journal of the Social Sciences and the Arts* (spring 1970). The complete document is reprinted in Anaya and Lomelí (1989, 1–5).

10   Quoted in Flores (1971a, 2).

11   Flores (1971a) allows us to date Chicana feminism's emergence prior to the official birth of Aztlán in 1969–70 as she writes that "discussion on the role of Mexican women has been going on for the last two or three years. There have been numerous attempts, on the part of women, in general Chicano organizations to express themselves as a group" (2). Also of interest in this article is its concluding report on the formation of the Comisión Femenil Mexicana on 11 October 1970, "in order to terminate exclusion of female leadership *in the Chicano/Mexican movement* and in the community" (2). The Comisión's last resolution was to "explore ways to establish a relationship with other women's organizations and movements" (3).

12   "[R]einitiating of the feminist movement in the United States after a long pause, a pause which Raza women have not known since our effort to obtain equality and justice for our people has never stopped."

13   "[T]oday it is dangerous as Raza women to not know our history which

shows us NOT THAT WE ARE *cause* and *victims* of so-called 'machismo' which others have invented and with which the real bandits of western films wish to characterize and divide us, . . . but rather speaks of a tradition of uninterrupted participation at every level. . . ."

14   Further details regarding the history of the Chicana feminist movement until 1976 can be found, among other sources, in Cotera (1976). Alma A. García (1989) provides a survey of some of the decade's Chicana feminist intellectual production. On the relations between the (white) women's movement and the Chicana movement, see Cotera (1980).

15   To cite Rincón, for example: "If she also happens to be of Mexican descent her battle seems almost insurmountable, and yet today the sisters are working to develop a strategy that will enable us to be women people, rather than chattels or pets; and, at the same time not to so radically disturb the balance of the man-woman relationship that we become neuters" (1975, 36). Much more subtle in her contradictory allegiance to idealized traditional constructions of family, Longauez y Vásquez developed her feminist arguments as follows:

> How the Chicana woman reacts depends totally on how the "Macho" Chicano is treated when he goes out into the so-called "Mainstream of Society. . . . When a family is involved in a human rights movement, if it is Mexican-American there should not have to be a definition of a woman's role. We should get down to the business at hand. Do we want a liberation for the Raza? Is this supposed to be a total liberation? . . . The woman must help liberate the man and the man must look upon this liberation with the woman at his side, not behind him, following, but alongside of him, leading. The family must come up together. The Raza movement is based on Brotherhood. Que no? We must look at each other as one large family. . . . When we talk about equality in the Mexican-American movement we'd better be talking about TOTAL equality, beginning right where it all starts, AT HOME." (1975, 34)

16   Therese Meléndez Hayes (in *Capirotada* 1977, 3).

17   "You are my mother,/You are my sister,/You are my love,/You are a Chicana Woman."

18   "Because I am a lesbian this culture of mine rejected and expulsed me from its breast. I sought refuge with my lesbian sisters, and because I am a Chicana—of dark skin, rare tongue and customs—speech was denied me. The very initiative of other of my Chicana sisters was torn out leaving us like dead women lifting the banners of life . . . without will.

"I anxiously await the awakening of our spirit—a spirit trampled so many times—to begin to enrich our Chicana/o culture and to show our people our woman's power and integrity: Mothers, Lesbians, Chicanas. As Women."

19   For fine discussions of Hernández's and López's feminist revisions of Chi-

cana/o Guadalupe imagery, see Yarbro-Bejarano (1993, 15, 17; 1995, 183–87), Chabram-Dernersesian (1992, 91–94), and Trujillo (1998).

20   1975, etching and aquatint, 9 × 12 inches, collection of the artist. The image is reproduced in Griswold del Castillo, McKenna, and Yarbro-Bejarano (1990, 324).

21   Etching, 9 × 12 inches, collection of the artist (ibid.).

22   My thanks to the wonderful African American artist, Valerie Maynard, whose own work powerfully rethinks dominant ideas of gender, nation, and freedom, for elucidating this gesture's significance and for suggesting Thompson's (1984) work on the topic. See, for example, pages 13 and 29 regarding its significance in Yoruba cultures of Africa and its diaspora.

23   The three portraits are oil pastel on paper, 32 × 24 inches, collection of the artist. The images are reproduced in Griswold del Castillo, McKenna, and Yarbro-Bejarano (1990, 64, 326). Also see López (1978). The triptych is listed in this exhibition catalogue, as part of a series of five pieces collectively called "Our Lady of Guadalupe: Mujer Mestiza." López writes: "Because I feel living, breathing women also deserve the respect and love lavished on Guadalupe, I have chosen to transform the image. . . . As Chicanos we need to become aware of our own imagery and how it functions. We privately agonize and sometimes publicly speak out on the representation of us in the majority culture. But what about the portrayal of ourselves within our own culture? Who are our heroes, our role models? . . . It is dangerous for us to wait around for the dominant culture to define and validate what role models we should have. As a Third World woman I am particularly aware of the oppressive nature of those images."

24   My reading of the triptych reflects the historically contextualized vocabulary of identity of the Mexican American community, where the Mexican immigrant might never cease to identify as a mexicana/o (i.e., not now or ever a U.S. American, regardless of citizenship); those born in the United States or educated early on here, that thus identify with a "Mexican American" politics of identity, particularly the generations that came of age between 1930 and 1960; and Chicana/os, a term that as of the mid-1960s came to signal political opposition to U.S. assimilationist policies and the marginalized place of Mexican Americans in U.S. society. In addition to Acuña (1981), other historical resources are Martínez (1992), Muñoz (1989), and Mario T. García (1989).

25   See Fregoso's groundbreaking work on Chicana video and film practices: "*Agueda Martínez* represents the life of the common everyday woman whose life experience and struggle are just as heroic as those of the 'exceptional' individuals. Like [Sylvia Morales's 1979 film] *Chicana, Agueda Martínez* challenges dominant assumptions about Chicanas as passive and subservient, for the film is an elegant portrayal of a self-sufficient woman.

. . . The form of the film's imagery articulates the matrilineal heritage of many Chicanos and Chicanas in the United States" (1992, 177–78). Fregoso's acute observations of the film are true of the aesthetics and politics of "Victoria F. Franco" as well and speak to the shared feminist tactics of Chicana artists of the late 1970s.

26 Serigraph, which I discovered printed on a postcard by Tea Lautrec, San Francisco, and reproduced on the cover of Trujillo (1991).

27 Carla Trujillo observes that "the fold of La Virgen's robe, the glowing aura around her, and the placement of the hands and face appear to transform La Virgen into a large, powerful vagina" (1998, 225). Yvonne Yarbro-Bejarano's reading of the serigraph is that "Together the image of the Virgin and the sheer size of the image construct the lesbian body-as-altar, while the lesbian context [on the cover of *Chicana Lesbians*, 1991] presses the religious icon transgressively into the representation of lesbian desire" (quoted in Trujillo 1998, 218–19).

Bloody Metaphors and Other Allegories of the Ordinary

Elspeth Probyn

There is nothing like moving to another country to make you feel really stupid. Without turning what I hope is a temporally limited term into a story of tragic proportions, I feel incredibly maladroit within the jangle of everyday life. Some of the cultural objects and practices that I encounter are disconcertingly familiar from remembrances of a British childhood: dishwashing soap bottles that come in straight opaque plastic rather than the American clear curves, getting a cup of hot sweet tea on the beach from an elderly man who calls me "Love." As the familiar comes to seem far off, the strange becomes near: a state of cultural confusion that can be most clearly heard on my tongue as my accent veers all over the place, trying to put long a's where they just don't belong.

In short, my move from Québec to Australia has been an immersion course in the ways in which the ordinary can sometimes loom up, not becoming so much extraordinary as emmerdant and annoying—when the taken-for-granted isn't. Humbling, it is a salubrious experience for someone involved in the study of culture, and perhaps should be mandatory for those in cultural studies—like walking around blindfolded on National Blind Awareness days. It makes me wonder at the extent of my masochism in the light of a move from a milieu that I had studied and lived for years into another, and one, moreover, that runs on a self-assurance about the evidentness of the ordinary.[1] But it is an ordinary that I find appealing. In the brief time that I have been here, I have been fascinated by examples of the ordinary in action. I read the reactions to Frank Moorhouse's comments on Australian cultural cringe; I listen to ordinary Australians on radio talkback shows outraged at Rupert Murdoch, who continues to intervene in the country's matters long after he renounced his citizenship; I ponder editorial cartoons on "tall poppies," and try to figure out whether the incessant repetition of one's given name by people in the service industries is a national obsession with equality or just a nice gesture.

If my argument here has little to do with Australia, being a hemisphere away has helped to clarify and rearrange some of the ideas that I wish to present. For my topic here is the ways in which Québec routinely comes dressed in gendered and sexualized metaphors. As such, it is part of my ongoing preoccupation about what different national regimes incorporate as ordinary. Here I rely on two Webster's dictionary definitions of ordinary; the first is the common sense of that which is "to be expected," and the second recalls the root *ordo*, designating "having or constituting immediate or original jurisdiction . . . belonging to such jurisdiction." Thus the ordinary has for me a combined valence: as that which a group, collectively constituted in their relation to an original jurisdiction, comes to take as expected. In turn, jurisdiction reminds us both of the space in which power is exerted and the modes through which it is carried. The ordinary then compels a mode of analyzing the particularities of a culture by way of imbrication within the very folds of belonging under study. For me at least, it is difficult to envisage studying the cultural practices and discourses that a group or nation takes as ordinary without being already within its limits. This is of course a liminal research position as one both is of, and at the same time is at a different relation of proximity to, the boundaries of the ordinary. But this liminality suggests to me a critical practice whereby one is positioned within national dreams. Or as Foucault says, "the anthropological significance of the history of dream teaches us that it is at once revelatory of the transcendence of the world, as well as a modulation of this world in its substance, [caught] on the element of its materiality" (1994, 88).

It follows that different orders of national dreaming will turn on singular figures. As Meaghan Morris writes in her article "On the Beach," "Yet today, a problem of nationality can still be framed as a scene of white, male Ordinariness; still today, a subject in a state of confusion may dispassionately be described as 'running around like a headless chook'" (1992, 452). If this expression captures how I sometimes feel, more importantly Morris's argument also helps me to think about the current figuring of the Québécois nation. Her article problematizes the relation between national figures ("the ordinary Aussie bloke") and a level of materiality that is again and again displayed in the routine and expected statements, images, expressions, and so on of a given nation.

In turn, the critical task I set for myself is that of engaging with those fragments that litter national byways in order to draw a composite of certain tangible ways in which nations constitute themselves—to ask what or who becomes the expected figure within given national regimes.

For, in one of the many twists in contemporary cultural theory, it seems that as the nation as concept has once again returned to prominence, the material specificity as well as the very level of ordinariness that it requires and that as a concept it supposedly describes get left behind. For instance, Benedict Anderson has made into something of a cliché the idea that nations are imagined into being. However, perhaps of more interest is the equivalence, which Anderson mentions in passing, of nation and gender: "The formal universality of nationality as a socio-cultural concept—in the modern world everyone can, should, will 'have' a nationality, as he or she 'has' a gender—vs. the irremediable particularity of its concrete manifestations" (1983, 14). While I respect the import of Anderson's argument, I want to ask what or whom is being nominated as the universal? For a feminist, it is hard not to feel that once again women in the guise of gender are being wheeled in as evidence of a universal materiality while the nation floats off as the abstract. In fact, it would be really paradoxical that the concrete social category of gender is taken as a universal condition if it were not for the way in which nations seem to inevitably come draped in feminine metaphors.

However, if the general idea of nation (and especially minor ones) as an abstract "she" is quite common, the local conditions that produce certain nations often disrupt such generalities. In the case of Australia, Morris cites Donald Horne's idea that "The image of Australia is of a man in an open-necked shirt solemnly enjoying an ice-cream. His kiddy is beside him" (Morris 1992, 451). She then argues that the man on the beach works as a chronotope, enabling us "to think about the cultural interdependence of spatial and temporal categories in terms of variable relations" (460). If, in Morris's argument, it is the image of the ordinary white male on the beach that figures the temporal and spatial relations of Australian nationalism, the very etymology of ordinary already carries a sense of the space that orders the limits of that which can then be taken on as the expected. Perhaps part of my fascination for Québec lies in the way that the extraordinary is routinely tied to banal stories of origin, a jurisdiction that is ordered by the privileged metaphor of the wound (*la blessure*) and women. As Micheline Cambron argues, the dominant mode of Québécois nationalist discourse is nostalgic, whereby "every choice is a loss and, although painful, the refusal to choose is unthinkable . . . a disjunction . . . an 'unhealable wound,' a 'sore' on the side of [the nation's] conscience" (1989, 186).

If it is common to refer to nations in gendered terms, what I wish to do here is raise the ways in which quite fantastic images of the nation as female are rendered quite ordinary. As such, they order the limits of what can be taken as Québécois (an efficient strategy of inclusion and exclusion), as they also demonstrate that alternative conceptions of social relations are to be expected. In simple terms, I want to argue for a way of analyzing the nation that takes up common metaphors as evidence of a collective struggle over what is to be considered allowable and ordinary. For instance, there is a double feminization at work in the Canadian and Québécois contexts that routinely renders Québec the downtrodden wife to her uncaring brute of a husband, Canada, while in turn English Canada is habitually portrayed as the defenseless female to the American hulk: the poor beaver to the preying eagle. It is a metaphorization that is further inflated by the common trope of Canada and Québec as continually in the throws of separation and divorce. These metaphors are then often taken as referring to an immanent ground of meaning, one that is fixed by a static equivalence of nation, femininity, and vulnerability. In moving beyond a metaphorical analysis, I want to raise the way in which the bleeding wound operates as a chronotope and puts into play female sexuality as the privileged mode of arranging the temporal and spatial interrelations that comprise the Québécois national. In Nietzsche's terms, through generations and centuries of use, metaphors become part of the taken for granted trappings of nationhood: "Poetically and rhetorically intensified, metamorphosed, adorned, and after long usage seem to a nation fixed, canonic and binding; truths *are* illusions of which one has forgotten that they are illusions; worn-out metaphors" (1972, 5). The particularity of a discrete and historical nation is thus subsumed, its singular conditions of possibility are generalized through metaphors of gender. It is of the utmost importance that we disturb these discursive modes. The movement of equivalence introduced by such metaphoric work allows for different orders of violent generalization. Be it in the quotidian analogies of Québec's language laws to the policies of Nazi Germany, to the way in which precise designations such as the Holocaust are attached to quite other situations, the metaphorizing of nation allows for quick labels and hinders the necessary concrete analysis of particular nationalist regimes. Very disembodied nations are produced as everywhere and nowhere; along with the very utility of the concept of gender, the nation as female is emptied of any material evidence of its historical production.

To substantiate, I return to the Québécois scene. From my experience of living inside the wound, as Québec continually moves uncertainly toward yet more referendums on sovereignty,[2] it strikes me that an ulcer—not life-threatening but banally irritating—might be a more apt metaphor. However, it is to the wound that writers of various stripes return: from Fredric Jameson's characterization of Hubert Acquin's prose —one of the preeminent Québécois writers—as "a garish surface . . . the smears of an open wound" (1983, 216), to Arthur Kroker's (1984) quite brilliant account of Canada and Québec as the historical bleeding wound carved in the aftermath of the encounter of empires: French, English, and the indigenous nations. "Nation" as a wound that never quite heals: scabs picked open by suburban decisions to build a golf course on the Mohawks' sacred grounds at Oka which resulted in near civil war; skin rubbed raw by Western Canadian rednecks stomping on the fleur-de-lys; and then, from the other side of Québec's provincial borders, many Canadians consider the separatist Bloc Québécois (her Majesty's Loyal Opposition in the federal House of Commons) as an unlanced boil on the Canadian national psyche.

Heady terms (so to speak) for a territory usually seen by the outside world as safe, if boring and cold. However, they are heartfelt and historical manifestations of the forces that make Canada and Québec the colonial happenstance that they are today. If they can be seen in action in any number of ways, from government statements to graffiti, here I privilege the ways in which televisual images fuel the gendering of the nation in ways that may be deeply threatening to perceived notions of both gender and nation.

In order to understand the extraordinary nature of what is considered ordinary in Québec, one needs to acknowledge that one of the particularities of the Québécois social is the predominance of locally produced television. Even as it is caught within the network of North American popular culture, Québec continually reproduces its "distinct" culture through an interconnected web of cultural production financed by government agencies and sponsored by private francophone businesses eager to be part of the present enterprise of heritage building. Moreover, studies and informal polls reveal that francophone Québécois are incredibly loyal to francophone popular culture, and actually prefer local programs to, say, a French-dubbed version of *Melrose Place*. As several of my colleagues have demonstrated (Allor 1993; Saint-Jacques and De la Garde 1992), the Québec cultural scene is marked by a *métissage* at the levels both of production and consumption. On the one hand, the production of Québécois fictional television brings together novelists, sports journalists, theater actors and directors, film and television actors, all proudly promoted by regional hardware store chains, paint and bread companies.[3] At the level of consumption, given the size of Québec's cultural pool, television viewers easily connect with their favorite actors across any number of cultural forms and productions and, given the sort of "down-home" behavior of Québécois stars, they may bump into them at local bars (having literally run into someone I took to be an ex-student only to realize he was a famous actor, I can attest that this can be disconcerting).

If the métissage of cultural production is one line in the weaving of Québec's singular distinctness, the ubiquity of historical drama captures some of the backwardness and forwardness, *le va et vient*, of a national desire to become a fully modern and normal nation. The abundance of television series that resolutely turn to the past encourages a popular narrative about the past, present, and future of Québec that would be definitely modernist in its teleological thrust, if it were not for the way in which the nation is rearranged by the excess of the texts themselves. In turn, if prime-time narrative television compulsively revolves around the trope of Woman in the founding of the nation, viewed in the context of other social tendencies, the metaphor may become threatening. In other words, if the movement of metaphorizing the nation in terms of woman would generally serve to displace actual historical women, the historical and social force of women in Québec society redirects this movement and reveals the very materiality of women in forging the nation. In addition, metaphors of the nation as female play to a Québécois audience well versed in popular representations of the absence of men in Québécois nation-building. For instance, when the noted playwright Michel Tremblay is asked why there are no male characters in his plays, he replies, "Because there *are* no men in Québec" (Schwartzwald 1991, 180).[4] Thus again, at a very routine level, it seems that the representation of Québec as organized around and by women is so accepted that it barely merits any academic or public comment.

Perhaps due to my liminal position, I am continually drawn to the singularity of Québécois images, and I turn now to some televisual texts that reveal standard configurations of nation, gender, and sexuality. The texts that I cite should be seen as examples that commingle in the Québécois every day; if I privilege them, they are but fragments in the on-going fabrication of a social imaginary. I commence with the example of *Shehaweh*, a prime-time historical drama that aired on Radio-Canada.[5] Directed by Jean Beaudoin and starring Marina Orsini (who reappears in any number of television series and ads for a local pharmacy chain), this series inverts the usual direction of colonization, the sort of representations that reproduce an ideology of *terra nullius*. In this version we open with a panorama of everyday life before contact. In the space of a few minutes we pass from an idyllic and originary scene, to depictions of violence amongst the First Nations to the fateful arrival of the white man, a journey from the open space of Indian life, down the Saint Laurent to Ville Marie (now Montréal) and then presumably back up the river and across the ocean to France. The figure through whom this potted history is told is that of a young Huron girl who is kidnapped by French henchmen only to be "civilized" in the French royal court before being returned to La Nouvelle France so that she can teach her people the merits of Empire. The series opens with a long pan of a Huron village, lingering on the domestic activities of the women. The focus then turns to a young girl, Shehaweh, who as she fishes reaches down to find blood between her legs. The women of the village gather around her and, in untranslated Huron, presumably comfort her in the ways of womanhood. All within a time frame of several minutes, we cut to the arrival of rival warriors (who are presumably Mohawk, although there is no indication of the exact identity of the actual native nations portrayed). Shehaweh is then taken off only to meet a worse fate when French trappers overwhelm the warriors and drag her off to Ville Marie. The entire opening moves smoothly from pastoral scenes of the village to the choreographed violence of the Frenchmen; as Shehaweh struggles and screams, the fade-out carries the scream to the next scene.

To say the least, this is a disturbing and bizarre telling of the contact between empires and nations that is the ground of modern Québec. From the first menstrual blood that flows down her thighs to the violence of the French *courreur-de-bois, Shehaweh* wants to be read as a sympathetic recounting of the coming together of nations. It is of course performed within the codes of colonialism that foreground violence as a necessary part of historical life. However, rather than documenting the murderous assault on native life, it gestures toward the assimilation of native peoples and the French conquerors (who are in turn conquered by the English) as a fait accompli, a deplorable but ineluctable fact of the present-day nation. Furthermore, the series desperately offers itself to be read as a rather strained inclusion of the First Nations within the nationalist trope of the "unhealable wound," a staging of commiseration between two oppressed peoples filmed against the splendor of the North, native land already stamped as Québécois property. To put it mildly, this is an ambiguous position of nationalist enunciation dependent on a certain suspension of historical fact. Moreover, despite the use of indigenous languages and an elder who introduces each episode (firmly anchored with the logo of the sponsor, Bell Canada), naturally it is a white Italo-Québécoise (Orsini) who plays the Indian princess.

As such it is yet another document of the European colonization of the Americas, one that coexists uneasily with statements about the historical rights of Francophones to the territory that is variously claimed by Québec, by Canada, and by several of the First Nations. As the leader of the Bloc Québécois, Lucien Bouchard, puts it, Québécois sovereignty is an inalienable right stemming from historical occupation: "It is necessary because we are a people, we have always felt and behaved as one, we live on a territory where our ancestors settled almost 400 years ago . . . we have a culture that is distinctly ours, and we have, as official language, French, sacred heritage of the struggles, the fidelity and the courage of 12 generations" (*The Gazette*, 4 November 1995, B3).

If elsewhere the ease of these proprietary colonial claims might astound, the heroic terms of Bouchard's statement must be heard within the discursive context of nation, gender, sexuality, and otherness that operates in Québec, a near pathological wish for marginalia. While the term "marginal" may sound like a quaint and old-fashioned complaint, spoken with a Québécois accent it continually reproduces an epistemology held in place by the accepted constructions of history, gender, sexuality, and race. Thus, nationalist debates in Québec routinely run on the accepted refrain that Québec is a specific culture, a "distinct society," and are grounded in an equivalence between language and colonization that are then taken as evidence of Québec's vulnerability within the Canadian and North American context. In turn, and as we have seen in the case of *Shehaweh*, popular representations portray Québec's specificity as marginal to the majority, or as marginal to other marginals (a nation of others), as peripheral to the center, as the violated female to the invincible male.

This mobilization of tropes could be seen as evidence for Anderson's implicit acceptance of the *normal* equivalence of nationhood and gender. But, as Partha Chatterjee cogently puts it, the question of *whose* imagined community must be continually asked; I would add of *whose* gender. In his reading of Indian and Bengali anticolonial nationalism, Chatterjee raises the ways in which the project for sovereignty was carried out in two distinct domains: the material, which he terms the outside, and the spiritual or the inside: "The colonial state, in other words, is kept out of the 'inner' domain of national culture . . . If the nation is an imagined community, then this is where it is brought into being" (1993a, 3). Chatterjee makes this distinction in order to create an analytic space for the consideration of the singularities of non-Western nationalisms. For, as he argues, contra Anderson, "If nationalisms in the rest of the world have to choose their imagined community from certain 'modular' forms already made available to them by Europe and the Americas, what do they have left to imagine?" (5).

But perhaps part of the problem is that nationalisms tend to lack imagination, preferring to settle down into the accepted. Much as I find Chatterjee's argument illuminating, I want to trouble his metaphorical assumptions by introducing some feminist concerns into this spatial dichotomy of the inside, spiritual center of the nation placed in opposition to its material outside. While it may be empirically true that in certain historical colonized situations, different forms of spirituality have protected against complete cultural annihilation, this order also recalls too vividly the ways in which women traditionally have been hidden away as the inside while men depict themselves as securing the outside of the nation. In the case of Québec, these gendered lines of national delineation are very much in play even as they seem to be going astray. Or is it that Québec nationalism wants it both ways? For it is clear that the outside of the nation is more or less secured and established now as francophone: at a material level, nearly all the top fifty business figures are francophone men, but the inner, "spiritual" discourses of the nation continue to be figured in the terms of gendered marginality—which is to say, female and vulnerable. While this may suit some nationalist discourses in Québec (basically, it allows for a modality that one could characterize as cultural "whinging," after the Australian expression), in turning to my next example, we may see that the very allegorical force of feminized metaphors may also skewer the traditional outside-inside arrangement of the nation.

Touted as a feminist historical drama, *Les filles de Caleb*, directed again by Beaudoin and shown on Radio-Canada, is one of the most successful television series ever produced in Québec, garnering three and a half million viewers for each episode (about three-fourths of the total francophone population). The story is organized around two of my favorite tropes: horses and schoolteachers. The heroine is Émilie, an independent schoolmarm who in the early 1900s raises a large family mainly by herself while her husband, Ovila, is either off drinking or working up North or both. A titillating scene occurs halfway through the series when a direct parallel is enacted between Émilie and a brood mare: a long scene where shots of the mare being mounted continually segue into close-ups of Ovila nuzzling Émilie from behind, creating a nervous sexual tension that is broken by the arrival of Émilie's sister, who is destined to become a nun. In the rather incestuous, intertextual cultural context of Québec, this scene, which aired at 8 P.M., caused all sorts of fun, including a spoof that had Émilie as dominatrix demanding that Ovila "do as the horses did," to which Ovila, played to the hilt as the village idiot, can only whinny. To only slightly paraphrase Orsini's comments when interviewed on English Canadian national radio, "Sex between humans and animals is beautiful and natural."

Les filles de Caleb then spawned the sequel *Blanche*, after the next in a series of novels by Arlette Cousture. It is an interesting take on Québec's movement into modernity that portrays a nation's historical emergence as equivalent to Émilie's daughter's failed attempt to become a doctor. Refused entrance into McGill University's Medical Faculty (the series makes it deliberately ambiguous as to whether this refusal by the bastion of English Québec is due to her gender or her ethnicity or both), Blanche finds fame and fulfillment as a nurse in the wild west of Québec, the Abitibi, which was settled by *les colons* between the wars.

Within the discourses of nationalism, it might be tempting to say that in the analogy of Blanche's career and the settling of modern Québec we have empirical proof of the equivalence of nationhood and gender. Thus, in a sweeping way, one could argue that these representations of the nation in emergence must of necessity pass through the figure of women in order that Québécois national identity be recognized as immutable, as fully universal as that of other modern nations. In psychoanalytic terms, the prominence of the "wound" metaphor would then serve to reproduce the truth of Québec as inevitable, even trans-historical in its mission to enter the symbolic as a modern nation-state. In the immortal words of René Lévesque, Québec's mission and destiny are rolled into one: "Nous avons un rendezvous normal avec l'histoire" ("We have a normal rendezvous with history"). These words were pronounced during a very moving moment immediately following the failure of the 1980 referendum, and they capture both the teleological thrust and the constant circling around the metaphor of the bleeding wound that are indeed integral elements within the discursive web of the Québécois nation. Only in sovereignty will the wound begin to heal, a refrain that could be heard in Jacques Parizeau's first words as premier when he exhorted Québec to become *normal*.

However, while these discursive turns may be present in much learned and accepted nationalist refrains as they seek to portray Québec as constantly threatened, the banal repetition of the trope of female sexuality also reveals a situation quite outside the confining terms of a universal feminine vulnerability. The very concreteness and the ubiquity of images of women in charge returns me to the ordinariness that national regimes seek to instill even as they are carried by it: the highly sexed Québécoise as the force that propels Québec into normality. It follows that the predominance of these images of the nation as a desiring woman allows for some rather interesting depictions of male sexuality. It is not surprising that in the accepted exclusion of so-called normal men from the sexualized relation of nation and women, what we have is a plethora of images of gay men and the nation. As Robert Schwartzwald (1991) has convincingly argued, male homosexuality was the favored trope for nationalists in the 1950s and 1960s and was circulated in order to explain Québec's inability to decide to become separate, arguments that were couched in psychoanalytic ideas of infantile sexuality. Both the Catholic Church and its priests (those "men in dresses," as they were called) and the federalist regime were seen as emasculating true Québécois men, denying them access to the Symbolic and a separate identity. Canadian federalists, be they francophone (like the traitor, Pierre Elliott Trudeau) or anglophone, were commonly called tapettes, fifis, or fags— the figures who stood in the way of ascension to proper national hetero-sexuality.

This absolute acceptance of the normality of Catholicism, nationalism, and sexuality can be seen in any number of reworkings of the past.
In *Les filles de Caleb*, and following the clergy's commandment that
women populate the land with numerous offspring (what was called
"the revenge of the cradle"), Émilie may reproduce the nation, but she
seems to get more fun out of it than the official metaphor of the bleeding wound would have us believe. In *Blanche*, her daughter rides away
from men and priests as she gives women advice about contraception,
overriding the Catholic Church and threats of excommunication.

If the priests in *Blanche* are sanctimonious, elsewhere they also get up
to a bit of fun. One of my favorite moments in *Montréal, P.Q.*, a really
trashy *téléroman* set in the 1940s, has a priest fondling a garter belt as
we watch him having a wet dream (and the camera has us actually positioned on top of him). In a recent series, *Miséricorde*, nuns get into the
act. Here Marina Orsini reappears with Nathalie Mallette (who played
Émilie's sister in *Les filles*), this time as nuns rebelling against modern
parents who want their daughters to advance in the newly secular state
of Québec. Set in the *yé-yé* or hippie period of the 1960s, the series portrays the overthrow of the Church's power during the Quiet Revolution,
the crucial period when Québec turned from years of Catholic darkness
(*la grande noirceur*) and struggled to emerge as a modern secular state.
This historical period is told across the lives of two nuns in a convent,
one of whom sets losing *her* virginity as her historical mission in life.
The writers of *Miséricorde* (the sports journalist Réjean Tremblay of *Les
filles* and his partner, Fabienne Larouche) explain that the inspiration
for the series came from a defrocked nun who confessed to Larouche:
"After having made love, I told him that I was a virgin and a nun. The
man replied to me: 'You sure french-kiss well for a nun!' [Tu frenches
bien pour une soeur]" (Montour 1994, 14).

As Soeur Édite fucks to an entire rendition of *Ave Maria*, it would
be easy, if not facile, to read her as metaphor for Québécois modernity.
However, what I find more intriguing is the gaze that passes between
the two nuns. As she looks with longing and defiance, Nathalie seems
more interested in Marina's reaction than in Gildor Roy's actions (and
given his prominence as a country-and-western star as well as being
the darling of the stage, cinema, and television, this is a bit of a treat).
Within the Québec context, the intertextual relations are clear: if, in
Les filles de Caleb, it is Nathalie Mallette, destined to become a nun,
who looks on as Marina Orsini engages in horseplay, here it is Marina

who watches as Nathalie has sex on the kitchen table in the galley of a boat (as one of my students put it, she really polishes that table). Sadly, Soeur Édite is traumatized by the event and eventually kills herself by throwing herself off the choir parapet in front of all the praying nuns.

While I could continue to enumerate other images, I want to return to the question of the very ordinariness that they express and are part of. Against a certain elevation and abstraction of the nation both in academic writing and in Québécois political discourses, I want to argue that these images direct us to what Achille Mbembe calls the banality of postcolonial power. These images work to make Québec's *devenir-nation*, or becoming-nation, "fully real, turning it into a part of people's common sense not only by instilling it in the minds of its *cibles* (or 'target population'), but also in the imaginary of an epoch" (Mbembe 1992, 2). As Mbembe argues, the question of what constitutes "the art of governing" introduces an epistemological shift from the usual binaries of "resistance/passivity," "conservative/progressive"—which, as he bluntly puts it, "cloud our understanding of postcolonial relations" (3). It also allows us a way out of traditional gender-weighted dichotomies. For instance, the common placement of women as the sanctified guardians of cultural tradition is considerably shifted in the face of the very ordinariness of women merrily screwing across, and indeed portrayed as, Québécois history.

Following Foucault's theory of governmentality as *la conduite des conduites*, the conduct of conduct, Nikolas Rose and Peter Miller argue that "Power is not so much a matter of imposing constraints upon citizens as of 'making up' citizens capable of bearing a kind of regulated power" (1992, 174). If elsewhere (Probyn 1996), I enter more fully into implications of using governmentality as an optic to analyze modern national forms of power, here I want to draw attention to the construction of a certain mode of governmentality that turns on figuring women's sexuality as central to and as an ordinary part of a national regime of self-constitution. To paraphrase Rose and Miller, in Québec, female sexuality becomes a privileged site not of restraint and repression but of the banal—the construction of ordinary citizens capable of bearing the knowledge of women's sexuality. Again, in Québec this is not only an abstract and philosophical affair; it is also a pragmatic and daily preoccupation of how to produce sovereign citizens, or yet more directly, how to get the majority to vote for independence: a sort of instrumental affectivity.

Beyond reading these images of women as metaphors that would express a latent and authentic meaning of the Québécois nation, I propose that we see them as allegories that serve to figure the boundaries of what is acceptable to the nation. As such they continually oscillate between what is considered to be the jurisdiction of the national and what is expected of and by the nation. Far from discounting the historicity of the forces that continually reproduce the nation, in studying how certain images are put forth as ordinary we can begin to comprehend the ways the configurations of the Québécois state of a nation in becoming, a governmental project whereby *le devenir de Québec* is increasingly heard in the terms of *un projet de société.* In part, this cry of a "societal project" was the outcome of the recent public assemblies held throughout the province, which the Parti Québécois had hoped would lead to massive support of immediate separation. However, what emerged was a public demand to consider the interrelationship of such diverse elements as the role of women, of native peoples, land rights, economics, free trade, the rights of gays and lesbians, and more—in short, questions about how distinct factors of Québec society would be conjugated as Québec becomes normal.

In arguing that in Québec the representation of women's sexuality operates as a privileged form of governmentality, I seek to avoid the type of distinctions and hierarchies too often at play within the discussion of nation, the type of argument that separates out questions of sexual difference from those "harder" ones of national difference, that considers television as a subset of cultural difference which in turn is analyzed merely as a kind of afterthought or frosting on the more serious matters of state policy and power. My espousal of the ordinary and the refusal of any inner national truth then entails an analytical commitment to the meticulous study of the nation in all its singularity, a singularity that, as Foucault argues, cannot be found in "deciphering signs through a system of differences." Instead, "the thickness of analogies . . . real and virtual, perception and wish, past and fantastic . . . only has value as movements of passage, relays rather than signs, traces of footsteps" (1994, 277).

This attention then yields a nation not as the heroic emergence of destiny, nor as the downtrodden and oppressed minority, but as a historical and material configuration that from its colonial, violent folds produces national manners of being and modes of becoming. It should be clear that a study of the ordinary within such regimes does not

condone the banality of xenophobia, racism, and gyno- and homophobia that is also a part of the Québécois everyday. Rather, I continually
seek ways of contesting such eruptions by raising the grounds that attest to their very extraordinary nature. If my turn to the ordinary is
a bit bizarre given the years I have spent teaching students to render
the familiar *unheimlich,* the exigency of intervening in the direction of
nationalist debates compels a precise analysis of the limits of the acceptable. Without eulogizing *le peuple,* it is salutary to remember that
polls regularly show that public opinion on matters ranging from abortion to the rights of gays and lesbians is substantially more progressive
than what politicians regularly state society will accept.

Thus, from within this nation fueled by metaphor, I endeavor to trace
a layering of the social as surface, a surface written with historical preoccupations, riven with virtual possibilities, marked by footsteps that
may lead to other modes of being a nation. As I have tried to show, the
Québécois national surface is produced and traced by televisual images
of horses and nuns fucking, of menstruation and rape, of masturbating
priests, of sincere accounts of lesbians within the traditional Québécois
family, of gay men adopting children, of s/m "made in Québec." Simply
put, these images speak of some of the vectors and engagements of Québec in the midst of becoming, lines of flight that gesture toward a wish
for a more ethical way of being a new nation. At least this is my hope
and the wager I seek to articulate. If the future of the nation is far from
clear, nor can it be predicted, at least the metaphor of "bleeding wound"
has been cauterized and the sisters are fucking its history.

Notes

I wish to thank the University of Western Sydney, Nepean for inviting me as
a Visiting Fellow and thus giving me the space in which to rethink Québec in
Australia. This research was funded by the FCAR—Programme de subvention
aux Équipes, and by the Social Sciences and Humanities Council of Canada.

1   A recent Australian film, *Hotel Sorrento* (directed by Richard Franklin), bears
    witness in interesting ways to the accepted place that the ordinary has within
    Australian culture. This story of three grown-up sisters revolves around banal
    tales of jealousy and misunderstandings, which one of the sisters has turned
    into a best-selling novel. The film's climax coincides with a rather wonder-
    ful twist when the novel is declared by the Booker committee to have been
    plagiarized from an English novel. In a nutshell, the film captures some of
    the tensions in contemporary Australia around questions of how a culture is

represented and by whom. The fact that a faraway group of cultural critics can dismiss the autobiographical anguish as the work of a British novelist sums up even as it takes in other directions some of the problems of ordinary Australian-ness.

2   The first referendum on Québec sovereignty was held in 1980: the "yes" side was led by the popular premier, René Lévesque, with the "no" side headed by Prime Minister Pierre Trudeau. The upshot was a no vote against sovereignty although, as the present situation demonstrates, the issue was hardly put to rest. The last referendum took place on 30 October 1995, but the results were hardly conclusive, with an extremely marginal win by the no side (.5 percent). In fact, the leader of the federal opposition, Lucien Bouchard, pledged to carry on until separation was assured and Premier Jacques Parizeau resigned, but not before he blamed "anglophone monied interests and the ethnic vote" for the defeat.

3   See Martin Allor's (1993) analysis of Québec Inc., the term for the emergent francophone business elite and its implication in cultural production. An example of the métissage at the production level can be seen in the very popular television series, Scoop, which is set in a very lightly fictionalized scene of daily newspapers (L'expresse and Scoop), is cowritten by a sports journalist, Réjean Tremblay, features actors like Roy Depuis, who can be found simultaneously acting in the latest film or theater production or in commercials. It is in turn sponsored by the bread company, Weston, and La Presse, the largest francophone daily newspaper. This is only the tip of the structural métissage, as the series routinely turns on actual news stories and portrays the imbrication of Québec business in the cultural life of the nation.

4   While I am unable to enter into the terms of Robert Schwartzwald's article, his work on Québec's "inverted fictions" of homosexuality has directly inspired my own arguments.

5   The major television networks in Québec are Radio Canada (SRC), the French-language homologue of the Canadian Broadcasting Corporation (CBC), federally funded and with commercials; Radio Québec, the Québec state-run television channel, with a mandate for quality and educational programming; and Télévision Quatre-Saisons, a private, commercial, and French-language network.

Chicana Feminism: In the Tracks of "The" Native Woman

Norma Alarcón

As Spain prepares to celebrate the quincentenary of "the discovery," contemporary Chicanas have been deliberating on the force of significations of that event. It took almost four hundred years for the territory that today we call Mexico to acquire a cohesive national identity and sovereignty. Centuries passed before the majority of the inhabitants were able to call themselves Mexican citizens. As a result, on the Mexican side of the designation Mexican American, Chicanas rethink their involvement in the capitalist neocolonization of the population of Mexican descent in the United States (Barrera et al. 1972).

In the 1960s, armed with a post–Mexican American critical consciousness, some people of Mexican descent in the United States recuperated, appropriated, and recodified the term Chicano to form a new political class (Acuña 1981; Muñoz 1989). Initially, the new appellation left the entrenched (middle-class) intellectuals mute because it emerged from oral usage in the working-class communities. In effect, the name measured the distance between the excluded and the few who had found a place for themselves in Anglo-America. The new Chicano political class began to work on the compound name, eager to redefine the economic, racial, cultural, and political position of the people. The appropriation and recodification of the term Chicano from the oral culture was a stroke of insight precisely because it unsettled all of the identities conferred by previous historical accounts. The apparently well documented terrains of the dyad Mexico/United States were repositioned and reconfigured through the inclusion of the excluded in the very interiority of culture, knowledge, and the political economy. Thus, the demand for a Chicano/a history became a call for the recovery and rearticulation of the record to include the stories of race/class relations of the silenced, against whom the very notions of being Mexican or not-Mexican, being American or not-American, being a citizen or not a citizen had been constructed. In brief, the call for the story of Chicana/os has not turned out to be a "definite" culture, as some dreamed. Rather, the term itself, in body and mind, has become a critical site of political, ideological, and discursive struggle through which the notion of "definitiveness" and hegemonic tendencies are placed in question.

Though the formation of the new political Chicano class has dominated many men, Chicana feminists have intervened from the beginning. The early Chicana intervention is available in the serials and journals that mushroomed in tandem with the alternative press in the United States in the 1960s and 1970s. Unfortunately, much of that early work by Chicanas often goes unrecognized, which is indicative of the process of erasure and exclusion of raced ethnic women within a patriarchal cultural and political economy. In the 1980s, however, there has been a reemergence of Chicana writers and scholars who have not only repositioned the Chicano political class through the feminist register but who have joined forces with an emergent women-of-color political class that has national and international implications (McLaughlin 1990).

The United States in the 1980s was, according to the Reagan administration, the decade of the Hispanic—a neoconservative move assisted by the U.S. Census Bureau (Giménez 1989) and the mass media, to homogenize all people of Latin American descent and occlude their heterogeneous histories of resistance to domination—in other words, the counterhistories to invasions and conquests. At the same time, in the 1980s, a more visible Chicana feminist intervention has given new life to a stalled Chicano movement (Rojas 1989). In fact, in the United States, this appears to be the case among most raced ethnic minorities. By including feminist and gender analysis into the emergent political class, Chicanas are reconfiguring the meaning of cultural and political resistance and redefining the jointure of the term Mexican American (Moraga and Anzaldúa 1981; Alarcón 1989, 1990).

To date, most writers and scholars of Mexican descent refuse to give up the term Chicana. Despite the social reaccommodation of many as Hispanics or Mexican Americans, it is the consideration of the excluded evoked by the name Chicana that provides the position for multiple cultural critiques: between and within, inside and outside, centers and margins. Working-class and peasant women, perhaps the "last colony," as a recent book announces (Mies et al. 1989), are most keenly aware of this. As a result, when many a writer of such racialized cultural history explores her identity, a reflectory and refractory position is depicted. In the words of Gloria Anzaldúa:

She has this fear
that she has no names
that she has many names
that she doesn't know her names
She has this fear
that she's an image
that comes and goes
clearing and darkening
the fear that she's the dreamwork inside someone else's skull . . .
She has this fear that if she digs into herself
she won't find anyone
that when she gets "there"
she won't find her notches on the trees . . .
She has this fear that she won't find the way back. (1987, 43)

The quest for a true self and identity, which was the initial desire of many writers involved in the Chicano movement in the late 1960s and early 1970s, has given way to the realization that there is no fixed identity. "I," or "She" as observed by Anzaldúa, is composed of multiple layers without necessarily yielding an uncontested "origin." In the words of Trinh T. Minh-ha, "Things may be said to be what they are, not exclusively in relation to what was and what will be (they should not solely be seen as clusters chained together by the temporal sequence of cause and effect), but also in relation to each other's immediate presences and to themselves as non/presences" (1989, 94). Thus, the name Chicana, in the present, is the name of resistance that enables cultural and political points of departure and thinking through the multiple migrations and dislocations of women of "Mexican" descent. The name Chicana is not a name that women (or men) are born to or with, as is often the case with Mexican, but rather is consciously and critically assumed and serves as a point of redeparture for dismantling historical conjunctures of crisis, confusion, political and ideological conflict, and contradictions of the simultaneous effects of having "no names," having "many names," not "know[ing] her names," and being someone else's "dreamwork." However, digging into the historically despised dark (prieto) body, in strictly psychological terms, may get her to the bare bones and marrow, but she may not "find the way back" to writing her embodied histories. The idea of plural historized bodies is proposed with respect to the multiple racial constructions of the body since "the discovery": to name a few, indigenous (evoking the extant as well as extinct tribes), criolla, morisca, loba, cambuja, barcina, coyota, samba, mulatta, china, chola. The contemporary assumption of *mestizaje* (hybridism) in the Mexican nation-making process was intended to racially colligate a heterogeneous population that was not European. On the American side of the compound, *mestizas* are nonwhite, thus further reducing the cultural and historical experience of Chicanas. However, the mestiza concept is always already bursting its boundaries. While some have "forgotten" the mestiza genealogy, others claim as indigenous, black or Asian ones as well. In short, the body, certainly in the past five hundred years in the Americas, has been always already racialized. As tribal "ethnicities" are broken down by conquest and colonizations, bodies are often multiply racialized and dislocated as if they had no other contents. The effort to recontextualize the processes recovers, speaks for, or gives voice to women on the bottom of a historically hierarchical economic and political structure (Spivak 1988).

It is not coincidental that as Chicana writers reconstruct the multiple names of the mestiza and Indian, social scientists and historians find them in the segmented labor force or in the grip of armed struggles. In fact, most of these women have been (and continue to be) the surplus sources of cheap labor in the field, the canneries, the maquiladora border industries, and domestic service. The effort to pluralize the racialized body by redefining part of their experience through the reappropriation of "the" native woman on Chicana feminist terms marked one of the first assaults on male-centered cultural nationalism on the one hand (Alarcón 1989), and patriarchal political economy on the other (Melville 1980; Mora et al. 1980; Córdova et al. 1986; Ruiz and Tiano 1987; Zavella 1987).

The native woman has many names also—Coatlicue, Cihuacoátl, Ixtacihúatl, and so on. In fact, one has only to consult the dictionary of *Mitología Nahuátl*, for example, to discover many more that have not been invoked. For many writers, the point is not so much to recover a lost "utopia" or the "true" essence of our being, although, of course, there are those among us who long for the "lost origins," as well as those who feel a profound spiritual kingship with the "lost"—a spirituality whose resistant political implications must not be underestimated, but refocused for feminist change (Allen 1988). The most relevant point in the present is to understand how a pivotal indigenous portion of the mestiza past may represent a collective female experience as well as "the mark of the Beast" within us—the maligned and abused indigenous woman (Anzaldúa 1987, 43). By invoking the "dark Beast" within and without, which has forced us to deny, the cultural and psychic dismemberment that is linked to imperialist racist and sexist practices is brought into focus. These practices are not a thing of the past either. One has only to recall the contemporary massacres of the Indian population in Guatemala, for example, or the continuous "democratic" interventionist tactics in Central and South America, which often result in the violent repression of the population.

It is not surprising, then, that many Chicana writers explore their racial and sexual experience in poetry, narrative, essay, testimony, and autobiography through the evocation of indigenous figures. This is a strategy that Gloria Anzaldúa uses and calls "La herencia de Coatlicue/The Coatlicue state." The "state" is, paradoxically, an ongoing process, a continuous effort of consciousness to make "sense" of something; she has to "cross over," kicking a hole out of the old boundaries of the self and slipping under or over, dragging the old skin along, stumbling over it (Anzaldúa 1987, 48–49). The contemporary subject-in-process is not just what Hegel would have us call the *Aufhebung*—that is, the effort to unify consciousness "is provided within a radical recomprehension of the totality" (Warren 1984, 37)—as tenuously, Chicana's consciousness, which is too readily viewed as representing "postmodern fragmenting identities," entails not only Hegel's *Aufhebung* with respect to Chicanas' immediate personal subjectivity as raced and sexed bodies, but also an understanding of all past negations as communitarian subjects in a doubled relation to cultural recollection, and remembrance, and to our contemporary presence and non/presence in the sociopolitical and cultural milieu. All of which together enables both individual and group Chicana positions previously "empty" of meanings to emerge as one who has to "make sense" of it all from the bottom through the recodification of the native woman. As such, the so-called postmodern decentered subject, a decentralization that implies diverse, multiply constructed subjects and historical conjunctures, in so far as she desires liberation, must move toward provisional solidarities, especially through social movements. In this fashion, one may recognize the endless production of differences to destabilize group or collective identities on the one hand, and the need for group solidarities to overcome oppressions through an understanding of the mechanisms at work on the other (McLaughlin 1990; Kauffman 1990).

The strategic invocation and recodification of "the" native woman in the present has the effect of conjoining the historical repression of the "noncivilized" dark woman—which continues to operate through "regulative psychobiographies" of good and evil women such as that of Guadalupe, Malinche, Llorona, and many others—with the present moment of speech that counters such repressions (Spivak 1989, 227). It is worthwhile to remember that the historical founding moment of the construction of mestiza(o) subjectivity entails the rejection and denial of the dark Indian Mother as Indian, which has compelled women often to collude in silence against themselves, and to actually deny the Indian position even as that position is visually stylized and represented in the making of the fatherland. Within these blatant contradictions, the overvaluation of Europeanness is constantly at work. Thus, Mexico constructs its own ideological version of the notorious Anglo-American "melting pot," under the sign of mestizo(a). The unmasking, however, becomes possible for Chicanas as they are put through the crisis of the Anglo-American experience where ("melting-pot") whiteness, not mestizaje, has been constructed as the Absolute Idea of Goodness and Value. In the Americas, then, the native woman as ultimate sign of potential reproduction of *barbarie* (savagery) has served as the sign of consensus for most others, men and women. Women, under penalty of the double bind charge of "betrayal" of the fatherland (in the future sense) and the mother tongues (in the past sense), are often compelled to acquiesce with the "civilizing" new order in male terms. Thus, for example, the "rights" of women in Nicaragua disappear vis-à-vis the "democratizing" forces, notwithstanding Sandinista intentions (Molyneux 1985). In this scenario, to speak at all, then, "the" native woman has to legitimize her position by becoming a "mother" in hegemonic patriarchal terms, which is near to impossible to do unless she is "married" or racially "related" to the right men (Hurtado 1989). As a result, the contemporary challenge to the multiple negations and rejections of the native racialized woman in the Americas is like few others.

For Chicanas, the consideration of the ideological constructions of the "noncivilized" dark woman brings into view a most sobering reference point: the overwhelming majority of the workers in maquiladoras, for example, are mestizas who have been forcefully subjected not only to the described processes but to many others that await disentanglement. Many of those workers are "single," unprotected within a cultural order that has required the masculine protection of women to ensure their "decency," indeed to ensure that they are "civilized" in sexual and racial terms. In fact, as Spivak and others have suggested, "the new army of 'permanent casual' labor working below the minimum wage . . . [are] these women [who today] represent the international neo-colonial subject paradigmatically" (Spivak 1989, 223). These women (and some men), who were subjected to the Hispanic New World "feudal mode of power" (which in Mexico gave way to the construction of mestizo nationalism) and who were subjected to an Anglo-American "feudal mode of power" in the isolation of migrant worker camps and exchange labor (which in the United States gave rise to Chicano cultural nationalism of the 1960s), in the 1990s find themselves in effect separated in many instances from men who heretofore had joined forces in resistance. Though work in the field continues to be done with kinship groupings, the "communal form of power" under the sign of the cultural nationalist family may be bankrupt, especially for female wage-workers. Although, of course, the attempt to bring men and women together under conservative notions of the "family" continues as well. In this instance, "family" may be a misnaming in lieu of a search for a more apt term for communitarian solidarity.

Whether as domestic servants, canners, or in the service industry in the United States, or as electronic assemblers along the U.S./Mexican border, these "new" women-subjects find themselves bombarded and subjected to multiple cross-cultural and contradictory ideologies, a maze of discourses through which the "I" as a racial and gendered self is hard put to emerge and runs the risk of being thought of as "irrational" or "deluded," in their attempt to articulate their oppression and exploitation. In the face of Anglo-European literacy and capitalist industrialization that interpellates them as individuals, for example, and the "communal mode of power" (as mode of defeudalization; Spivak 1989, 224), which interpellates them as "Mothers" (the bedrock of the "ideal family" at the center of the nation-making process, despite discontinuous modes of its construction), the figure and referent of the Chicana today is positioned as conflictively as Lyotard's "differend." She is the descendant of native women who are continuously transformed into mestizas, Mexicans, émigrés to Anglo-America, Chicanas, Latinas, Hispanics—there are as many names as there are namers.

Lyotard defines differend as "a case of conflict, between (at least) two parties, that cannot be equitably resolved for lack of a rule of judgment applicable to both arguments. One side's legitimacy does not imply the other's lack of legitimacy" (1988, 11). In appropriating the concept as a metonym for both the figure and referent of the Chicana, for example, it is important to note that though it enables us to locate and articulate sites of ideological and discursive conflict, it cannot inform the actual Chicana differend engaged in a living struggle to seize her "I" or even her feminist "We," to change her circumstances without bringing into play the axes in which she finds herself in the present—culturally, politically, and economically.

The call for elaborated theories based on the "flesh-and-blood" experiences of women of color in *This Bridge Called My Back* (Moraga and Anzaldúa 1981) may mean that the Chicana feminism project must interweave the following critiques and critical operations: (1) multiple cross-cultural analyses of the ideological constructions of raced Chicana subjects in relation to the differently positioned cultural constructions of all men and some Anglo-European women; (2) negotiation for strategic political transitions from cultural constructions and contestations to "social science" studies and referentially grounded Chicanas in the political economy who live out their experiences in heterogeneous social and geographic positions. Though not all women of Mexican/Hispanic descent would call themselves Chicanas, I would argue that it is an important point of departure for critiques and critical operations (on the jointure/bridge) that keep the excluded within any theory-making project. That is, in the Mexican-descent continuum of meanings, Chicana is still the name that brings into focus the interrelatedness of a class/race/gender and forges the link to actual subaltern native women in the U.S./Mexico dyad. (3) In negotiating points 1 and 2, how can we work with literary, testimonial, and pertinent ethnographic materials to enable Chicanas to grasp their "I" and "We" in order to make effective political interventions? This implies that we must select, in dialogue with women, from the range of cultural productions, those materials that actually enable the emergence of I/We subjectivities (Castellano 1990).

Given the extensive ideological sedimentation of the (silent) Good Woman and the (speech-producing) Bad Woman that enabled the formations of the cultural nationalistic "communal modes of power," Chicana feminists have an enormous mandate to make "sense" of it all, as Anzaldúa desires. It requires no less that the deconstruction of paternalistic "communal modes of power," which is politically perilous because often they appear to be the "only" model of empowerment that the oppressed have, although they have ceased to function for many women as development and postindustrial social research indicates. Also, it requires the thematization and construction of new models of political agency for women of color, who are always already positioned cross-culturally and within contradictory discourses. As we consider the diffusion of mass media archetypes and stereotypes of all women which continuously interpellates them into the patriarchal order according to their class, race (ethnicity), and gender, the "mandate" is (cross-culturally) daunting. Yet, "agents provocateurs" know that mass media and popular cultural production are always open to contestations and recodifications that can become sites of resistance (Castellano 1990).

Thus, the feminist Chicana, activist, writer, scholar, and intellectual on the one hand has to locate the point of theoretical and political consensus with other feminists (and "feminist" men), and on the other continue with projects that position her in paradoxical binds: for example, breaking out of ideological boundaries that subject her in culturally specific ways, and not crossing over to cultural and political arenas that subject her as "individual/autonomous/neutralized" laborer. Moreover, to reconstruct differently the raced and gendered "I's" and "We's" also calls for a rearticulation of the "You's" and "They's." Traversing the processes may well enable us to locate points of differences and identities in the present to forge the needed solidarities against repression and oppression. Or, as Lorde (1984) and Spivak (1988) would have it, locate the "identity-in-difference" of cultural and political struggle.

Note

I would like to thank Gloria Anzaldúa, Rosa Linda Fregoso, Francine Masiello, and Margarita Melville for their reading and comments on this essay. Responsibility for the final version is, of course, mine.

Re-Imagining Chicana Urban Identities in the

Public Sphere, *Cool Chuca Style*

Rosa Linda Fregoso

The pachuco is one of the principal actors in the Chicano narrative of cultural affirmation and resistance. He performs as a legendary figure of counterhegemonic masculinity for Chicano nationalists who see in him the embodiment of revolutionary identity and identification. Since the 1960s, pachuco adulation has proliferated to many sites of cultural politics, inside academia, within commercial popular culture and community-based art. Inventively crafted as an urban warrior by movement intellectuals, his vestments and mannerism—cool detachment, zoot suits, ducktails, khakis and GI T-shirts, hip demeanor, suave and daring stance—inspire masculine visions of streetwise opposition to the disciplinary regimes of power. The figure of the pachuco riddles the plots of Chicano movement plays and films, his image appears center stage on colorfully etched murals, and melancholic poems confer him such legendary status that he continues to animate pages of novels, lyrics in rap songs, images on the screen.

In this thickly woven narrative of cultural politics, his female counterpart, the pachuca, is described cursorily. While he is the subject of public culture and politics, she remains his dangling object, unseen and unnamed within Chicano movement strategies insofar as their asymmetrical constructions of cultural and political resistance identities relegate the pachuca to an exotic image for public and private consumption. We have thus seen her body painted next to Aztec gods on murals, recognizable by her style: hair in a long ratted and sprayed beehive, with more hair draping over her shoulders; her face caked with makeup and shellacked lipstick. Her body adorns the hood of lowrider cars. Or, with a permed curly layered hairstyle, ruby-red polished nails, short, tight skirt and halter top, revealing the body's full curves, she's inside *Low-rider* magazine as a pinup. And her image gazes back at us from under a crisp white T-shirt where she rests as a tattoo on the body of a man.

The production of her eroticized image predates the current fascination and commodification of the "gangsta" style in mainstream popular culture. So too does her tragic performance in public as a social subject. Since the 1930s, pachucas, the predecessors of *cholas* and of today's homegirls, have hung out in the public domain of barrios like Maravilla, in southern California, as members of girls' clubs or what is currently referred to as girl gangs. Yet she stands figuratively on the margins of literary and film testimonies on la pachucada, subservient to masculine versions of the gangsta life and lifestyle. The violence and abuse she has witnessed remain unknown. Fashioned as a deviant in studies about adolescent girl gangs, her story remains untold and untheorized.[1] Throughout this discussion, I explore what it is that the pachuca, chola, homegirl as a historical subject and as a producer of meaning offers to feminist discourse and what she teaches us about opposition and resistance, not just to "la vida loca" (the "crazy life") but to "la vida dura" (the "hard life").

The Girls My Mother Warned Me About[2]

Where I grew up in South Texas, pachucas were disliked by our parents. As a young Catholic-school girl, I was afraid of but also fascinated by pachucas, for they were the female image, the embodiment, of urban "toughness" and "coolness." Every morning I walked to Holy Family School dressed in navy blue pleated-skirt uniform and black-and-white oxfords, admiring the pachucas who pranced down to public school. I could not help but notice them dressed in their stylish clothes, wearing vibrant makeup and ratted hairdos. Pachucas were loud and boisterous, hanging out after school, sometimes at the *tiendita*, often on a street corner, smoking cigarettes while I walked home sucking on a five-cent pickle. In my barrio on the west side, people called them "piranhas" because they fought as a group. I was not allowed to play with them, yet my first lesson in sex education came from a pachuca named Mary Ester.

With peroxide-orange hair, big light brown eyes circled by Maybelline black eyeliner, eyebrows shaped and painted like wings, reddish orange lips, and a teased beehive hairdo that my mother said was a nest for cockroaches, la Mary Ester was a *guera* (a light-skinned girl) who lived across the street from my gramma's house in Corpus Christi. I once heard she was my tio's *movida* (lover). Yet what I remember most about Mary Ester was how she disturbed my childhood innocence, teaching me the meaning of that popular lyric, "Let me tell you about the birds and the bees." One day I was walking down the street with her when Mary Ester asked me about the due date for my mother's baby. "What baby?" I responded. "The one in her stomach, *mensa* (dummy). That's why she's so fat. Don't you know anything about the birds and the bees?" I didn't, except that they were somehow related to "a thing called love." On that same day, I learned about the sexual taboo. As I stood in my gramma's dark, enclosed kitchen, proudly conveying my new discovery and deconstruction of the song about the birds and the bees to my mother, gramma, and tio Pepe, they stared down distressingly at me. A nine-year-old girl's thrill of learning was suddenly displaced by shame and guilt for solving the mysteries of the flesh. Yet I never forgot Mary Ester's casual frankness, nor her role in unlocking my sexual curiosity. I was always fascinated by that pachuca masquerade she wore in public, by how she had made her face into her canvas. She died several years later of a drug overdose.

Another pachuca named Gloria taught me the meaning of female solidarity. When I was fifteen years old, gang-banging, or group rape, was spreading throughout Corpus. A group of guys got a girl high on drugs, drove her to the beach, then raped and abandoned her. One Saturday night, I was hanging around the Carousel dancehall, stoned on "reds," walking from car to car, smoking, drinking, and listening to music. Gloria and a friend were there as well. She did not like me; I could tell by the way she glared at me. I was friends with her ex-boyfriend, one of two brothers I knew who were drug dealers. That Saturday night one of the brothers invited me to go cruising: "Maybe the beach," he said. Right before I entered that tan Chevrolet station wagon, Gloria drove up and yelled, "Get in the car. I'm gonna take you for a ride." Without hesitating or protesting, I followed Gloria, who took me home and on the way told me that the guys, including my friends, the two brothers, were "preparing a gang-banging," with me as their victim. I knew she was right. The hurt and terror I felt drove me away from my Carousel hangout. I even quit doing drugs. And all that summer I wondered why Gloria had intervened to save me. What I didn't understand then was Gloria's gift to me: a pachuca's sense of female solidarity.

In some Chicano *familias,* mothers warn their daughters about lesbians. In mine, I was cautioned about pachucas—*por ser muchachas corrientes y callejeras* (cheap street-roaming girls). They fought like guys and would stand up to anybody's provocation. And, most of all, the street was their turf. Indeed, the street constitutes the social geography of urban space, the arena where pachucas access public life. But the streets are also contested semiotic terrains within the public sphere, functioning, in the words of Nancy Fraser, as "culturally specific rhetorical lenses that filter and alter the utterances they frame" (1994, 86). In the eyes of parents, the streets are sites of danger, where young girls become pachucas and callejeras. For pachucas, the street is an arena where they appropriate public space. Refusing to stay in the place assigned to them by Chicano society, pachucas are trespassers in public spaces, violating the boundaries of femininity.

In my childhood, pachucas were often viewed by adults as transgressive girls who disturbed private and public patriarchy, la familia, and the Catholic Church. They threatened the foundations of la familia's gendered structure by speaking and acting in the public sphere. Mary Ester disrupted my family's acquiescence to the Church's moral prohibitions regarding sexuality. In public, she spoke openly about her sexual knowledge. And, on the streets of Corpus Christi as well, Gloria subverted patriarchal misogyny. She had intervened to stop men from inflicting their powerful violence and privilege on my body. In public spaces, both of these young women exhibited this mastery over and resistance to the sanctimony of patriarchal culture and religion.

I now understand the reason for parental scorn. In their appropriation of the public sphere, pachucas set a "bad" example. Most important, in their rebellion, pachucas failed to do what the Chicano family demands of girls and women. They rejected and challenged parental norms by refusing to stay inside the home. Their provocative language and dress style served to further refute la familia's authority. Boldly displaying their sexuality, pachucas refused to be confined by domesticity. The pachuca is therefore the place that marks the limits of la familia and is also the one who introduces disorder into its essentially patriarchal project.

Gendered Territoriality

The confinement of girls and women to domesticity is not endemic to Chicano familias, but is an inherent feature of modern capitalist societies as well as others throughout history. It is intimately linked to women's subordination in societies that, as Nancy Fraser explains, are premised on both the separation of the public from the private spheres, as well as on the "separation of the official economic sphere from the domestic sphere and the enclaving of childrearing from the rest of social labor" (1991, 122).

Fraser's work on contemporary social theory is particularly useful for exploring the construction and enactment of social and cultural identities within the public sphere. She takes issue with the tendency in feminist scholarship to collapse the entire arena outside the home into the single concept of the "public sphere." Following the theoretical model developed by Jürgen Habermas, Fraser conceptualizes classic capitalist societies as comprised of two levels of interrelated public/private separations: "systems" and "lifeworld spheres." At the level of systems, the division is between the state, as a "public" system, and the "(official) capitalist economy," as a "private" system of market relations. At the level of lifeworld spheres, the division separates family, or "private" lifeworld sphere, from the "public" lifeworld sphere, which Fraser defines as a "space of political opinion formation and participation" (Fraser 1991, 122–24). In this manner, Fraser departs from feminist theorists who define the "private" realm solely in terms of the home or the family. In Fraser's view, the private realm is more than the home, for the private encompasses both official economy of paid employment (the private system of market relations) as well as the family (the private lifeworld sphere).

Thus for Fraser, the public sphere is not an "arena of market relations." Rather it is comprised of the state (as a public system) and the public lifeworld sphere. With this qualification in mind, Fraser defines the public sphere as an arena of "discursive relations." In Fraser's words, "It [the public sphere] designates a theater in modern societies in which political participation is enacted through the medium of talk. It is the space in which citizens deliberate about their common affairs, hence, an institutionalized arena of discursive interaction" (Fraser 1994, 75). The distinction Fraser makes between the two levels of public/private separations is important to my work because in order to support their families, Chicana working-class women are allowed to work outside the home in the "private" official economy of paid employment. My concern in this essay is with the social and cultural prohibition of women's access to the public sphere of the "streets" and "discursive relations."

Giving Habermas's insights a feminist twist, Fraser explores the gendered aspects of each of these spheres. She explicitly underscores the masculine subtext of the citizen's role in the public sphere and the feminine subtext of the child-rearing role in the familial or private lifeworld sphere. According to Fraser, in defining citizenship, modern capitalist societies invest a higher value on the soldiering role rather than on what she terms "life-fostering child-rearing." In so doing, modern societies privilege the public (masculine) citizen-subject in the formation of the nation-state. Indeed, male dominance is intrinsic rather than accidental to classic capitalism precisely because it is structural and "premised on the separation of waged labor and the state from childrearing and the household." It is an institutional arrangement, namely the domestication and separation of child rearing and household work from the rest of social labor that for Fraser marks "the linchpin of modern women's subordination." As Fraser adds, it is in the public sphere as citizens and in the private (official) economic sphere as producers that men are the privileged subjects of discourse and social relations. In sharp contrast, women's role and function are confined to the private domestic sphere of the family and consumption (Fraser 1991, 122–129).

Chicanas' confinement to domesticity is not simply derivative of the division of labor in advanced capitalist societies, but rather is intensified by the dual legacy of Catholicism and the Spanish Conquest. In this respect, Jean Franco's study of gender and representation in Mexico offers a valuable insight. Franco traces the immobility of women in Latin American society, what she terms their "territoriality" within Latin America, not simply to Catholic hegemony but to the inheritance of Spanish pre-Cortesian culture: "Here we should keep in mind the privatized and inward looking Hispanic house and the fact that the virtual confinement of married women to the home had not only been required by the Church but was also intended to insure the purity of blood that Spanish society had imposed after the war against the Moors" (1988, 507).

Mexican women's and Chicanas' confinement to domesticity is thus aggravated by the syncretism of Catholicism's view about the proper place of women in the social order and the Spanish crown's anxieties around *pureza de sangre* (purity of blood). These premodern prohibitions remain submerged in memory and are resurrected to confront other "threats" to patriarchal order. For in the span of five hundred years, Spain's anxiety and fear of racial mixing has been reworked and sublimated into a concern for girls' and women's safety, and the home plays a central role in this rearticulation. Thus, even though Chicanas are permitted to work outside the home, as potential wives young Chicanas are instructed to view the home in feminine terms as a "safe" haven and the public sphere of the streets as "dangerous" or "male" terrain. In this respect, the genealogy of Chicanas' territoriality, their immobility, their confinement to the home can be traced essentially to earlier prohibitions against miscegenation. A masculine and racist project indeed! Masked as a concern for their safety, the confinement of girls to the home is first and foremost about protecting sexual property, about policing sexuality. And this is precisely the masculine familial project that pachucas interrupted and disrupted. Their bodies refused to be contained by domesticity or limited by the prevailing orthodoxy of appropriate female behavior.

Chicana Urban Identities

In Chicano nationalist discourse, Chicanas can occupy only one position, either as the self-renounced female, *la madre abnegada* (suffering mother), the passive virgin, or the embodiment of female treachery and sexual promiscuity, respectively sublimated into the either/or binary of *"virgen de guadalupe/la malinche."* Chicana feminist contestation of the myth of a monolithic, univocal Chicana either/or identity revisions figures such as la malinche or la virgen de guadalupe into symbols of oppositional practice and resistance. Within the Chicana feminist deconstruction of Chicano familial discourse, the figure of the pachuca, chola, or homegirl is inadvertently overlooked as an agent of oppositional practices, despite her notable contribution to the politics of resistance. Yet, Chicana urban identities are in fact represented vividly as subjects of narrative discourse in creative works by Carmen Tafolla, Laura del Fuego, and Mary Helen Ponce.[3]

Tejana poet and performance artist Carmen Tafolla wrote one of the first movement poems on pachucas in 1975 as part of her "Los Corts (Five Voices)." She continued to map the cultural space of pachucas with the poem "and when I dream dreams," which defamiliarizes the bucolic space of Rhodes Jr. High through the innocent denunciation of a young Chicana:

I never graduated to a
Cafeteria Guard,
who knows how they were picked
We thought it had something to do
with the FBI
or maybe the principal's office.
So we got frisked,
Boys in one line,
Girls in another,
twice every day
entering lunch and leaving
Check—no knives on boys.
Check—no dangerous weapons on girls
(like mirrors,
    perfume bottles,
        deodorant bottles,
            or teased hair.)
So we wandered the halls
    cool chuca style
    "no se sale"
    and unawares,
never knowing
other junior highs were never frisked
never knowing
what the teachers said in the teacher's lounge
never knowing we were (s'posed to be)
the toughest junior high in town. (1992, 95–96)

In this testimony by a young pachuca growing up during the 1960s, Tafolla's poem renders a pachuca style in the rhythm and rhyme of the poem and, more significantly, the poet poignantly communicates a pachuca's subjectivity and agency, located in the narrator's deliberate account of the criminalization of pachucas by the educational system. Ten years later, Laura del Fuego wrote *Maravilla*, a novel in which the subversive potential of pachuca's desire and pleasure is explicitly brought into focus.

Maravilla tells the story of a young pachuca growing up in East Los Angeles during the 1960s. A member of the Las Belltones East LA girls gang, the main character, Consuelo, or Cece, interrogates Catholic prohibitions against corporal pleasure in the following way:

> According to the Catholic church, there are two categories of sin—venial and mortal. Venial being less serious of the two, sort of like a misdemeanor, with mortal sin being more like a felony.
>
> I used to lie in bed wondering what category the sin of masturbation fell into . . . especially after having brought myself to orgasm, with my hand rigid from applying constant friction to my clitoris. I began to think that, if I only played with myself and stopped before reaching that little, gratifying explosion, it might be classified as a venial instead of the deadly mortal. (1989, 49)

Exploring her own body and affirming it as the site of sexual pleasure, she openly circumvents Catholicism. In an earlier part of the novel, Cece innocently experiences her first sexual encounter in her home with a girlfriend, Liz:

> When we reached my house, we went into the bathroom and locked the door. She pulled her panties down and sat on the toilet seat, lifting her skirt, arching her legs open. I could see the tiny opening covered with fuzz above her ass. I'd never seen it quite like that.
>
> "That's it," she said.
>
> I felt dizzy and my stomach was queasy.
>
> "Do you want to touch it?" she asked.
>
> My hand jerked back. She took hold of it, pressing it against the throbbing spot, helping me push in the tip of my finger. It was soft and mushy. For a minute, I couldn't tell if I was the one sitting on the toilet or standing up. The room pitched and I fell to my knees in front of her. Someone was rattling at the door. (33)

As a further affront to Chicano patriarchal values, Cece openly combines her interest in boyfriends with an attraction to and admiration of girls:

> There was a quick, sarcastic ring to her voice, and she had the greatest tits in the world, which she accented whenever she had the chance. But the reason I fell in love with Gerry wasn't because of her tits but because of her laugh. I loved her laugh, raucous and daring. I recog-

nized it in a group even when I couldn't see her. I was familiar with little things about her like the way she lifted a soda bottle to her lips with her pinkie extended and the sexy way she swung down the streets, languidly swaying her hips, holding her books close to her breasts. (37)

Though *Maravilla* stops before consumating homosexual desires, these scenes of Cece's homoerotic pleasures and her homosocial bonds with other girls nonetheless disclose the novel's homosexual subtext. In this manner, del Fuego's *Maravilla* openly introduces disorder into the Chicano family's essentially masculine and heterosexual project. By hanging out with girlfriends, cruising the streets, or fighting rival gangs, Cece and her cohort of pachucas refuse to be contained in the home or limited by the prevailing views of female comportment. As a pachuca, Cece openly expresses a young woman's sexual pleasures and desires despite Chicano culture's prohibitions. Unfortunately, the pachuca as social subject would appear quite differently on the screen in the gang genre.

Screening the Homegirl

Early debates in cinema studies underscored the invisibility, but also the visibility, of certain kinds of images of Chicanas and Chicanos in mainstream media. The gangsta trope, for instance, has been deployed extensively since the 1940s as the way to make Chicanos visible in U.S. popular culture. And this deployment has not been the sole purview of the dominant culture, for in contesting mainstream representations, Chicano filmmakers such as Luis Valdez and Edward James Olmos resort as well to the gangsta trope. As usual, mainstream and oppositional films succeed in marginalizing the female gang member vis-à-vis the male character. Yet despite the erasure and denial of the chola as narrative subject, what does stand out is her figuration in peculiar kinds of ways.

When I was a child, the term "pachuca" was used interchangeably with "puta." There is a scene in Luis Valdez's classic film *Zoot Suit* where the mother of the main character, upon witnessing her daughter's 1940s pachuca dress style, makes precisely that equation by saying: "Pareces puta . . . pachuca!" Thus, the fusion of the pachuca dress style with that of the hooker motivates me to read the image of the pachuca-chola-homegirl through historical and cultural discourses as well as through social and feminist theorizing about the subject, in order to analyze and interpret the visual strategies chosen to construct her image in cinema, in those spaces where she figures as object of cultural discourse. What is being played out on the body of the home-girl? What kinds of social and cultural meanings is masculinist ideology mapping onto her image?

In mainstream "gangxploitation" films like *Boulevard Nights, The Warriors,* and *Bound by Honor (Blood In, Blood Out),* the chola is inci-dental to the narrative, appearing textually as an appendage, as female props draped around the body of male gang members. In the 1988 film *Colors,* by Dennis Hopper, the homegirl has a speaking part, the sem-blance of a narrative voice. A film about Chicano gangs in Los Angeles, *Colors* is told from the point of view of the LAPD. The trope of misce-genation is a major subtext, dealing with the romance between chicana homegirl Luisa (played by the Cuban actress Maria Conchita Alonzo) and Danny (played by Sean Penn). In the first part of the film, Luisa ap-pears as the nice, subservient, sexy-but-not-too-promiscuous girl from the barrio—a demeanor designed to emphasize her passivity, thereby making the brown woman appealing to the white cop. By operating as the translator for the gang world, the homegirl facilitates white male penetration into the world of the other. However, as we learn by the sec-ond half of the film, Luisa's accommodation has been just a masquerade.

Responding to a drive-by shooting in the barrio, Danny and other law enforcers walk in on a party at a gang member's home. As Danny ap-proaches the bedroom, a black man walks out. Inside the room Danny finds Luisa, who has shed her previous homely "good-girl" attire. Danny watches as Luisa, in heavy makeup, teased hair, wearing the provocative dress typical of cholas, is donning her hose. To Danny's dismay, Luisa violently and aggressively confronts him as he walks out of the house.

Luisa's initial subservience in the film masks the underside of a native woman, for as the bedroom scene illustrates, passivity and accommo-dation figure as disguise. Beneath the passive acquiescence, Luisa sur-faces as a hypersexual object—the embodiment of unbridled sexuality, betrayal, and deceit. The end of the film demonizes Luisa, reinscribing her as threat to the white race, an inscription serving to legitimate U.S. society's historic prohibition of mixed-race unions. Yet, the film also recapitulates Hollywood's fascination with the trope of miscegenation and the "forbidden other": the mythic native woman figured in *Colors* as the homegirl of the Studio's imagination.

Does the pachuca-chola-homegirl fare any better in Chicano productions? Partly in response to films such as *Colors*, Chicano cultural workers have focused their attention on countering the pejorative image of pachucos as incorrigible deviants within the dominant culture and media. In poetry, theater, and film, this refashioning of the pachuco as urban warrior and antihero has centered exclusively on male identities. (I have written elsewhere about this reformulation as well as production of the subject of Chicano nationalism; Fregoso 1993). This masculine subject found its narrative expression in characters of the public sphere: males operating outside the home, in the streets, in the recording industry, and as urban warriors against threatening external institutional forces such as the police, the media, and the state. Chicano feature-length productions are marked by a strict gender division between the public sphere and the private domestic sphere, thereby mapping an artificial separation between them. Despite critiques by feminists about the role such separation plays in the subordination of women, the stories told by Chicano films are particularly forceful in affirming and adhering to that gendered social division. For example, while Chicano male identity and subjectivity are depicted as products of the public sphere, the female subject is absent from that space. Her presence is contained in domesticity as mother, wife, girlfriend, caretaker. Just as in the experiential realm, so too in Chicano media representation, woman's containment to the private sphere is buttressed by the extratextual forces of the church and la familia—forces dictating a specific subject location for Chicanas.

The pachuca has appeared in two such films: *Zoot Suit* and *American Me*. In *Zoot Suit*, she is again imaged in terms of the strategy of containment, appearing only in limited scenes and roles. Consequently, for all the differences in politics between *Colors* and *Zoot Suit*, both are akin in their imagery of the homegirl.[4] While three pachucas have speaking parts in *Zoot Suit*, my focus is on la Berta, who appears in the dance hall and whose love interest in the main character, Hank. Berta is depicted as a pathetic, "not-chosen-as-the-annointed-lover" of Hank. She is promiscuous, exaggerating her character traits as a pachuca.

Berta's overstated pachuca style is most evident when she approaches Hank and Della on the dance floor. Obviously drunk, Berta circles around the dancing couple, hanging onto Hank, who openly expresses his annoyance. Berta's provocative facial and bodily gestures make explicitly obvious her jealousy of Della and desire for Hank. Directing rude and obnoxious comments to the couple as she flaunts her body, Berta ends by saying: "I hope she [Della] knows the difference between being cool and being culo [piece of ass]."

Hank's sister also exhibits the style of the pachuca, yet it is la Berta who embodies the lifestyle: she is in control of her own sexual desires. Yet, the filmmaker deploys a standard virgin/whore distinction in order to punish Berta for exhibiting her desires in public. She is reprimanded for her transgression through an imaging strategy that ridicules her, depicting her as exaggerated and hypersexed. By deploying this narrow strategy of containment, the filmmaker prohibits any meaningful expression of Berta's complex sexuality. In so doing, *Zoot Suit* illustrates the extent to which female desires and explicit female sexuality threaten the familial order. Yet as the impropriety of her clothing style and her provocative gestures and language illustrate, la Berta represents a threat to both la familia and the Church's orthodoxy of female comportment. Just as in the social realm, the pachuca of *Zoot Suit* figures as a subject whose personal style and lifestyle, whose very presence on the dance floor, contest her exclusion from the public sphere.

In the film *American Me*, the homegirl, Julie (Evelina Fernandez), appears as a *veterana*, that is to say not as an actual but as a former, rehabilitated chola. In this film we witness a distinct form of the "strategy of containment," for her status as former chola demonstrates the filmmaker's inability to handle the inscription of a chola on the screen. Although the chola is part of Julie's past identity, she does not manifest that aspect of her character on the screen. Indeed, throughout the film Julie has masked this identity, remaking herself into a different form of femaleness: a mother. What is most significant about the film's articulation of the "strategy of containment" is the site where Julie's identity as a chola is made known to spectators.

Toward the end of the film, Julie is in her bedroom dressing for work. Viewers hear the voice-over of Santana's farewell letter. A shot of Julie combing her hair before a mirror ends as she stares at her hand. There, between her thumb and index finger, is an insignia testifying to her membership in *la primera* gang. Before leaving the room, Julie covers the cross tattoo on her hand with skin-toned makeup.

By masquerading and shielding the mark on her body, Julie demonstrates the extent to which social identity is not stable, but rather is a production that is fluid and provisional. Yet because the act of veiling and unveiling her identity takes place in the space of the bedroom, the film locates the chola subject in the private sphere of domesticity. By prohibiting its unveiling in the public sphere, *American Me* exemplifies and suggests just how threatening the performance of chola identity can be to Chicano society. The film reinforces society's censure that the Chicana can only be a chola in the interior space of the bedroom.

I concluded my book, *The Bronze Screen*, with a reading of the film *American Me*. Lamenting the film's erasure of the female subject, I ended with the following words:

> Who is this new subject, this Chicana whom Edward James Olmos claims is the heroine of *American Me*, the hope in our barrios? His story ends before hers can begin. In the final close-up shot of a cross tattooed on Julie's hand resides her untold story. It is the history of Chicana membership in gangs that unfolds not on the screen, but in my mind. The final weathered look in Julie's eyes sparks the painful silent memory of the female gang members I have known: Chicanas surviving and resisting la vida dura (the hard life). I often wonder why the story of Julie's oppression and resistance, why the pain of her rape is not up there, on the Hollywood screen, looking at me. (Fregoso 1993, 133–34)

That story of Chicanas surviving la vida dura would appear on screen in 1994. Three decades after Herbert Biberman's feature film, *Salt of the Earth*, focused exclusively on Chicana identities, thereby enabling Chicana subjectivity on the screen, another white director attempted a similar project. Alison Anders's *Mi Vida Loca* tells the story of young Chicana gang members, homegirls with names like Mousie, Sad Girl, and Whisper, who live in Echo Park, L.A. As I have written elsewhere, *Mi Vida Loca* is a splendid contradiction (Fregoso 1995). It is the first commercial film to focus entirely on Chicana gang members. The film faithfully renders the style, stance, posture, gestures, mannerisms, and speech of so many pachucas-cholas-homegirls I have known throughout the years. Yet its daring and gritty realism is so partial in its one-sided view of la vida loca, or what I prefer to call la vida dura.

Reviews of the film have been mixed.[5] Professional film critics have trashed *Mi Vida Loca* on political and ideological grounds. Writing for the *Los Angeles Times*, Kevin Thomas points to the filmmaker's paternalism as well as to the fact that the film confirms negative stereotypes of Chicanas as welfare dependents (1994). Pat Dowell further blasts the film's nihilism, its downbeat resolution (1994). It should come as no surprise that a Latina critic would launch the usual "negative stereotype" accusation. Writing on behalf of the "Latino" community, Rose Arrieta disapproves of the film for playing "on every stereotype 'mainstream' America thinks about urban gang life," and urges the portrayal of Chicanos as something else besides gang members (1994). In the United States as well as abroad, others fault the film for depicting teenagers without ambition, "drifting downward into chaos and dead-end lives."

I am less concerned with these types of objections, as hopelessness and helplessness is in fact pervasive among inner-city youth. Therefore, unless we deal directly with the very serious social, economic, and structural problems of the inner city, a positive or uplifting ending to a gang film would make no difference in the lives of young gang members. Even though I too desire the production of films that show Chicanas and Chicanos as characters other than gang members, filmmakers such as Anders cannot be held responsible for the widespread dissemination of these images in popular culture. Though it is true that in choosing a subject, Anders took advantage of the current fascination and commodification of the gangsta style in mainstream culture, *Mi Vida Loca* is not the usual gangxploitation film.

In fact, *Mi Vida Loca* is the first Hollywood film to take homegirls seriously, detailing the gangsta life of the Echo Parque Locas. At first glance, it seems as though the story is told from a homegirl point of view. The film opens with frames of the iconography of a vibrant barrio. It portrays homegirls who are fiercely independent, struggling as single teenage mothers whose boyfriends or husbands have ended up in prison or the grave. In terms of the politics of representation, that is, in the context of other portrayals of Chicana homegirls, *Mi Vida Loca* appears to have all of the essential ingredients.

In the first place, through its exclusive focus on relations among teenage girls, the film enables a Chicana homosocial perspective to emerge for the first time on the big screen. The film begins by telling the story of two childhood friends, Sad Girl and Mousie (Angie Aviles and Seidy Lopez). The girls are lifelong friends whose friendship ends when they both end up pregnant by the same homeboy, Ernesto (Jacob Vargas). Mousie and Sad Girl's fatal showdown at a barrio vacant lot has a surprise resolution when Ernesto is gunned down by one of his despised customers, a white female druggie. This ironic twist in the plot propels the story in a different direction and opens up a space for narrating a tale of female bonding and collectivity, not just between Sad Girl and Mousie, but among the homegirls in general.

It is Giggles, a veterana just released from prison, whose words about female solidarity consolidate the homosocial space created in the film. On their trip home after picking up Giggles from prison, the Echo Park Locas stop for a bite to eat. Inside the diner, as the homegirls share news about their lives, an argument about Ernesto erupts between Sad Girl and Mousie. Giggles interrupts them with the following words: "Girls, you don't ever throw down with a homegirl over a guy. Guys come and go. They ain't worth it." From this point on, *Mi Vida Loca* unfolds as a sisterhood saga, portraying young Chicanas whose lives are marked by camaraderie, affection, struggle, and survival.

The film is shot in a style Anders calls "romantic realism," where camera movements follow characters' emotions. The film's cinematographer, Rodrigo Garcia (son of writer Gabriel García Márquez), effectively mixes low-angle close-ups with opalescent and luminous shots. Structurally, the film disrupts conventional narrative coherence. Rather than presenting a single unifying thread, *Mi Vida Loca* features three interlocking stories, giving the film its episodic quality. Besides the main story line described earlier, a minor plot features an epistolary romance between La Blue Eyes and El Duran, who is in prison. A final plot line revolves around Ernesto, a homeboy obsessed with a lowrider truck.

The film's ethnographic-documentary texture derives from its use of six different narrators. Voice-over narration is often self-reflexive, exhibiting a subjective quality. At other times, the narration is informational and descriptive, further accentuating the film's ethnographic-documentary character. Another significant feature of the film derives from the fact that multiple narrators, framing shifting points of view, disrupt spectator identification with a single cinematic position. Textual reality is presented first through Sad Girl's point of view, then through Mousie's vision, followed by Ernesto's, so that identification with spectators shifts from one character to another. For example, at one point, the story is told from Ernesto's point of view; when he is killed, spectator identification shifts back to a homegirl point of view. Thus, in contrast to the single narrative point of view and/or character identification typical in most conventional films, *Mi Vida Loca* constructs multiple positions from which viewers can identify with its narrative reality. In so doing, the film offers a collective subjectivity that destabilizes and challenges the individualism typical in Chicano gang films. In other words, by depicting subject formation through shifting perspectives, the film enables a space for collective Chicana urban identities shamefully neglected in other films about gangs.

The film created decisive instances of cinematic identification, as is evident in Keta Miranda's observation that homegirls derived pleasure from seeing "themselves" on the screen represented with such fidelity.[6] In circulating alternative images of homegirls, *Mi Vida Loca* fulfills homegirls' desire for representation and opens up a discursive space in which homegirls may reclaim and affirm their authority as subjects in history and producers of meaning. At the San Francisco Film Festival's screening of the film in 1994, during the question-and-answer session, the following comments by a member of Oakland's Da Crew girls' gang were directed at Anders: "The movie was really down. . . . Why didn't you show the girls really throwing down? And why did they throw down over a boy? You know, we wouldn't throw down over a guy." And while Chicana homegirls welcomed and celebrated their arrival on the screen as subjects of cinematic discourse, they objected forcefully to the details in the film's multiple plots.

For all its feminist politics, its aesthetic and narrative innovations, *Mi Vida Loca* succumbs in some respects to conventional film antics. Sad Girl's final statement, "Women don't use weapons to prove a point; women use weapons for love," has the melodramatic flavor of a Mexican soap opera. And the final scene, which depicts the drive-by shooting of Sleepy's daughter, gives the film a classic Hollywood ending. More substantive critiques of the film come from the gang members themselves, who have taken issue with the filmmaker's depiction of their lives. Among Chicana homegirls' objections to the film are that: (1) homegirls don't get pregnant from the same guy, they have more respect than that; (2) a homeboy does not become obsessed over a lowrider truck at the expense of his kids' welfare; and (3) rival gangs fight over turf, never over a car (Sharer 1994 and Cobo-Hanlon 1994). In fact, the film's three interlocking stories reflect autobiographical experiences from the life of the filmmaker. A victim of unrequited love, Anders transformed a romantic episode in her past into the epistolary affair between La Blue Eyes and El Duran. A short script written by her former boyfriend, Kurt Voss, inspired the lowrider truck segment. And the subplot in which the two homegirls discover that they both have become pregnant after having intercourse with the same man is taken from a story that her daughter heard on the streets.

In *Mi Vida Loca*, Chicana homegirls are portrayed as independent and self-sufficient young women whose survival depends on a bond and camaraderie with their cohorts. For them, the familial contract is not an option, since the Chicano family is portrayed as either dysfunctional or nonexistent in their lives. And this is part of the film's problem, for while the heterosexual nuclear family may not figure prominently in the lives of these women, in reality there is an alternative form of family unit operative in the barrio. Anders misses the reality that the sisterhood so eloquently captured in the film is not created in a vacuum. Those who decide to create stories and films about Chicanas ought to understand that the girls' survival in the barrio depends heavily on the kinship of older, compassionate and understanding women who have also resisted and survived la vida dura. For reasons that are unclear, Anders chose to portray Chicana teenagers as self-sufficient, having little interaction with adults. Untold is the story of the elaborate extended family of mothers, grandmothers, and aunts, who visit them in jail, bail them out, and help deliver, feed, and take care of their babies. At the San Francisco Film Festival's screening of the film, Anders told the audience: "My goal was to humanize people who don't get represented on the screen." Although Anders misses crucial elements of Chicana homegirl reality, *Mi Vida Loca* nonetheless serves as an effective vehicle for my discussion of the pachuca-chola-homegirl because the film opens up a space for the refashioning of Chicana urban identities.

What is the nature of that space that *Mi Vida Loca* enables? As we know, social identities are both produced and constituted experientially, in the public sphere as well as within and through representational forms (Hall 1989). In cultural forms and practices, subject formation is also depicted for us textually in their narratives. *Mi Vida Loca* makes manifest these processes textually as well as through the spectator positions that the film enables and constitutes. As the images on the screen demonstrate, the film challenges the artificial division between the public and the private sphere, where men and women are assigned "appropriate" terrain. In the film, the production of Chicana urban identities takes place simultaneously on the streets and in the domestic site of the home, thereby positing the body of the homegirl as a disruption of those spaces restricted by gender. One scene in the film in particular obliterates the public/private split completely. In an interior domestic scene, the veterana Giggles organizes the Echo Park Locas. At this meeting, a dozen or so homegirls sit around the living room, smoking, drinking beer, and discussing the main issue before them: what should be done with Ernesto's truck. Earlier, their male counterparts had met on the streets in a vacant lot to consider the same issue, whereas the locas met inside a home. Yet, in this particular case, the home is not linked to women's subordination and containment; instead, the film transforms this privatized space of the home into a public sphere of "discursive interaction." Departing from the usual treatment in Chicano films, the home in *Mi Vida Loca* functions as the arena where, through the medium of talk, homegirls are acting as citizens deliberating an issue. In organizing the homegirls, Giggles has symbolically channeled them into the collective public sphere of action. They may be mothers, but these young women are neither confined by, nor contained in, domesticity.

My reflections on Chicana homegirl-chola-pachuca have attempted to underscore the ways in which the physical body of this historical figure contributes to Chicana feminist discourse, and the manner in which her very presence disrupts la familia. The inability of masculine cultural discourses thus far to portray Chicana urban identities, restricting them to the narrow private sphere of the home, derives, in my view, from the threat to the Chicano "family romance" that her presence represents. Her comportment registers the outer boundaries of Chicana femininity; her body marks the limits of la familia; her masquerade accentuates her deviance from the culture's normative domestic place for women. And perhaps the production of pachuca-chola-homegirl subjectivities has not been celebrated by many of us precisely because her body defies, provokes, challenges as it interrogates the traditional familial basis of our constructions of the Chicano nation.

Notes

The line given in the title of this essay, "cool chuca style," is taken from Carmen Tafolla's poem "and when I dream dreams" published in *Sonnets of Human Beings and Other Selected Works* (1992). This article was greatly improved by comments, support, and encouragement from the following friends and colleagues: Angie Chabram-Dernersesian, Iris Blanco, Alvina Quintana, B. Ruby Rich, Herman Gray, Keta Miranda, Janet Bergstrom, Margarita de la Vega Hurtado, Yvon Yabro-Bejarano, Ellie Hernandez, Tomas Almaguer, Pat Zavella, and Maria Elena de las Carreras de Kuntz.

1 In terms of the research on girl gangs, the exception to this neglect by feminists is the new body of work by a recent generation of Chicana graduate students, including Keta Miranda of UCSC, whose research on Oakland's Da Crew girls gang treats these adolescent girls as producers of meaning. Discussion of Chicana cholas and homegirls is also found in Harris (1994) and Moore (1991).

2 Taken from the title of the anthology, *Chicana Lesbians: The Girls Our Mothers Warned Us About*, edited by Carla Trujillo (1991).

3 See del Fuego (1989) and Ponce (1989).

4 The main political difference between the films is that of point of view. *Colors* is told from the perspective of law enforcement officers, whereas *Zoot Suit* is told from the point of view of Chicano pachucos.

5 Initially I wrote a favorable review that aired on National Public Radio's *Latino USA* during the summer of 1994. Other favorable reviews include Kort (1994); Salas (1994); and Rich (1994, 1995).

6 Keta Miranda is a graduate student in the History of Consciousness Department at the University of California, Santa Cruz, who is conducting an ethnography on the Da Crew girls gang. She took several girls to screen the film at the San Francisco Film Festival as well as to academic conferences, where they have shared their experiences with many of us. I have benefited enormously from their insights and from Keta's observations on girl gang members. I would also like to thank Sylvia Escarcega-Judge, a graduate student in the Department of Anthropology at the University of California, Davis, whose insightful comments on a shorter published version of this research forced me to rethink some of my previous formulations. At her insistence, I reformulated this section to include some account of the agency and subjectivity of "actual" (not simply discursive) girl gang members.

A Guest at the Wedding: Honor, Memory, and

(National) Desire in Michel Khleife's *Wedding in Galilee*

Mary N. Layoun

> We carry in our worlds that flourish
> our worlds that have failed.
> > —Christopher Okigbo,
> > "Lament of the Silent Sisters"

> Huná nahnu qaruba hunák
> Here we are near there
> > —Mahmud Darwish,
> > "Here We Are Near There"

Desire is often and almost proverbially formulated as in opposition to some more properly biological need, and that desire as for something absent or missing or lacking. Further, desire is proposed as itself a representation of that absence or lack through the attempt to imagine its satisfaction. In this formulation, desire, then, is an imaginary depiction of its own fulfillment. To push this proposition yet further, desire can be a productive way to account for the workings of narratives of nationalism—as an attempt to imagine its own fulfillment, which fulfillment is most often depicted as in and by a sovereign and independent state, though this perhaps preemptive fulfillment is scarcely the only desire to which nationalism addresses itself.

In the late twentieth century, this is, on one level, only too obvious. For the claims and aspirations of nationalism are still familiar, sometimes excruciatingly so. But the impossibility of a static reiteration of nineteenth-century nationalism is clear in what is a decidedly trans- if not postnational moment. While the meanings and workings of the global or the transnational are fiercely debated and debatable, the economic and political exhaustion of older notions of the nation-state—as of its necessary counterpart of modernity—are apparent. Yet, the call of nationalism as a preferred self-image—problematic and vexed as it is—still typically asserts the coherence, continuity, and integrity of a nation's past and of that nation's relation to a distinct language, culture, and land. This story of the past is cited as legitimation for a demand for autonomy or independence or, at least, a change in political status for the designated nation. And this call is made notwithstanding diverse national populations, languages, and cultures or the ineluctable workings of transnational capital and the sometimes massive disruptions and migrations of peoples. Even if the national present must be acknowledged as one ineluctably complexified culturally, socially, ethnically, and racially, the national past still resides in popular imagination as a differently configured one.

Nationalism, then, of both the nineteenth and the twentieth centuries, and perhaps in the late twentieth century more than ever, is a masterful effort of narrative construction. Like all narrative, nationalism tells a story by articulating diverse but presumably linked elements. And not by chance, it also constructs and privileges—sometimes as virtually omniscient—its own narrative perspective. Narratives of nationalism propose a grammar of the nation. That is, they propose the correct and orderly placement and use of the constituent elements of the nation. And, not least of all, that grammar prescribes the proper and acceptable definition and situation of gendered citizens. It also, of course, prescribes the definition and situation of noncitizens.

But in addition, nationalism also and necessarily articulates a rhetoric of the nation. The rhetoric of nationalism-as-narrative persuades and convinces its multiple audiences—its implied readers and listeners— of the efficacy and desirability of its terms and of the necessary and "natural" relationship between those terms. The call of rhetoric is not as of the letter and word of proper order (as grammar), but with letters and words and representations as persuasion and likely possibility (as rhetoric).

If nationalism is, then, articulated as a narrative, the tactical and strategic maneuvers of and within those narratives and among contesting narratives are a significant commentary on the workings of nationalism as it is told, heard, retold, practiced, and repracticed. Or, put differently, nationalism is simultaneously both ideological and utopic narrative. All nationalism. It seeks to contain the present as it constructs a legitimating past and as it projects a future for which the present is but a prelude. It follows then that a crucial part of negotiating nationalism, literally and figuratively, is located in a critical understanding of the complexity of this narrative process and in the construction, deconstruction, and reconstruction of (perhaps only parts of?) the dominant national narrative. The rhetorical attempt of nationalism-as-narrative, arguably of all narrative, is to give the impression of coherence, of the legitimate authority of the narrator (however that authority might be construed), of the truth-value of the stories told, and not least of all, to situate the implied narrative audience in particular ways. Clearly, these attempts will always be contradictory, full of gaps and slippage. Therein lies the vulnerability of nationalism-as-narrative, perhaps of any narrative. But there too—in those moments of narrative slippage and contradiction, or, if you like, in those moments of narrative silence—lie possibilities of recasting or at least of renegotiating nationalism-as-narrative, rhetorically and perhaps grammatically as well.

This process of renegotiation takes place not only in the historical, legal, and political domain and in their documents. Cultural and literary narratives too can be read as attempts to negotiate, to counter, to reimagine, to articulate differently the dominant narratives—literary and cultural as well as national or transnational—in which they participate and the boundaries those narratives draw and seek to maintain. Such narrative negotiation is contestatory and acquiescent, often simultaneously. And while my focus here will be on a distinctly cultural text, Michel Khleife's *Wedding in Galilee*,[1] historical or legal or political texts are no less subject to these narrative processes—if not to the specificities of literary and cultural variations.

In the consideration that follows of a distinctly cultural and decidedly "textual"—if cinematic—Palestinian narrative, then, my point is not to propose the Palestinian authenticity or the quasi-anthropological value of Khleife's film. Nor is it to propose the film as some sort of direct proposition about the extratextual Palestinian situation. Rather, I want to propose, in a discussion of the imaginary and impossible suggestions of Khleife's *Wedding in Galilee*, the ways in which cultural and literary texts can afford a space for questions and propositions that are precisely impossible to articulate in the contemporary political or social sphere. It is those impossible fictions, in their very fictiveness and impossibility, that can suggest to us a story we might not have heard before, a dream we might not have dreamed, a proposition—in *Wedding in Galilee* about gendered (meta)nationalism—we might not yet have considered. It is precisely in this impossible imaginary, or, if you like, in this splendidly figural aspect, that a literary or cultural text can articulate otherwise nationalism and gender, the state and the citizen, sexuality and honor. It is precisely in this impossible imaginary too that the literary and cultural text can articulate other notions of community, other notions of honor, other notions of gendered citizenship than the predominant or putatively commonsense ones. Of these former we are in fierce need. As we are in fierce need of an uncommon or a new common sense.

The wedding is an overwhelmingly familiar trope in Palestinian literature, song, and popular imagination, and that trope took a notable turn, after 1948. In the subsequent economy of conjugal relations, that moment of the establishment of the state of Israel in Palestine was cast as a "coercive conjugal separation." As even the titles of popular poems from the post-1948 period suggest—'Abd al-Latif' Aql's "Love the Palestinian Way" or Mahmud Darwish's "Blessed Is That Which Has Not Come," with its invocation of "the Palestinian wedding without end" of his "Lover from Palestine"—the bride or beloved is typically the land of Palestine, the groom or lover is the Palestinian. But what appears to be almost mundanely familiar and even common sense in this image—the union of or wedding between a man and a woman, an exiled lover and his beloved, a Palestinian and Palestine—is distinctly more vexed on closer consideration.

Yet this prosaic image of the conjugal union of man and woman as a trope for the union of national citizen with national territory under the authority of a national state is at the heart of virtually all nationalist rhetoric. (And it has situated itself as well and with considerable regularity at the heart of nationalist grammar as state order.) This vexed trope is arguably the generative basis for the absence and longing on which national desire is erected. And, following mundanely on the terms of that trope, the representation of the fulfillment or consummation of desire is possession and control of the land-as-woman. The profoundly problematic nature of this latter equation is by now patent; increasingly there are challenges to its putative naturalness. Yet its currency in the economy of nationalist rhetoric and grammar continues. A pressing question in this context is certainly what this trope of conjugal union silences or effaces. And *Wedding in Galilee* is an instructive answer, though hardly the only one, to just this question. For in the Palestinian instance, there is a premier obstacle to possession-of-the-woman/land-as-national-fulfillment. Rather obviously, the fertile, virginal (if violated), and desirable woman/land that "belongs to" the virile (if exiled) male lover/citizen is differently occupied. Namely, Palestine is also Israel and the as-yet-still-occupied Israeli territories.

So this trope, discrepant from the beginning, has come to be as debated in the Palestinian context as it is familiar. And it is precisely in this context of vexed familiarity and debate that Khleife's 1987 Belgian-French coproduction of *Wedding in Galilee* is situated. It subtly if substantially frustrates the conjoining of the formerly separated man and woman as a trope for Palestinian nationalism. The film itself as a narrative representation of the fulfillment of national and sexual desire is equally a trenchant suggestion of an absence or lack that cannot be made present. This apparently abstract proposition takes a distinctly concrete turn in the national/sexual contradiction that propels the latter half of the film. The antithesis or resolution of absence in this instance is not, in any event, presence. Rather, it is the continuation of desire itself—a desire for something else beyond the consummation of a "national" wedding.

So then, the putative fulfillment of national/sexual desire in the conjugal union of bride and groom is drastically and suggestively recast in Khleife's *Wedding in Galilee,* for that consummation cannot take place as expected. In the face of the burden of his father's dreams, the expectations of the Palestinian community, the growing and clamorous tensions and barely foiled plans for violence outside the wedding chamber, and his own rage and frustration, the bridegroom is impotent. And so to "protect the honor and dignity of everyone" (*karamat lil-al-kull*), the bride, Samia, takes her own virginity, asking as she prepares to do so: "If a woman's honor is her virginity, where is the honor of a man?" *Haithu*—where, she asks, not what. She knows *where* her virginity is and, seizing the male prerogative, she takes it herself. Samia takes possession of her own honor—if, as she says, "Woman's honor is her virginity." But what of Ádil, her young bridegroom? Or of his friends, angry victims of Israeli military rule? What of the older generation of Palestinian men? The predication of the wedding night—or of the allegorical union of Palestinian (male) with (a female) Palestine—on the groom's possession of the bride and on that possession or taking and its object (female virginity) as a mark of honor are here radically undermined.

This then is a rather different rendition of "the Palestinian national struggle" than that which might be more familiar to some from media broadcasts and newspaper accounts. It is also a rather different rendition from that series of gendered national equations noted above. And so for some segments of a Palestinian audience, Samia's actions toward the end of the film are its most scandalous moment. Yet it is simultaneously one of the film's most adamant accounts of "struggle." It is, however, one that occurs behind closed doors, in the house of the patriarch, witnessed only by the frustrated and temporarily impotent bridegroom. But it is precisely this aspect of national struggle in containment that follows on and recasts a more prosaic understanding of gendered national struggle. The trope of national/sexual possession is transmuted. In her literal and metaphoric self-consummation, Samia claims Palestine—herself—for herself. And that taking suggests further a vision of self-possession that is simultaneously sensual, sexual, and personally and communally political. Yet, outside the bridal chamber, the wedding guests and the larger community know nothing of this. They know only that tradition has been maintained. The bloodied bridal sheets are displayed in demonstration of the virginity of the bride, the virility of the bridegroom, and "the honor of everyone."

But, courtesy of the camera, peering into the bridal chamber, watching from behind the bride's back—the only guests at the wedding afforded this voyeuristic view—the film's audience knows differently. And to witness Samia's act of self-possession is to be compelled to reconsider the significance of the wedding itself. It is to be compelled to reconsider as well the significance of the gendered national trope that would postulate the consummation of national desire in the possession by a man of a woman.

But it is not only Samia's unanswered question and her act of self-possession that force a reconsideration of the national narrative and notions of community, memory, and honor. There are other noteworthy instances of visual reformulation of the dominant national trope in *Wedding in Galilee*. One of these is the very movement of the camera itself in the framing and telling of the story. To turn for a moment to the beginning of the film, the sounds and images that might be expected to frame a wedding celebration are not the first ones audible in the film's opening sequence. Rather, it is the sound of military jets buzzing the landscape. The first frames are of the exterior of the Israeli military headquarters. The camera subsequently moves inside to a waiting room in the offices of the military commander. This move from outside to inside and out again—here from the skies dominated by Israeli jets to the exterior façade of the military headquarters to the interior workings of military rule to the outside of the building again—marks the visual organization of the film throughout.[2] And, like the trope of the wedding consummated, this structural device is strategically though ambiguously reversed in conclusion. If it is on the inside that potentially radical transformation of desire and imaginary figures of its satisfaction occur, if it is on the inside that the dominant narratives of nation, family, and gendered community are contested and enacted differently, on the outside the dominant narrative arguably continues to hold sway. Yet, the disturbingly familiar and vexed implications of this construct are themselves breached in the film. Is the interior a site of the challenge to the dominant scheme of things and the exterior a site of the apparent maintenance of that dominant scheme? Or is it otherwise? I bracket this question only for the moment. For there are a number of crucial instances in and aspects of the film that suggest an answer.

Let me return for a moment to the opening of the film in the military governor's office and the exchange between the *mukhtar* (the headman or "mayor") of a Palestinian village in the Galilee, Salim Saleh Daoud, and the military governor. As you might expect from the film's title, the mukhtar comes to request permission for an exemption from the military restrictions that forbid public gatherings so that he can hold a traditional village wedding for his eldest son. And as you might also expect, the mukhtar's request is denied in the name of Israeli (military) law and order and, as the military governor insists, because Palestinians have not demonstrated "respect for Israeli will." The implicit formula here for soliciting the "benevolence" of the ruler/occupier toward the ruled/occupied is one that is reiterated later in the film and within Palestinian society between man/husband and woman/wife. But in the opening, the references are clearly to military rule and national aspirations and (tradition) in opposition to that rule. An aide to the governor, however, comes up with a brilliantly Machiavellian idea. He suggests that the governor agree to a permit for the wedding but only if the Israeli military governor and his entourage be invited to the wedding. To their surprise, the mukhtar agrees. But he has a condition of his own: "You've told me your terms; let me tell you mine—that you will stay for the *entire* wedding"—that is, you will behave as a proper and respectful guest at the wedding.

The bargain is struck and the mukhtar leaves the military headquarters, boards a bus, and returns to his village. In what is the paradigmatic visual organization of the film, the camera moves from the bus and the exterior landscape as it travels through the countryside to the interior, now the courtyard of the mukhtar's home. There his mother sits with her grandchild, Daoud's youngest daughter, telling her a story about the communal murder of an adulteress's son. This scene and its (ironic) commentary on marital and communal law and order and the consequences of their violation is the first thing that greets Daoud on his return home and is the first interior scene juxtaposed to his opening encounter with Israeli military law and order. The scene then reverts to Daoud's bus ride back to the village and his voice-over interior monologue as the camera pans the landscape, its olive trees, its goat herds, and its fields. This is interrupted temporally and spatially again by a scene in the interior of Daoud's house, his bedroom, where he explains to his wife that he had to invite the military authorities to the wedding in order to get permission for the celebration. "What's your opinion?" he asks her. "It's your decision," she responds. "But," she adds meaningfully, "try not to cause a split in the family because of this."

On this warning, the scene returns to the mukhtar's bus ride, then to his bedroom again, back to the bus, and finally to the main room of Daoud's home and the reedy voice of his old father singing. The room fills quickly with male relatives for the family meeting convened to discuss the wedding of Daoud's son and the invitation that had to be extended to the Israeli military authorities. The film cuts back to the bus ride back to the village and the landscape of the countryside; it moves back to the main room of Daoud's house and his formal invitation to the wedding to all of his kinfolk. Heated disagreement erupts over the invitation to the Israeli military to the wedding and over holding an elaborate wedding at all in a time of occupation and military rule. An angry refrain echoes throughout the room: "At what cost, this wedding?" In response, Daoud recounts to the assembled men a recurring dream in which his grandfather appears to him dressed in white and urges him to hold a traditional village wedding for his son with singing, dancing, an elaborate feast, and with the young women dressed in their most beautiful clothes. And Daoud reminds the men of the traditional extension of village hospitality at a wedding, which would include even enemies.

As if in counterbalance to the men's indictment of the circumstances of the wedding, Daoud's old father reminisces to Hassan, Daoud's youngest son, about the multiple occupations of Palestine. There were the Turks ("When the Turks were here they despised the Arabs"), the British, and now the Israelis. And, in a reiteration of proverbial Arab hospitality, echoing his son Daoud's acceptance of an Israeli military presence at the wedding, the old man, in apparently senile confusion, tells Hassan, "If my home were nearby, I'd go and bring you some raisins." "But grandfather," the young boy responds with a smile, "this is your home, so where are my raisins?" Such "senile" interruptions by the grandfather and the grandmother are, more properly, punctual reminders of alternative ways of seeing the present in light of the past. Their disruptive outbursts of apparent senility are simultaneously astute commentary on what no one else wants to admit or remember. Daoud himself, standing in the courtyard of his house, responds to his mother's advice about quickly marrying off Sumaya, the mukhtar's lovely and bold older daughter, with the observation that "the old woman only seems to be senile but is in fact clever as a fox."

But inside the house, the men of the family argue; some walk out angrily, others continue to dispute Daoud's decision. The camera moves back to the bus ride once again and an identification check by an armed Israeli soldier of Palestinians on the bus. The bus finally arrives in the village and, as he steps down, Daoud invites everyone to his son Ádil's wedding the following Friday. As he walks to his house, and over the ululations of the women on the bus, a megaphone from a military jeep declares an early curfew in the village. Although the first third of the film moves back and forth between the present of the mukhtar's bus ride back to his village and the future of his arrival home, from the narrative time of that arrival, *Wedding in Galilee* proceeds in fairly linear temporal fashion. A more historically shaped temporal disruption of the film's narrative present is marked in the persons of the mukhtar's parents rather than in the movement of the camera itself. From this point on, the camera's oscillation is spatial—between interior and exterior—rather than temporal.

And so as time begins to unfold in a more linear fashion, the day of the wedding dawns, and the festivities and the tensions begin to accelerate. In the context of precisely this tension—particularly that between the Palestinians and the Israeli military—Tlali, an Israeli woman soldier, faints at the wedding from the long day of drink and food and heat. She is taken away to an upstairs bedroom by the Palestinian women of the house. The women gather around the bed where Tlali lies, reciting a passage from the Koran to protect her. One of the older women massages Tlali's neck and chest and loosens her military uniform. And then the women leave the room, leaving Tlali to sleep and two or three of the younger women to watch over her. Outside, Sumaya, the mukhtar's lovely and bold older daughter, playfully taunts the Israeli soldier waiting anxiously for Tlali to reemerge. "We're going to cut her heart out and eat it," she tells him in Arabic (which he cannot understand). Sumaya continues to tease him, telling him that if he wants to dance at her brother's wedding he will have to take off his military uniform. The silly banter of a playfully mocking young woman. But in fact, there is someone who removes her military uniform to participate in Ádil's wedding: not the young soldier whom Sumaya teases, but Tlali, who loses consciousness in one (exterior) setting and regains it in another (on the inside).

Tlali's initially involuntary crossing over from the more public space of the courtyard where the wedding proper is taking place to an inner room of the mukhtar's house allows another kind of opening to emerge in the story of *Wedding in Galilee*, another visual rendition of gendered community and the nation—though a decidedly more private one. That rendition is, for a moment, a women's story. The second time we see Tlali in the upstairs bedroom, she has awoken and is transfixed by the sensual time and space in which she finds herself. She gets up from the bed where she was sleeping, looks around her, and stretches out on the cool stone floor, tracing the texture of its stones with her fingertips.

But, as in the story of Samia's self-possession, the story of Tlali and the Palestinian women is one framed and at least partially contained by the different and male organization outside the inner room. The very movement of the camera makes this narrative containment visually apparent: the camera advances from men dancing in the bright sunlight of the courtyard to the bridegroom Ádil's face in their midst to the men dancing again, then it cuts to the inside of the house and the room where Tlali has been sleeping. Now the light changes from that of the bright sun to a softer and ever so slightly blurred shade of yellow, filtered delicately through the curtains at the windows. There is gentle laughter in the background and the sound of bracelets jangling faintly against one another. One of the young women sifts dried rose petals through her fingers from a bowl on the tabletop, letting the fragrant petals drop slowly back into the bowl. This is one of the film's most sensual markers in the effort to visually account for smell and touch. With the help of her young Palestinian counterparts, Tlali removes her military uniform and puts on a thoub, an embroidered Palestinian dress. At the heart of the Palestinian wedding, there is, for a moment, a sensual and improvisational community of Israeli and Palestinian women for whom exclusionary nationality is suspended. Tlali *does* dance at Ádil's wedding, in the company of women on the inside of the house, unnoticed by her male counterparts or by the Palestinian men. That this moment is severely constrained is clear from that characteristic (almost nervous) movement of the camera from this suggestive scene inside the house of gently laughing women who do not speak each other's language but have managed to communicate nonetheless to the growing tensions outside the house, as the tensions that underlie the wedding gather momentum.

This nascently transnational community among women stands out against the familial community of her new husband into which Samia enters. It stands out as well against the community of national oppression of Palestinians by Israelis and the potential for violent opposition to that oppression, which is signaled by the young Palestinian men who are Ádil's cohorts in the film. And it stands out against Israeli national community with its own internal ethnic and religious tensions. If inside the house there is for a moment a different order—one not necessarily predicated on national desire but on desire and longing for community of a different sort—that community is abruptly interrupted and reframed by events outside. And it is not only the threat of the young Palestinian men's retaliation against the Israeli military that overshadows both this sensual community and the wedding and union of Ádil and Samia; there are other grim reminders of the fierce foreclosure of alternative community. The social and sexual order of a society under siege, the burden of claustrophobic and loveless marriages—these markers too clutter the landscape of *Wedding in Galilee* in the desperate plotting of the young Palestinian men for reprisal, in Sumaya's attempts to refuse the stifling burden of traditional women's roles, in the frightened and lonely weeping of a wife assaulted by her husband.

Yet this grim foreclosure is qualified by the repetition of two crucial images and moments in the film. The least obvious of these repetitions is perhaps the most suggestive: the duplication of Samia's bridal dance by Tlali. Implicitly but nonetheless clearly, there are, then, two brides at this Palestinian wedding. One, Samia, is Palestinian; the other is Tlali, the Israeli soldier. And, other than the implied audience for the film afforded by the camera eye, there is only one person in the film who recognizes the parallel between Samia and Tlali. He interrupts the dance of both women swaying with candles in their hands. It is the same Israeli soldier whom Sumaya teases outside the room where Tlali sleeps. It is this Israeli soldier who interrupts the dance of Samia as he searches for Tlali inside the house. Samia is framed in the doorway, surrounded by a group of Palestinian women, two candles in her hands. Following this intrusion by the Israeli soldier, Samia's mother-in-law decides that the time for the consummation of the wedding has come. Samia extinguishes the two lit candles by stepping on the flames, presumably marking the transition from one life to another. When we next see someone (another "bride") swaying with two lit candles in her hands, it is Tlali frozen in the doorway as the same Israeli soldier who burst in on Samia and her company of women, bursts in on Tlali and her female Palestinian companions.[3] But Tlali's candles are not ritually extinguished to mark a transition from one life to the next. She drops the candles as the Israeli soldier, presumably her admirer, roughly grabs her arm and pulls her from the room.

These two moments are at a considerable distance from one another in the film, but the repetition is distinct nonetheless. And, as if to subtly underscore the connection, the scene in which Tlali is framed in the bedroom doorway as a second bride follows immediately on that in which, in another bedroom of the mukhtar's house, Samia takes her own virginity. The camera moves from behind Samia's back to the window of the bridal chamber directly to the door of the room where Tlali is dancing with the other young Palestinian women in attendance. Dressed in Palestinian clothes, dancing gently with the lit candles in her hand, Tlali's stance marks the vexation of the land-as-woman trope. It marks the vexation of the wedding and conjugal consummation as trope. It marks the vexation of male possession of female honor—even as it reenacts that possession. Palestine/Israel has two brides. What happens, then, to the nationalist trope of the reunion of Palestinian man with Palestine-as-woman? With which woman is national desire to be satisfied? (And why with woman at all?) Of course, the conventional answer to that question is clear. But in spite of the abrupt interruption of the sensual and nonexclusive community of women, the suggestion of alternatives to the present order of things remains a flickering image.

The rather more grim conclusion of the film and of the wedding in which the guests are forced to scatter as Israeli troops reenter the village, firing their weapons as they reoccupy the village streets, cannot quite manage to efface that glimmering image of another kind of community. That that other community is not simply a nationalist one is figured precisely in the repetition of the same stance by the Palestinian and the Israeli women and by the gentle seduction that allows both Israeli and Palestinian women to briefly enact a community not of honor but of gently shared sensuality and pleasure.

Finally, in the triple repetition of the night reveries of the mukhtar as he watches his sleeping youngest son, Hassan, there is a further and equally striking instance in *Wedding in Galilee* of the play of other desires, of inside and out, of visual and verbal reiteration, of dreams and memory and the burden of both, and of desire that will not be simply satisfied. Each instance of the scene functions as punctuation of sorts for the film, introducing another crucial turn in events. The setting is always the same. In a dimly lit room, the mukhtar murmurs tenderly over his sleeping son: "How strange that every time I want to tell you a beautiful story, one you've never heard before, you're asleep in my arms. What are you dreaming? Are your dreams like mine? Why is it that I want you to learn my story by heart?" The third and final time in which this scene occurs is near the end of the film. It is immediately preceded by long, dark shots of the increasing turmoil and agitation outside as the wedding guests wait clamorously for the climax of the wedding in a demonstration of its consummation. The Israeli soldier who has waited anxiously for the reappearance of Tlali searches for her in the dark corridors of the mukhtar's house. He pauses outside the window of the room where the mukhtar murmurs over his sleeping son. This time, though, Hassan wakes up and faces his father without speaking. The mukhtar asks him if he fears his father, and Hassan darts out of the room in response. The scene immediately following this is in the wedding chamber as Samia takes her own virginity. The mukhtar's dreams are, in that room too, both a fearful burden and a charge. But he will never know how honor is maintained or who sustains his dreams. Only Ádil and the implied audience for the film are witness to what actually happens inside the wedding chamber. So, in addition to its grammatical function within the film, the repetition of this scene also gestures strategically toward the film's implied audience—those voyeuristic wedding guests who have followed the rapid, fluctuating movement of the camera inside and out, close up and far away, from men to women, from Israelis to Palestinians, until finally the darkness and confusion close in at the end of the film.

The wedding is over; sheets are displayed; the union of bride and groom has been consummated; the honor of everyone is upheld. And the Israeli military reoccupy the village; jeeps rush through the streets as shots are fired into the air. The film closes with a prolonged shot of the long gauntlet that the Israeli military, now only arguably wedding guests, walk as they leave the village. The shot is punctuated by Tlali still in Palestinian dress walking next to her compatriots. But as the Israeli military take control once again over the streets and the outside, and as the Palestinian wedding guests rush to their houses, there is one Palestinian figure who runs outside. That is Hassan, the mukhtar's young son, witness to his father's frustration, his sister's desire, his brother's impotence, his mother's interventions, his grandfather's memories, the wedding guests' tensions. It is Hassan who weaves in and out of the wedding, darting from one place to another, carrying messages, overhearing whispered conversations. Hassan, like the Israeli soldier, is witness to more of the disparate events of the wedding and thus potentially at least to their significance than almost anyone else there. In the closing frames of the film, in the dark night, he runs to the olive grove, away from the house, away from his family, reclaiming in a small way his residence on the outside. Perhaps because he is too young or perhaps because he will (re)tell the story differently, he does so without metaphorizing his action as an act of possession or the land as woman and bride. His is a young and prepubescent challenge to the dominant scheme(s) of things, Palestinian and Israeli. And it is one that defiantly takes place on the outside.

The charge of, the terms for, bearing witness, like the terms for being a wedding guest, are perhaps to stay until the end; to recognize, to remember, to "know by heart" the stories that unfold there; and—at least implicitly—to retell the story. How will the story be retold? In simple repetition of a single point of view? That of the mukhtar? Of his old father? Of the Israeli military governor? Of Samia or Sumaya? Of Tlali? Of the insistently mobile camera eye (not unlike the insistent mobility of Hassan himself)? Or will it be told otherwise? *Wedding in Galilee* offers its audience visual complicity but not identification with any one of the guests at the wedding. There is no special insight into what occurs in the minds of the wedding party. The audience is conspicuously cast as an observer, an eavesdropper, a distanced eye and ear to the wedding in Galilee. The only interior monologue available is that of the mukhtar to his young son. For although Hassan sleeps, the audience does not. How then will they (we) retell the story of *Wedding in Galilee?* As a story of national oppression and resistance, of the recreation of a traditional wedding, of patriarchal repression and abuse, of women's occupation differently of patriarchal space? What is the proper role and adequate response of the wedding guest? The film presents a range of positions to choose from. But finally it privileges the visual image of Samia and Tlali—the two brides, the dreams of the mukhtar, and the mobility of Hassan and of the camera itself. The desire that punctuates *Wedding in Galilee* is not only for the consummation of a marriage, for the liberation of an occupied land and its people, for the celebration of honor maintained. It is not only for the fulfillment of national aspirations. Or, perhaps, to imagine the fulfillment of that desire is simultaneously to imagine its limits—as in the suggestion of the two brides or in the reminders of other kinds of conjugal unions whose consequences are rather more grim. To imagine the articulation of desire and its fulfillment otherwise—as in the otherwise of the old grandfather's and grandmother's memories, as in the otherwise of the brief moment of community among an Israeli and Palestinian women.

Though it might seem perverse to suggest *Wedding in Galilee* as a marker for national narratives that are not only marked by desires for a state, for freedom from an occupier's oppression, for citizenship, I would nonetheless make that suggestion. And another as well. That is, that it is equally there, circulating among those other desires that are not simply a desire to occupy the gendered subject position of the nation-state that nationalism and its narratives can point to communities and social organization organized otherwise. Perhaps this is the charge, the terms, of being a guest at the wedding, of being a witness to the story of *Wedding in Galilee.* But those terms are as dependent on the retelling of those stories as on the reading of and listening to them in the first place. If "we carry our worlds that have failed in our worlds that flourish," as the Nigerian poet Christopher Okigbo suggests, it might then be possible, even in a failed dream or world, to see otherwise. "Here we are, near there."

Notes

1   *Wedding in Galilee.* Dir. Michel Khleife. Marissa Films, 1987.

2   The predominance of particular conceptions of interior and exterior in other Palestinian texts and situations is also discussed in Layoun (1991).

3   The figure of this Israeli soldier is an interesting and ambiguous one. As he searches for Tlali in the dark passageways of the house, he listens at the window of the room in which, for the third and final time, the mukhtar repeats his desire to be remembered to his sleeping son. And he listens as well outside the room in which Samia takes her own virginity. More than any other single guest at the wedding, this soldier has seen the crossing over of boundaries between tradition and the present, between male potency and female possession, between transgression on the inside and the maintenance of honor on the outside, and of course between Israeli and Palestinian. But the consequences of the Israeli soldier's involuntary witnessing of these scenes is never clearly registered in the film. Yet privileged witness/wedding guest he indubitably is.

II

The Production of Nationness:

Reading Regulatory Practices

Seduction and the Ruses of Power

Saidiya Hartman

I went to converse with Celia (defendant) at the request of several citizens. The object of my conversation was to ascertain whether she had any accomplices in the crime. This was eight or ten days after she had been put into the jail. I asked whether she thought she would be hung for what she had done. She said she thought she would be hung. I then had her tell the whole matter. She said the old man (Newsome, the deceased) had been having sexual intercourse with her. That he had told her he was coming down to her cabin that night. She told him not to come and if he came she would hurt him. She then got a stick and put it in the corner. He came down that night. There was very little fire in the cabin that night. When she heard him coming she fixed the fire to make a little light. She said his face was towards her and he was standing talking to her when she struck him. He did not raise his hand when she went to strike the first blow but sunk down on a stool towards the floor. Threw his hands up as he sunk down. . . . The stick with which she struck was about as large as the upper part of a chair, but not so long. . . . She said after she had killed him, the body laid a long time, she thought an hour. She did not know what to do with it. She said she would try to burn it. (*State of Missouri v. Celia*, 1885)[1]

In nineteenth-century common law, rape was defined as the forcible carnal knowledge of a female against her will and without her consent.[2] Yet, the actual or attempted rape of an enslaved woman was an offense neither recognized nor legislated by law. Rape was not simply unimaginable because of purported black lasciviousness, but its repression was essential to the displacement of white culpability that characterized both the recognition of black humanity in slave law and the designation of the black subject as the originary locus of transgression and offense.

The cases of *State of Missouri v. Celia* and *George v. State* averred that the enslaved, in general, and captive women, in particular, were not appropriate subjects of common law, thus not protected against rape. The rape of enslaved women was not an offense in either common law or slave statute. However, the repression or effacement of rape can only in part be explained by the inapplicability of common law to the enslaved. Rather, the repression and negation of this act of violence is central, not only to the pained constitution of blackness, but to the figuration and the deployment of sexuality in the context of captivity. The disavowal of rape most obviously involves issues of consent, agency, and will, which are ensnared in a larger dilemma concerning the construction of person and the calculation of black humanity in slave law.[3] Moreover, this repression of violence constitutes female gender as the locus of both unredressed and negligible injury.

The dual invocation of person and property made issues of consent, will, and agency complicated and ungainly. Yet the law strived to contain the tensions generated by this seemingly contradictory invocation of the enslaved as property and as person, as absolutely subject to the will of another and as actional subject, by recourse to the power of feelings or the mutual affection between master and slave, and the strength of weakness or the ability of the dominated to influence, if not control, the dominant. Just as the dual invocation of the slave as both property and person was an effort to wed reciprocity and submission, intimacy and domination, the legitimacy of violence and the necessity of protection, so too the law's nullification of the captive's ability to give consent, or act as agent, and the punitive recognition or the stipulation of agency as criminality, or both, reproduced the double bind of the bifurcated subject and intensified the burdened personhood of human chattel.

If the definition of the crime of rape relies on the capacity to give consent or to exercise will, then how does one make legible the sexual violation of the enslaved, when that which would constitute evidence of intentionality, and thus evidence of the crime, the state of consent or willingness of the assailed, opens a Pandora's box in which the subject formation and object constitution of the enslaved female are no less ponderous than the crime itself? Or when the legal definition of the enslaved negates the very idea of "reasonable resistance"?[4] Or when violence is inextricable from enjoyment and the "blood-stained gate of slavery" a primal scene of sexual domination? Can the wanton and indiscriminate uses of the captive body be made sense of within the heteronormative framing of sexual violation as rape? If a crime can be said in fact to exist, or is at all fathomable within the scope of any normative understanding of rape, it perhaps can only be apprehended or discerned precisely as it is entangled with the construction of personhood in slave law, and the punitive stipulation of agency as abasement, servility, or criminality.

What Thomas Jefferson termed the boisterous passions of slavery, the "unremitting despotism" of slaveowners and the "degrading submissions" of the enslaved, were curiously embraced, denied, inverted, and displaced in the law of slavery (Jefferson 1787, 162). The boisterous passions bespoke the dilemma of enjoyment in a context in which joy and domination and use and violation could not be separated. As well, this language of passion bespeaks an essential confusion of force and feeling. The confusion between consent and coercion, feeling and submission, intimacy and domination, and violence and reciprocity constitutes what I term the discourse of seduction in slave law.[5] The discourse of seduction obfuscates the primacy and extremity of violence in master-slave relations and in the construction of the slave as both property and person. To paraphrase John Forrester, seduction is a meditation on freedom and slavery, and will and subjection in the arena of sexuality (1990, 86). Seduction makes recourse to the idea of reciprocal and collusive relations, and engenders a precipitating construction of black female sexuality in which rape is unimaginable. As the enslaved female is legally unable to give consent or to offer resistance, she is presumed to be always willing.[6]

If the legal existence of the crime of rape depends on evaluating the *mens rea* and *actus rea* of the perpetrator, and, more important, the consent or nonconsent of the victim, then how does one grapple with issues of consent and will, when the negation or restricted recognition of these terms determine the meaning of enslavement?[7] If the commonplace understanding of "will" implies the power to control and determine our actions and identifies the expressive capacity of the self-possessed and intending subject, certainly this is far afield of the conditions and terms of action available to the enslaved. Yet the notion of the will connotes more than simply the capacity to act and do; rather, it distinguishes the autonomous agent from the enslaved, encumbered, and constrained. Furthermore, the extremity of power and the absolute submission required of the slave not only renders suspect, or meaningless, concepts of consent and will, but the sheer lack of limitations regarding the violence "necessary" to the maintenance of slave relations, that is, black submission, unmoors the notion of "force." What limit must be exceeded in order that the violence directed at the black body be made legible in the law? In the case of slave women, the law's circumscribed recognition of consent and will occurred only in order to intensify and secure the subordination of the enslaved, repress the crime, and deny injury. For it asserted that the captive female was both will-less and always already willing. Moreover, the utter negation of the captive's will required to secure absolute submission was identified as *willful* submission to the master in the topsy-turvy scenario of onerous passions. Within this scenario, the constraints of sentiment were no less severe than those of violence. The purportedly binding passions of master-slave relations were predicated on the inability of the enslaved to exercise his or her will in any way other than serving the master, and, in this respect, the enslaved existed only as an extension or embodiment of the owner's rights of property. To act outside the scope of willful submission was to defy the law. The surety of punishment awaited such transgressions.

The Violence of the Law

In the *State of Missouri v. Celia (a slave)*, Celia was prosecuted for the murder of her owner, Robert Newsome. The first time Newsome raped Celia was on the day he purchased her. He only stopped four years later when she killed him. Celia was found guilty by the court and sentenced to death by hanging. Although her attorney argued that the laws of Missouri concerning crimes of ravishment embraced slave women as well as white women and that Celia was acting to defend herself, this argument was rejected by the court. *Missouri v. Celia* raises critical questions about sexuality, agency, and subjectivity. Perhaps this is why the case was never reported or published. Certainly, the fact that this case was neglected for over 145 years—it was not cited in any legal index but abandoned in a file drawer at the Callaway County Courthouse—is significant. Cases involving cruelty of a sexual nature were often underreported or omitted from the report of cases.[8] The few cases involving issues of rape and sexual violence that are available in legal indexes, not surprisingly, are civil cases concerned with the recovery of damages for the loss of slave property, or criminal cases in which the enslaved and their "crimes," usually efforts to resist, defend against, or flee from such violations, are on trial. For example, *Humphrey v. Utz*, a case in which a slave owner sued his overseer for the death of a slave brutally beaten by the overseer and subjected to a range of cruelties, including having his penis nailed to a bedpost, like *Missouri v. Celia*, was also omitted from the state report of cases. It similarly illuminates the regularity of sexual violence directed at the enslaved and the obscene way in which these atrocities enter the legal record as suits for damages to property or criminal charges made against the enslaved.

As *Missouri v. Celia* demonstrated, the enslaved could neither give nor refuse consent, nor offer reasonable resistance, yet they were criminally responsible and liable. The slave was recognized as a reasoning subject who possessed intent and rationality solely in the context of criminal liability; ironically, the slave's will was acknowledged only as it was prohibited or punished. It was generally the slave's crimes that were on trial, not white offense and violation (which were enshrined as legitimate and thereby licensed), nor the violence of the law, which in the effort to shift the locus of culpability is conceptualized here in terms of the crimes of the state.[9] In positing the black as criminal, the state obfuscated its instrumental role in terror, projecting all culpability and wrongdoing onto the enslaved. The black body was simply the site on which the "crimes" of the dominant class and of the state were externalized in the form of a threat. The criminality imputed to blacks disavowed white violence as a necessary response to the threatening agency of blackness. I employ the terms "white" culpability and "white" offense because the absolute submission mandated by law was not simply that of slave to his or her owner, but the submission of the enslaved to all whites.

The assignation of right and blame, privilege and punishment, was a central element in the construction of racial difference and the absolute distinctions of status between free white persons and black captives. As the case of *State v. Tackett* made clear, "The relation between a white man and a slave differs from that, which subsists between free persons." In this case, the Supreme Court of North Carolina reversed a lower court ruling that convicted a non-slaveowning white for the murder of a slave. (*State v. Tackett* also involved the sexual arrangements of slavery and the conjugal relations of the enslaved, although they were considered incidental to the case. Daniel, the murdered slave, had accused Tackett of "keeping his [Daniel's] wife, Lotty," and threatened to kill him if he did not leave Lotty alone.) The court held that common law standards of provocation and mitigation were not applicable to the relation between a white man and a slave: "The homicide of a slave may be extenuated by acts, which would not produce a legal provocation if done by a white person" (*State v. Tackett*, 1 Hawks 210, December 1820). The extenuating circumstances included arrogance, insult, trespass, and troublesome deportment. Acts of homicide, battery, and mayhem were sanctioned, if deemed essential to proper relations of free white persons and black captives and the maintenance of black submission.[10]

White culpability was displaced as black criminality, and violence legitimated as the ruling principle of the social relations of racial slavery. Newsome's constant violations were eclipsed by the criminal agency of Celia. *Missouri v. Celia* illustrates how difficult it is to uncover and articulate the sexual violation of enslaved women, exactly because the crime surfaces obliquely and only as the captive confesses her guilt. Ultimately, the motive for Celia's act was deemed inadmissible, and her voice usurped and negated: her white inquisitors spoke for her during the trial. As neither slaves nor free blacks were allowed to testify against whites, the "crime" that precipitated the murder of Newsome was denied.

To assert that Celia was raped is to issue a provocation. It is a declaration intended to shift our attention to another locus of crime. It is to envision the unimaginable, excavate the repressed, and discern the illegible. It is to reveal sentiment and protection as the guise of violence in the legal construction of the captive person and, in particular, the slippage of desire and domination in the loosely constructed term "sexual intercourse." In the trial record, the "sexuality" of Celia was ensnared in the web of others' demands, and the trace of what I risk calling her "desire" only discernible in the compliance and defiance of these competing claims.[11] As the trial record stated, Newsome had been having "sexual intercourse" with Celia, he "forced her" on the day he purchased her, and last, George, Celia's enslaved companion, "would have nothing to do with her if she did not *quit* the old man." Coercion, desire, submission, and complicity are the circulating terms that come to characterize, less the sexuality *of* Celia, or the enslaved female, than the way in which she is inhabited by sexuality and her body possessed (Foucault 1978, 75–132). Simply put, Celia embodied the vested rights of others.

The abjection of the captive body exceeds what can be conveyed by the designation or difference between "slave" women and "free" women. In this case, what is at issue is the difference between the deployment of sexuality in the contexts of white kinship (the proprietorial relation of the patriarch to his wife and children, the making of legitimate heirs, and the transmission of property) and black captivity (the reproduction of property, the relations of mastery and subjection, and the regularity of sexual violence), rather than the imputed "freedom" of white women. The en-gendering of race occurs within these different economies of constraint and by way of divergent methods of sexual control and domination. Kinship and captivity designate radically different conditions of embodiment that reveal the determinancy of race in the deployment of sexuality and underline the particular mechanisms through which bodies are disciplined and regulated.

The (re)production of enslavement and the legal codification of racial subordination and sexual subjection depended on various methods of sexual control and domination: antimiscegenation statutes, rape laws that made the rape of white women by black men a capital offense, the sanctioning of sexual violence against slave women by virtue of the law's calculation of negligible injury, the negation of kinship, and the commercial vitiation of motherhood as a means for the reproduction and conveyance of property and black subordination (Morgan 1979).[12] *Alfred v. State* illuminates the convergence of these varied techniques in maintaining the domination of the enslaved and cultivating the pained and burdened personhood of the enslaved. In *Alfred v. State,* Alfred, a slave, was indicted for the murder of his overseer, Coleman. A witness testified that Alfred admitted having killed the overseer: "The defendant wanted to introduce a witness on his behalf, a slave named Charlotte, who stated that she was the wife of the prisoner . . . Prisoner's counsel then proposed to prove, by Charlotte, that about nine or ten o'clock in the morning . . . (the overseer) Coleman 'had forced her to submit to sexual intercourse with him'; and that she had communicated the fact to the prisoner before the killing" (*Alfred v. State,* 37 Miss 296, October 1858). Although the defense attempted to introduce Charlotte as a witness and thereby prove that Alfred's action was motivated by the rape of his wife, the district attorney objected to Charlotte's testimony. The court sustained the objection, the prisoner was convicted and sentenced to be hanged.[13]

What is at issue here are the ways in which various mechanisms of sexual domination act in concert—the repression of rape, the negation of kinship, and the legal invalidation of slave marriage. In this instance, sexuality is a central dimension of the power best exercised over and against the slave population and entails everything from compulsory couplings to the right to manage life.[14] Charlotte's testimony was rejected because her relation to Alfred had no legal status, and thus it could not provide an alibi or motive for Alfred's action. The disallowance of the marital relation, in turn, rendered superfluous Charlotte's sexual violation.[15] In the rejection of Charlotte as witness, her status as wife and partner of Alfred was negated, her rape displaced as adultery and then dismissed, and the violence that catalyzed the overseer's murder repressed.

The defense's argument focused on the violation of Alfred's rights as a "husband" rather than the rape of Charlotte. It is significant that the rape of Charlotte is interpreted narrowly within the frame of "outrages of conjugal affections" and as adultery. Alfred's counsel unsuccessfully argued that "the humanity of our law . . . regards with as much tenderness the excesses of outraged conjugal affections in the negro as in the white man. The servile condition . . . has not deprived him of his social or moral instincts, and he is as much entitled to the protection of the laws, when acting under their influence, as if he were freed." The discussion of a husband's, even a slave husband's, conjugal rights supplants the rape of Charlotte.[16] In all likelihood, the court denied Alfred the right to vindicate this outrage because the decedent was white. However, in cases of this nature involving other slaves, the court sometimes recognized the husband's exclusive sexual rights in his wife and "the sudden fury excited by finding a man in the very act of shame with his wife" (Keith v. State, 45 Tenn [5 Cold.] 35, 1867). Ultimately, the motive for Alfred's act was deemed irrelevant because of the need to maintain black subordination and the presumably negligible status of the injury.

Alfred v. State illuminates the legal mechanisms by which sexuality and subordination are yoked in securing the social relations of slavery. On the one hand, the management of slave sexuality indifferently translates the rape of slave women simply as adultery or sexual intercourse; on the other, it refuses to recognize or grant any legitimacy to relations forged among the enslaved. The rape of black women exists as an unspoken but normative condition fully within the purview of everyday sexual practices, whether within the implied arrangements of the slave enclave or the plantation household. This is evidenced in myriad ways, from the inattention to the commonplace evasion and indirection of polite discourse, which euphemized rape as ravishment and sex as carnal knowledge, to the utter omission and repression of the crime in slave statute and case law. In this case, the normativity of rape is to be derived from the violence of the law—the identity or coincidence of legitimate uses of slave property and what Spillers terms "high crimes against the flesh" (1987, 47). The normativity of sexual violence establishes an inextricable link between racial formation and sexual subjection. As well, the virtual absence of prohibitions or limitations in the determination of socially tolerable and necessary violence sets the stage for the indiscriminate use of the body for pleasure, profit, and punishment.

The legal transposition of rape as sexual intercourse affirms the quotidian character of violence and shrouds this condition of violent domination with the suggestion of complicity. Sexual intercourse, regardless of whether coerced or consensual, comes to describe the arrangements, however violent, between men and enslaved women.[17] What does sexuality designate when rape is a normative mode of its deployment? What set of effects does it produce? How can violence be differentiated from sexuality when "consent" is intelligible only as submission? How can we discern the crime when it is a legitimate use of property? Or when the black captive is made the locus of origin for liability?[18] Does the regularity of violation transform it into an arrangement or a liaison from which the captive female can extract herself, if she chooses, as a lover's request or adultery would seem to imply? Can she use or wield sexuality as a weapon of the weak? Do four years and two children later imply submission, resignation, complicity, desire, or the extremity of constraint (McLaurin 1991, 121)?

It is this slippage that Celia's act brings to a standstill through the intervention of her will or what inadequately approximates desire. To speak of will or desire broaches a host of issues that revolve upon the terms, dimensions, and conditions of action. Moreover, the term "will" is an overextended proximation of the agency of the dispossessed subject/object of property, or perhaps simply unrecognizable in a context in which agency and intentionality are inseparable from the threat of punishment. It is possible to read this act as liberating the captive body, however transient this liberation, or as a decisive shift in embodiment, a movement from Newsome's Celia to Celia's body, though my intention is merely to underscore its complexity. The full dimensions of this act and the resignation, courage, or glimpse of possibility that might have fueled it defy comprehensive analysis, since we only have access to Celia's life as it has been recorded by her interrogators and rendered as crime. The fateful negotiation of autonomy at the site of the expended and exploited body affirms both the impossibility of consent and the struggle to mitigate the brutal constraints of captivity through an entitlement denied the captive—no, the prerogative of refusal. Ultimately, Celia was hanged for this refusal. This effort to claim the body and to possibly experience embodiment as full, inviolate, and pleasurable, not as an extension of another's will or right nor as a condition of expenditure or defilement, led Celia to construct a boundary at the threshold of her cabin that would shield her from the tacit violence seen as "befitting" the relation of slaveowner and enslaved female. As Leon Higginbotham notes, the Missouri court in pronouncing Celia's guilt "held that the end of the slavery system is not merely 'the [economic] profit of the master' but also the *joy* of the master in the sexual conquest of the slave" (1989, 694). Thus, Celia's declaration of the limit was an emancipatory articulation of the desire for a different economy of enjoyment.

The Bonds of Affection

The effacement of rape in the context of enslavement concerns matters of necessary and tolerable violence, the full enjoyment of the slave as thing, and the form of captive embodiment. The eliding of rape must also be considered in relation to what is callously termed the recognition of slave humanity, and the particular mechanisms of tyrannical power that converge on the black body. In this instance, tyranny is not a rhetorical inflation, but a designation of the absoluteness of power. Gender, if at all appropriate in this scenario, must be understood as indissociable from violence, the refiguration of rape as mutual and shared desire, the wanton exploitation of the captive body tacitly sanctioned as a legitimate use of property, the disavowal of injury, and the absolute possession of the body and its "issue." In short, black *and* female difference is registered by virtue of the extremity of power operating on captive bodies and licensed within the scope of the humane and the tolerable.[19]

The violence commensurate with the exercise of property rights and essential to the making of perfect submission was dissembled in regard to sexual violation by black female "excesses"—immoderate and overabundant sexuality, bestial appetites and capacities that were most often likened to the orangutan, and an untiring readiness that was only to be outstripped by her willingness.[20] Lasciviousness made unnecessary the protection of rape law, for insatiate black desire presupposed that all sexual intercourse was welcomed, if not pursued. The state's crimes of omission and proaction, the failure to extend protection and the sanctioning of violence in the name of rights of property, disappeared before the spectacle of black concupiscence. The nonexistence of rape as a category of injury pointed not to the violence of the law but to the enslaved woman as guilty accomplice and seducer. However, the omissions of law must be read symptomatically within an economy of bodies in which the full enjoyment of the slave as thing depended upon unbounded authority and the totalizing consumption of the body in its myriad capacities.[21]

The construction of black subjectivity as will-less, abject, insatiate, and pained, and the instrumental deployment of sexuality in the reproduction of property, subordination, and racial difference usurped the category of rape. Sexuality formed the nexus in which black, female, and chattel were inextricably bound, and acted to intensify the constraints of chattel status by subjecting the body to another order of violations and whims.[22] The despotic ravages of power made violence indistinguishable from the full enjoyment of the thing. The tensions generated by the law's dual invocation of property and person, or by "full enjoyment" and limited protection to life and limb, were masked by the phantasmal ensnaring agency of the lascivious black.[23] Rape disappeared through the intervention of seduction—the assertion of the slave woman's complicity and willful submission. Seduction was central to the very constitution and imagination of the antebellum South, for it provided a way of masking the antagonistic fissures of the society by ascribing to the object of property an ensnaring and criminal agency that acted to dissimulate the barbarous forms of white enjoyment permitted within the law.

The discourse of seduction enabled those like Mary Boykin Chestnut, who were disgusted and enraged by the sexual arrangements of slavery, to target slave women as the agents of their husbands' downfall. The complicity of slave women displaced the act of sexual violence. According to Chestnut, decent white women were forced to live with husbands degraded by the lowliness of their enslaved "mistresses": "Under slavery, we lived surrounded by prostitutes, yet an abandoned woman is sent out of any decent house. Who thinks any worse of a Negro or mulatto woman for being a thing we can't name?" (1949, 21). The sexual exploitation of the enslaved female, incredibly, served as evidence of her collusion with the master class and as evidence of her power, the power both to render the master weak and, implicitly, to be the mistress of her own subjection. The slave woman not only suffered the responsibility for her sexual (ab)use, but was blameworthy because of her purported ability to render the powerful weak.

Even those like Fanny Kemble, who eloquently described the "simple horror and misery" that slave women regularly experienced, were able to callously exclaim, when confronted with the inescapable norma-tivity of rape and the "string of detestable details" that comprised the life of enslaved woman, after yet another woman, Sophy, shared her ex-perience of violation: "Ah! but don't you know—did nobody ever teach any of you that it is a sin to live with men who are not your husbands?!" (1984, 270).[24] Sophy appropriately and vehemently responded: "Oh, yes, missis, we know—we know all about dat well enough; but we do any-thing to get our poor flesh some rest from the whip; when he made me follow him into de bush, what use me tell him no? He have strength to make me" (270).

The equivocations that surround issues of consensual sexual relations under domination, the eliding of sexual violence by the imputation of the slave woman's ensnaring sexual agency or lack of virtue, and the presumption of consent as consequence of the utter powerlessness of her "no," the "no means yes" philosophy, are important constituents of the discourse of seduction. In a more expansive or generic sense, seduc-tion denotes a theory of power that demands the absolute and "perfect" submission of the enslaved as the guiding principle of slave relations, and yet seeks to mitigate the avowedly necessary brutality of slave rela-tions through the shared affections of owner and captive. The doctrine of "perfect submission" reconciled violence and the claims of mutual benevolence between master and slave as necessary in maintaining the harmony of the institution. The presumed mutuality of feelings in maintaining domination enchanted the brutal and direct violence of master-slave relations. The term "seduction" is employed here to des-ignate this displacement and euphemization of violence, for seduction epitomizes the discursive alchemy that shrouds direct forms of violence beneath the "veil of enchanted relations," that is, the reciprocal and mutual relations of master and slave (Bourdieu 1977). This mining of the discourse of seduction attempts to illuminate the violence obscured by the veil through an interrogation of the language of power and feelings, specifically the manipulations of the weak and the kindheartedness and moral instruction of the powerful.

The benign representation of the paternal institution in slave law constituted the master-slave relationship as typified by the bonds of affection, and thereby transformed relations of violence and domination into those of affinity. This benignity depended on a construction of the enslaved black as one easily inclined to submission, a skilled maneuverer wielding weakness masterfully, and as a potentially threatening insubordinate who could only be disciplined through violence. If what is at stake in social fantasy is the construction of a nonantagonistic, organic, and complementary society, then the ability of the South to imagine slavery as a paternal and benign institution and master-slave relations as bound by feelings depended on the specter of the obsequious and threatening slave (Žižek 1989, 126).[25] For this Manichaean construction undergirded both the necessary violence and the bonds of affection set forth in slave law. As well, this fantasy enabled a vision of whiteness defined primarily by its complementary relation to blackness and by the desire to incorporate and regulate black excess. Seduction thus provided a holistic vision of social order, not divided by antagonisms and precariously balancing barbarism and civilization, violence and protection, mutual benevolence and absolute submission, and brutality and sentiment. This harmonious vision of community was made possible by the exercise of violence, the bonds of affection, and the consonance of the weak and the powerful.

How does seduction uphold perfect submission and, at the same time, assert the alluring, if not endangering, agency of the dominated? It does so by forwarding the strength of weakness. As a theory of power, seduction contends that there is an ostensible equality between the dominant and the dominated. The dominated acquire power based on the identification of force and feeling. As Baudrillard writes, "Seduction play(s) triumphantly with weakness" (1979, 83). The artifice of weakness not only provides seduction with its power but defines its essential character, for the enactment of weakness and the "impenetrable obscurity" of femininity and blackness harbor a conspiracy of power (83). The dominated catalyze reversals of power, not by challenges presented to the system, but by succumbing to the system's logic. Thus power comes to be defined not by domination, but by the manipulations of the dominated. The reversibility of power and the play of the dominated discredit the force of violence through the assertion of reciprocal and intimate relations. In this regard, the recognition of the agency of the dominated and the power of the weak secures the fetters of subjection while proclaiming the power and influence of those shackled and tethered.

The proslavery ideologue George Fitzhugh, like Baudrillard, also celebrated the reversibility of power enacted through surrender. In *Cannibals All! or, Slaves Without Masters*, Fitzhugh argued that the strength of weakness disrupts the hierarchy of power within the family as well as the master-slave relationship. Appearances conspire to contrary purposes, thus the seemingly weak slave, like the infant or (white) woman, exercises capricious dominion: "The dependent exercise, because of their dependence, as much control over their superiors, in most things, as those superiors exercise over them. Thus and thus only, can conditions be equalized" (1971, 204–5). Seduction appears to be a necessary labor, one required to extend and reproduce the claims of power, though advanced in the guise of the subaltern's control and disruptions: "The humble and obedient slave exercises more or less control over the most brutal and hard-hearted master. It is an invariable law of nature, that weakness and dependence are elements of strength, and generally sufficiently limit that universal despotism, observable throughout human and animal nature" (205). If, as Fitzhugh insists, the greatest slave is the master of the household and the enslaved rule by virtue of the "strength of weakness," then, in effect, the slave is made the master of her subjection.

As Fitzhugh envisioned, kindness and affection undergirded the relations of subordination and dependency. As a model of social order, the patriarchal family depended on duty, status, and protection rather than consent, equality, and civil freedom. Subjection was not only naturalized but consonant with the sentimental equality of reciprocity, inasmuch as the power of affection licensed the strength of weakness. Essentially, "the strength of weakness" prevailed due to the goodness of the father, "the armor of affection and benevolence." The generosity of the father enabled the victory claimed by the slave, the tyrannical child, and the brooding wife. The bonds of affection within the slaveholding family circle permitted the tyranny of weakness and supplanted the stranglehold of the ruling father. Ironically, the family circle remained intact as much by the bonds of affection as by the tyranny of the weak. Literally, the *forces* of affection bound the interests of the master and slave in a delicate equilibrium, as one form of strength modified the other (Fitzhugh 1971, 204). Thus, we are to believe that the exercise of control by the weak softens universal despotism, subdues the power of the father by commanding his care, and guarantees the harmony of slave relations.

Seduction erects a family romance, in this case, the elaboration of a racial and sexual fantasy in which domination is transposed into the bonds of mutual affection, subjection idealized as the pathway to equality, and perfect subordination declared the means of ensuring great happiness and harmony. The patriarchal model of social order erected by Fitzhugh marries equality and despotism through an explicit critique of consent, possessive individualism, and contractual relations (Pateman 1988, 66–67). Feelings rather than contract are the necessary corrective to universal despotism, therefore duty and reciprocity rather than consent provide the basis for equality. The despotic and sovereign power celebrated by Fitzhugh could be abated only by the bonds of affection, a phrase that resonates with the ambivalence attendant to the attachments and constraints that characterize the relation of owner and object.

If a conspiracy of power resides within seduction, then questions arise as to the exact nature of this conspiracy: Who seduces whom? Does the slave become entrapped in the enchanted web of the owner's dominion, lured by promises of protection and care? Does the guile and subterfuge of the dependent mitigate the effects of power? Are the manipulations and transgressions of the dominated fated to reproduce the very order presumably challenged by such actions? Or do such enactments on the part of the owner and the enslaved, the feigned concessions of power and the stylized performance of naïveté effect any shifts or disruptions of force, or compulsively restage power and powerlessness?

Seduction reifies the idea of submission by proclaiming it the pathway to ostensible equality, protection, and social harmony. As expounded by proslavery ideologues like Fitzhugh or as a legal principle guiding master-slave relations, seduction professed that power and protection were acquired through surrender. The tautology reiterated: the dominated exert influence over the dominant by virtue of their weakness, and therefore more formal protections against despotism or guarantors of equality are unnecessary, if not redundant. The insinuation that the dominated were mutually invested in their subjugation recast violence in the ambiguous guise of affection, and declared hegemony rather than domination the ruling term of order.[26] The assertion that coercion *and* consent characterized the condition of enslavement can be seen in the implied and explicit promises of protection extended by the law.

The incessant reiteration of the necessity of submission—the slave must be subject to the master's will in all things—upheld it as the guiding principle of slave relations if not the central element in the trinity of savagery, sentiment, and submission. Slave law ensured the rights of property and the absolute submission of the slave while attending to limited forms of slave subjectivity. The law granted slaveowners virtually absolute rights and militated against the abuses of such authority by granting limited protection to slaves against "callous and cold-blooded" murder, torture and maiming, although procedural constraints, most notably the fact that a slave or free black could not act as witness against a white person, acted as safeguards against white liability and made these laws virtually impossible to enforce. In the effort to attend to the interests of master and slave, the law elaborated a theory of power in which the affection of slaveowners and the influence of the enslaved compensated for its failures and omissions. It contended that affection and influence bridged the shortcomings of law concerning the protection of black life. The ethic of perfect submission recognized the unlimited dominion of the slaveowner, yet bounded this dominion by invoking the centrality of affections in regulating the asymmetries of power in the master-slave relation.[27] The dual existence of the slave as property and person and the interests and absolute dominion of the slaveowner were to be maintained in precarious balance by forwarding the role of affection in mitigating brutality.

The case *State v. Mann*, although it doesn't specifically involve issues of sexuality or rape, is important in considering the place of affection, violence, and surrender in the law. Mann was indicted for assault and battery upon Elizabeth Jones's slave Lydia, whom he had hired for a year: "During the term, the slave had committed some small offence, for which the Defendant undertook to chastise her—that while in the act of so doing, the slave ran off, whereupon the Defendant called upon her to stop, which being refused, he shot and wounded her" (*State v. Mann*, 2 Devereaux, December 1829). The lower court convicted Mann, finding him guilty of "cruel and unwarrantable punishment, and disproportionate to the offense committed by the slave." However, in an appeal to the North Carolina Supreme Court, the decision was reversed. Though the

liability of the hirer, Mann, to the owner for an injury presumably im-
pairing the value of slave property was left to general rules of bailment,
the charges of criminal battery were overturned. Even if the injury diminished the value of slave property, it was not indictable as cruel and
unreasonable battery. The court held that the power of the master was
absolute and not a subject for discussion (*State v. Mann* 267).

The higher court ruling held that the master had absolute power to
render the submission of the slave perfect; yet it was also argued that the
harshness of such a principle would be regulated, not by existing legislation but by feelings—the benevolence and affection between master
and slave and the ruling moral code. In other words, the court considered affection to be an internal regulating principle of slave relations.
The Supreme Court reversed the decision of the lower court on the following grounds: the power of the master had to be absolute in order "to
render the submission of the slave perfect," although "as a principle of
moral right, every person in his retirement must repudiate it. But in
the actual condition of things it must be so." Yet the harshness implied
by this difficult yet unavoidable decision would be regulated by "the
protection already afforded by several statutes [which made it illegal to
murder slaves in cold blood] . . . the private interest of the owner, *the
benevolence toward each other, seated in the hearts of those who have
been born and bred together,* [and] the . . . deep execrations of the community upon the barbarian, who is guilty of excessive cruelty to his
unprotected slave" (*State v. Mann* 267; emphasis mine).

Although the court acknowledged that the scope of such absolute
rights of property left the enslaved open to violent abuses, it also recognized that the right to abuse had to be guaranteed for the perpetuation of the institution, for the amorphous "public good" mandated the
absolute subordination of the enslaved. The opinion amended this brutal admission with the assurance that the rights of ownership generally
precluded such abuses because of self-interest, that is, pecuniary considerations. The rights of ownership permitted any and all means necessary to render perfect submission; however, it was hoped that the use of
excessive force was unnecessary because of the reciprocal benevolence
of master-slave relations.

Rather than distinguish between implied relations and absolute dominance or separate affection from violence, the court considered them
both essential to the maintenance and longevity of the institution. In

short, the ethic of submission indiscriminately included absolute power and human feelings. The court admitted that the obedience of the slave was "the consequence only of uncontrolled authority over the body." How else could perpetual labor and submission be guaranteed? The services of one "doomed in his person and his posterity" and "without knowledge or the capacity to make anything his own, and to toil that another may reap the fruits," could be expected only of "one who has no will of his own" and "who surrenders his will in perfect obedience to that of another" (*State v. Mann* 266). To be sure, the power of the master had to be absolute to produce this surrender of the will.

Not only was perfect submission an ordering principle of the social, to be accomplished by whatever violent means necessary, regardless of how brutal, but this conceptualization of power relations depended on feelings, not law, to guarantee basic protections to the enslaved. Submission encompassed not only the acquisition of power, but explicitly addressed the power of affection in influencing relations between master and slave, although the court distinguished between slavery and the domestic relations of parent and child, tutor and pupil, and master and servant to which it was frequently compared. The centrality ascribed to the role of feelings implicitly acknowledged the unrestricted violence the *Mann* opinion had licensed, yet minimized the consequences of this through an appeal to "moral right" rather than the actual condition of things. Feelings were to balance the use and role of force. As Judge Ruffin stated: "I must freely confess my sense of the harshness of this proposition; I feel it as deeply as any man can; and as a principle of moral right every person in his retirement must repudiate it. But in the actual condition of things it must be so."

The importance attributed to the intimacies of domination illustrate the role of seduction in the law. As the opinion clearly stated, power resided not only in the title to slave property, but in the bonds of affection. Feelings repudiated and corrected the violence legitimated by law. Material interests and mutual benevolence would "mitigat[e] the rigors of servitude and ameliorat[e] the condition of the slave," and protect the slave from the ravages of abuse unleashed by the ruling. In other words, the brutal dominion guaranteed by the law was to be regulated by the influence of the enslaved—their pull on the heartstrings of the master. Slave law contradictorily asserted that absolute dominion was both necessary and voluntary. The intimacy of the master and the slave purportedly operated as an internal regulator of power and ameliorated the terror inherent to unlimited dominion. The wedding of intimacy and violent domination as regulatory norms exemplifies the logic through which violence is displaced as mutual and reciprocal desire.

The significance attributed to feelings, attachment, and the familiarity of domestic slavery rendered domination in a heartwarming light. The power of influence invested in the enslaved—the power of the weak to sway the powerful—and the place attributed to feeling in regulating the excesses of market relations refigured relations of domination and exploitation in the garb of affection, family, and reciprocal obligations. Such reasoning held that violence was both necessary and tolerable while insisting that feelings determined the character of the master-slave relationship and informed social, familial, and political organization. In short, slave relations were dependent upon and determined by "the action taking place in individual hearts" (Tompkins, 1985, 128).

The contradictory appeal to the public good contended that public tranquility required violence and, at the same time, served as the guarantor that this entitlement to virtually unlimited power need never be exercised. The invocation of the public good authorized necessary violence and established minimal standards for the recognition of slave humanity. Just as the appeal to the public good mandated absolute submission, it also required that certain provisions or protections be granted to the enslaved, such as housing, clothing, food, and support for elderly and infirm slaves. Yet this concern for the welfare of the enslaved and the provisions granted them should not be mistaken for rights. As a judge commented in another case that hinged on determining degrees of necessary and excessive violence, though the excessive violence "disturbed the harmony of society, was offensive to public decency, and directly tended to a breach of peace," the rights of the slave were extraneous to such considerations: "The same would be the law, if a horse had been so beaten. And yet it would not be pretended, that it was in respect to the rights of the horse, or the feelings of humanity, that this interposition would take place" (*Commonwealth v. Turner*). The public good mandated absolute submission and minimal protections intent upon maintaining harmony and security. Even when the entreaty made in the name of the public good acted minimally on the behalf of the enslaved, it did so, not surprisingly, by granting these limited entitlements in a manner that "recognized" black humanity in accordance with minimal standards of existence. This truncated construction of the slave as person rather than lessening the constraints of chattel status enhanced them by making personhood conterminous with injury.

Although the public good putatively served as the arbiter of care and coercion, the precarious status of the slave within this sphere raises questions about the meaning of a slave's personhood, the protections advanced on his or her behalf, and the limited concerns of public decency. Contrary to pronouncements that sentiment would abate brutality, feelings intensified the violence of law and posed dire consequences for the calculation of black humanity. For the dual existence of the slave as object of property and person required that the feelings endowed the enslaved be greatly circumscribed. While the slave was recognized as a sentient being, the degree of sentience had to be cautiously calibrated in order to avoid intensifying the antagonisms of the social order. How could property and person be reconciled on the ground of mutual benevolence and affection? How could the dual invocation of humanity and interest be sustained?

The dual existence of the slave as person and property was generated by the slave mode of production.[28] The law attempted to resolve the contradiction between the slave as property and as person/laborer or, at the very least, to minimize this tension, by attending to the slave as both a form of property and a person. This effort was instrumental in maintaining the dominance of the slaveowning class, particularly in a period of national crisis concerning the institution. The increasing recognition of slave person from 1830 to 1860 was an effort to combat the abolitionist polemic about the degradations of chattel status and the slave's lack of rights.[29] In any case, the dual invocation of slave law was neither a matter of an essential ethical contradiction nor a conflict between bourgeois and slave relations, but an expression of the multivalence of subjection. The dual invocation quite easily accommodated the restricted recognition of slave person and the violence necessary to the accumulation of profit and the management of a captive population. For the figuration of the humane in slave law was totally consonant with the domination of the enslaved. The constitution of the slave as person was not at odds with the structural demands of the system, nor did it necessarily challenge the social relations of the antebellum world.

Rather, the dual invocation of law designated the limits of rights of ownership, and extended and constricted these rights as was necessary for the preservation of the institution. On one hand, there was increased liability for white violence committed against slaves; on the other, the law continued to decriminalize the violence thought necessary to the preservation of the institution and the submission and obedience of the slave. If anything, the dual invocation of law generated the prohibitions and interdictions designed to regulate the violent excesses of slavery and at the same time extended this violence in the garb of sentiment. The recognition of the slave as subject and the figuration of the captive person in law served to explicate the meaning of dominion. To be subject in this manner was no less brutalizing than being an object of property.

In the arena of affect, the body was no less vulnerable to the demands and the excesses of power, for the bestowal that granted the slave a circumscribed and fragmented identity as person in turn shrouded the violence of such a beneficent and humane gesture. Bluntly stated, the violence of subjection concealed and extended itself through the outstretched hand of legislated concern. The slave was considered subject only insofar as he or she was criminal(ized), wounded body or mortified flesh. This construction of the subject seems rather at odds with a proclaimed concern for the "total person." However, it does not mean that the efforts to regulate the abuses of slavery were any less "genuine," but that in the very efforts to protect the enslaved from the ravages of the institution, a mutilation of another order was set in motion. Protection was an exemplary dissimulation, for it savagely truncated the dimensions of existence, inasmuch as the effort to safeguard slave life recognized the slave as subject only as she violated the law or was violated (wounded flesh or pained body). Thus rendered, person signified little more than a pained body or a body in need of punishment.[30]

The designation of person was inescapably bound to violence, and the effort to protect embodied a degree of violence no less severe than the excesses being regulated. Despite the law's proclaimed concern for slave life or recognition of black humanity, minimal standards of existence determined personhood. *For the recognition of the slave as person depended upon the calculation of interest and injury.* The law constituted the subject as a muted pained body or as a body to be punished; this agonized embodiment of subjectivity certainly intensified the dreadful objectification of chattel status. Paradoxically, this designation of subjectivity utterly negated the possibility of a nonpunitive, inviolate, or pleasurable embodiment, and instead the black captive vanished in the chasm between object, criminal, pained body, and mortified flesh.[31] The law's exposition of sentiment culminated in a violent shuttling of the subject between varied conditions of harm, juggled between the plantation and the state, and dispersed across categories of property, injury, and punishment.

The Measure of Humanity

In *Inquiry into the Law of Negro Slavery,* Thomas Cobb explicated the conditions in which the dominion of the master and the person of the slave were to be accommodated in the law. In examining the dual character of the slave, as person and property, and the particular dimensions of personhood in common law and slave statute, Cobb contended that the slave was recognized first as person and second as property, largely because in all slaveholding states, "the homicide of a slave is held to be murder, and in most of them, has been so expressly declared by law"; and even when not expressly declared by law, the principles of Christian enlightenment extend protection to life and limb (Cobb 1858, 84). Notwithstanding, he argued that slaves were not proper subjects of common law and proposed a minimal definition of protection of life and limb.

The calculation of slave existence was determined by base conditions necessary for functioning as an effective laborer, and the extent of protection to life and limb decided by diminutions in the value of capital. Within these boundaries, degrees of injury and magnitudes of labor decided the meaning of a slave's personhood. It is difficult to acknowledge this savage quantification of life and person as a recognition of black humanity, for, as argued earlier, this restricted stipulation of humanity intensified the pained existence of the enslaved. This scale of subjective value was a complement rather than a corrective to the decriminalization of white violence. Ironically, the recognition of slave personhood tacitly and covertly licensed the decriminalization of white violence. Despite the fact that the recognition of slave humanity was intended to establish criminal liability for acts of violence committed upon slaves, in the end it relied on diminutions in the value of property in determining and recognizing injury. In other words, the "corrective" resembled the ailment to the degree that the recognition of slave humanity reinscribed black life as the owner's property. For the scale of subjective value was inescapably bound to the use and value of property. The consequence of this construction of personhood intensified injury in the very name of redress. Moreover, the selective inclusion of the slave into the web of rights and duties that comprised the common law demonstrated the tentativeness of this recognition of personhood.

Not surprisingly, Cobb's calibrations of injury severely circumscribed the dimensions of personhood in its dismissal of sexual violence as an "offense not affecting the existence of the slave" (1858, 90). This simultaneously made the body prey to sexual violence and disavowed both the violence and the injury. The ravished body, unlike a broken arm or other site of injury, did not bestow any increment of subjectivity because it did not decrease productivity or diminish value—on the contrary, it might actually increase the female captive's magnitude of value—nor did it apparently offend the principles of Christian enlightenment. It was declared to be inconsequential in the calculation of slave subjectivity, and not within the rights and protections granted the enslaved:

> If the general provision of the law against murder should be held to include slaves, why not all other penal enactments, by the same course of reasoning, be held to include similar offences when committed on slaves, without their being specifically named? . . . The law by recognizing the existence of the slave as person, thereby confers no rights or privileges except such as are necessary to protect that existence. All other rights should be granted specially. Hence, the penalties for rape would not and should not, by such implication, be made to extend to carnal forcible knowledge of a slave, that offense *not affecting the existence* of the slave, and that existence being the extent of the right which the implication of the law grants. (Cobb 1858, 83)

Concerned with this lapse in slave law, the neglect of sexual injury and the failure to protect slave women from rape, Cobb stated that "although worthy of consideration by legislators," it need not cause undue concern because "the occurrence of such an offense is almost unheard of; and the known lasciviousness of the negro, renders the possibility of its occurrence very remote" (1858, 99). As the black male's nature made "rape too often an occurrence," the black female's imputed lasciviousness removed it entirely from consideration. It is not simply fortuitous that gender emerges in relation to violence; that is, gender is constituted in terms of negligible and unredressed injury and the propensity for violence. The en-gendering of race, as it is refracted through Cobb's scale of subjective value, entails the denial of sexual violation as a form of injury while asserting the prevalence of sexual violence due to the rapacity of the negro. While Cobb's consideration of sexual violation initially posits gender differences within the enslaved community in the heteronormative terms of female victim and male perpetrator, ultimately the "strong passions" of the negro, in this instance, lust and lasciviousness, ultimately annul such distinctions and concomitantly any concerns about "the violation of the person of a female slave." Since, according to Cobb, blacks were endowed less with sexuality than criminality, they were in need of discipline and punishment rather than protection, for as sexual subjects they were beyond the pale of the law and outside the boundaries of the decent and the nameable.

In *George v. State,* George, a slave, was indicted for rape under a statute making it a crime to have sex with a child under ten years of age. The Mississippi Supreme Court overturned a lower court ruling that convicted George for the rape of a female slave under ten years old and sentenced him to death by hanging. The attorney for George cited Cobb's *Law of Slavery* in his argument before the court. He argued that "the crime of rape does not exist in this State between African slaves. Our laws recognize no marital rights as between slaves; their sexual intercourse is left to be regulated by their owners. The regulations of law, as to the white race, on the subject of sexual intercourse, do not and cannot, for obvious reasons, apply to slaves; their intercourse is promiscuous, and the violation of a female slave by a male slave would be mere assault and battery" (*George (a slave) v. State,* 37 Miss. 317, October 1859). According to George's attorney, the sexual arrangements of the captive community were so different from those of the dominant order that they were beyond the reach of the law and best left to the regulation of slaveowners. The Mississippi Supreme Court concluded that based on a "careful examination of our legislation on this subject, we are satisfied that there is no act which embraces either the attempted or actual commission of a rape by a slave on a female slave. . . . Masters and slaves cannot be governed by the same common system of laws: so different are their positions, rights, and duties." The lower court's judgment was reversed, the indictment quashed, and the defendant discharged on the grounds that "this indictment cannot be sustained, either at common law or under our statutes. It charges no offence known to either system." The opinion held that slaves were not subject to the protection of common law, and that earlier cases in which whites were prosecuted for the murder of slaves under common law were founded on "unmeaning twaddle . . . 'natural law,' 'civilization and Christian enlightenment,' in amending propio vigore, the rigor of the common law."

If subjectivity is calculated in accordance with degrees of injury, and sexual violation is not within the scope of offenses affecting slave existence, what are the consequences of this repression and disavowal in regard to gender and sexuality? Does this callous circumscription of black sentience define the condition of the slave female, or does it radically challenge the adequacy of gender as a way of making sense of the inscription and exploitation of captive bodies? Does the enslaved female as a consequence of this disavowal of offense thereby occupy a particularly circumscribed scope of existence or personhood? Does she exist exclusively as property? Is she insensate?

The "too common occurrence of offense" and an "offense not effecting existence" differentiated what Cobb described as the strongest passion of negroes—lust—into gendered categories of ubiquitous criminality and negligible injury (1858, 40). Such designations illuminate the concerted processes of racialization, accumulation, engenderment, domination, and sexual subjection. Here it is not my intention to reproduce a heteronormative view of sexual violence as only and always directed at women, or to discount the "great pleasure in whipping a slave" experienced by owners and overseers, or to eliminate acts of castration and genital mutilation from the scope of sexual violence, but rather to consider the terms in which gender, in particular the category of "woman," becomes meaningful in a context in which subjectivity is tantamount to injury. The disavowal of sexual violence is specific not only to female engenderment but to the condition of enslavement in general. In cases such as *Humphrey v. Utz* and *Worley v. State*, essentially what was being decided was whether acts of genital mutilation and castration, (legally defined as acts of mayhem) were crimes when perpetuated against the enslaved or acts of just and reasonable violence. Obviously, the quotidian terror of the antebellum world made difficult the discernments of socially tolerable versus criminal violence. How does one identify "cruel" treatment in a context in which routine acts of barbarism are considered not only reasonable but necessary?

To return to the central issue, the law's selective recognition of slave personhood in regard to issues of injury and protection failed to acknowledge the matter of sexual violation, specifically rape, and thereby defined the identity of the slave female by the negation of sentience,

an invulnerability to sexual violation, and the negligibility of her in-
juries. However, it is important that the decriminalization of rape not
be understood as dispossessing the enslaved of female gender, but in
terms of the differential production of gendered identity or, more specifically, the adequacy or meaning of gender in this context. What is
at stake here is not maintaining gender as an identitarian category but
rather examining gender formation in relation to property relations, the
sexual economy of slavery, and the calculation of injury.

The disregard of sexual injury does not dispossess slave women of
gender; rather, it is an index of ultimate and extreme possession. In this
case, possession occurs not via the protections of the patriarchal family
and its control of female sexuality, but via absolute rights of property.
What is precariously designated "woman" in the context of captivity is
not to be explicated in terms of domesticity or protection but in terms
of the disavowed violence of the paternalist injunction of slave law—
the sanctity of property and the necessity of absolute submission. In
this context, the instrumental deployment of sexuality operated in disregard of white regulatory norms such as chastity and marriage. Within
this economy, the conveyance of property did not require legitimate
issue, as it did within the confines of the patriarchal family. This was
evidenced by the court's description of slave children as neither illegitimate nor bastards, but as simply "not legitimate."[32]

It is necessary to belabor the issue for too often it has been argued that
the enslaved female exists outside of the gendered universe because she
was not privy to the entitlements of bourgeois women within the white
patriarchal family. As a consequence, gender becomes a descriptive for
the social and sexual arrangements of the dominant order rather than an
analytic category. As well, it enchants the discourse of protection and
mystifies its instrumental role in the control and disciplining of body
and, more importantly, maintains the white normativity of the category
"woman." What I am attempting to explore here is the divergent production of the category woman rather than a comparison of black and white
women, which implicitly or inadvertently assumes that gender is relevant only to the degree that generalizable and universal criteria define a
common identity. Can we employ the term woman and yet remain vigi-
lant that "all women do not have the same gender?" (Brown 1995, 39), or
"name as 'woman' that disenfranchised woman whom we strictly, historically, geopolitically *cannot imagine* as a literal referent," rather than
reproduce the very normativity that has occluded an understanding of

the differential production of gender (Spivak 1993, 139)? Nor should it be assumed that "woman" designates a known referent, an a priori unity, a precise bundle of easily recognizable characteristics, traits, and dispositions, and thereby fail to attend to the contigent and disjunctive production of the category. In short, woman must be disassociated from the white middle-class female subject who norms the category.

In light of these remarks, what does the name woman designate within Cobb's restricted scope of subjective value? Does it merely mark the disavowed violence and pained condition of enslavement or make palpable the negligible injury? Does the condition of the enslaved female suggest an obtuseness to pain and injury? By interrogating gender within the purview of "offenses to existence" and examining female subject formation at the site of sexual violence, I am not positing that forced sex constitutes *the* meaning of gender, but that the erasure or disavowal of sexual violence engendered black femaleness as a condition of unredressed injury, which only intensified the bonds of captivity and the deadening objectification of chattel status.[33] Unlike the admittedly indispensable and requisite violence of *State v. Mann*, or the protections extended to other forms of injury, and the criminalization of particular acts of violence (homicide, mayhem, and battery), despite the procedural restrictions that made prosecution extremely difficult, if not nearly impossible, rape was unredressed and disavowed. Ironically, the intervention of affection and the calculation of black sentience intensified the violence legitimated within the scope of the law, and, in this way, the effort to regulate violence simply underscored the categories of unredressed injury. In the very effort to recognize the slave as person, blackness was reinscribed as the pained and punitive embodiment of captivity and black humanity constituted as a state of injury and punishment.

Notes

1   *State of Missouri versus Celia (a Slave)* File 4496, Callaway County Court, October Term, 1855. Callaway County Courthouse, Fulton, Missouri. All quotes are from the case record; however, Melton McClaurin's *Celia, a Slave* (1991) brought the case to my attention.

2   See *Cato (a Slave) v. State*, o Fla. 163, 182 (1860).

3   Slave law encompasses both the slave statutes of the South and precedents established in case law. I do not intend to suggest that this is a unified body

of material or that there are not differences, inconsistencies, and contradictions across jurisdictions. However, I am concerned with the exemplary and characteristic features of slave law as they effect the construction of black subjectivity, sexual violence, and other categories of injury.

4   In accordance with the common law definition of rape, the raped woman must, in effect, prove she was raped by giving evidence of "reasonable resistance."

5   The role of seduction in rape cases has previously been examined along the lines of "no means yes" by Susan Estrich (1986) and Catherine MacKinnon (1983). My emphasis is different here. It is not simply a matter of a woman's "no" not being taken seriously, or of unveiling the crime when "it looks like sex." What is at issue here is the denial and restricted recognition of will or submission because of the legal construction of black subjectivity and the utter negation of the crime. As well, by exploring rape and sexual domination in the frame of seduction, I risk being accused of conflating the two or of effacing the violence of rape through such framing. I share the reasonable discomfort with the juxtaposition of rape and seduction because it shifts the focus from violence to women's culpability or complicity; however, this is exactly what is at stake in this exploration: the ways in which the captive is made responsible for her undoing and the black body made the originary locus of its violation.

6   This presumption of consent is also crucially related to the pathologizing of the black body as a site of sexual excess, torpidity, and sloth. See Jordan (1968).

7   I am working with legal definitions of rape to demonstrate that the sexual violation of enslaved women was not encompassed by the law. It is not only that they are not protected by the common law or slave statute, but that the extremity of socially tolerable violence throws into crisis notions of force and will. Thus, the violence and domination they are commonly subjected to falls outside of the legal constituents of rape as a consequence of the sheer extremity of violence that is normative in their case (Bessmer 1976; Edwards 1981; Eisenstein 1988; Estrich 1987; Smart 1989; Tong 1984).

8   Judith Schafer's work on the antebellum Supreme Court of Louisiana documents this. See Schafer (forthcoming). One case that she has unearthed, *Humphreys v. Utz*, involved an owner's suit against an overseer for the death of a slave who was brutally beaten and suffered cruelties including having his penis nailed to a bedstead.

9   Crime isn't employed here in accordance with traditional legal usage, but as a way of challenging and interrogating the logic of property, the use of chattel persons, and the contradictions of slave law. For a discussion of state crime, see Barak (1991) and George (1991).

10   There were criminal sanctions against homicide and violent assaults on
     slaves. However, extreme and torturous violence was legitimated if exer-
     cised to secure submission. See *Ex parte Bolyston, State v. Mann, Oliver v.
     State.* As well, the procedural discrimination that prohibited blacks from
     testifying against whites made these statutes ineffective if not meaningless.
     Cases in which owners were prosecuted for murder and battery were cases
     involving violence that was so extreme that the "enormities" involved were
     "too disgusting to be particularly designated." See *State v. Hoover,* 20 N.C.
     396, 4 Dev. & Bat. 504 (1839). On the "legitimate uses" of slave property as
     regards sexual abuse and domination, see Goodell ([1853] 1968, 86).

11   I use that term cautiously in light of Hortense Spillers's admonition about
     how "dubiously appropriate" sexuality is as a term of "implied relationship
     and desire in the context of enslavement." See Spillers (1987).

12   As Margaret Burnham notes, "in contradistinction to the common law, the
     slaveholding states all adopted the civil rule, partus sequitur ventrem—the
     issue and descendants of the slaves follow the status of the mother" (1987,
     215). See also Getman (1984, 115–52).

13   *Alfred v. State,* 37 Miss 296. The case was appealed in an appellate court
     on grounds concerning the county of juror selection, the competence of a
     biased juror, Alfred's confession, adultery as a defence for the murder, and
     the exclusion of Charlotte's confession. The higher court upheld the ruling
     of the lower court.

14   Here I am dealing with the "menace to life" that characterizes sovereign
     power, but also its control and management of life in the case of the en-
     slaved population. Thus, I am arguing that the modality of power operative
     on the enslaved combined features of modern and premodern power. See
     Foucault (1978, 133–59).

15   In *State v. Samuel,* 19 N.C. (2 Dev. & Bat.) 177 (1836), Samuel was convicted
     of murdering his wife's lover. On appeal of this conviction, his attorney ar-
     gued that his wife's testimony against him should have been barred by the
     marital privilege. The court held that "the privilege is grounded on the legal
     requirement of marital permanence, it ought not to be held to apply where
     no contract exists to require such permanence. . . . Hence a marriage de
     facto will not, but only a marriage de jure, will exclude one of the parties
     from giving evidence for or against the other."

16   Hazel V. Carby notes that in abolitionist discourse and in slave narratives,
     "the victim (of sexual violence) appeared not just in her own right as a figure
     of oppression but was linked to a threat to, or denial of, the manhood of the
     male slave" (1987, 35).

17   Nor were enslaved women protected from rape and sexual violation per-
     petuated by enslaved men.

18 The rape of black women is registered in case law almost exclusively in contexts in which they or their husbands and lovers are being prosecuted for crimes that would otherwise be recognized as self-defense.

19 I argue that sexual violence is crucial to the construction and experience of gender for black women, unlike Elizabeth Fox-Genovese, who argues that sexual violation of slave women demonstrated that they were somehow without gender or endowed with a lesser gender, since their sexual violation defied the "appropriate gender conventions" of the dominant class. Fox-Genovese fails to consider that gender is not a preexistent unity but is overdetermined by other social practices and discourses: "Violations of the (gender) norm painfully reminded slaves that they did not enjoy the full status of their gender, that they could not count on the 'protection'— however constraining and sometimes hypocritical—that surrounded white women" (1988, 193).

20 See Jordan (1968) and Jefferson ([1801] 1982).

21 In *Commonwealth v. Turner*, 26 Va. 560, 5 Rand. 678 (1827), the court upheld the master's right to extreme forms of punishment. The only dissenting justice argued that a slave was entitled to protection as a person "except so far as the application of it conflicted with the enjoyment of the slave as a thing." William Goodell noted: "Another use of slave property is indicated in the advertisements of beautiful young mulatto girls for sale; and by the fact that these commonly command higher prices than the ablest male labourers, or any other description of slaves. . . . Forced concubinage of slave women with their masters and overseers, constitutes another class of facts, equally undeniable. . . . Such facts in their interminable varieties corroborate the preceding, and illustrate the almost innumerable uses of slave property" ([1853] 1968, 86).

22 Though I am focusing on female bodies, we must not lose sight of the fact that men were also the objects of sexual violence and (ab)use. I am not arguing that female gender is essentially defined by violation; rather, I am interrogating rape within the heterosexual closures that have traditionally defined the act, the role of violence in the reproductive economy of the plantation household, and the constitution of black subjectivity, particularly the construction of female gender, in the context of the law's calculation of personhood in accordance with degrees of injury.

23 As Slavoj Žižek writes, social fantasy "is a necessary counterpart to the concept of antagonism, a scenario filling out the voids of the social structure, masking its constitutive antagonism by the fullness of enjoyment" (1990, 254).

24 Kemble, noting the inappropriateness of this response, described it as foolish and as a weary reaction to the "ineffable state of utter degradation."

25 Žižek (1989, 126). In the North, whiteness and freedom were also defined in contradistinction to black enslavement.

26 Hegemony encompasses coercion and consent, as opposed to direct and simple forms of domination, which rely solely on force and coercion. See Gramsci (1971).

27 I argue that the theory of power and the ethic of submission at work in law are aspects of nineteenth-century sentimental culture. For an extensive discussion of submission as an ethic of nineteenth-century culture, see Douglas (1977) and Tompkins (1985).

28 The contradiction between property and person is also generated by "two distinct economic forms . . . the form of property and the labour process," since the slave was both a "form of property (with a value in circulation) and . . . [a] direct producer (as the producer of value in some definite activity of labouring" (Hindess and Hirst 1975, 129).

29 However, manumission became more difficult during this period and codes regulating slave gatherings became more severe.

30 See Scarry (1985, 108–9) for an examination of the relation between nation, body, and culture.

31 The mortified flesh refers both to the "zero degree of social conceptualization" and to the condition of social death. Spillers writes: "Before the 'body' there is the 'flesh,' that zero degree of social conceptualization that does not escape concealment under the brush of discourse. . . . though the European hegemonies stole bodies . . . out of West African communities in concert with African 'middlemen,' we regard this human and social irreparability as high crimes against the flesh, as the person of African females and African males registered the wounded" (1987, 67). Though I do not distinguish between the body and the flesh as liberated and captive subject positions, I contend that the negation of the subject that results from such restricted recognition reinscribes the condition of social death. See Patterson (1982).

32 *Andrews v. Page*, 3 Heiskell 653, 1871.

33 This encompasses the construction of rape as a capital offense when committed by black men, and the castration of black men as a preventive measure against such "sexual immodesty," as well as the magnification of injury through the omission of rape as an offense effecting the enslaved female's existence.

From Nation-Church to Nation-State:

Evolving Sex-Gender Relations in Québec Society

Danielle Juteau

Rethinking "Race," Ethnicity, Nation, Gender, and Sex

Social formations are conceived here as formed by analytically distinct and empirically interwoven systems of social relations. Each system of social relations can be understood historically in terms of the conditions of its production, reproduction, and transformation, as well as in terms of the construction and transformation of the meaning and content of categories such as "race," ethnicity, nation, sex, and gender, which are not transculturally and transcendentally fixed (Hall 1990).

Social class, sex-gender, ethnic, and national relations, among others, interact and intersect in such a way as to produce a multiplicity of positions, overlapping categories and fluctuating boundaries, and an "intricate experiential nexus of (often contradictory) heterogeneous differences" (de Lauretis 1988, 161). The structure of complex totalities cannot be reduced to a single line of determination but can be examined in terms of horizontal and vertical forms of articulation. The various types of interrelated social divisions must be examined at all levels of the social formation, without flattening the mediations among the determining instances (Hall 1986, 10).

This means that relations among social classes cannot be theorized as economic instances while representations and practices predicated on sex, gender, "race," and ethnicity are reduced to the ideological level. Although it is now generally accepted that neither "race" nor sex and gender can be reduced to class, social scientists such as Anthias and Yuval-Davis (1992, 75) affirm that "race" and class should not be treated as distinct social relations and that gender involves representations and practices that originate in social relations including class and "race" and ethnicity. While they accept the need for examining the mediations among different vertical instances of the social formation, such as the economic, the political, and the ideological, they prefer to reduce their horizontal analysis to one system. In other words, they argue that one should recognize the existence of one, rather than many, empirically interacting and intersecting systems of social relations. In my view, this single-system approach masks the very processes underlying the construction of categories such as "race" and sex and the specific relations in which they are grounded. Before proceeding with the articulation of categories, it is first necessary to find where they emerge from. To do so, it is more useful to adopt a relative autonomy model, positing the existence of analytically distinct and interrelated sets of social relations. This allows us to uncover their respective underpinnings, as I argue with respect to "race"-ethnicity-nation on the one hand, and sex-gender on the other.

Ethnic and National Relations: A Transversal Analysis

Although "races," ethnic groups, and nations cannot be reduced to one another (Omi and Winant, 1994), they have important points in common inasmuch as they usually refer to communities of history and culture.[1] While the notion of "race" involves a specific type of ideological construct (i.e., "race" is defined as involving biological differences), ethnic groups and nations are usually seen as groups possessing common ancestors and the capacity for self-reproduction. In my own work, ethnic and national relations are theorized as social relations of communalization which constitute and unite, within a common material and symbolic universe, groups of a cultural tradition having a subjective belief in a common origin. This belief, as pointed out by Weber ([1921] 1978), is typically triggered by social and political inequalities. Ethnic and national relations correspond to a mode of social classification and hierarchical ordering which derives from the construction of cultural or national origin and belonging. It is in the context of these relations that the criteria, traits, attributes, and labels defining national and ethnic groups and boundaries and serving as a basis for communalization are chosen (Juteau-Lee 1983). Ethnic and national groups can thus be viewed both as elements and as products of this system of social relations.

Accounting for the production, reproduction, and transformation of ethnicity and ethnic boundaries entails analyzing the ethnic social formation in terms of a set of interrelated social structures. The transformation of ethnic social relations refers to the transformation of ethnic differentiations and hierarchizations. These hierarchized differentiations refer to an order of rank, privileges, and an unequal distribution of power, prestige, and possessions (Simon 1983, 9). National and ethnic groups share many similarities, but they can be differentiated in terms of levels of organizational capacity and types of political project (Juteau-Lee 1983). Nations refer to "the idea of a powerful political community of people," a state that may already exist or may be desired. In short, the concept of nation seems to refer to a specific kind of pathos that is linked to political power; the more power is emphasized, the closer the link between nation and state appears to be (Weber 1978, 397–98). As we shall see, nations possess different forms of nationness.

This perspective emphasizes the production, reproduction, and transformation of both ethnic and national boundaries and the stuff from which they are made. Ethnic relations include cultural, ideological, political, and economic dimensions. Ethnic relations do not simply derive from class relations; they possess their own basis and dynamic. While ethnicity is rejected as a primordial element, it is treated here as more than an aspect of consciousness, a label, or a resource. The production of ethnicity is examined in terms of the material practices, relations, and circumstances in which it emerges and operates. Through processes of monopolistic closure, ethnic relations affect the distribution of resources such as economic and cultural capital, the division of labor, the formation of social boundaries, the definition of political issues and ideologies related to forms of pluralism, and so forth. In other words, ethnic social relations structure the entire social formation.

I turn now to a closer examination of the construction of sex-gender relations, another transversal system of social relations that cuts across society as a whole and is comprised of many dimensions: the economic, the political, the cultural, the ideological, and the subjective.

Sexage, or the Social Relations Constructing the Category of Sex

Masculinity and femininity are now usually theorized as acquired traits added on to the differentiated categories of male and female. Gender would thus involve representations and practices that originate in social relations including class, "race," and ethnicity (Anthias and

Yuval-Davis 1992). One of the problems stemming from this unified system approach is the inability to identify the specific relations constitutive of the sexual categories themselves, which are considered to be given and self-evident, originating in biological differences. The link established between biological differences and categorization is seen as inevitable, resting on existing sexual differences and on the centrality of reproduction. The authors who develop an approach focusing on analytically distinct systems of social relations and who adhere, implicitly at least, to a relative autonomy model transcend the analysis of gender to examine the formation of sex classes.

Not unlike racial categories, sexual categories are constructed within a social relation of appropriation constituting sex classes. Guillaumin (1978a) uses the term "sexage" to describe this social relation of appropriation.[2] It is only after the constitution of these sex classes that biological sex (like skin color) is adopted as a criterion for identifying the boundaries between the socially constructed categories of women and men. It is because women are appropriated physical entities that they are turned into things in the realm of thought. This naturalist ideology operates in different ways. In some cases, physical characteristics such as sexual anatomy are seen as causing domination. However, many social scientists now disassociate gender from sex and recognize that women's subordination does not rest upon a biological basis. Nonetheless, the strength of the idea of nature is such that sexual categories still seem self-evident and self-explanatory. Real biological differences are thought to bring about the construction of sexual categories as well as the insertion of human beings to these categories. Yet, as Guillaumin points out, it is because certain humans are appropriated that they are constructed as females: It is not because one is female that one is appropriated, but one is female because one is appropriated.[3] This rejection of the naturalist discourse completely destructures the dominant mode of explanation. The social appropriation of women comprises an ideological and a material dimension. As we have seen, the ideological dimension is exemplified in the discourse on their specific nature and in the use of biological sex as a marker of socially constituted categories. It is intrinsically linked to the material dimension which involves the appropriation of their bodies and labor power.

In what follows I argue that there are several systems of sexage which evolve as a function of the diverse modalities of appropriation, in both their private and collective forms. Moreover, location in class, national, ethnic, and "racial" systems, and in the specific institutions through which the appropriation of women and their labor occurs (church, capital, state, family), combine in such a way as to foster empirically diverse sex-gender systems as well as a variety of locations within them. I develop this argument by a discussion of how changes in the dominant mode of production in Québec modified the relationship between church and state. This engendered new forms of nationness, the transformation of the sex-gender system, and a major reorganization in women's work and positions.

Sexage 1: Class, Sex-Gender, and the Nation-Church

THE CONSTITUTION OF THE FRENCH CANADIAN NATION[4]

As the British immigrants came to British North America after the cession of New France to England in 1763,[5] one of the conquered and subordinate groups, descendants of the colonizers from France, were identified and defined in terms of their differences: language (French) and religion (Catholic). These attributes were soon considered, by insiders and outsiders, to represent their essence, and the struggle to maintain them created a community called the French Canadian nation. This national community kept relatively distinct social boundaries, and its nationness included diverse characteristics: a relatively autarkic economy, the preponderance of the Church as a central political actor, a discourse emphasizing a cultural mode of nationhood, and, as we will see, a specific form of sex-gender system.

Up until the end of the nineteenth century, French Canadian families generally lived in rural settings (on farms or in small parishes) and led a relatively autarkic existence (Juteau 1993). Work performed by husbands and sons in the logging industry supplemented the farm income. Some men worked as unskilled laborers in the primary sector, notably in mining or lumbering. Men and women also provided cheap and docile "manpower" for businesses developing in urban centers. This French Canadian nation was inseparable from the Church, which functioned as an apparatus equivalent to the state, that is, as a centralized agency of regulation (Laurin-Frenette 1978). The Church extended its power by gaining control over educational and other social matters as well as family life. Belongingness to the nation manifested itself through adherence to the Catholic religion and, secondarily, to the French language.

French Canadians were also united through a common discourse; the nation was envisaged as a *Volknation* based on common ancestry.[6] Belongingness to the nation was perceived in an essentialist and static manner; one was born a French Canadian and did not become one. The Church maintained and preserved social institutions in the name of national specificity, thereby ensuring its control over the nation as well as the reproduction of its power. Economic exploitation was left to the English-speaking capitalist class.

French Canadian women were involved in the biological, social, and ideological reproduction of the nation and nationality (Juteau-Lee 1983). Their extremely high birthrate ensured what was called "the revenge of the cradles." In 1931, 20.4 percent of married women had six or more children; in 1961, the proportion was 11.3 percent overall and 23 percent in rural areas (Laurin, Juteau, and Duchesne 1991, 303). Furthermore, by socializing newborns, women furnished the work serving to humanize and ethnicize them.[7] Women were crucial to the social and ideological reproduction of the nation. As a consequence, they were strongly controlled. Those responsible for producing little French Canadians who were to become and behave like true little French Canadians, the guardians of the "race," had to be guarded themselves (Juteau-Lee 1983). Mothers thus stood at the center of the nation, both dominated and praised to the skies.

In the middle of this center and rising above all other women, stood the nuns: women in convents, in schools, in hospitals, in orphanages, in psychiatric wards, in nursing homes, in presbyteries, living in cities and in villages across Québec, Canada, the United States, and even throughout the world. Over the decades they came to number in the thousands (forty thousand at one stage), and in 1941 they accounted for 3 percent of all women in Québec aged fifteen years or more.[8] Veiled, celibate, sometimes cloistered, and having pronounced vows of chastity, poverty, and obedience, these women worked day and night without pay in female religious orders, which constituted vast employment ghettos contained within the Church.[9] They "manned" the institutions controlled by the clergy, thereby allowing the Church to exercise its power over French Canadian institutions and the French Canadian nation.

WOMEN AND THE CONSTRUCTION OF THE NATION

A specific sex-gender system developed within the boundaries of this nation-church. It was characterized by a complex division of labor among women resulting from the articulation of various systems of social relations. Women who entered the convent were recruited mainly from within the boundaries of the French Canadian nation (Laurin, Juteau, and Duchesne 1991, 298), which at the time included not only Québec (94.2 percent were from Québec) but also Francophones living in the other provinces and even in the United States (Franco-Americans). They came largely from the peasantry (which is overrepresented in relation to total population) and blue-collar milieux (which is underrepresented). They grew up in small towns; more than 70 percent of the nuns came from areas with fewer than five thousand inhabitants (340). Finally, 80 percent of the nuns came from the 20 percent of families with more than six children (308–17). More precisely, 39.6 percent were from families with six to ten children, and 36.2 percent were from families with eleven to fifteen children (302). Ethnic and national relations, social class, and region combined so as to define specific social milieux more receptive to God's calling, which produced women who "chose" to become nuns. For example, a woman's chance of hearing the voice of God was higher if her father was a French Canadian farmer or a blue-collar worker residing outside large centers than if her father was an English Canadian or even a French Canadian medical doctor practicing in the metropolis, and if her mother had sixteen children rather than two.

The French Canada that existed until the first half of the century yields a fascinating picture of the interrelation between two categories of women—nuns and laywomen working in the home as wives and mothers—whose bodies and labor power were controlled and appropriated through the Church. Mothers ensured the biological reproduction of the nation and the reproduction of nationality in the name of a nationalist-conservative ideology of *survivance*.[10] For their part, the nuns, those women who chose the religious life, came from the "surplus" children produced by married women. Their size encouraged by the Church, big families provided the same Church with women who became nuns. Their unpaid labor, carried out in the name of God and for his glory, rendered operative the social institutions that underlay the (male) Church's power base.

A strict division of labor between these two fractions of the sex class was established. Mothers and nuns were united and interrelated within the same sex-gender system. Working without pay, they cared for all the dependent members of that society, either as housewives in the home or as nuns outside of the home. Nuns looked after those unattended by mothers: the sick, the old, the mentally or physically handicapped, orphans, the so-called deviants such as unwed mothers and prisoners, and the adult male clerics who, in the Catholic church, were "deprived" of the services of a wife. Because their work was often accomplished within the boundaries of Church-operated institutions such as schools and hospitals, many of the French Canadian women not confined to the home were also kept away from the external and "dangerous" influences of capitalist, non-Catholic, and Anglophone milieux. Intrusions from the outside world were kept at a minimum, thereby ensuring the reproduction of the nation both in objective and subjective terms. More than any other women in Québec, nuns epitomized and embodied the French Canadian nation. They were the signifiers of its boundaries, so much so that when I first moved to English Canada, I would run up to a nun every time I saw one, assuming I could exchange a few words in French with a compatriot.

Meanwhile, the clerical elite condemned women's paid labor. As a result, a smaller proportion of married women were in the labor force in Québec than in Canada: in 1931, women represented 7 percent of the total labor force in Québec and 10 percent in Ontario; in 1941, 7.3 percent of married women in Québec and 15 percent in Ontario were in the labor force. Paid work was more or less incompatible with marriage, and most salaried female workers were single. In certain occupations, female workers were fired when they married. But some women did work outside the home,[11] and I will now compare their occupational distribution to that of the nuns.

NUNS AND PAID FEMALE WORKERS: THE IMPACT OF DIFFERENT ORGANIZATIONAL STRUCTURES

In 1941, when female religious orders were at their height, 3 percent of women aged fifteen years and over in Québec were nuns (Laurin, Juteau, and Duchesne 1991, 224). This constituted 11.8 percent of the female labor force (229) and represented almost a third (31.8 percent) of female workers between the ages of forty-five and fifty-four (232) in that province (see table 1).

Table 1 shows the impact of organizational structures on the labor accomplished by women. The jobs held by paid female workers and their distribution both differ from and resemble those held by the nuns. During the period covered by our study (1901–1971), close to 40 percent (last nine categories) of the nuns performed domestic labor such as cooking,

Table 1. Occupational Distribution of the Female Labor Force (Total and Religious) by Percentage, Quebec, 1911–1971

	1911		1921		1931	
	Nuns	Total L.F.	Nuns	Total L.F.	Nuns	Total L.F.
Managerial	20.8	2.7	22.0	2.4	20.8	1.5
Professional and technical	36.3	13.5	39.4	22.5	40.2	18.0
Clerical	2.1	6.1	2.5	13.5	2.2	14.1
Sales	—	5.7	—	5.6	—	6.0
Service and recreation occupations	34.7	36.1	29.7	24.7	29.6	32.9
Transport and communications	0.3	1.3	0.2	2.4	0.2	2.0
Farmers	0.1	3.1	0.7	2.6	0.7	2.3
Other primary occupations	0.0	0.0	0.0	0.0	0.0	0.0
Craftsmen and prod. process workers	5.8	31.4	5.5	25.5	6.2	19.7
Laborers	—	0.1	—	0.8	—	3.3
Unspecified	—	—	—	—	—	0.0
Total	100	100	100	100	100	100

Sources for total labor force: Census of Canada, 1971, cat. 94–716, table 1; Census of Canada, 1911, vol. 6, Occupations, table 5; Census of Canada, 1921, vol. 5, Occupations, table 4.

housekeeping, and laundry. Another 40 percent had professional jobs (second category), mainly as teachers. The remaining 20 percent (first category) were in charge of organizing these activities and managing their institutions. They held mainly middle and senior management positions: heads of religious orders and directors of organizations such as hospitals, orphanages, and schools (Juteau and Laurin, 1997). Our findings can be briefly summarized as follows:

1. In both cases, the level of concentration is high. The great majority of nuns worked in the liberal and technical professions, services, and administration. These three categories account for roughly 90 percent of job occupations for the period under study: for example, 91.8 per-

1941		1951		1961		1971	
Nuns	Total L.F.	Nuns	Total L.F.	Nuns	Total L.F.	Nuns	Total L.F.
19.1	1.9	20.8	3.0	22.6	3.1	19.4	2.8
40.2	16.6	41.1	15.4	40.2	16.5	37.4	16.2
3.2	14.2	2.9	22.5	4.0	25.2	8.7	29.3
—	5.6	0.1	6.6	0.0	6.4	—	5.4
29.5	32.1	28.6	20.4	27.9	21.1	28.7	15.4
0.4	1.3	0.3	2.5	0.8	2.0	0.5	1.1
0.7	1.3	0.3	2.2	0.1	3.2	0.2	2.1
0.0	0.0	0.0	0.0	0.0	0.0	0.0	0.0
6.9	24.6	5.8	24.0	4.4	18.1	5.2	12.3
—	2.1	—	2.2	—	1.4	—	1.3
—	0.3	—	1.3	—	3.2	—	14.0
100	100	100	100	100	100	100	100

Source for the religious labor force: Juteau, Laurin, and Duchesne, *Database on Religious Communities, Quebec, 1901–1971.*

cent in 1911 and 90.7 percent in 1961. The exception is 1971, with 85.5 percent. For the most part, salaried employees were distributed among four occupational categories: the liberal and technical professions, office work, services and recreational activities, and trades. The level of concentration was slightly less than was the case for nuns. These four categories accounted for roughly 80 percent of all workers, except in 1971 with 73.2 percent.

2. Both nuns and paid workers can be found in the professions and in the services, accomplishing to a certain extent women's traditional work: teaching, nursing, and providing services. But nuns are highly

represented in administrative positions, while paid workers are in blue- and pink-collar work. What is striking is the low level of nuns doing clerical work; except for 1971, it remains at or under 4 percent. Our data indicate that in 1961, 40 percent of female administrators in Québec were nuns (Juteau and Laurin, 1997). Furthermore, the administrative positions held by nuns were important: they managed and often owned hospitals in which the combined number of personnel and patients could reach three thousand individuals, and schools that offered numerous programs and took in boarders; they managed religious orders comprising up to two thousand nuns, large real estate holdings, and other investments. These were by no means "mom-and-pop" operations run on a shoestring. For their part, laywomen in the paid labor force held clerical positions or were employed in manufacturing activities.

3. The stability of the nuns' occupational distribution contrasted sharply with the movement of paid workers and is related to the distinct structures within which they evolved.[12] Nuns' work, which is unpaid and organized by the Church, takes place outside the embrace of capitalist social relations. As such, their occupational distribution was not directly subjected to the major fluctuations affecting the French Canadian economy. Only after the state assumed complete control of health, educational, and social services did this system break down.[13]

INTERCONNECTED AND STATIC CATEGORIES OF WOMEN

Sexage 1 is characterized by the absence of officially accepted birth control, of secular marriages, of recognized divorces, of the right to vote at the provincial level until 1940. Some called it a matriarchy, because women assumed sole responsibility for running the home and social institutions. This system comprises a relatively strict division of labor among the three different and interconnected categories of women that collectively form a sex-class: mothers and wives in the home, nuns, and a small proportion of salaried workers. The coherence and effectiveness of this system of sexage rested on the functional differentiation among the fractions of the sex-class. Its organization was static, and movement among compartments was kept to a minimum: a woman was either a mother and wife or a nun; before marrying or entering the convent, and exceptionally after marriage, she was allowed to work. These three distinct empirical configurations were predicated on specific modes of appropriation of their labor and specific combinations of social relations. Both housewives and nuns shared the work of providing physical, emotional, and intellectual care to human beings; in both cases, their work was appropriated, that is, unpaid and not subjected to a contract or a time limit. This central characteristic points to the specific relation constituting the sex-gender system and sex-classes. This unpaid labor, which was performed in various settings and under different rules and organizational systems, points to the distinction between private and collective modes of appropriation. Nuns were not submitted to the private form of appropriation and therefore escaped the work of biological reproduction and providing sexual services. Their position also differed from that of paid female workers, whose work was exchanged for a wage. As such, the latter's work is exploited but not appropriated. Women's work in the public sphere is thus determined both by capitalist social relations and by sex-gender relations; consequently, their position in the paid labor force differs substantially from that occupied by men (Walby 1986, 1990).

The nuns represent a paradoxical category of women, both more and less controlled than other women. While housewives experience collective appropriation that is contradicted by private appropriation,[14] paid workers experience the contradiction between social appropriation and paid work. The nuns, on the other hand, experience collective appropriation not contradicted by either private or paid work. During the time they belong to a religious order, women do not acquire economic capital necessary to escape appropriation. If and when they leave the convent, it is difficult for them to make use of the cultural capital they have acquired. As long as women remain unpaid workers in an employment ghetto contained within the boundaries of the Church, it is not threatening to allow them to hold top administrative positions and to be upwardly mobile. But when the jobs held by nuns become salaried, guess who will get them?

Sexage 2: Sex-Gender in the Nation-State[15]

The previously described sex-gender system did not immediately break down as industrialization and urbanization radically altered relations between French and English Canadians. While the expansion of Anglo-American capitalism eroded the basis of the dominant mode of production, pushed French Canadians out of their autarkic existence, and "integrated" them into the system of capitalist exchange, industrialization gave birth to a new ethnic division of labor (Juteau 1993).

Meanwhile, there was a significant decrease in the number of women entering the convent and a decline in the birthrate (Laurin, Juteau, and Duchesne 1991, 203), and women entered the labor market in increasing numbers. Nevertheless, the overall position of female religious orders remained relatively stable, as did their internal structure. But these social forces eventually sapped the material foundations of the old forms of social organization and weakened the Church's power base. As the power of the provincial state increased, as it took over control of educational, health, and social services institutions, the female religious orders disintegrated and the total number of nuns declined dramatically (Laurin, Juteau, and Duchesne 1991, 199–223).

The modernization, expansion, and bureaucratization of the Québec state apparatus gave way to a growing emphasis on territory and to the emergence and development of a new national community: les Québécois, a community excluding all French Canadians living outside Québec (Juteau-Lee 1983). A new vocabulary arose alongside these new boundaries. Just as Negroes in the United States became Blacks, French Canadians became Québécois. To this changing collective identity corresponded new forms of political consciousness. The new nationalism was essentially a secular ideology, anti-imperialist and oriented toward decolonization, national liberation, and self-determination.

These changes were accompanied by strong labor and feminist movements, variously liberal, radical, and marxist. The liberation of women was often seen as inextricably tied to that of the nation, and Québécois women formed their own feminist associations. The civil code was first reformed in 1964; divorce was made possible and accessible, means of contraception were generalized, abortion was legalized, the birthrate continued its long decline, women were elected to parliament, and changes were made to the legal system with regard to divorce settlements and so forth.

In addition, nuns left their convents, seemingly attracted to the freedom of the outside world, access to paid labor, and the possibility of expressing their sexuality. In fact, something else was happening as the state took over and modernized the institutions formerly controlled by the Church. This takeover, in the case of health care at least, involved a power struggle opposing not only the state and the Church but the latter and the female religious orders. The male elite of the Catholic Church did not fight the state as it took over, with the help of the unions, their hospitals. Their hospitals? In fact, the hospitals belonged in large part to the female religious orders, as did their management and the jobs involved. Nuns, that is women, first lost their administrative positions and then their property.[16] In 1961, as we have seen, 40 percent of female administrators in Québec were nuns (Marquis 1987). Today, most senior administrators in hospitals are men, as are health care system bureaucrats. While men, both former clerics and laypersons, monopolized senior management jobs both within these institutions and throughout the expanding civil service, nuns were replaced by laywomen (paid female labor) at the middle and lower echelons of the system. Thus, the transformation of the nation, the modernization and secularization of Québec, did bring about an improvement in women's status. But it was also accompanied by a loss of managerial positions in health, educational, and social services sectors.

The system of sexage did not disappear, but its forms and its specific substructures changed. The reorganization of women's work in Québec involved a shift from three relatively distinct categories of female workers to two categories: unpaid laborers in the home and paid laborers. It also established a new relationship between them. The participation of women in the labor force increased (from 34.6 percent in 1971 to 40.6 percent in 1981 and 45.0 percent in 1991), as did their participation in the labor force, which increased from 39.9 percent in 1971 to 51.8 percent in 1981 and 59.9 percent in 1991. Only 25.7 percent of women in the labor force in 1991 had never married. Paid labor became a dominant structure of the sex-gender system.[17] While the division of labor among women became blurred, the amount and nature of the work furnished by women as a whole remained practically unchanged. Women shifted from one location to another in an unending circular movement (Juteau and Laurin 1989b).

The importance of the state also increased: now unemployment payments, aid for dependent children, and other forms of public assistance provide women with the minimum necessities of life that neither their employers, fathers, husbands, nor lovers give them over the long term. The state is actively involved in compensating for the growing pauperization of women; neither marriage nor paid employment seem to suffice. But this is another story.

The forms of private appropriation have become varied. In addition to the traditional family, one finds common-law unions, reconstituted families, single-parent families, and so on. Although women still carry out most of the material and emotional work demanded for the upkeep of their partners and children, their subsistence and that of their children are only partially assured by their partners, who expect the woman also to have a paying job. Moreover, this support lasts only for the period of their union.

Pressures to have children are stronger than ever. Every woman must want motherhood at any price, even if she limits herself to one child, as is often the case. Even though fertility and birthrates have declined, more women are now involved in biological reproduction. Now we are all nuns, wives, lovers, mothers, housekeepers, volunteer workers, and paid workers. Freedom to move from one location to another is what makes this sex-gender system work. It is now through the state that men partly compensate for the losses that the new modalities of appropriation bring to women.

Finally, an alarmist discourse on the possible disappearance of the nation still exhorts women of French Canadian ethnicity to have more children in order to ensure the material and ideological reproduction of the nation. This is yet another neverending story. As recently as October 1995, one of the leaders of the campaign for Québec sovereignty encouraged women of the "white race" to produce more children, thereby allowing French Canadians to maintain demographic control within the province. And, on referendum night,[18] a disappointed premier of Québec and leader of the independentist Parti Québécois, Jacques Parizeau, commenting on the results showing 50.4 percent of the population against separation, said that "we" had lost the referendum because of money and the ethnic vote. Although his comments created a furor, and although he was generally criticized, the words stay with us and remind us of the close connections among nationalism, nation, history, ancestry, the reproduction of the nation, and its reproducers. Once again, in a very different setting, women of the "right" ethnicity are urged to become biological reproducers so as to ensure the reproduction of the nation.

Concluding Remarks: On Sexual Categories

Changing forms of nationness have substantially modified the sex-gender system in Québec society, transforming the relationship between private and collective appropriation and between social appropriation and paid employment. New structures have become dominant in defining and organizing the sex-gender system, as paid labor and the state replaced the Church while former structures such as the family became less important in their modified forms.

I have focused on women belonging to one national group because for the most part it was their labor power that was accessible to the Church. By following them across time, I could indicate how positions occupied in different systems of social relations interact in such a way as to produce diverse modalities of appropriation. This analysis could be pursued in many directions: by looking at the women who are not nuns and at women who belong to other ethnic and national groups; by examining in greater detail the new system of sexage briefly sketched in this article; by looking at other structures such as paid labor, the state, violence, and sexuality. Sex-gender systems evolve constantly as a result of changes in their dominant structures and their articulation. Furthermore, as we have seen, the different modalities of appropriation produce a multiplicity of distinct locations and a diversity of life experiences: in the case of women, having twelve children and not having children; the combination of unpaid labor and administrative positions; a strict sexual division of labor and occupational mobility.

Last, and importantly, it allows me to rethink the relationships among the sexual division of labor, sex, and gender. The articulation between sex and gender is complex and multifaceted. A person with a male body, for example, can feel that a woman inhabits his/her body; s/he can also choose to behave or not to behave as a male. In her discussion of this double inversion occurring with transvestites, Butler (1990) argues that gender need not be superimposed mechanically upon sexual categories. In the case of the Catholic Church during the period covered by our study, sexuality is, in a manner of speaking, transcended. Nuns are constructed as unsexed women: their hair is partly or totally covered, they are veiled, and their bodies are hidden behind multiple layers of long skirts, as prescribed by strict regulations defined by the male clergy. No makeup, perfume, nail polish, or other frills are allowed. For their part, priests and other male clerics are also constructed with a specific masculinity. They wear long black skirts, show well-manicured hands, and, as they rise in the hierarchy, the body is covered with colorful tissues and purple and gold embroidery, rings are worn, and ornaments become more festive. Importantly, the robes dissimulate the male sex. Gender is used here to mask sex. Interestingly, the body, the sex that is dissimulated, is one that is not used. Celibacy is the rule: Catholic priests and nuns neither have sex nor procreate. Indeed, they are removed from procreation and child raising in order to perform a better job as clerics. In one respect, biological sex is completely irrelevant. In another, however, it is very much at the heart of the matter.

For it is females who become nuns, and males who become priests. Biological sex becomes a discriminatory criterion, the basis for the institutional assignment of workers to different places and positions. Although biological differences clearly have nothing to do with the work performed, the division of humans into two biologically differentiated categories serves to determine who does what in the Church, who exercises power and who is controlled. Nuns look after the sick and other dependents, while male religious orders such as the Jesuits teach in colleges and priests run the Vatican. This supports the claim that the construction of sexual categories originates in a sexual division of labor rather than the opposite. It also supports the hypothesis that sexual categorization on the basis of biological differences is an ideological construction legitimating the sexual division of labor that produces and reproduces sex-classes. Sex-classes originate in social relations that are distinct from those constitutive of classes as well as of ethnic, national, and racialized groups. These latter, as I have shown, were interlocked in such a way in Québec that changes in the dominant mode of production transformed national boundaries and the sex-gender system.

Notes

This paper is based on a project made possible by research grants obtained from the Social Science Research Council of Canada and the Fonds des chercheurs et d'aide à la recherche du Québec. It was carried out with my colleague, Professor Nicole Laurin, and the help of six research assistants. The data are mainly from a representative sample of twenty-four religious orders and thirty-seven hundred nuns working in Québec over a period of seventy years (1901–1971). For each nun, information was collected on her father's occupation (data on mothers were, unfortunately but not surprisingly, absent), her education level upon entering the convent, her education after entering the convent, her first job in the convent and subsequent occupation for each decade, and the place where this work was performed. Collecting and analyzing these data required three years of full-time work and was supplemented by census data. Many of the ideas presented here were discussed with my colleague, but I assume full responsibility for the present interpretation.

1 A somewhat similar position is developed by Anthias and Yuval-Davis, who argue that "race" is a boundary that refers to a particular construction of a collectivity (1992, 2).

2 Unpaid labor, Guillaumin points out, is an indicator and an expression of a specific type of social relation that is distinct from capitalist social relations in which labor power is paid. The social relations between the sexes are conceived as class relations having their origin in the processes of production and reproduction of goods and of human beings; its agents are men on the one hand, and women on the other. Female agents are appropriated in their physical and psychological individuality, as are, consequently, their labor power and the products of their bodies and of their work. Guillaumin calls this relationship collective appropriation. Private appropriation, which puts some women into a relation with some men, mainly in marriage and the family, is a particular and restrictive form of collective appropriation. For a more detailed presentation of this author's pathbreaking work, see my introduction "Reconstructing the Categories of Sex and Race" in Guillaumin (1995).

3 And it is not because you are black that you become a slave but because you are a slave that black designates a category.

4 For a longer discussion of the processes underlying the construction of the nation as well as the changing forms of nationness, see Juteau (1993).

5 One of the first group of English speakers to settle were the Loyalists leaving the United States after the American Revolution.

6 Ethnic nations define belongingness in terms of common ancestry and blood ties while *Staatnations* emphasize territory and participation in a common polity; in reality, both aspects often coexist, as pointed out in Gilroy's critique of the racialization of national boundaries (1987). This corresponds to the distinction made by A. D. Smith (1986) between ethnic and territorial nations.

7 Socialization can be conceptualized as a labor process, a double process of humanization and ethnicization inseparable from a social relation involving physical, affective, and intellectual upkeep.

8 These data are presented and analyzed in Laurin, Juteau, and Duchesne (1991).

9 The sexual division within the Catholic Church is extremely rigid. Women are barred from the priesthood, the positions of religious and political power. Furthermore, male religious orders are more specialized in higher education than primary and secondary education, and hardly ever in providing social services and physical care.

10 *Survivance* (survival) was the first main ideology to characterize French Canadian political thought. Articulated mainly by the ruling elite (clerical

and petit bourgeois), it advocated the maintenance of the distinct boundaries of the French Canadian nation, which entailed the maintenance of
specific cultural attributes and the rejection of change.

11 According to Statistics Canada (Census of Canada, 1911, vol. 6, Occupations, table 5; Census of Canada, 1921, vol. 4, Occupations, table 4; Census
of Canada, catalogue 94-716, table 1, includes the years 1931–71), the following number of women were in the Québec labor force: 95,635 in 1911,
132,615 in 1921, 200,863 in 1931, 259,312 in 1941, 340,591 in 1951, 478,694
in 1961, 717,485 in 1971. For the same years, the number of nuns calculated
on the basis of our representative sample is as follows: 9,486 in 1901, 13,249
in 1911, 18,460 in 1921, 24,427 in 1931, 30,238 in 1941, 33,665 in 1951, 35,078
in 1961, 28,320 in 1971.

12 The proportion of workers in each category varies for each decade. As well,
the order in which these four categories appeared changed. In 1911, the
latter accounted for 87.1 percent of salaried workers, distributed as follows:
services and recreational activities were the most important with 36.1 percent of this labor force, for the most part domestic workers. This was followed by trades workers with 31.4 percent, and far behind the liberal and
technical professions with 13.5 percent and office work with 6.1 percent. In
1921, 86.2 percent of workers fell into these four categories. However, trades
are now the most important (25.5 percent), followed closely by service work
(24.7 percent) and the liberal and technical professions (22.5 percent). Office
work (13.5 percent) remained in fourth position. With the numbers for office
work and the professions increased considerably, those for the services and
trades dropped.

Overall, this trend held for the period under study. The services and trades
categories continued to decrease and the office work category increased,
which functioned to change the respective positions of these categories
over the decades. It should be noted, however, that the number of professional workers began to decrease after 1921. It went from 22.5 percent of
this labor force to 18 percent in 1931, and finally stabilized at 16.2 percent.
The proportion of service workers decreased considerably, going from 24.7
percent in 1921 and remaining in first position until 1941 (32.1 percent) to
21.1 percent in 1961 and 15.4 percent in 1971). During this period, the proportion of trades workers remains relatively stable, going from 25.5 percent
in 1921 to 24 percent in 1951 and dropping to 18.1 percent in 1961 and 12.3
percent in 1971. The most spectacular transformation occurred in the case
of office workers, who were in fourth position until 1941 and reached the
second position in 1951 and the first position from 1961 on. This category
went from 6.1 percent in 1991 to 25.2 percent in 1961 and 29.3 percent in
1971. Throughout these eight decades, the sales clerk category remained in

a stable fifth position, far behind the fourth category, with roughly 6 percent of the labor force.

13 This occurred at the beginning of the 1960s with the election of a new government under the slogan "Il faut que ça change" (Things must change). What has been referred to as the Quiet Revolution marked the beginning of a new era in which the state replaced the Church as the dominant apparatus and took control of social services.

14 This idea of contradiction is found in Guillaumin's work (1978a). While all women belong to the sex-class (that is, all women are appropriated and provide without pay the labor necessary for the upkeep of human beings), some women belong to one man. In addition, paid labor contradicts appropriation, because persons belonging to others are in principle not free to sell their labor power. Women's changing position in the labor market has modified the sex-gender system.

15 For a longer analysis of these processes, see Juteau and Laurin (1989b).

16 This occurred through a process called the "clause de désintéressement." For a more detailed analysis, see Juteau and Laurin (1989a).

17 Interestingly, the proportion of women in administrative categories has now reached 10.2 percent, and these positions usually do not involve the power and responsibility of positions previously held by nuns.

18 On 31 October 1995, residents of Québec who were Canadian citizens voted in a referendum on the separation of Québec from Canada. This was the second referendum to be held. The first one took place in 1980.

Women Between Nation and State in Lebanon

Suad Joseph

Compulsory Nation-States

The nation-state has been a "compulsory" model for former colonies, according to Sami Zubaida (1988, 121). Modern states define themselves through constitutions, the main purpose of which is to articulate the nature of their relationships with their citizens. The modern nation-state has been modeled on the Western European experience, particularly, Zubaida contends, the French Jacobin model. This model has entailed a number of key constructs that are of interest to understanding the position of women caught between nation and state in Lebanon: the notion of the people as a nation; the notion of the sovereignty of the people as a nation; the notion of the state as the sum total of its individualized citizens (Zubaida 1989, 121).

If, as Zubaida claims, the nation-state has become a compulsory model for former colonies, then I would suggest that citizenship also has become compulsory. One must belong to a nation-state to have a political identity, to have mobility, and to have rights to resources, services, and protection vis-à-vis international relations. If citizenship in a nation-state has become the venue defining membership in the world community, then the manner in which nation-states define citizenship and structure membership in their political communities becomes crucial for understanding women's positions globally. Citizenship defines identity—who you are, where you belong, where you come from, and how you understand yourself in the world. Rights vis-à-vis the state flow from the state's definition of its citizenry.

Nation-state building projects in Southern states have been shaped not only by Western models,[1] but also by local forces. To assume that Southern peoples absorb Western ideas unmediated by their own histories and cultures would be to disregard the agency of those peoples. At the same time, to excavate the origins of ideas in order to exorcise a culture of impurities is a nostalgic exercise premised on the false assumption that a people can claim an unadulterated moment in a pristine past. Often, assertions of the origins of ideas or theories are deployed in contestations over authenticity that lock the contestants in dead-ended essentializing strategies of combat. As Edward Said eloquently argues, however, theory travels (1983, 226). The evolution, migrations, and applications of an idea are a set of stories in some ways shaped, but not determined, by its origins. To specify the Western origins of the construct of nation-state is only to historically and culturally situate it, not to judge or reject it. My concern is to unpack the untheorized coincident constructs embedded within the nation-state (as implemented in Lebanon) as they pertain to women.

To assess women's position in these compulsory nation-states in the South, we need to analyze the dynamics of nation building as at once separate from and mutually shaping and shaped by the dynamics of state building.[2] These processes in Southern countries differ significantly from Western experiences, because states were often imposed upon Southern peoples by colonizing powers. Southern states often grouped peoples who neither thought of themselves as a nation nor had any previous experience of statehood. If the nation-state is always an imagined community, as Benedict Anderson argues (1983), building Southern nation-states has required massive imagination to transform the disparate communities into nations that fit states. As Partha Chatterjee observed, however, the imagination of Southern states has been colonized (1993a, 5). They have been pressured to imagine their communities in European forms and to naturalize the European as the true nation-state.

Alien in their origin, Southern states often have stood, as Zubaida argues, external to their communities (1988, 124). Yet state structures and institutions have been embraced by local elites strategizing for a space in local and global politics. In the process of creating their states, local elites have created institutions and policies aimed at creating the political communities to uphold their states. Control of critical resources and coercive instruments has facilitated elites' interventions in local communities to build national communities. The character of local elites, their coherency of structure and purpose, and the resources available to them have shaped their nation-state building projects. The more politically and socially unified the elite and the more resources available to them, the more they have been able to channel primordial into national communities. Alternatively, the less unified and endowed, the more difficult has been the molding process. Similarly, the character, coherency, and resources of local communities have shaped their capacity and will to resist or cooperate as communities with the elite's project. At times, as I argue for the Lebanese case below, the nation being built by communities at local levels does not correspond to the nation being built by the state elites.

In many Southern countries, women have been caught between nation building and state building projects. Often identified as symbols of their communities, control of their bodies, behavior, production, and reproduction has become a site of contestation or organizing between state and local leaders in their competing or compatible projects. Women's views on and responses to the maneuvers of state and local leaders are often mediated through the very structures and processes used to control them—kinship, religion, political and social leadership networks, and local community relations.

The notion of the nation-state as a compulsory model therefore raises critical issues concerning women. Middle Eastern societies have adopted most of the principles of the Western nation-state in their constitutions, and the ideas have continued to influence political actors, ideologies, and practices in the region. Middle Eastern states and political actors, however, have greatly departed from the model, particularly in arenas affecting women.

In this chapter, I analyze some of the problems in this compulsory model of nation-state and the implications of this model for women in Lebanon. I analyze the character and structure of the nation the Lebanese elite tried to build in the postindependence period (post-1943). I use my research in an urban working-class neighborhood of Greater Beirut to address the experience of some women caught between nation and state formation.

I caution against generalizing from Lebanon to other Arab states and the dangers of essentializing the cultures and politics, however. We need to ground theory in culturally and historically specific contexts. From such grounding we can more accurately account for local dynamics, avoiding unfounded universalisms that are often projections and generalizations from the experience of the theorizing nation.

I argue that the Lebanese state built during the French Mandate and refined by the Lebanese elite after independence was premised on the notion of a nation fragmented by religious communities. The Lebanese elite, themselves fragmented, defined their nation as a collection of communities recruited by religious sectarian affiliations. The state institutionalization of religious fragmentation militated against the development of a nation unified by common culture and subsidized sectarian institutions and identities. Therefore, unlike in the Jacobin model, the Lebanese were not individualized citizens of a political community but stood before the state as members of prescribed sectarian communities. As Zubaida notes, for members of nation-states to become individualized citizens who are equal before the law, they have to be divested of statuses derived from communities (1988, 126). The Lebanese state not only did not divest its members of communal statuses, but institutionalized those statuses, thus reinscribing many of the concomitant constructs and dynamics.

The institutionalization of nation defined as a collection of religious communities, I contend, reinforced already existing and contributed to the growth of new patriarchal and parochial institutions and structures that further subordinated women. Built into public, sectarian, and lay leadership patterns were the idioms, moralities, and dynamics of patriarchy.

In local communities, women were both shaped by these elite nation-building strategies as well as resistant to them. Paradoxically, the very structures of domination opened spaces for maneuvering against the constraints of the structures. The competition and conflicts among the elite, their strategies of pulling the center of power away from the state toward themselves personally, and the poverty of public resources allowed citizens to maneuver among political leaders, among political institutions, and among political identities. In the maneuvering, national identity became a fluid, continually renegotiated set of positionalities flowing from strategic personalized relations. Women maneuvered in these spaces, as did men, and in much the same ways as did men. Given the patriarchal public and private institutions through which they had to move, however, women and juniors were structurally disadvantaged relative to men and seniors.

I problematize the construct of nation-state from the experience of women in the urban working-class neighborhood of Camp Trad, Borj Hammoud, where I have conducted research since 1971. The women's responses I discuss here, shaped by their kin, social, political, and local community relations, were quite variable and do not exhaust the range of responses of women in Lebanon from different classes, regions, religions, and national origins. In outlining some of these responses, I caution *against* seeing women in Lebanon as a homogeneous category, coherently defined and affected by elite (themselves fragmented) strategies (which were often contradictory) and uniformly responding in consistent ways. Class, region, religion, and national origin intersected with the always shifting sets of relations to help create and constrain women's responses to state elite policies and strategies.

Nation in the Lebanese State

BOUNDARIES OF NATION, OF STATE

I began research in Lebanon because I was interested in understanding how states constructed their citizens through processes that institutionalized identities. In 1971, when I began working in Camp Trad, Lebanon was a new state, less than thirty years old. While the area and peoples of Lebanon have had long historical experiences with statehood, the boundaries of the state and the definitions of the political community have shifted many times. Like most Southern states, the contemporary boundaries of Lebanon became fixed only with independence. The fixing of the boundaries, however, did not fix the population, citizen or noncitizen. A country of little over three million in 1970, Lebanon had about a million residents (citizen and noncitizen) of non-Lebanese origins.

The area of Lebanon historically has witnessed ongoing movements of peoples; it has been one of the most intersected crossroads of the world. As people moved, settled, integrated, and moved again, so did cultures, ideas, and identities. The area of Lebanon has been marked by fluidity of peoples and identities. And, in this too, Lebanon was not unique, but perhaps a more condensed version of a larger world story.

NATIONALITIES IN THE LEBANESE STATE

During the massacres of Armenians during and after World War I, hundreds of thousands of Armenians were admitted into Lebanon as citizens. Civil disturbances in Syria led many more Armenians to flee to Lebanon as noncitizens, though some succeeded in obtaining Lebanese citizenship. By the 1970s, the Armenians were several hundred thousand, enough to have one representative in the Lebanese parliament.

Shortly after Lebanese independence, the founding of Israel brought hundreds of thousands of Palestinians to Lebanon. Most settled in refugee camps. Expecting to return to Palestine, most did not claim Lebanese citizenship. Historically, there has always been significant movement of peoples between the areas of Lebanon and Palestine. Many of those living in Palestine had Lebanese origins. Some Palestinians obtained Lebanese citizenship on the basis of origin or through other means. By the 1970s, there were over three hundred thousand Palestinians in Lebanon.

Lebanon in the 1960s had also become a political refuge and economic haven for Syrians, Jordanians, Egyptians, and Iraqis. By the 1970s, there were about five hundred thousand Syrians working in Lebanon, as well as many other Arab nationals. These people, however, rarely obtained citizenship.

Lebanese citizenship became extremely difficult to obtain as political contestations over representation and distribution of state resources heated up in the 1960s and 1970s, the period just before the outbreak of the civil war in 1975. With these migrations into and out of Lebanon, it is not surprising that citizenship, membership in the national community, and the nature of the national community became contested issues in the 1970s and remain so today. As in most Southern countries, a central question remains: What does it mean to be Lebanese?

THE STATE CREATES THE NATION

The Lebanese state defined its citizenry in terms of a representative system, with a directly elected parliament, a president elected by the parliament, a prime minister appointed by the president, and a cabinet appointed by the prime minister. The parliament represented all religious sects based on their demographic distribution in the population. From independence in 1943, the formal distribution had been fixed according to the last official census carried out in 1932.[3]

The Lebanese state carried the legacy of Ottoman and French rule, which had essentialized and reified sectarianism as a core component of political identity, citizenship, and representation. From the seventeenth to the twentieth century, various European powers had tried to obtain a foothold in the Middle East by turning religious sects into client communities. They built on the Ottoman millet system (a system more for taxation than for governance) that had organized membership in the empire by religious communities. In the process, competing European powers increasingly politicized religious identity as political identity by playing their sectarian-defined client communities against each other.

INSTITUTIONALIZING NATIONAL FRAGMENTS

Heirs, products, and participants in this political legacy, the elite of the young Lebanese state institutionalized religious identity as political identity. Themselves fragmented by a history of sectarian competition and shifting alliances and with minimal social, economic, and natural resources available to forcefully mold alternatives, the Lebanese elite defined membership in the political community through membership in religious sects. To belong to the national community and gain rights of access and representation, the newly created state required its citizens to belong to a religious community. It became a nation of fragments (Chatterjee 1993a).

The Lebanese state required citizens to carry identification cards. Among the vital information displayed on each citizen's ID card was his or her religion. The identification of citizens by religion on their IDs made "killing by the card" possible during the civil war. For a period of time, various militias put up roadblocks in the neighborhoods they controlled. Those crossing their road checks were at times killed if they were of the "wrong" religion. Clever Lebanese carried several forged cards. A nation institutionalizing fragments could kill by fragments.

SECTARIAN REPRESENTATION

Seventeen different religious sects were formally recognized in Lebanon for purposes of political representation. Representation of the religious sects in parliament was based on their distribution in the population, fixed according to the last official census in 1932. Electoral districts allocated representatives based on their population. The representatives were then allocated on the basis of the formal distribution of religious sects in that district.

For example, if a district had a population including 50 percent Sunni, 25 percent Maronite, 10 percent Shi'a, 5 percent Greek Orthodox, and 5 percent a combination of Druze, Roman Catholic, Armenian Orthodox, and others, that district would have to be represented by two Sunni, one Maronite, and one Shi'i. The Greek Orthodox, Druze, Roman Catholic, Armenian Orthodox, and others could not serve as representatives from that district. The political practice had been for politicians to offer voters slates including candidates from each of the allocated sects. In such a hypothetical district, each competing slate would consist of two Sunnis, one Maronite, and one Shi'i. All citizens of each district, however, voted for all candidates, not only those of their own sect.

The rationale for sectarian representation, established in the French Mandate period, was that religious sects had different needs and interests that were best represented by members of their own communities. The rationale assumed the homogeneity and unity of each religious community. It also disguised the patriarchal structure that upheld the communities. The implications for women in this state which defined the nation by its religious fragments were played out in civil (personal) status laws (family law), in laws of citizenship, and in patronage politics. The formal agencies, as well as the political processes, of the state institutionalized fragmented identities and legal possibilities.

THE NATION AT THE MARGINS

It is by understanding the elite's construction of the nation as a collection of fragments that we can begin to understand marginalities in Lebanon. Among the Shi'a, legally defined (by the 1932 census) as the third largest group in numbers (by the 1970s, they had become the largest, however), the leaders spoke of being marginalized because they were not adequately represented in parliament or in distribution of government resources. The Druze leadership, though powerful, were sandwiched between the larger Sunnis and Shi'a (and often rejected by both). The Sunnis, though the majority in the Arab world, were concerned about being pushed out by the Shi'a in Lebanon. The leadership of the Maronites, defined as the largest sect with the greatest political power (by virtue of their grip on critical state offices and institutions), continually addressed the fear of being engulfed as a Christian minority in the surrounding Muslim Arab world. Marginality defined the nation. The leadership spoke of their communities as living at the margins by defining different arenas of nationhood—the Lebanese, the Arab, the Islamic nation. As sectarian communities, none expressed confidence of position or tenure at the center. However, laypeople in Camp Trad, as I discuss below, spoke a different and more diversified discourse.

PATRIARCHY IN THE NATION IN THE STATE

By passing its citizens through the portals of religion, the Lebanese state reinforced patriarchy and the gender/age hierarchy embedded in those religious communities. I define patriarchy as the privileging of males and elders (including elder women) and the mobilization of kinship idioms, structures, and moralities in service of a system of gender/age domination. Elite patriarchy, religious institutional patriarchy, and lay patriarchy mutually reinforced each other in the reproduction of gender/age domination.

RELIGION AS CIVIL STATUS

The Lebanese state elite implemented their fragmented-nation vision in a number of ways. Crucial to the institutionalization of this nation as religious fragments was the delegation to the sectarian communities of sole legal authority over matters of personal status or civil status. Personal status laws, also called family law, covered marriage, divorce, child custody, and inheritance. Lebanon had no civil personal status laws. In this regard, Lebanon was like all other Middle Eastern states (including Israel) except Tunisia, Turkey, and Yemen. In the case of Lebanon, with seventeen formally recognized sects, there were seventeen different laws of marriage, divorce, child custody, and inheritance.

The delegation of legal authority over matters of personal status to religious institutions meant that women and men in Lebanon neither had a common set of laws in these matters nor did they have recourse to the state in their disputes with these laws. Women in different religious communities experienced different legal realities from which they had no civil recourse, for which there was no unified body of codes as a common referent. As Yolla Sharara argued (1978), women in Lebanon, as a result, did not feel the impact of the state in their lives so much as they felt the impact of the men of their religious communities. It was a system that offered fewer options for women than for men. The sectarian system of family law fed into the fragmentation of the collectivity at one level; at another level, this system reinforced the shared national commitment to patriarchy.

RELIGIOUS INSTITUTIONS AS PATRIARCHAL

Clerics in all churches in Lebanon were exclusively male. In addition, clergy in all religious institutions, to greater and lesser degrees, were all hierarchically organized. Religious institutions were a system of male authority that reinforced the privileging of male and elder authority in the patriarchal kin system.

RELIGIOUS INSTITUTIONS SUPPORT KINSHIP

Religious institutions supported kinship through their direct support of family relations, their use of kin idioms, and their support of patriarchy and patrilineality. Religious institutions attempted to help integrate persons in their families, taught respect of family, celebrated family love, loyalty, and responsibility. In dispute situations, clergy invariably intervened in favor of stabilizing family relations.

In addition, all religious institutions supported kinship through the use of kin idioms and the privileging of kin relations. Christians typically addressed their priests as *abuna* (father). While Muslims referred to their clerics as *sheikh*, the relationship enacted in the cleric-layperson relationship was modeled on a father-child relationship, as in the Christian churches. Clerics referred to a parishioner as *ibni* (son) or *binti* (daughter). The privileging of kinship entailed the bolstering of patriarchy, because the kinship system was patriarchal.

RELIGIOUS INSTITUTIONS SUPPORT PATRIARCHY

The religious institutions were not only themselves patriarchal, but they supported domestic and public patriarchy. Religious institutions supported the subordination of women and juniors to men and elders in most respects. The interventions of clergy in family disputes serve mostly to reinforce the authority of males and elders. In addition to such direct support of seniors, fathers, uncles, and brothers, clergy supported patriarchy through their support of patrilineality. While patriarchy (privileging of males and seniors, legitimated by kin idioms and morality) and patrilineality (reckoning descent through male lines) should not be conflated analytically, in practice socially and politically in Lebanon they operated to reinforce each other.

RELIGIOUS INSTITUTIONS SUPPORT PATRILINEALITY

Both Muslims and Christian churches assumed that children belonged to their father and their father's lineage, thereby supporting patrilineality. While laws differed from sect to sect, in general, religious institutions assumed that children became members of their father's lineage and supported the claims of the father's lineage over a mother's claim to children. In divorces, Muslim women eventually lost possession of and control over children.[4] Many women avoided divorce for fear of losing their children. Such was the strength of the patrilineality supported by Muslim religious institutions that a Muslim man's parents and siblings had rights over his children at his death superseding those of their mother. While Christians varied in their laws concerning custody, they too shared the assumption that children belonged to their father and their father's lineage.

Religious institutions supported patrilineality also by privileging kin endogamy. The preferred marriage pattern among Muslims has been for marriage between paternal parallel cousins. In some regions of Lebanon, Muslim religious institutions supported a man's right of first choice in marrying his father's brother's daughter. While the ideal marriage (between the children of brothers) accounted for few marriages in Lebanon, other kinds of kin endogamy accounted for a significant number of marriages. Even when matrilineal kin endogamy was practiced, the outcome was still to privilege kinship, though it may not have been patrilineal kinship. In so privileging kinship, religious institutions reinforced the control of patriarchs over women and juniors.

This was predominantly a Muslim pattern in Lebanon. The Christian churches formally disallowed close cousin marriage. The reality, however, was that close cousin marriage (patrilineal and matrilineal) was relatively common among Christians as well.

RELIGIOUS INSTITUTIONS AND THE FRAGMENTED NATION

Religious institutions' control of civil law reinforced patrilineality in a number of other ways. The absence of civil marriage and divorce laws meant that citizens were subject to the regulations of their churches in terms of whom and how they could marry and divorce and how custody over children was adjudicated. Most religious institutions preferred religious endogamy. Minimally that meant that churches pressured persons to marry at least within their large religious rubric. Muslim clerics encouraged Muslims to marry other Muslims; Arab Christian churches encouraged Arab Christians to marry other Arab Christians; Armenian Christian churches encouraged Armenian Christians to marry other Armenian Christians. At times, clergy even discouraged marriages across religious sects within the religious rubric. Maronite clerics historically have at times discouraged marriage to Greek Orthodox, Druze clerics have discouraged marriage to Shi'a, and so forth. I documented a number of cases in my research of clergy acting aggressively to prohibit marriage outside their sect. The Christian sects were the most aggressive, and among these the most aggressive were the Armenian Christian churches. At times, religious institutions worked hand in hand with sectarian political parties to dissuade persons from marrying outside their sects. Several instances were reported to me in which the Dashnag Party send thugs to "persuade" an Armenian man from marrying out or an Arab man from trying to marry in.

A person wanting to marry outside his or her religious sect or rubric could do so only with the permission of either the husband's or wife's religious institution. If both churches refused the intersectarian or interrubric marriage, the couple might have to leave their religious community to marry in a third sect, if cooperative clerics could be found. If none could, the marriage could not be carried out.

PATRILINEAL RELIGIOUS IDENTITY

These constraints operated to control the behavior of women more than that of men. It was assumed, in intersect and interrubric marriages, that the woman would change her religion to that of the man. This practice made the consequences of intermarriage negligible for men, but often profound for women. That is, a woman usually lost her religious identity in an intersect marriage, but a man rarely did. Further, because children were assumed to belong to the religion of their fathers, a woman marrying out could not formally pass on her religious heritage to her children, but a man could.

As a result, men had more marriage choices than did women. Communities kept closer guard of the marriages of their women than they did of their men. Men's intersect/interrubric marriages added new members to the religious community. Women's community exogamy led to a loss for the religious community and the nation that built itself on religious communities.

PATRILINEAL POLITICAL IDENTITY

The alliance between the Lebanese state and religious institutions to funnel citizenship through religious sects meant that the state and religious institutions reinforced children's identification with their father. Children were assigned the religious identity of their father by both religious institutions and the state. Receiving a religious identity through the father meant that children also were assigned the political identity of their father. Because citizenship was identified through religion, the source of religious identity was also the source of political identity.

The partnership of the state and religious institutions along these lines went further. Persons got Lebanese citizenship only through their father and husband. A woman could not pass on her Lebanese citizenship to her children or her husband. While a woman would not be penalized by loss of her own citizenship if she married a noncitizen, she would be penalized in loss of national identity common with her children. A woman's father, brother, and husband could pass on their national identities to their children, but she could not.

That is, national identity in the Lebanese state was patrilineal, and political identity came through a male genealogy. The Lebanese nation was constructed as descending through a series of patrilineal lineages, a male descent line, a patrilineal genealogy. It was kin-based and masculinized. One belonged to a male-defined kin group to belong to a religious sect to belong to the nation. Religious institutions and the state allied in reinforcing patrilineality to the degree that patrilineality for children was the only avenue to nationality. Citizenship in the Lebanese state was not only an assertion of rights vis-à-vis the state, but a claim by a patriarchal kin group and a religious community on persons.

With the abatement of the civil war in 1991, the Lebanese elite is strategizing to rebuild the Lebanese nation and state. Having lost several hundred thousand lives during the war, perhaps an equivalent number through migrations, and hundreds of thousands of nonnationals (Syrians and Palestinians particularly) through flight, the elite must revitalize membership in the national community. Citizenship is once again a national question. Of the numerous current proposals, one suggests allowing women to confer citizenship on their children. While the outcome of this debate is yet to unravel, there are a number of interesting dynamics involved. For example, this proposal has received less attention than those proposing to grant citizenship to Lebanese émigrés and to Palestinians who had lived in Lebanon prior to 1948. Ravished by the civil war, there is no women's movement in Lebanon mobilizing around this issue. Additionally interesting is the quick mobilization of religious institutions to find members of their religious communities among Lebanese émigrés and others communities for whom they can gain citizenship.

CIVIL SOCIETY AS A SITE FOR STATE ACTION

Civil society is a key arena for the construction of a state's relationships with its citizenship. I use civil society to mean the array of nongovernmental organizations (unions, professional associations, service organizations, and the like) whose activities buffer citizens from the state's arbitrary exercise of power (Sadowski 1993). The state elite has fragmented the nation by delegating state resources to the private sector rather than building state institutions that could create a national culture. The state subsidized private schools, private charities, private hospitals, private cultural clubs, private youth groups, private social service agencies.

The implications for women were profound. Most of these agencies in the private sphere were run by religious institutions or persons affiliated with religious institutions, and they often catered to their own religious communities. As a result, the private sector, the sphere of civil society that might have offered alternatives to women, was often (though not exclusively) organized by religiously identified agencies, with the blessing and financial support of the state. Some communities were remarkably proactive in institutionalizing the separation of their members from the national community. Armenians, for example, built low-income housing for poor Armenians to pull them out of the heterogeneous working-class neighborhoods; at times, they used public monies to do this. This was possible because of the franchise the state gave for displays of sectarian solidarity.

Yet, paradoxically, the very structures of elite and state fragmentation that trapped women in patriarchal kin and religious communities and relationships also created spaces for maneuvering. Conflicts within the elite, the inability of any elite fragment to gain hegemony, their lack of public resources, and the elite's practice of decentering the state by diverting state resources into private channels allowed multiple opportunities for maneuvering and negotiating. Both women and men maneuvered in this system. Given the predominance of patriarchy in both public and private arenas, however, women's latitude for negotiations was more limited than men's.

Camp Trad

While the state formally and legally structured a fragmented nation underpinned by patriarchy, the lived reality of the nation's people was far more complex than the state definition. In Camp Trad, I found that religion was only one of many factors that shaped identity and channeled political and social behavior. In addition, despite the formal fragmentation, there were commonalities of culture and practice that had long existed, as well as new commonalities emerging in heterogeneous neighborhoods like Camp Trad. Such shared experiences and viewpoints, lived in the day-to-day lives of people like those in Camp Trad, went against the grain of the institutional structure of the state and the elite's construct of the nation. Below, I discuss the tensions and opportunities stemming from the political and social realities of working-class women in Camp Trad.

Camp Trad housed Lebanese, Syrians, Palestinians, Jordanians, Greeks, and Egyptians of every religious sect. Armenians dominated the municipality of Borj Hammoud and, like other ethnic groups, were also composed of different religious sects (Orthodox, Catholic, Protestants). Identities operant in the neighborhood were multiple and shifting.

A woman might think of herself as a member of her kin group, her natal village, her religious sect (Maronite, Druze, Sunni, etc.), her religious rubric (Christian, Muslim), her ethnic group (Armenian, Kurdish), her national community (Syrian, Lebanese, Palestinian), or supranational community (Arab, pan-Christian, pan-Muslim). These identities were held simultaneously by persons in Camp Trad. Women, as did men, used their identities situationally. A Lebanese Shi'i woman interacting with a Sunni woman might identify as a Muslim to link herself with her neighbor. She might identify herself as Lebanese to connect with non-Muslim Lebanese. She might identify as an Arab to facilitate relationships with Jordanians or Egyptians.

The nation as an Arab nation crossing state boundaries was the central construct of a pan-Arabist movement that had for decades moved and mobilized peoples throughout the Middle East. The nation as a Muslim nation crossing state and regional boundaries was another construct on the rise in the 1970s. These and other forms of identification had concrete institutional structures to adhere to. Political parties, states, and revolutionary movements used these labels to mobilize and moralize followings. Women, as did men, called these labels into play, as needed, to create relationships for sociability, economic advantage, and political networking. Therefore, in practice, the nation was a moving set of identities crystallized periodically for specific purposes, then flowing again through the matrices of both situational and long-term relationalities. The fluidity of national identification allowed women, as well as men, to negotiate alliances, shift loyalties, and procure advantages as they needed.

Of importance is that these identities were simultaneously felt. Though often conflictual, the multiple identities were sustained and called forth as needed. The hierarchy among the identities, if it existed in the minds of the women in Camp Trad, was not fixed. Perhaps, though, primary among the identities was that of kinship. Kinship identity, in fact, entailed and proscribed other identities. By being a member of a kin group, one became a member of a religious sect and ethnic and national or pan-national community. Patrilineal kinship chartered a course of multiple memberships. The nation defined as fragments probably reinforced patrilineal kinship as much if not more than religious communities because one entered sects through kinship.

In Camp Trad, on a day-to-day basis, women prioritized their kin affiliations. For many, however, kin were not nearby. Thus, neighbors came to play the role of kin. They often said to each other and to me, "A neighbor who is near is better than a brother who is far." Proximity affected who visited whom, who befriended whom, and who impacted whom on a day-to-day basis more than any other factor. Given the heterogeneity of the neighborhood, women readily moved among the multiple identities to engage each other in relationships of intimacy, exchange, reciprocity, and support. Intense relationships developed among the neighborhood women helping each other socially, economically, politically, emotionally, and spiritually. They needed each other and they used each other regardless of formal definitions of difference.

I have elsewhere analyzed at depth the impact of these women-based networks on local culture, social organization, and political dynamics (Joseph 1977, 1978, 1983). I have argued that women's networks were crucial in reinforcing commonalities of culture that already existed as well as in creating new commonalities. Family structures and dynamics, values concerning child rearing, attitudes about proper gender relations, views about social decorum, and opinions about political and

economic events were shared, disputed, discussed, digested. In the processes of their intense sociability, women were significant actors in the
production and reproduction of a common local culture. This was not
new, as people in heterogeneous villages and urban areas have always
crossed boundaries transporting their ideas, learning of others' ideas,
and creating new ideas as they moved. Boundaries have always been
porous in this area of the world, and religion has always been only one
of many identities available and embraced. But it has been an identity continually reinscribed in the minds and bodies of laypeople by
ruling elites—Ottoman, European, and Lebanese. The Lebanese elite
acted within frameworks they inherited as well as ones they helped
to create. These frameworks, however, did not describe or contain the
range of identities and practices of people in Camp Trad.

Indeed, in Camp Trad, and I imagine in most heterogeneous neighborhoods throughout Lebanon, people had much more in common than
their formally defined differences would suggest. Furthermore, differences of interest and perspective within the formally defined boundaries of sameness (religious sects) were greater than the formal definitions articulated. In part, this was because the axes of sameness and
difference were far too complex, contradictory, and changing to be encompassed within any single vector.

I have argued that the intersectarian relations and culture that
was emerging in these neighborhoods, largely as a result of women's
networks, was partly responsible for the concerted attacks to purify
neighborhoods like Camp Trad during the civil war (Joseph 1983).
Heterogeneous neighborhoods, in offering women and men both the
opportunity and the need to create relationalities across boundaries,
became a threat to state leaders who conceived of the nation as fragments and molded their power by encouraging differences within the
nation. The nation that was emerging in such neighborhoods was not
the nation constructed by the elite. Calls for secularization of the political system had been mounting in the early 1970s, coming especially
from the underrepresented Shi'a. I have suggested that the elite with
the most to lose from the demise of the fragmented nation (especially
the Maronite Christians) moved to preempt the emergence of the new
nation (Joseph 1983). What has not been visible, however, was women's
central role in creating this new nation.

Despite the spaces for maneuvering available to women in Lebanon,
they were nevertheless disadvantaged relative to men. Whether oper-

ating in patron-client relationships, negotiating services through private agencies, or pleading their cases before public offices, women confronted the ever present dominance of patriarchal structures, idioms, and moralities. Political, religious, and social leaders preferred dealing with men (although they did deal directly with women as well). In a situation of conflict, men's views and needs tended to be privileged over those of women. Leaders at times required the intervention of fathers, brothers, and husbands before negotiating with women.

The circumstances, however, varied for women of different religious sects, ethnic communities, social classes, and nationalities. Women were not a homogeneous category with a homogeneous set of experiences and interests, neither in Camp Trad nor in other parts of Lebanon. Middle- and upper-class women could and did maneuver with greater independence than did working-class women. In some situations, Christian women had more spaces for movement than Muslim women. Armenian women in Camp Trad had more services available to them and therefore could operate within more spaces.

Syrian and Palestinian women in Camp Trad were often disadvantaged by their noncitizen status. Palestinian women had recourse to their militias, the United Nations–sponsored UNWRA (United Nations Relief and Works Agency) services, and the services offered by the PLO (Palestine Liberation Organization), which acted as a government within a government. Yet these too were all patriarchal in organization and orientation. Syrians lacked not only citizenship but also any other formal agency addressing their needs. They negotiated through their family, village, and regional ties as well as their neighborhood-based relationships. Again, most of these privileged males and elders.

At times, it seemed that the kinship anchor of patriarchy was the winner in the fragmented nation. Patriarchal kinship, more than religion, ethnicity, class, or region, was the conduit to resources and relationships. And it was perhaps because public and private agencies acknowledged and valorized kinship relationships and idioms that women continually had to call upon patriarchal relationships to mediate their interests in the Lebanese nation-state.

Between Nation and State: Women

If the nation-state is a compulsory model (Zubaida 1988) and the nation is an imagined community (Anderson 1983), then Partha Chatterjee's

(1993a, 3) question "Whose imagined community?" is particularly relevant for Southern women. States imposed by colonial regimes are inherited by new (or old) elites who must construct nations. The elites may participate in shaping the colonial heritage and reinscribe its outlines in the minds and bodies of citizens of their nation. The colonial legacy and the character of an elite's state-building project (Kandiyoti 1991) are crucial to the nation that is built.

Invariably, tensions within the elite, contradictions in their strategies, and resource problems leave negotiating spaces. Women operate in the spaces between state-building and nation-building projects. Their beliefs and practices are shaped by the structures within which and between which they operate. They are caught in between by nation-building projects that reinscribe or produce patriarchal structures and practices. Yet often, concertedly or inadvertently, women become prime actors in the construction of new cultural forms. It is these possibilities and realities that need to be understood and made apparent to empower women. As Chatterjee argues, Southern women, along with men, must reclaim their imaginations to create political communities in which their agency and subjectivity is freed from regimes of domination.

Notes

I am indebted to Deniz Kandiyoti for helpful discussions related to this paper.

1   I use South and Southern states to refer to societies and states with a nineteenth- or twentieth-century colonial experience whose economies and political structures are still, to a significant degree, controlled or regulated by external powers, particularly by Northern states, the advanced industrialized states, and often excolonial states.

2   Although I use the term "women," I caution against any essentialization of the category of women. Women are not an undifferentiated classification of people (Yuval-Davis 1995). Their positions and interests are shaped by class, religion, tribe, ethnicity, nationality, region, and education, among other factors. With this caution in mind, it is still useful and necessary to use the category of women for macrolevel discussions of nation-state building processes. This is so in large part because nation-states often, particularly in their legal structures, systematically treat women as a category differentiated from men. Women, as women, come to have or not have certain rights—such as voting, the right to divorce, the right to custody over their children, and the like. It is at this level of analysis that much of the discussion in this essay is aimed.

3   The official numerical rank order of the religious sects has been first Maron-
    ites, then Sunnis, Shi'a, Greek Orthodox, Druze.

4   In most Muslim family codes in cases of divorce, children are allowed to
    stay with their mothers through early childhood, typically, until age seven
    for boys and nine for girls.

Relational Positionalities of

Nationalisms, Racisms, and Feminisms

Daiva K. Stasiulis

Feminists everywhere face a complicated process in positioning them-selves vis-à-vis nationalism and nationalist politics. The ambiguous re-lationship between feminism and nationalism resides in the histories of relations between the two wherein "nationalism has both made possible forms of activism for women which were previously impossible, and simultaneously limited their horizons" (Hall 1993, 100). There are forces that bind women to nations, nation-states, and nationalist struggles, but equally there are forces that divide women and feminists from nation-alism and nationalist struggles and that limit their options for self-determination.

The already ambiguous relationship between nationalism and femi-nism is further complicated by the reality of competing nationalist and nation-building projects mapped within the same geopolitical space. Whether or not a nationalist movement hinders or furthers a move-ment toward women's emancipation among women defined as part of that nation is a separate question from whether a nationalist movement may oppress women who are defined as outside that nation, and who may have their own nationalist or communal self-determination aspi-rations. The answer to the second question depends in part on whether nationalism is inherently exclusionary, or whether, alternatively, it is capable of recognizing and validating other nationalisms and ethnic mi-nority claims, together with the demands of women's liberation within these competing national/ethnic projects. The degree to which a par-ticular nationalism is open or oppositional to the communal projects of those who are not part of the dominant ethnicity is also dependent on the larger societal project (neoliberal, social democratic, fascist, etc.) to which nationalism is wedded.

A feminism nurtured within one national sovereignty movement can be oppressive for other groups of women (and men) seeking self-determination as nations or peoples. The recognition of the oppressive consequences of one feminist/nationalist project for women found at the margins or exterior to the envisioned nation may be viewed minimally as unnecessarily complicating or diverting of energies, or maximally as a threat by members of that feminist/nationalist movement. Acknowledgment of a narrative that allows for an interplay between marginality/alterity and privilege is likely to be perceived, at least initially, as threatening and undermining of the claims for a movement that has henceforth and unproblematically defined itself as oppressed. In women's movements in North America, Britain, and Western Europe, white women, who had always already assumed their status as an oppressed group within patriarchy, initially responded with shock, confusion, and hostility to allegations and analyses by women of color of their role as oppressors within relations of race and colonialism and discourses of Eurocentrism. Yet through turbulent struggles, racial and ethnic multiplicity and the contradictions that flow from racialized and ethnic relations have increasingly been defined as constitutive of the heterogeneous character of women's movements.

The recognition of the power relations reflected in the racial and ethnic multiplicity of women and women's movements has spawned significant developments in feminist theorizing, challenging any attempt to universalize the category "woman." It has also led to the creation of new mechanisms and agendas within feminist organizations aimed at forging a more inclusive politics. Yet the conflicts and contradictions associated with mediating the competing claims of nationalist feminisms, or competing feminisms conceived within antagonistic projects of national self-determination (and minority rights), are less adequately theorized or politically resolved.

The dilemmas faced by women's movements in dealing with simultaneous nationalist and ethnic minority claims within the same geopolitical space suggest the need to develop a conceptual apparatus that can analytically deal with not merely the *plurality* but also and more importantly the *positionality* of different nationalisms, racisms, ethnocultural movements, and feminisms *in relation to one another*. Such an approach is essential in order to understand the possibilities and limitations of transnational and interethnic solidarities within women's movements, through highlighting the extent to which feminist projects are complementary or contradictory. Elements of such a framework have been suggested by some feminists, critical race scholars, and activists working on producing an understanding of women's oppressions and identities in the context of multiple and complex webs of social relations and discourses. This framework will be elaborated and developed in the context of women's politics in Canada, with a focus on Québec, where feminisms intersect in complex ways with nationalist, sovereignty, and ethnolinguistic/racial rights projects.

O Canada! How Many Nations?

There is a growing sense among Canadians that their country is coming apart at the seams.[1] This pessimism arises out of the despair over global trends such as jobless growth and the demise of Canada's social welfare system. Universality and national standards in health care and social security are jeopardized by substantial cuts in social services, harnessed to a neoliberal agenda of the federal and provincial governments. This national pessimism also reflects a growing lack of confidence in the ability of politicians to sustain the model of Canada as a civic or territorial nation in the face of the demands of francophone Quebecers and First Nations peoples for recognition as distinct peoples and self-determination,[2] and of the claims of ethnocultural and "visible" minorities for full citizenship rights and more than a token multiculturalism.[3] Rather than the model federation often vaunted internationally, achieving unity through a celebrated racial and ethnocultural diversity, the country is riven by seemingly irreconcilable claims to national sovereignty and minority rights. As one wag recently put it, "Canada is the only constitution without a country" (Colombo 1996, 21).

Feminist and women's politics in Canada have been inflected and shaped by these nationalist, racial, and ethnic forms of conflict. Canadian women's movements can be read in terms of several overlapping histories that both vigorously championed and challenged the matrix of racial/ethnic, gendered, and class power relations inscribed in Canada's history as a settler society (Stasiulis and Jhappan 1995, 119–20). Like other settler societies, Canada's development has occurred within a historical context in which "Europeans . . . settled, [in which] their descendants have remained politically dominant over indigenous peoples, and [in which] a heterogeneous society has developed in class, ethnic and racial terms" (Stasiulis and Yuval-Davis 1995, 3). Canada's settler colonial history is distinguished, however, by the fact that it involved a history of *dual* European—French, followed by British—settler colonization.

Within some settler societies, divisions between different feminist and women's politics have followed the schisms in power relations, worldviews, and living conditions between indigenous peoples and the colonial settlers/immigrants. This form of *bicultural feminism* is most apparent in Aotaearoa/New Zealand where Pakeha (non-Maori, primarily European-descent) feminists have come to respect the fact that Maori (indigenous) feminists view their struggles as intimately tied to Maori culture, spirituality, and self-determination (Larner and Spoonley 1995, 59; Larner 1995, 185). In Mexico, in spite of the significance placed within Mexican nationalism upon *mestizaje*—the process of racial and cultural miscegenation—the fault line in women's politics has followed the division between the lives of more rural indigenous peoples and those of more urban-based descendants of Spanish settlers (Gutierrez 1995). Within Palestine/Israel, the feminist politics of Palestinian and Jewish Israeli women have been sharply divided and shaped by the Zionist settler project and indigenous resistance to it such as the Intifada (Abdo 1994; Abdo and Yuval-Davis 1995).

The indigenous/settler schism is not the only national/ethnic division, however, to mold the priorities, objectives, and conflicts within women's and feminist politics in settler societies. The nonindigenous or settler population in most settler societies is never or rarely composed solely of descendants of the colonizing settlers and hence members of the ethnically hegemonic group(s). Ethnic and racial heterogeneity is the historical product of nation-building projects that relied on the importation of cheap but often ethnically less desirable labor. Much of this immigration was subjected to restrictive and often unfree terms of entry, such as head taxes and indentured status, designed to discourage long-term settlement. These less desirable immigrants, many of whom stayed, had unequal access to settler and citizens' rights. The women's politics of those previously on the margins of feminist politics in settler societies—indigenous women, women of color, and ethnically nondominant immigrant women—have increasingly called attention to the injustice of differential, racist, and sexist citizenship. One objective of these politics has been to transform "mainstream" feminism into more pluralist, inclusive, and antiracist directions.

The lines of division and accommodation within women's politics in Canada have mirrored the significant divisions among peoples or nations, as well as exclusion and subordination of racial/ethnic minority communities stemming from the country's history as a dual settler society. The discussion below outlines the forms and sources of some of these divisions, as well as recent attempts to bridge them. It then examines the ways in which women's politics in Canada have intersected with the politics of nationalism, racism, and minority rights to come to a position of pluralism, without yet offering the means of reconciling the contradictions stemming from the relational positionality of different ethnonational and minority communities. A brief discussion is obviously unable to do justice to the rich history and ideological diversity of Canadian feminism, or the variegated ways in which women have participated in the country's nationalist and ethnic minority politics and in sustaining their national/ethnic communities. My analyses are thus necessarily selective and schematic, teasing out the implications of women's ties to nationalist and self-determination movements for the aspirations of other women who are also located and mobilized not only as feminists, but also as members of colonized, oppressed, or ethnically hegemonic communities.

Canada has had a unique colonial settlement history in the sense that it is the outcome of the settler projects of two competing colonizing powers—France until the mid-eighteenth century, and Britain thereafter. Following the British military defeat of the French in the Conquest of 1760, the French surrendered to the British, but subsequently became subordinate partners in nation building.[4] Much of Canadian political history and the character of federal institutions can be seen as giving credence to the notion that Canada was built by these two settler societies or "two founding races/nations," a discourse that makes no mention of either indigenous peoples or the diversity in national origins of settlers beyond the British and French who helped populate and develop Canada.[5]

The agreement reached with Anglo politicians was that French elites and the Catholic Church would rule inside Québec, although this meant that they were rendered relatively powerless in the wider industrial capitalist project of Canada as a whole.[6] Historically, women in French Canada (including francophone women outside of Québec) have thus had to wrestle with the discrimination against Francophones where the English language and Anglo-Saxon Protestant culture were hegemonic. They have also had to confront and overcome constraints placed on women's roles by the patriarchal Catholic clergy and social doctrine.

"Nation building" in Canada under the aegis of British, local colonial, and later dominion elites entailed the development of immigration and other policies that favored Britain, even though the 1867 British North American Act had created federalism as an accommodation of French Canada. Shortly after confederation, French Canadian politicians constructed a "compact theory" of the federation that introduced the concept of "two founding races" (which, following the discrediting of race theories after World War II, was renamed "two founding nations").

The "two founding nations" concept, which had lain dormant since the development of multiculturalism policy in the 1970s, has recently enjoyed a renaissance in the efforts of Québec sovereignists to secede from Canada and of federalists to persuade Québec to stay. With the growth of the independence movement in Québec since the 1960s, an important shift occurred in the identity of the francophone founding nation from "French Canadian" to "Québécois."[7] This shift signified a desire on the part of francophone Quebecers, the large majority in that province,[8] to distance themselves from a French Canadian identity that was associated with submissiveness to Anglo rule, traditionalism, and elitism (Cardinal 1995, 285).[9] It also reflected the growing assertiveness of the provincial Québec state in promoting the economic, political, linguistic, and cultural interests of francophone Quebecers. A significant piece of legislation, symbolic of this new proactive stance, was Bill 101, the Charter of the French Language, passed by the Parti Québécois government in 1977, which transformed Québec into an officially French-speaking society.[10]

The real possibility of Québec's secession from the rest of Canada in the foreseeable future has raised anew the question of the definition of the "Québec nation." While the political discourse in Québec does not exclusively define the Québec nation in ethnic terms, ethnic nationalism, defined in terms of the history of Anglo domination, French ancestry, French language, French culture, territory, and sense of destiny, clearly underlies much of the contemporary Québec sovereignist movement. Within Québec's contemporary political culture, ethnic appeals are commonly made for public support of the secessionist strategy.

Several of the top leadership of the ruling Parti Québécois (and its sister federal party, the Bloc Québécois) have made remarks indicating their perception of the Québec nation as synonymous with francophone Quebecers, and indeed with "old stock francophones" (*Québécois de souche*), or descendants of the white settlers of New France. On the eve of the 31 October 1995 referendum on Québec sovereignty, when Quebecers very narrowly voted to remain within Confederation, an embittered Premier Jacques Parizeau declared, "We have been defeated . . . by money and the ethnic vote." Such remarks, while shocking in their open contempt for nonfrancophone minorities, were consistent with Parizeau's stated belief that the "Québécois" referred not to all residents of Québec but to "Québécois de souche" (Grand Council of the Crees 1995, 23, n. 23). Bernard Landry, deputy premier of Québec, left the Immigration portfolio after accusations that he had ranted to nonfrancophone hotel employees about "immigrants" who had deprived the "yes" forces of a victory (Authier 1995, A3). Midway through the referendum campaign, Lucien Bouchard, then leader of the federal Bloc Québécois party (who succeeded Parizeau as Québec premier in January 1996) lamented that Québec women had the lowest fertility rate of the "white races" (Tu 1995, D1). Bouchard's remarks not only defined Quebecers racially in terms of white skin color, but also resuscitated the notion that the primary obligation of women to their nation resided in their biological baby-making capacity. Feminists have identified and critiqued women's role as biological reproducers of ethnic/national collectivities as one of the major roles consigned to women within patriarchal nationalist projects (Anthias and Yuval-Davis 1989; Korac 1996). Indeed, Bouchard's comment harkens back to the pronatalist, nationalist discourse that was central to the *revanche des berceaux* (revenge of the cradle) strategy for the cultural survival of a rural, Catholic, francophone society, promoted by a conservative Catholic clergy in Québec. The extraordinarily high birthrates of Québec women between the 1880s and 1950s were also part of a settlement strategy based on "low technology family-based agriculture in which children's labour was a productive resource" (Maroney 1992, 32, n. 13). In the 1960s and 1970s, clerical nationalist pronatalism and the image of Québec women as mothers of the French Canadian "race" had been sharply attacked by Québec feminists who objected to the "maternal essentialism" inherent in such images (Maroney 1992, 12). The remarks by the soon-to-be premier Bouchard again focused on the reproductive capacities of white Québec women in biologically reproducing the white, francophone Québec nation.

Quite apart from racialist remarks made by nationalist politicians, the policies toward Aboriginal peoples, Anglophones, and allophones (people with mother tongues other than French or English) have defined the ethnic boundaries of the Québec nation. Anglophones in Québec continue to have protection of their linguistic and educational rights in such Québec language legislation as Bill 101, reflective of the recognition by Québec politicians of their status as one of the two "founding nations" or, in the context of the Québec nation, a "national minority." Historically, it was also the Anglos who supplied much of the capital for Québec's economic development, a fact that accords them some special recognition from Québec governments, who are eager to stem the tide of capital flight from the province. Yet in spite of certain legislated guarantees for Anglophones, the independence movement has fueled anxiety about their future in a sovereign Québec, precipitating an exodus particularly marked at the time of the election of independentist governments (in 1976 and 1993) and during the time of sovereignty referenda (in 1980 and 1995).[11] It has also provoked the formation of a militant anglophone rights movement, hyperbolically contesting what it calls Québec's "linguistic racism" and calling for partition of non-francophone territories from an independent Québec (Tu 1996a, A1, A5).

While Québec governments have begrudgingly accepted the presence of Anglophones in Québec, the fear that the "declining birthrate [among Francophones] and the rising tide of non-francophone immigration will dilute the French presence in North America" has shaped the policy of recent Québec governments toward ethnocultural and especially non-francophone minorities (Ignatieff 1993, 117). Immigration policy in Québec since the 1970s has been geared to maximizing the selection of French-speaking immigrants.[12] Provincial policies regulating immigration, language, and "cultural communities" of successive Québec governments since the Quiet Revolution of the 1960s have reflected the primacy of protecting the cultural and linguistic integrity of a francophone Québec, located in the context of anglophone hegemony within the rest of Canada and south of the Canadian/Québec border.

Since its beginnings in a federal royal commission in 1967 which sought to develop policies for Canada based on its *bi*cultural and *bi*lingual character, federal multiculturalism policy has encountered vociferous opposition in Québec. The policy of multiculturalism, which responded to the sense of exclusion of non-Anglo, non-French groups, was perceived as an outrage by francophone Quebecers who viewed it as "a policy that placed their culture on a par with that of minority ethnic groups and that betrayed the conception of Canada as a country built upon two 'founding nations'" (Carens 1995, 67). Successive Québec governments have opted instead for the term "interculturalism" in policies geared toward integrating immigrants. Under a Liberal Québec government, interculturalism and other Québec government initiatives toward minority ethnic groups sought to develop a "recognition of the pluralist reality" of Québec (Québec, Ministere des communautés culturelles et de l'immigration 1990, 1991). Given the paramount concern with the protection and enhancement of the cultural and linguistic rights of francophone Quebecers, however, state policies on ethnic pluralism within Québec are bound to be "impregnated with political ambiguity" (Labelle 1990, 151; translation mine).

Moreover, not unlike some of the cynical election-time, vote-gathering uses of the federal policy of multiculturalism, recent appeals of the Québec government to forge links between new immigrants and established francophone Quebecers have been clumsy and have utilized offensive stereotypes. For instance, a $1.2 million advertising campaign launched by the Québec government six months prior to the 1995 sovereignty referendum used posters and television commercials that drew on Orientalist and other racialized stereotypes of immigrants from Asia, the Middle East, and Africa. The texts accompanying the smiling faces of people depicted from these areas referred to "almond eyes," "kinky hair," and "Oriental charm," with each stereotype followed by "Québec heart" (Block 1995). For many ethnic minorities, who, alongside anglophone and First Nations voters, voted overwhelmingly to reject Québec sovereignty in the last referendum, the belief resides that they are "acceptable as long as they don't get in the way of the aspirations of the [francophone] majority" (Tu 1995, D1).

The extent of openness or exclusion in the Québec nationalist project to nonfrancophone and racial minorities is tied to the layering of discourses—some open and some very bounded and exclusionary—within the ethnic definition of the ideal Québec nation. As suggested by Etienne Balibar, the fictive ethnicity that is indispensable to the construction of the ideal nation is produced through different articulations of a "predominantly linguistic ethnicity" and an ethnicity that is "predominantly racial" (Balibar 1991, 97). Linguistic ethnicity is more open to acquisition, for example through schooling, as well as participation in other common economic and political institutions, especially for second-generation immigrants. By "racial ethnicity," Balibar means "all kinds of somatic or psychological features, both visible and invisible, [which] may lend themselves to creating the fiction of a racial identity and therefore to representing natural and hereditary differences between social groups" (1991, 97). Whereas linguistic ethnicity is open, this second mode of "ethnicization" is exclusionary, suggesting the transmission of a "substance both biological and spiritual" inscribing individuals in a circle of extended kinship. Balibar contends that linguistic ethnicity is insufficient to produce ethnicity as the language community "assimilates anyone, but holds no one" (99). In this instance, speaking French does not a Québécois make. The principle of racial ethnicity provides that extra degree of "particularity . . . principle of closure, of exclusion" for a language community to be an ideal nation (99).

Located within a sea of Anglophones in North America, the preservation of the French language as the language of the streets, schools, shops, state institutions, and commerce has been central to the definition of the Québec nation. Indeed, citing documents on cultural policy of the Parti Québécois, some observers claim that the *sole* defining characteristic of the sovereignist's view of Québec's culture is the French language, thus permitting all immigrants and cultural minorities to contribute their multicultural heritage to the Québec identity (Whitaker 1995, 197). This interpretation, however, does not do justice to the much fuller construction of Québec's uniqueness, for example, the definition of Québec as a "distinct society" which emerged in the failed 1992 constitutional reform package, the Charlottetown Accord. "Distinct society" makes explicit mention not merely of the French language, but also of Québec's unique tradition of civil law and its culture. In the minds of most people within Québec, the Québec nation is intimately connected to the preservation and development of a historical culture and historical grievances shared by the descendants of the original French settlers. Emblazoned on every Québec license plate is "Je me souviens," referencing a collective memory of "the Conquest," the British military defeat of the French on the Plains of Abraham in 1760 (Carens 1995, 70–71). The contemporary sovereignist movement is fueled by a sense of injustice and the perception that the French were dominated politically, economically, and linguistically, indeed "colonized" by the British for two centuries. The anxiety expressed by some nationalists for the survival of the French linguistic and cultural presence in North America, however, places barriers in the way of extending cultural rights that would maintain the distinctiveness of other ethnocultural groups and thus transform the Québec symbolic order in multicultural directions.

The Québec state thus faces a dilemma in formulating policies to integrate and inculcate a sense of belonging among immigrants to the Québec nation. If what it means to be Québécois is based primarily or exclusively on the French language, there is greater scope for developing more inclusive and pluralist policies toward individuals and communities who are not descended from the French settlers. An explicit part of the agenda among some progressive organizations in Québec, including women's organizations, is the construction in a reflexive and self-conscious manner of a more pluralist conception of Québec identity that integrates the diverse communities of modern Québec (Juteau 1992; Juteau and McAndrew 1992; Balthazar 1994; Forum pour un Québec féminin pluriel 1994). As linguistic ethnicity does not offer a sufficiently bounded sense of belonging, however, many Québec nationalists are likely to continue to invoke the stronger claim for distinctiveness of the Québec nation based on an attachment to symbols and culture associated with settler mythology. Yet it is precisely this more exclusionary form of "racial ethnicity" that privileges Québécois de souche and "whiter" groups over more recent and racialized immigrants and prevents the latter's identification with the projects of Québec nationalists, including the secession of Québec from Canada.[13]

A major obstacle to moving from an ethnic to a civic or territorial form of nationalism in Québec also exists in the hegemonic social vision to which Québec nationalism is now harnessed. While Québec unions and other progressive social movements envision a social democratic blueprint for Québec's future, the governing nationalist party (the Parti Québécois) is now driven by the interests of the economically and financially mature francophone business community, which is anxious to position itself more favorably within the international market. Global imperatives are implicated in the shift from the more social democratic view of citizenship characteristic of Québec's recent history to a more market-based conception of "citizen-as-customer," whose rights and access to previously public goods is predicated on an unequal command of property and ability to pay. The character of Québec identity that results from a probusiness neoliberal nationalism, what Daniel Salee (n.d.) refers to as *l'homo québecensis*, discounts, ignores, and silences many identities such as those of immigrants, Aboriginal peoples, women, the poor, youth, Anglo-Quebecers, and so on.

Questions of exclusion from the definition of the Québec nation for ethnocultural and racial minorities have centered on language and cultural rights, and racism—for example, in coercive policing of the black communities, in the controversy within Québec schools over the *hijab* worn by some Muslim girls, and in the color symbolism of *pure laine* (literally, "pure wool") Quebecers, referring to the descendants of the original French settlers. Issues of language and cultural rights are also important for indigenous peoples, or First Nations, particularly as the language laws of a sovereign Québec would further threaten indigenous languages that have survived centuries of colonization and linguistic suppression. Yet for Aboriginal peoples, it is the territorial boundaries and legal jurisdiction of the Québec nation claimed by sovereignists, rather than language policies, that have been the major source of conflict. For Aboriginal groups, the claim by Québec nationalists that an independent Québec would entail establishment of a single Québec nation based on its current provincial boundaries is a neocolonialist stance. This claim denies indigenous peoples, including the Crees, Inuit, Naskapi, Mikmaq, Maliseet, Mohawk, Montagnais, Abenaki, Algonquin, Atikawekw, and Huron, their rights to self-determination in their homelands, which are at least partially within the geographic boundaries of the province (Turpel 1992). These peoples define their survival as distinct societies and cultures in terms of their ability to retain control over their lands and territories.[14] Yet the integrity of Aboriginal traditional territories in Québec, as elsewhere in Canada, has been continuously undermined by governments representing the interests of white settlers and corporate interests.[15]

The infringement on indigenous peoples' rights to self-determination by the nationalist project of another people (francophone Quebecers) with whom the indigenous are linked within colonialism presents one of the clearest instances within Canada of the intimate, constitutive relationship of racism to nationalism. This should not be read, as it often problematically is, especially in the froth and accusatory tone of debates over Québec secession, as indicating that Quebecers are individually more racist than other Canadians (Conlogue 1996, A12). There is no evidence to support this view. Rather, the lesser sympathies re-

cently shown by francophone Quebecers to Aboriginal collective interests (compared with other Canadians) reflect the difficulties of reconciling Aboriginal interests within the context of the sovereignist project
of Québec nationalism.[16]

As expressed by Balibar, racism is "always in excess" of nationalism,
"but always indispensable to its constitution and yet always still insufficient to achieve its project" (1991, 54). Robert Miles compares the
continuous ideological articulation of the ideas of "race" and "nation"
to the play of a kaleidoscope, with each merging "into one another
in varying patterns, each simultaneously highlighting and obscuring
each other" (1993, 55, 76). This is a useful metaphor, suggesting the distinct yet overlapping genealogies of nationalisms and racisms specific
to particular regions and that form the impetus for movements of inclusion and exclusion in "national" communities and the creation of
separate nation-states. The complementarity of racism to nationalism
in the Québec sovereignist project involves the systematic denial and
subordination of the rights to self-determination of colonized and less
empowered peoples that stems from the single-minded pursuit of self-
determination by a more powerful people. This relationship becomes
apparent when the nationalist and justice claims of each collectivity—
"Québec" and "Aboriginal" (Cree, Mohawk, etc.)—are considered in a
framework of relational positionality, rather than in isolation from each
other, or as parallel histories.

Relational Positionality

"Relationality," "positionality," and "relational positionality" are concepts developed by antiracist and postcolonial feminists to explain the
fluidity of individual and group identities at the crossroads of different
systems of power and domination. They refer to the multiple relations of
power that intersect in complex ways to position individuals and collectivities in shifting and often contradictory locations within geopolitical
spaces, historical narratives, and movement politics. Avtar Brah uses
the concept of positionality to examine the particular relation of different racisms with respect to one another, which she posits is a necessary
prelude to "analysis of the interconnections between racism, class, gender and sexuality" (1991, 62). She acknowledges the shared features of
the historical experiences of the Irish and "black" (including African
Caribbean and South Asian) groups in Britain, such as the history of

being colonized and subjected to racism and class exploitation (see also Miles 1982). Notwithstanding these similarities in antiblack and anti-Irish racisms, Brah highlights the need to locate these two racisms in relation to each other in the context of British society. Viewed relationally, the "whiteness" of Irish people places them in a dominant position vis-à-vis black people as constructed through discourses of antiblack racism (Brah 1991, 62).

A relational approach to historical oppressions of different ethnicities is also creatively employed in Shohat and Stam's (1994) supple discussion of representation in Hollywood films of racially and ethnically marginalized communities. The specificity of representation of European Jewish immigrants, for instance, was inscribed in a contradictory manner by ethnic-religious relations (their Jewishness in the context of anti-Semitism), race (their whiteness), and corporate power (their concentration within the top ranks of the American film industry). In contrast, African Americans had little power over their own self-representation. Their blackness made it impossible (collectively) to "pass" for the socially normative ethnicity, and their relentlessly oppressed status meant that Hollywood offered a segregated space for bit characters and gross caricatures, while commonly appropriating without acknowledgment African American music and culture (Shohat and Stam 1994, 223–30).

Chandra Mohanty draws attention to the "complex relationality" within systems of domination such as colonialism, imperialism, racism, and capitalism which mean that "systems of racial, class and gender domination do not have *identical* effects on women in third world contexts" (1991, 13). In an article on racial and ethnic multiplicity in women's politics, Susan Friedman elaborates on the work on relationality developed by Mohanty and others in viewing the dynamics of contradictory subject positions through narratives or "scripts of relational positionality." Such scripts offer an understanding of "the interplay of privilege and alterity" by acknowledging that power flows in more than one direction, so that the oppressed can also be the oppressor, the victim, victimizer, depending on the particular axis of power (race, gender, class, sexuality, religion, etc.) one considers (1995, 15, 18).[17] Friedman points out that scripts of relational positionality destabilize organizational strategies: How can one organize politically if everyone belongs to multiple groups? (1995, 18) This dilemma is particularly poignant for many "mixed-race" individuals—whose hybrid cultural heritage, in addition to class, gender, and so on place their multiple identities on both sides of the oppressor/oppressed divide — with the attendant risk of neutralizing a focused sense of injustice that underlies many progressive social movements (see also Jhappan 1996).[18]

Friedman's discussion shares with several other feminist theories of location, positionality, and standpoint a focus on the individual rather than collectivities as the subject of multiple and contradictory subject positions (Bannerji et al. 1991; de Lauretis 1986; Larner 1995). By way of contrast, Brah's and Shohat and Stam's discussions of relational positionality of racisms and ethnicities suggest the need to comprehend the links in discourses, representations, and relative claims of oppression and rights of different peoples or collectivities. Central to my interpretation of relational positionality is also a rejection of poststructuralist deconstructions that deny the material bases for power relations, however complicated their discursive representations. The relative merits of the arguments for secession of Québec, and national self-determination of Aboriginal peoples, are illuminated within a framework of relational positionality of the movements for self-determination of francophone Quebecers and Aboriginal peoples.

Relational Positionality of Ethnonational and Multicultural Claims

While several Aboriginal leaders have acknowledged the cultural, linguistic, and sociological distinctiveness of French Canada or francophone Quebecers and their right to self-determination, they argue that indigenous peoples have prior and stronger claims. First, while Quebecers base their claim to the right to secede on the basis of their distinct status as a people or nation, indigenous peoples claim a natural and unceded or *inherent* and continuing right to self-government based on their historical status as self-governing and distinct peoples (Jhappan 1993, 235–36). Second, while Québec's rights to self-determination and secession are often stated in historical terms that include "washing away the inequities and humiliations suffered by their ancestors," Aboriginal peoples dispute claims made by the Québécois that they have been *colonized* (Derriennic, quoted in Grand Council of Crees 1995, 124). In contrast, indigenous peoples in Québec, as in the rest of Canada, have experienced both external and internal forms of colonialism, to which the Québec government has been a party; they have notably yet to witness political decolonization (Frideres 1993, 3–5; Grand Council of Crees 1995, 237, 371; Turpel 1992).

Third, unlike Quebecers, who have an entire provincial state for the exercise of internal self-determination, indigenous peoples have continuously been denied their rights to self-determination through colonialist policies, practices, and attitudes (Grand Council of the Crees 1995, 89). A central difference between Aboriginal peoples and the Québécois resides in the vastly greater capacity of the Québécois to advance the protection of their cultural and linguistic identities through the agency of the Québec state. Aboriginal peoples lack any similar political instruments of political and economic self-determination, and must live in a context whereby "dominant white majorities (both Canadian and Québécois) have imposed structures of law, politics and economics upon them that sometimes expressly deny their identity and sometimes actively seek to repress it" (Whitaker 1995, 206).[19] This does not mean that Aboriginal peoples have been passive; indeed, Mohawk and other indigenous nationalisms were nurtured out of resistance to the Canadian state (Alfred 1995). The material and political resources for resistance of First Nations peoples are, however, much weaker than for francophone Quebecers.

Fourth, principles of redistributive justice provide support for the need to give top priority to the political aspirations of Aboriginal peoples over other ethnonationalist projects.[20] According to all measures of economic well-being and social distress, the peoples of the First Nations remain the most economically disadvantaged collectivity in Canada. As constitutional expert Peter Russell writes, "In socioeconomic terms it is the Native component of the population . . . that suffers the greatest deprivation of equality and the continuing imposition of non-Aboriginal rule over the Aboriginal peoples constitutes Canada's most serious constitutional injustice" (quoted in Grand Council of Crees 1995, 372). In contrast, although historically francophone Quebecers have experienced wage and employment discrimination in comparison to Anglophones, this is no longer the case. Indeed, by the 1980s, bilingual Francophones in Québec earned higher incomes than bilingual Anglophones (Laczko 1995, 23); thus, arguments of redistributive justice do not currently support the case for Québec sovereignty.

The prosovereignty Québec government has relied on a "double standard" in advocating self-determination for Québec but refusing any similar right for the indigenous populations of the region (Grand Council of the Crees 1995, 105). While the Québec National Assembly has formally recognized Aboriginal peoples in Québec as distinct "nations," "for [the Parti Québécois government and] many Québec sovereignists, the status of 'nations' for Aboriginal peoples, is of a secondary order and . . . there are only 'two founding nations' (i.e., English and French Canadians) in Canada" (14).[21] Aboriginal peoples throughout Canada have long argued that the concept of "two founding nations" is an offensive colonialist myth that obliterates Aboriginal presence, rights, and status and the role taken by Aboriginal peoples in the "founding" of the country's history, economy, cultural character, and well-being (Come 1995; Jhappan 1993, 238).[22] The laws and policies enacted by colonial and Canadian governments signified that they regarded indigenous peoples as inferior to settler populations and a hindrance to settler colonization. Ironically, the insistence of Québec nationalists that there are only two founding nations has led to an appropriation of indigenous status by francophone Quebecers while denying pride of place within Canada's foundational myths to the actual first peoples.[23]

Immigrants and their descendants with origins other than English or French have also objected to the exclusionary nature of the "two founding nations" concept in Canada's symbolic/cultural order, although their criticisms have been more muted and taken less seriously in the arenas of constitutional, federal, and provincial politics. Unlike Aboriginal peoples, non-French, non-English groups have not claimed a constitutional status or territorially based rights as separate peoples or nations. This does not mean, however, that certain groups arriving during crucial phases in Canadian nation building, such as the approximately 170,000 Ukrainian peasants who formed agricultural settlements during the turn of the century in the prairies, did not develop a sense of group self-identity as a "founding people" (Swyripa 1993, 5).[24]

Since its establishment as official federal government policy in 1971, multiculturalism was supposed to be the policy that made palatable for ethnic minorities their exclusion from the settler society "two founding nations" construct. The fact that it was wedded, as an afterthought, to the construct of a "bilingual and bicultural" Canada, rather than replacing French/British dualism, has inherently limited the possibilities of public support for cultures and peoples at odds with British and French Canadian institutions (Gabriel 1996, 179–80; Stasiulis 1988). At most, what is officially provided is the carving out of "a precarious area of diversity on the margins of a predominantly assimilationist structure" (Parekh, in Gabriel 1996, 181). The constitutional, administrative, and popular status of multiculturalism has been demoted with the national unity crisis trained on Québec's status within or secession from Confederation, the revitalization of the "two founding nations" discourse, and the heightened expression, with racist overtones, of intolerance for "too much diversity" (Abu-Laban and Stasiulis 1992).

The virtual disappearance of multiculturalism from official state discourses is ironic given Canada's continuing reliance on immigration for population and economic renewal. As important, immigration has become more diverse in its ethnic and racial makeup and has departed from the ideals of white European Christian supremacy and preference for white, British, and northwestern European immigrants woven into Canadian immigration policy throughout most of its history. Since the early 1970s, non-European regions such as the Caribbean, South and Central America, Africa, the Middle East, the Pacific, and especially Asia have overtaken Europe as regional sources for Canadian immigration.[25]

The attribution of the label "founding people" outside Québec, which historically referred to the British, is completely removed from the actual mix of cultures and hybrid sensibilities of many Canadian residents, particularly of "global cities" such as Toronto and Vancouver. In effect, it resuscitates an ethnic-national label for what has become, through ethnically heterogeneous immigration, a territorial nation, united by economic and political ties. It also effaces the struggles of many non-British communities against forms of racism that flourished in white settler British colonies.

Dialectics of Racial/Ethnic Multiplicity and Power in Women's Politics

Women's movements in Canada have historically participated in reproducing the essentialist roles attributed to women and the racist biases of the (dual) white settler society nation-building project. In a process particularly marked over the past fifteen years, the voices and politics of women from racially and ethnically marginalized communities have critiqued and then redefined the agenda of "mainstream" Canadian feminism, empowered by the growth of movements for Aboriginal rights, Québec independence, immigrant rights, and antiracist movements. The trend toward greater inclusiveness has involved contemporary feminist organizations in contesting the racial, gendered, and class notions of inclusion and exclusion involved in settler colonization. It has also brought to the fore the contradictions involved in privileging certain "people's" or national rights, with the effect of giving less attention and resources to the most marginalized and oppressed groups of women. Here, I explore how the intersection of racial/ethnic/national heterogeneity with women's politics has moved from a position of *exclusion* to *pluralism*, without yet grappling with the more complicated power dynamics of *relational positionality.*

The first wave of feminism (1880–1920) in Canada saw white, British Canadian women pressing for an increased public role, including exercise of the vote and involvement in immigrant selection, in order to fulfill their role as gatekeepers of the virtuous, British nation in Canada (Agnew 1996, 39–42; Roberts 1979; Valverde 1991). Organizations such as the Women's Christian Temperance Union gave a platform for eugenics arguments based on the new "scientific" racism, but mostly drew upon more conventional racism propagated by Christian missionaries, such as tropes that equated Christian Europe with light/morality and Africa with darkness/sin (Valverde 1992a, 17). Among the targets identified in the writings and speeches of feminist reformers were male immigrants from eastern Europe and China whose "depraved character" made them threats to the morals of "white" women and "unfit" to have the vote denied to "decent" Anglo-Celtic women (Palmer 1982, 39).

Aboriginal and non-British immigrants and African Canadian women were excluded from the early feminist organizations and typically encountered British Canadian women in unequal relations as employers (e.g., in domestic service) or as targets of mission- or church-related charity or reform work. When made aware of the concerns of non-British women, the organizations representing British Canadian women shied away from these concerns, fearing that they might tarnish the appeal of their causes, such as attaining the franchise for themselves (Frager 1992, 139). Ruth Frager describes the reluctance of female suffragists and other middle-class, British, Christian women's groups to support the union struggles of working-class Jewish Canadian women in the needle trades in the first four decades of the twentieth century, "nor did they make significant efforts to bring these female workers into the women's movement itself" (1992, 148).

The racial/ethnic barriers to participation and solidarity within first-wave feminism did not prevent spirited activism among non-British immigrant women. Some European women—particularly Finnish, Jewish, and Ukrainian—drew from homeland socialist and working-class traditions to become active in Canadian socialist organizations and the labor movement, albeit in separate language or ethnocultural locals (Frager 1992; Sangster 1989). For some women from ethnocultural minority communities, their attachment to the political traditions of their homelands was as important in shaping their involvement in politics in Canada as ethnolinguistic barriers and the racial/ethnic biases of British Canadian women's politics.[26]

The restricted extent and forms of organizing among the racially most marginalized groups, such as black and Asian women in the early twentieth century, were influenced by the sex-ratio imbalances within these communities shaped by racist immigration policies. Such policies sought to draw on the cheap labor of nonwhites but to prevent their permanent settlement. Thus, the small numbers of pre–World War II Chinese women were the product of a policy that imported Chinese male peasants as cheap laborers in British Columbia and kept women and children back home through prohibitive "head taxes" (Li 1988). In contrast, the migration of Caribbean women to perform domestic service in cities such as Toronto and Montréal, in a context where most Caribbean migration was prohibited by restrictive immigration laws, fostered black communities where women sought refuge from their loneliness and harsh lives in church and social clubs (Henry 1981, 14–15). In Canada as in the United States, the black-run Christian churches, such as the African United Baptist Church in Nova Scotia, provided an important "free space" for cultivating a tradition of black women's activism, leadership, and self-reliance denied by a racist society since the days of slavery (Hamilton 1993, 191).

In Québec, feminism had a distinctive chronology[27] and cultural traditions and reflected the status of the subordinate partner in the uneasy compromise between the two settler societies. The presence of dynamic and resilient female religious communities since the establishment of the French colony, with a central role in providing educational, health, and other services, meant that "strong, outspoken women were nothing new in French Canada, provided they were shrouded in habit and veil" (Lavigne, Pinard, and Stoddart 1979, 72; see also Juteau, this volume). French Canadian nationalism, which has been tied to many divergent projects of social reform and reaction ranging across the political spectrum, has served both to oppose and nourish movements for women's rights. The history of the Fédération Nationale Saint-Jean-Baptiste, which dominated laywomen's organizations from 1907 to its demise in 1933, is indicative of how a conservative, church-centered, and antifeminist nationalism won over feminisms focused on social reform projects (such as temperance, child welfare, working-class health, and "white slavery") and liberal political reforms (Lavigne, Pinard, and Stoddart 1979). The next surge of public feminism occurred in the late 1960s with the founding of the Fédération des femmes du Québec (FFQ), which at the time adopted a liberal feminist orientation. Dumont contends, however, that between the 1940s and 1960s, many women, rural and urban, were active within church-supported and dissident organizations (1992, 80–81). These women developed a "colossal network of women" and collective feminine consciousness that presaged the vitality of Québec feminism in the 1970s and 1980s.

Since the early 1980s, the fractured face of contemporary women's movements in Canada has reflected three important and linked trends. The first is the giving voice to the struggles of women tied to the survival and empowerment of their communities, with the most prominent communities defined in national and ethnocultural terms. The second is the trend toward greater inclusiveness within those organizations whose mandate is to represent all or a diversity of women.[28] Third, many of the conflicts, splits, and contradictions in present-day women's movements reflect the difficulties, and possibly the irreconcilability, of accommodating claims arising out of women's histories interpreted according to different positions of racial and ethnic collectivities in relation to Canada's historical development as a dual settler society.

The struggles for decolonization and emergence of Aboriginal nationalism in the 1960s and 1970s provided an important spur to the organization of overtly political organizations of First Nations, Metis, and Inuit women. Aboriginal nationalism has sought to maintain, reclaim, and rebuild indigenous forms of governance that had intentionally been undermined by Christian missionaries and outlawed by the colonial and Canadian governments. For example, until 1951 the Indian Act excluded women from the band electorate and barred them from public meetings, which did not, however, mitigate their active roles through often female-centered kin networks (Fiske 1995, 6).

For First Nations women, the fact that their own traditional forms of governance accorded them power, status, and respect, especially in communities with matriarchal traditions, distinguishes them sharply from women in non-Aboriginal, equality-seeking feminist movements (Turpel 1993, 182). Unlike women settlers who originated from patriarchal European cultures and subsequently fought for equality with men in their communities, First Nations women enjoyed considerable power and status in the governance, spiritual life, and organization of production in precontact societies. Indeed, some Aboriginal women writers have claimed that the liberal "equality" discourse, around which much of the non-Aboriginal women's movement has organized, is culturally inappropriate for First Nations women, who are committed to a "communitarian" notion of responsibilities to their peoples and to the land (179, 180, 184). Similarly, the types of action taken by non-Aboriginal feminists arising out of a Eurocentric and middle-class analysis of the oppressive nature of the nuclear family appear largely irrelevant to many First Nations women, who see their public politics to be an extension of their familial responsibilities as mothers, grandmothers, and aunties (181; Fiske 1995, 15; Krosenbrink-Gelissen 1993, 349).

The struggle that first thrust First Nations women into the political limelight was the fight to rid the membership sections of the Indian Act of gender discrimination in who was to be recognized as an "Indian."[29] Interestingly, it was this struggle that, however inappropriately, could be understood in terms of the rights of individual women rather than national or collective rights, which garnered the support of some non-Aboriginal feminist organizations such as the national umbrella organization, the National Action Committee on the Status of Women (NAC).[30]

Recently, some First Nations struggles, where women have played a central role, have garnered national and even international attention. These have included the resistance, leadership, and revitalization of traditional roles of Mohawk women as warriors in the face of a political and military occupation during the "Oka crisis" in Québec in 1990 (Goodleaf 1993). Also notable have been battles to reach a fragile balance of collective Aboriginal rights and individual rights for First Nations women in the constitutional forum. In the 1991–92 negotiations preceding the referendum on the Charlottetown Accord, NAC, dominated by non-Aboriginal women, worked closely with the Native Women's Association of Canada (NWAC). NAC supported NWAC's controversial demand that the Charter of Rights and Freedoms be applied fully to Aboriginal governments so as to protect the rights of women in male-dominated political structures (Jhappan 1993, 245–49).

For the most part, the activism of Aboriginal women occurs at more local (reserve and urban) community and less visible arenas, such as movements "to heal the wounds inflicted by an oppressive colonial past" (Castellano and Hill 1995, 232). These healing movements address such issues as the continuing apprehension of Aboriginal children by child welfare, family violence, and substance abuse, and the renewal of the spiritual, ethical, and linguistic foundations of Aboriginal cultures (232, 249; Kaye 1990). While recent statistics show that Aboriginal people have made significant gains in health and education over the past fifteen years (Platiel 1996), these gains are largely the product of self-reliance of First Nations' communities where women have played key leadership roles, rather than the equality-seeking Canadian women's movement, which has generally ignored addressing its Euro-supremacist and colonial roots (Goodleaf 1993, 240; Turpel 1993).[31] Monture-Angus (1995, 177) has argued that the label "Aboriginal feminist" has no meaning for her, a Mohawk woman, as her culture precedes her gender in shaping her experience. For many First Nations women who are woman-centered in their lives, identification with the mainstream or "white" Canadian feminist movement is prevented by the failure of non-Aboriginal feminists to examine their role in participating in and colonizing Aboriginal peoples, homelands, and natural resources (Goodleaf 1993, 240–41).

The efforts by feminists to address the schism between women from the two settler societies split territorially between Québec and "the rest of Canada" (ROC) have also been largely unsuccessful.[32] Given the dual French-British framework of Canadian politics, however, more effort has been expended by women's organizations, such as NAC, with its self-defined role as a "parliament of women," in addressing this ethnonational conflict than other forms of racial/ethnic difference. The establishment of the Royal Commission on the Status of Women in 1969, which was to bring liberal feminism, women's programs, and femocrats into the Canadian state, involved the activation of networks of influential women and the active cooperation between francophone Québec feminists and feminists in the ROC (Begin 1992, 25–26). "Dialogue was maintained into the 1970s between anglophone and francophone feminists" through the familiar approach in Canadian politics of "elite accommodation" (Vickers, Rankin, and Appelle 1993, 39).

Over the next fifteen years, the embrace of nationalism by francophone feminist groups in Québec such as the umbrella FFQ brought about a rupture with feminists in the ROC, represented by NAC. Québec francophone feminists, emboldened by Québec's relatively progressive legislation on women's, labor, and social rights have tied their feminist project to the Québec state, whose jurisdiction and power they have sought to expand (De Seve 1992b; Fédération des femmes de Québec 1990; Vickers, Rankin, and Appelle 1993, 267). Flashpoints signaling the divide between nationalist Québécois feminists and anglophone feminists have often involved constitutional politics that define a particular relation of loyalty to particular states. For instance, the struggle to enshrine women's formal rights to equality in Section 28 of the Canadian Charter of Rights and Freedoms was considered a major victory for equality-seeking feminists outside Québec, its success highlighted by the inability of American feminists to ratify the Equal Rights Amendment despite a protracted battle. The noninvolvement of nationalist feminists from Québec in this historic struggle was resented by feminists in the ROC, who failed to understand that Québec feminists, from their own point of view, were not choosing nationalism over feminism, but could not involve themselves in supporting a Constitution considered illegitimate by their own democratic institutions in Québec (De Seve 1992b, 114–15). The Québec-ROC schism among feminists deepened during the politics surrounding the 1990 failed Meech Lake Accord and the 1992 Charlottetown Accord (defeated in a national referendum), each of which were meant to bring Québec into the Constitution by enshrining its "distinct society" status. Over this time, the FFQ took an official stand supporting sovereignty, while NAC developed a position that supported a strong national government in order to protect national standards in beleaguered social programs. NAC's "no" position on the Charlottetown Accord was also motivated by its concern over the Accord's weak protection of Aboriginal women's rights.

Nationalist Québécois feminists have been critical of the failure of feminists in the ROC to recognize the "bi-national character of the women's movement in Canada," which means according the status of "national association" to the FFQ (De Seve 1992a, 111, 115). As De Seve articulates, misunderstandings among Canadian feminists are inevitable when they fail "to grasp that beyond a few bilingual spokespersons, the majority of Québécoises are exclusively French-speaking women with their own historical baggage; they are living under a distinct civil law code, being educated under a different system, becoming used to different 'maitres à penser' and, in general, living and thinking in a distinct cultural context" (1992b, 134).

In the meantime, NAC, which views itself as representing a pan-Canadian women's movement and which had been born within a liberal feminist framework, has moved a considerable discursive distance in adopting a "three nations" position in the constitutional debates leading up to the 1992 Charlottetown Accord (Vickers, Rankin, and Appelle 1993, 9). NAC's position was meant to recognize that the future welfare of different communities of women was tied to the granting of constitutional demands for greater autonomy of francophone Québec and First Nations peoples, as distinct from anglophone Canada. This position is *pluralist* in acknowledging the validity of Québécois and First Nations women's attachments to their national communities. The highly ambiguous and crude "three nations" formulation fails, however, to address *relations of power and/or colonialism* among ethnic/racial collectivities (colonized status of the Aboriginal peoples in relation to French and English) and conflicting demands among the "three nations" (a strong national state versus decentralization; Aboriginal versus Québec claims, etc.). In the constitutional forum, where "multiculturalism" had discursively disappeared, it also does not speak to the representation and interests of women of color, immigrant and refugee women who did not see themselves reflected in discourses of "two nations" or "three nations."[33]

For their part, women of color and immigrant women have been organizing, sometimes through their ethnocultural networks and sometimes in broader alliance with other women, to redress the conditions of their oppression and the racism faced by their communities.[34] Increasingly, women in African, Asian, and Caribbean communities are organizing to provide social services that are ethnospecific, antiracist and woman-centered, reflecting three sorts of principles: "first, the right to maintain their cultural distinctiveness; second, the right to equal treatment under the law; and third, the right to special programs (a form of affirmative action) designed to eliminate and compensate for the historical disadvantages resulting from race, class, and gender oppression" (Agnew 1996, 144). Women from these communities are asserting control over community and policy responses to sensitive issues such as domestic violence and female genital mutilation, which might otherwise be used to stigmatize these communities (194–223). As some of these communities are the product of recent migration to Canada, political activism is also directed toward reforming unjust immigration, refugee, and foreign domestic worker policies. The transnational character of families, communities, and political networks formed by many immigrant women has also provided an important basis for bringing Canadian feminist politics into transnational alliances.

Issues of racial/ethnic diversity and white solipsism, barely visible until the 1980s, have since rocked women's movements in many parts of Canada outside Québec, where feminism has been shaped less by binational issues than by diverse identity and diasporic politics and critical feminist perspectives, including (U.S.- and British-inspired) black and third world feminisms. Dealing with racism has made it incumbent upon white women, individually and collectively, to come to terms with the history of white, British-dominated women's organizations that in formative stages (such as the first wave) linked the racist and exclusionary behavior of white and ethnically hegemonic women to nation building.

The at least partially successful efforts to incorporate an antiracist sensibility within "mainstream" feminist organizations are increasingly apparent. They have reshaped abortion rights campaigns to take up analyses of the broader racist, sexist, and imperialist assumptions and practices (involuntary sterilization, Depo-provera, sex-selection technology, female genital mutilation) that have restricted the reproductive rights of women of color and third world women (Egan and Gardner 1994; Thobani 1992). In the arena of law and the courts, feminist organizations such as the Legal Education Action Fund, however tentatively, are attempting to address the erasure of racial minority women in law, as well as their own elitist, white, affluent image. They are considering "the complex interactions of race, sex, and the various other grounds of discrimination that are so much a part of the lived experience (as opposed to the legal analysis) of discrimination" (Duclos 1993, 40). In the realm of feminist publishing, following a period of explosive race politics, policies have been enacted to provide support for the voices of women of color by the previously white-dominated Women's Press (Stasiulis 1993).

This trend toward antiracist pluralism is best exemplified by the structural changes undertaken and issues championed by NAC, the largest umbrella feminist organization in Canada. Following ten years of lobbying by Asian, African, Caribbean, and First Nations women and the introduction of affirmative action policies, women of color now represent over a quarter of NAC's executive, major leadership positions, including the presidency, and an increasing number of member groups (Agnew 1996, 83–86; Whitla 1995, 248).[35]

One result of NAC's greater inclusiveness has been policies that are increasingly shaped to reflect the antiracist, feminist analyses, issues, positions, and strategies advanced by previously unrepresented minority and First Nations women.[36] With women at the helm who experience their lives as multiply constituted by intersections of race, gender, class, and other relations, NAC has made a significant epistemological shift in treating issues such as racism and First Nations, immigration, and refugee policies as feminist issues rather than human rights issues supported by women (Stasiulis 1987, 7; Valverde 1992b, 161). These developments have made the women's movement in the ROC more pluralist, participatory, and meaningful for greater numbers of differently located women. This tendency to democratic pluralism, however, has occurred without resolving the contradictions inherent in the historically structured positions of inequality of women's racial/ethnic communities, the relative merits of their claims for self-determination and entitlements, and the possibly negative implications for women from other communities of pursuit of feminist-nationalist projects.

Racial/ethnic diversity has also been addressed within the Québec feminist movement. For instance, the FFQ elaborated on its vision of a sovereign Québec in the brief submitted to the Belanger-Campeau Commission, convened by the Québec Liberal government in 1990 to discuss Québec's future after the failed Meech Lake Accord. This included recognition of the ancestral rights of First Nations, sensitivity in social service delivery to immigrant women's needs, nonracist principles in international aid, and an open immigration and refugee policy (Fédération des femmes du Québec 1990).

A conference organized by the FFQ, unions, and community groups in 1992 on "Un Québec feminin pluriel" marked real progress in recognizing and validating ethnic pluralism within the women's movement in Québec (Forum pour un Québec feminin pluriel 1994; Maroney 1992, 36, n. 60). Preparation for the conference involved extensive consultations with numerous women's groups across Québec and efforts to reflect within the coordinating committee the diversity of the women's movement, including representation of women from "ethnocultural communities." While First Nations women were not represented on the coordinating committee, they were involved in organizing a workshop at the conference.

The document produced from the 1992 conference, entitled *Pour changer le monde* (To change the world), offers a radical democratic vision of Québec's future, incorporating the goals of pluralism, ecofeminism, demilitarization, and empowerment through active participation and democratization of the institutions of civil society (Forum pour un Québec féminin pluriel 1994, 43). It explicitly critiques the hegemonic neoliberal view of the economy, which measures "success solely in terms of growth in production, productivity and profits." As I have argued above, the neoliberal agenda offers the least scope for pluralism within contemporary Québec nationalism in the sense of constructing so many excluded "others," making it significant that Québec women's organizations have explicitly rejected this societal project (33–34).

Ethnic pluralism is woven throughout the text of *Pour changer le monde* both as a description of the sociological reality of Québec, and as a fundamental value of the Québec women's movement (Forum 1994, 62). References are made to racist violence, "the lack of reflection of the pluralist reality of Québec" within educational institutions and mass media, the injustice of immigration laws that force women to remain with violent spouses, and the vulnerability of foreign domestic workers to the dictates of their employers. The "double oppression" is also mentioned of Aboriginal women, who are "most affected by an ensemble of socioeconomic problems: poverty, discrimination, suicide, alcoholism, family violence" (31, 57–58, 63, 112).

Pluralism implies that in relations with First Nations, "equality" does not mean "sameness" in treatment and that "we must resolve disputes between our 'peoples' " (Forum 1994, 63). It acknowledges that the Canadian and Québec governments have not recognized the right of Aboriginal peoples to self-determination or dealt with the obstacles to forms of development that correspond to their distinctive values, culture, and way of life. Yet the affirmation by the forum of the obligation to "recognize" First Nations is vaguely drawn and does not deal with the neocolonial presumptions within the Québec sovereignist project about Aboriginal peoples' inferior territorial and political sovereignty claims.

In an important sense, by acknowledging a lack of consensus on the question of Québec's independence, the feminist forum was exempted from dealing with the most vexatious of the contradictions posed by racial/ethnic pluralism in Québec. At the plenary, it was reported that "many participants, in particular Amerindians, women from ethnocultural communities and lesbians openly expressed their reticence towards subordinating the feminist societal project to a political choice in favour of, or against the sovereignty of Québec" (Forum 1994, 119). Although one participant is quoted as regarding the absence of consensus on "the national question" as a sign of the feminist movement's maturity, it might also be read as the incapacity to forge solidarity among women once the contradictions between their respective attachments to their ethnonational communities are politically foregrounded. Notwithstanding the expressed desire of the FFQ and the 1992 Québec feminist forum to embrace an inclusive politics of difference, the most public, organized, and "legitimate" face of feminism in Québec remains that of (white) francophone feminists. *Pour changer le monde* acknowledges that women from ethnocultural minorities do not yet identify with the Québec women's movement, at least not sufficiently to find their place within it. It also argues that the women's movement has not yet accepted an integrated form of belonging based on sex and ethnicity, suggesting an absence of consideration by the authors of the report of how the identities of many francophone Québec women are constructed through ethnic nationalism (129).

The concerns and identities of First Nations, immigrant, racial minority (francophone, anglophone, and allophone), and Anglo-Canadian women in Québec are relatively marginalized within normative Québec women's politics. Their marginalization reflects the difficulty among sovereignist francophone Québec women, who structure their politics around a combined sense of their own gender and national/linguistic oppression in Canada, to come to terms with the racial/ethnic exclusions flowing from their historical role as mothers and shapers of a subordinated white settler society. It is difficult to see how the FFQ could support the self-determination aspirations of, for instance, Cree women in Québec when the Crees have forcefully argued that the self-definition of Québec as a nation, and the Québec nationalist goal of secession of Québec, are inherently damaging to First Nations' sovereignty claims.

The overdetermination of the feminist movement by Québec nationalism was reflected in the response by Françoise David, the president of the FFQ, to the "catastrophic speech" by Premier Jacques Parizeau, who blamed the results of the 1995 sovereignty referendum vote on "money and the ethnics" (Hamilton 1996, 24). While the FFQ joined other organizations in denouncing the speech, the major concern expressed by David in a popular Canadian women's magazine was the false perception held by English Canadians of sovereignists as racists and xenophobes: "I am fed up with the federal government and the premiers humiliating us over that speech" (quoted in Armstrong 1996, 26). Absent from her remarks was a sense of the need among feminists who identify with the Québec sovereignist project to come to terms with the discrimination toward groups that have been excluded or marginalized by Québec nationalism.

Conclusion

The foregoing discussion provides an analysis of the challenges faced in developing a racially and ethnically inclusionary women's movement in settler societies where mainstream feminism has historically been shaped by white women's double positionality as both oppressed and colonizing. Feminist politics and organizations are increasingly compelled to consider women's attachment to collectivities including ethnic nations. In so doing, their efforts toward inclusion may express a pluralistic model of several nations within a state. While seemingly supportive of several liberation movements, such a model may submerge significant contradictions posed by the coexistence of contending nationalisms, as well as the inevitable exclusions of ethnic nationalism. Thus, the problematic notion of "three nations" supported by NAC, motivated by a desire to respect the distinct collective aspirations of Québec francophone and First Nations women, mystifies the power relations existing between peoples with conflicting nationalist claims (settler versus indigenous) and between the hegemonic "nation" and minorities or excluded "others."

On the eve of the third millennium, women's movements globally face limits to the diversity that can meaningfully be supported in their agendas. They are confronted by the hostility of international finance, states, and political climates to virtually all progressive causes, and the new reality (i.e., new in the more prosperous North) of severe funding cuts and "belt-tightening." For this reason, it is understandable that in the context of sharp ethnocultural, linguistic, and racial communal divisions among women, recent efforts to forge alliances among women from differently positioned communities have refocused their energies in struggles involving a shared agenda. This common ground exists in the need of all women to engage in building alternatives to the destructive trends of neoliberalism. Recently, this has occurred within Québec through the construction of a pluralistic radical democratic vision. It is also the direction taken by NAC, which in conjunction with the labor movement, organized a national "Bread and Roses, Jobs and Justice" march to Ottawa in June 1996, rallying thousands of women from across Canada and Québec to take up common cause in all of their splendid diversity.

Notes

I am indebted to Yasmeen Abu-Laban, Radha Jhappan, Anna Paletta, and the editors of this volume for their helpful comments on earlier drafts of this chapter.

1   In a nationwide poll taken in December 1995, nearly one in three Canadians expressed their belief that by 2000, Canada as a nation would cease to exist (Vincent 1995, A1).

2   Michael Ignatieff (1993) differentiates "ethnic nationalism," an "appeal to blood loyalty," which tends toward authoritarianism in its policies toward ethnic minorities, from "civic nationalism," which binds a multiethnic society through the sharing of democratic traditions and the rule of law rather than divisive inherited loyalties.

3   The term "visible minority" is a concept developed in the early 1980s within the Canadian federal bureaucracy to refer to people of nonwhite skin color or people of color. This term, which was (politely) meant to avoid mention of color or race, has been subjected to much criticism from grassroots organizations and people it was meant to designate. One criticism is that this term avoids recognition of the invisibility of racial minorities within high-level positions in the civil service and private sector.

4   The inclusion by British elites of the conquered French enemy in the founding of the modern Canadian state must be viewed in a context wherein other threats to the survival and profitability of the British Empire (such as the possibility of an American invasion) necessitated alliance and accommodation with the surviving French in Québec. From 1840 to Confederation in 1867, Québec (renamed Canada East) was joined to Upper Canada (Canada West) to form the single colony of Canada. The delegates from Québec took an active role in Confederation in 1867, and Quebecers "freely joined the Union of Canada in 1867, along with their counterparts in Ontario, New Brunswick and Nova Scotia" (Grand Council of the Crees 1995, 114–15, n. 408).

5   The indigenous peoples in Canada have undergone name changes "which

are not universally accepted—either by the indigenous population or the nonindigenous peoples" (Frideres 1993, 24). The term "Aboriginal" covers three categories of peoples—the Inuit (still referred to as Eskimo in the United States), Indian, and Metis (a people who developed out of the symbiotic relations between Europeans and Indians during the fur trade). The term "Indian" is itself a misleading legal fiction that masks the immense ethno-cultural, linguistic, economic, and political diversity of the first peoples, both at the time of "first contact" with Europeans and in the current day.

6   Although the aims of British policy at times vacillated between preserving and assimilating the French culture, the legal and institutional frameworks promoted formal respect for the French language and French cultural heritage. For instance, the 1774 Québec Act and the 1791 Constitutional Act accommodated French Canadians by respecting freedom of worship for Roman Catholics (who were chiefly of French descent), officially sanctioning the Catholic Church, retaining French civil law and the seigneurial landholding system, and granting the right of the predominantly French representative government to Lower Canada from 1791 to 1867.

The federal system created at Confederation (1867) and welcomed by Québec must also be seen in part as an accommodation of "the French fact," since Anglo politicians of the time (such as Canada's first prime minister, Sir John A. Macdonald) would have preferred a unitary state for economic and security reasons. From the political compromise reached with French officials, "the Québécois emerged with: a provincial state exercising jurisdiction over matters such as culture, language, education, immigration and civil law; the right to use French in the federal Parliament and courts; and what has turned out to be over-representation (relative to the proportion of the population) in the House of Commons, Senate and Cabinets. These arrangements did not put the Québécois free and clear of the domination of the Anglo-Canadian state, as the institutions and constitution created were based on the British model and passed by her Parliament. Nonetheless, one of the most enduring facts of Canadian federal politics and political elites has been respect for French-English bicultural traditions, and the need to achieve elite accommodation of French Canadians" (Stasiulis and Jhappan 1995, 110).

7   The change in self-identity of this population historically has been from canadien to la nation candienne-française to franco-Québécois to Québécois (Kymlicka 1995, 197, n. 2).

8   In 1991, 82 percent of Québec residents reported French as their mother tongue. Only 9.2 percent and 8.8 percent of Quebecers, respectively, reported English and "nonofficial languages" as their mother tongues (Tu 1996b, A6).

9   About one million Francophones in Canada live outside Québec, who, espe-

cially since the emergence of a Québécois identity, have developed their own set of identities as "Francophones outside Québec," or as "Franco-Ontarians," "Franco-Manitobans," les Acadiens, and so on.

10   This legislation limited English-language rights, decreed that the children of immigrants attend French schools, and stipulated that all commercial signage be in French only.

11   The insecurity regarding the future of Anglophones and Allophones in Québec was heightened immediately following the 1995 referendum, when five hospitals in Montréal were closed that served largely English-speaking and ethnic minority communities (Gray 1995, A3). The federalist sentiment of the vast majority of Anglophones (and Allophones) in Québec has also led to mobilization of forces supporting partition of those portions of the province that voted no from the territory that secedes from Canada. Partition has been dismissed as monstrous by the Parti Québécois, and is viewed as unacceptable among Québec nationalists and the majority of federalists.

12   In the 1970s, Québec negotiated the Cullen-Couture agreement with Ottawa, which secured the maximum control possible over immigration by a province within a federal system (Boase 1994, 392).

13   One recent study of 150 "Caucasian French Quebecers" in a multiethnic junior college in Montréal found that there was a "hierarchy of acceptance" of other ethnic groups that was racially based. Thus, these students perceived francophone, white Europeans more as "Quebecers" and less as "outsiders" than groups such as Haitians, Latin Americans, and Southeast Asians (Moghaddam, et al. 1994).

14   From the perspective of Aboriginal peoples, the principle of "territorial integrity" being invoked by the Parti Québécois government is a neocolonialist policy that continues centuries of racist, colonial policies by non-Aboriginal, including Québec, governments. Such policies involved "threats of dispossession, denial of title, unwarranted development projects, environmental degradation, or other unacceptable actions" (Grand Council of Crees 1995, 223). "Resource development in the traditional territories of Aboriginal peoples without their consent has been a major and enduring source of conflict with the Québec government" (398). With regard to the James Bay Crees and Inuit, conflicts have centered on the clear-cutting of forests and on hydroelectric development by Québec Hydro, which was originally initiated without regard to native rights, although it involved the flooding of a massive land mass that had traditionally been occupied and relied upon for subsistence production by the Crees and Inuit. Since the signing of the 1975 James Bay and Northern Québec Agreement, which had been negotiated under conditions of duress for the Aboriginal participants, the Crees have contended that this treaty has been interpreted by Québec and federal governments in a manner that "would suppress Cree values,

priorities and concerns" and would have adverse effects on the northern environment (250–51).

15 At issue for the Crees are the territorial extensions to Québec carried out in 1898 and 1912, which comprise two-thirds of the land area of the province today. These land areas, which constitute the traditional territories of the Crees and other indigenous peoples in northern Québec, were annexed to Québec without indigenous peoples' knowledge or consent (Grand Council of Crees 1995, 212). To the Aboriginal peoples, "the current provincial frontiers are arbitrary lines on a map, drawn by European newcomers who paid scant attention to the well-established territories of many native populations . . . who have inhabited the place continuously since the last ice age ended 10,000 years ago" (Come, in Grand Council of Crees 1995, 223).

16 In contrast, the aspirations regarding their political futures of Canadians outside of Québec, especially living in larger cities, would not seem (for now) to be as threatened by the self-determination goals of Aboriginal peoples. One national poll administered in August 1995, approximately three months prior to the Québec referendum, showed that Quebecers were more opposed than other Canadians to having Aboriginal laws replace federal and provincial laws. Québec respondents were also the least likely provincially to believe that Aboriginal issues should be treated as a high priority by the federal government (Aubry 1995, A14). Within Québec, a 1994 poll showed that 77 percent of Francophones, as compared to 28 percent of Anglophones, believed that federal programs for Aboriginal peoples should be diminished or even abolished (Bisson 1994, A1).

17 The example of a person with a contradictory subject position provided by Friedman is "a relatively dark-skinned Brahmin woman who moves back and forth between London and Calcutta. As a Brahmin she is privileged by caste; as a woman, she is oppressed. As a frequent traveller, she is well-off in class terms, but called black by the British and subject to the disorientations of a bicontinental postcolonial identity. As a dark-skinned woman, she is differently disadvantaged within the Indian context of colorism and the British context of racism" (1995, 15).

18 There are, however, many "mixed-race" people who develop a keen sense of political engagement precisely because they are privy to the bigotry of dominant groups. I wish to thank Yasmeen Abu-Laban for suggesting this point to me.

19 Most First Nations writers and constitutional experts agree that there has been little change in the paternalistic and racist governance of the Aboriginal population by Canadian governments in the past 120 years. In 1876, the Indian Act (amended in 1951 and 1985) consolidated colonial Indian policies and provided a totalitarian "cradle-to-grave" set of rules, regulations, and directives to manage Aboriginal peoples' lives. It also imposed discrimina-

tory, Eurocentric, and patrilineal standards for defining who was or was not a "status Indian" qualifying for benefits under the Indian Act, the result of which has been divisive and undermining of First Nations identity. This single, all-encompassing statute has been described by Aboriginal lawyer Mary Ellen Turpel as enveloped by "a web of racism and offensive legal fictions." Turpel further points out that "just to ponder the notion of a human being as 'non-status' . . . is offensive in the extreme" (1993, 177).

20   With reference to the Québec sovereignty debate, self-determination for indigenous peoples does not mean the establishment of independent states. Rather, it entails the right to choose the state under whose authority they live, including the right to remain within Canada. It also refers to " 'internal sovereignty' via new political arrangements and institutions by which Aboriginal peoples might govern their own internal affairs" (Jhappan 1993, 234). This is consistent with the more global observation that "indigenous peoples have overwhelmingly expressed their preference for constitutional reform within existing states as opposed to secession" (Daes 1993, 6, quoted in Grand Council of Crees 1995, 52, n. 190). Self-determination for First Nations in Canada allows indigenous peoples to determine their own destiny, "to freely flourish and interact by choice in the structures and institutions of Canadian society" (Turpel 1993, 191).

21   This hypocrisy is not, however, confined to the Québec government, but also characterizes the government of Canada's position. In spite of its unqualified recognition of "Aboriginal peoples" (Indians, Inuit, and Metis) in Canada's Constitution Act of 1982, within international forums the Canadian government has advocated that indigenous peoples not be referred to as "peoples" in international instruments (Turpel 1993, 13).

22   This "fiction" is said to continue the imperialist European doctrines of discovery and occupation which held that North America was, legally speaking, *terra nullius* (uninhabited land), and that the presumed nomadic life and "pagan" beliefs of Amerindians disqualified them from being classified as inhabitants in the European sense. Through such mythologies, Europeans fancied that they had legitimized both their "discovery" of and hence title over the land (as marked by symbolic acts such as flag raising)—and their de facto occupations (via the creation of settlements) (Richardson 1993).

23   Thus, Leslie Laczko contends that through British colonization of Québec, French Canadians became "simultaneously an *indigenous* subordinate group and a demographic majority with a wide if incomplete range of institutions" (1995, 15; emphasis added).

24   Ukrainian Canadians, particularly those who were fighting against the political subjugation and cultural-linguistic persecution in the Soviet Union, were at the forefront of the lobby for a multiculturalism policy in Canada,

committed to the public-supported preservation of ethnocultural communities (Swyripa 1993, 9).

25 Over the past five years, some European countries (e.g., Poland) have appeared among the top ten source countries for immigration. The majority of top source countries have, however, been on other continents. Thus, while European-born immigrants represented 90 percent of those who arrived before 1961, they accounted for only 25 percent of those arriving between 1981 and 1991. Of the 1.24 million immigrants who came to Canada between 1981 and 1991, six of the ten top source countries were Asian, with Hong Kong and China in the top three reported countries of birth. The top ten sending countries for Canadian immigrants in 1993, in descending order of importance, were Hong Kong, India, the Philippines, Taiwan, China, Sri Lanka, Vietnam, the United States, the United Kingdom, and Poland (Badets 1994, 29).

26 Swyripa writes of the politics of Ukrainian Canadian women in the interwar period, "The fact that Ukrainian-Canadian women organized outside the Canadian mainstream and within community structures under nationalist and progressive barriers confirmed at the outset the primacy of Ukrainian politics in dictating a role for their sex. Moreover, the individuals who formed the nucleus of a female organizational elite were shown to be motivated not by narrowly defined feminist goals but by the national or class goals of community agenda" (1993, 13).

27 For instance, the federal government and all provincial governments *except* *Québec* had extended the franchise to white women in the period between 1916 and 1922. Québec women did not receive the right to vote provincially until 1940.

28 Other identities besides those of nation, ethnicity, and race have defined communities of women who have been marginalized or rendered vulnerable in terms of immigrant status, disability, and sexual orientation (Vickers, Rankin, and Appelle 1992, 10).

29 Disregarding matrilineal or bilateral rules of descent and inheritance prevailing among many First Nations, the Indian Act decreed that legal status (and thus entitlement to many benefits such as housing, education, other social services, and exemption from federal taxes) was to be transmitted exclusively in the male line from one generation to the next (Weaver 1993, 95). The double standard of the Indian Act stipulated that Indian women who married nonstatus men would have their and their children's legal status revoked, whereas nonstatus (including non-Indian) women who married status men acquired status and benefited from federal Indian programs.

30 The fact that Bill C-31 (passed in 1985) revised rather than abolished the totalitarian divide-and-rule Indian policy and failed to give control over

First Nations' citizenship to Aboriginal political organizations provided grounds for active opposition to the legislation by many First Nations' political organizations (Fiske 1995, 18). While initially hailed as a victory for "nonstatus" women who gained access to Indian registration and band membership, the emerging consensus on Bill C-31 is that it has "exacerbated gender tensions by imposing severe restrictions on women's personal lives and by-bolstering state patriarchy" (Fiske 1995, 16; see also Monture-Angus 1995, 183; Weaver 1993, 97–105; Mercredi and Turpel 1993, 83, 88).

31   There remains a huge gap in life expectancy, living standards, and the administration of justice (such that First Nations women are 131 times more likely to be imprisoned in comparison with non-Aboriginal women!), indicating that the experience of Aboriginal peoples continues to be colored by the grief of being colonized—the "grief over overwhelming losses—of land, language and sustenance, of generations of children to residential schools, foster homes, and too often, violent death" (Castellano and Hill 1995, 249; Monture-Okanee 1992, 198).

32   I am deliberately using the awkward appellation "the rest of Canada" (ROC) rather than "English Canada" to refer to the nine provinces and two territories that along with Québec make up Canada. The term "English Canada" suggests a distorted view of the ethnocultural makeup of much of Canada and privileges the hegemonic English settler society.

33   For a fuller critical discussion of the ambiguities of the "three nations" view of Canada, see Cairns (1995, 161–75).

34   For instance, homeworkers in the garment trades and live-in foreign domestic workers are two groups of women, predominantly of third world origins, who are developing creative new models of organizing that reflect their uniquely vulnerable and isolated circumstances (Bakan and Stasiulis 1995; Borowy et al. 1993). Grassroots pressure by women of color workers has forced trade unions to take up campaigns that address simultaneously racism and sexism in hospitals and other sectors where racial minority women are concentrated (Leah 1989).

35   In 1993, Sunera Thobani, a Tanzanian-born single mother, was the first woman of color to be chosen president of NAC. In June 1996, the first black woman, Jamaican-born Joan Grant-Cummings, was elected by the membership to succeed Thobani.

36   Among the new issues taken up by NAC has been the strengthening of the rights of refugee women. Intense lobbying by NAC was instrumental in altering the guidelines used by the Canadian refugee board to interpret "social group" to include women fleeing from female-specific forms of violence and persecution, including rape, female infanticide, genital mutilation, bride burning, forced marriage, domestic violence, forced abortion, and compulsory sterilization (Mawani 1994).

Feminism-in-Nationalism: The Gendered Subaltern

at the Yucatán Feminist Congresses of 1916

Emma Pérez

Feminism causes divorce, feminine associations against marriage, and the vice of Lesbianism, which, by an immense mis-
fortune assumes large proportions in the cities.
— Ignacio Gamboa, *La Mujer Moderna*, 1906[1]

Ignacio Gamboa, essayist, wrote *La Mujer Moderna* to publicize convictions profoundly critical of feminism. Pamphlets such as his circulated in middle- and upper-class homes where women like those who
attended the Yucatán Feminist Congresses in 1916 may have praised
Gamboa, criticized him, or simply ignored him.

Tracking "things said" about feminism by the intellectuals and leaders of a historical event, in this instance, the Mexican Revolution, can
elucidate discursive formations. Often, what is recovered in such a Foucauldian "archaeology" of "things said" is not "genesis, continuity, or
totalization" (Foucault 1972, 138), but repetition. "Things said" are repeated without any kind of evolutionary or revolutionary transformation. It is as if the dialectic has failed women's voices. But has it? If
indeed we consider rhetoric about feminism within nationalist movements, we seem doomed to repetition over the centuries. How often
have feminists been accused of lesbianism and antimarriage sentiments
(as if either are insults), because they claim feminist identities? Almost
a century later, Gamboa's accusations are still hurled at feminists; however, social and political movements through the decades have opened
up spaces for feminists who no longer fear being silenced or censured
by ideologues who essentialize women's voices.

While the repetition of "things said" is engaging, the modicum of social change that can be traced, that is, if we want to trace change, is fundamental. Change can always be unveiled across the centuries, just as continuity can be hailed. Both are inherent tools for the historian, both are differential by degrees. My interest is always social change, but I also want to probe change as it is formed discursively, in the past, by the present.

As a historian, I have been trained to locate origins, to trace continuities and changes, and to unify that which seems out of synchronization, to categorize facts and words that seem to be "lost in space," lingering alone, anxious for a historian who will assign categories to these "things said." On the other hand, if one studies history only from a Foucauldian stance, to rupture totalities and dispute origins, one can become disillusioned; yet disillusion may be essential to interrogate differences and subjectivities in different ways, perhaps by crossing disciplines. The historian's subjectivity imagines and produces historiography, even when it is revisionist. The language of historiography is enunciated and repeated, authorizing systems of thought, which are not tested, nor do they interrogate the subject who utters privilege and authority. As Spivak reminds us, "the production of historical accounts is the discursive narrativization of events" and the assumption that the historian will tell "what really happened" in "value-neutral prose" (1988, 241) if theory is disregarded is itself a subject position that contributes to the discursive formation of a historiography that claims purity, the purity of knowledge, as if the documents spoke for themselves.

In this essay, I am concerned with tracking discursive formations of feminism during a nationalist moment, acknowledging my own subject position as a Chicana feminist historian with historical materialist tendencies. I want to contrast women's voices with men's as both articulated a nationalist revolution in Mexico from 1910 to 1920, but more specifically, I want to address the feminist narratives constructed at the Yucatán Feminist Congresses of 1916 to query systems of thought. As the gendered subaltern spoke interstitially,[2] a kind of "dialectics of doubling" yielded a politics of contradiction, a contradiction to and with male-centered policies.[3] It is as if women and men became each other's doubles in their rhetoric, especially as both were confronted with neocolonial and postcolonial political dynamics in their nation. The Yucatán Feminist Congresses became the spaces for "subaltern performative acts"[4] under the eyes of male leaders whose nationalist vision for women was quite specific.[5] While I do not intend to address the debate that questions whether "subaltern studies" may or may not be appropriate for Chicana or Latin American history, instead, I will refashion what is useful and defer to intellectuals of Latin American subaltern thought such as Florencia Mallon (1994), Gilbert M. Joseph and Daniel Nugent (1994), and many others who are engaged in the Latin American Subaltern Studies Group.[6]

Within this "doubling," this "double signifier," theorizes Homi Bhabha, a particular politics of the postcolonial is created. For Mexico, the neocolonial and postcolonial were at once at issue, hence forcing Mexicans to inhabit political positions. While Mexico had won its independence from Spain in 1821, two years later, the United States made it known to the world that Mexico was within the U.S. "sphere of influence." A few decades later, Mexico's dictator, Porfirio Díaz, welcomed the United States' corporate giants, selling them land at ten cents an acre. Minerals such as copper and silver and oil were extracted from the land and trains were built to transport these riches to the United States. Many Mexicans protested this neocolonial relationship, hence toppling the dictator Díaz would excise neocolonial compromises with the United States. The women and men of México who protested Díaz's near thirty-five-year regime conceded that they wanted Mexico for Mexicans (Hart 1987; Cordoba 1973; G. M. Joseph 1982).

A kind of doubling was in play for women and men in this specific nationalist movement as they allied politically, yet even within that "doubling," women's purpose was discursively constructed as they became symbolic representations for a nationalist cause. Women were left out and could speak only within and from interstitial spaces. There was no space for fusion or integration. Instead, feminism-in-nationalism would have to be articulated as the "intervention of the Third Space. It is that Third Space, though unrepresentable in itself, which constitutes the discursive conditions of enunciation" (Bhabha 1994, 37), and it was in that Third Space where the women of Yucatán found themselves reiterating, reassigning, rehistoricizing their symbolic place in the Revolution.

Elite male ideologues of the nation, such as Gamboa, spread rumor and antifeminism in Mexico just as Revolution began to stir. How was feminism going to be reconciled with the Mexico that would forge a new constitutionalist government? Would women's "femininity" become a symbol foregrounded in the construction of the new nation? Would women be relegated to traditional, gender-specific roles? How would women be included in the nationalist agenda? As an addendum? The Mexican Revolution, after all, was a constitutionalist revolution in which feminist activities were by no means bolstered. Women, however, such as those in Yucatán, may have attempted to reconfigure the nation-state, but they were restricted by the structures of the male-centralist itinerary for the Revolution. In other words, the male leaders of the Revolution envisioned a discursive order that bound women to "femininity." That is not to say that women held back or were passive. Women spoke, even if they were regulated and impeded by systems of thought enunciated by male revolutionaries. Could women have done more to disrupt these discursive formations? Weren't they also part of a social design that provided a forum like the feminist congresses to them? They were, most of them, middle class like the leaders of the Revolution. While the male leaders generated women's arenas, women's agency cannot be ignored. The Yucatecan women, at least some of them, created their own discursive agenda within that preconstructed domain. And given the political complexities of Mexico's history, its postcolonial relation to Spain since 1821, and its neocolonial relation to the United States since 1823, with the advent of the Monroe Doctrine, perhaps there were interstitial spaces where the women and men of the nation met, concurred, and spawned a new constitutionalist government. But again, despite the interstices of agreement, women, for the most part, were excluded from the nation's strategies except where men like Governor Salvador Alvarado sought women's backing. What were his words? How did he represent women and their duty to their nation? First, I'd like to sketch briefly Mexican feminist historiography.

In her study on the feminist movement in Mexico, Anna Macías posed that "feminism as it developed in Mexico from approximately 1870 to 1940, had a character all its own and bore only a faint resemblance to the feminist movement in the United States or northern Europe" (1982, 152). Feminism's resemblance to the movements in the United States and Europe can be attributed to two characteristics. First, an international feminist movement in the late nineteenth century made its way to third world countries by the beginning of the twentieth century. Mexico was such an example. The term and identity "feminista" appeared in Mexico by the early part of the century. Mexican women, however, did not become aware of gender-specific issues only through their contact with European feminists. Mexican feminism has always had its particular cultural forms. "Marianismo," as a form of feminism, empowered women in the household much in the same way that domestic feminism gave women power in U.S. homes in the mid–nineteenth century.[7] Second, the feminism of the era was linked structurally to the Mexican Revolution, a revolution overtly expressed as a nationalist, constitutionalist movement. Despite its socialist proclivities, Governor Salvador Alvarado's nationalist revolution sustained a capitalist economy in Yucatán during his tenure from 1915 to 1918. The feminist movement, led primarily by middle-class teachers, upheld reforms under that economy. The most glaring similarity between Mexican, U.S., and European feminism was a conviction for reforming gender inequalities in a socioeconomic system that was inherently unequal. Feminism in Yucatán was inextricably linked to an economy that sought reforms, not revolution, and the reforms excluded the voices of the marginalized.

For the feminists of Yucatán, liberal feminism defined their activities while a governor who called himself socialist enunciated and formed the discourse of that activism. In this instance, the nation's ideologues restricted and controlled gendered agendas. The gendered subaltern was heard from only under particular institutional circumstances where women performed liberal feminist discourse. What was women's potential for imputing leaders of the Revolution who already knew what women should say, do, and how they should react to the Revolution?

Yucatecan feminists were in a precarious position. While the predominantly middle-class teachers at the congresses disputed the injustices women experienced in society, the illiterate female population was kept from engaging in the discussion. Alvarado only permitted literate women to attend the congresses, hence the Mayas and mestizas who worked as domestic servants were not represented. This is not to say that the feminists did not debate vital issues for women. They were indeed acting in their gender's best interest when they advocated education, the vote, divorce laws, and property rights. Alvarado's moderate socialism braced the middle-class women's measures and, for women, he charted a scheme, an order, by which women's rights would be mapped out. He set the stage, building a particular discourse within a specific site. The nationalist movement, bent on liberal reforms, prohibited probing deeper into the country's contradictions.

Salvador Alvarado: Reconstructing "Femininity"

Perhaps less judgmental than Ignacio Gamboa and more concerned with granting women a space in the Revolution was the man who became governor of Yucatán in 1915. During his administration, moderate socialist governor Salvador Alvarado championed women's rights. From 1915 to 1918, the general called feminist and pedagogic congresses where such issues as suffrage, literacy, and higher education for women were debated.

To Governor Alvarado, education symbolized achievement, growth, and advancement for Yucatán's population. His gubernatorial career focused on a variety of reforms, but public education stood in the forefront. Throughout the nation, the Mexican Revolution had pushed education reforms forward. Antonio Manero, a member of Constitutionalist leader Venustiano Carranza's administration, initiated rhetoric about women that leaders like Alvarado appropriated. Manero stated, "Woman is the best educator of childhood and for that veritable ministry she ought also be instructed and prepared" (1915, 100). He charged that "Education should commence, then, in the good constitution of the home" to fulfill the "general temperament of the races which form a nation" (98). In essence, the Mexican revolutionaries expected women to be the moral guides of the nation.

Salvador Alvarado's education policies fill the pages of his study, *The Reconstruction of Mexico*. He published the volumes in 1919, as the violent phase of the Mexican Revolution approached its end. Having just stepped out of office, the former governor had used his position to shape ideas and experiment with them in the state. In the first volume, Alvarado outlined concepts for a renewed Mexico; in the second, the governor concluded, along with Antonio Manero, that "It is necessary to elevate the Mexican woman for the reconstruction of the country" (Alvarado [1919] 1980, 2: 120). He further insisted that the country's national pride rested in the "civilization" of the home. Classroom guidance, therefore, could serve to improve women's skills as homemakers, mothers, wives, and even teachers—all for the good of the country. Emphasizing women's femininity to reconstruct the nation apparently guided the former governor's vision for Mexican women and their future.

Alvarado's philosophy about women's "emancipation, independence, and citizenship" was a discourse that underscored his core beliefs—that educating women would, in turn, make them better homemakers. "We live in an epoch of women's emancipation," he began. "If a woman is to complete her responsibilities and if she is to exercise her rights, then, SHE MUST BE EDUCATED" (2: 115–16). With that education, she was destined to achieve two social functions: "To be the foundation of the family as she unites with a man to make a home. To be a producer and a worker before she unites with a man to make a family" (2: 107–8). The first function was the more important of the two, he claimed, because at home her true personality was revealed.

In a section entitled, "The Homemaker," his male-centralist discourse burdens the wife to sustain romance in marriage while she inhabits multiple roles to suit her husband's needs: "The bride ceases to be a bride the day after the wedding. However, if the bride is sustained in the wife, if the lover, the friend, the companion, the partner, the sister, mother and daughter are cultivated, then all that is feminine, everything sweet and beautiful in a woman will also be part of the wife. She and she alone will be her husband's mistress, absolutely and unquestionably" (2: 109).

How did Alvarado intend to cultivate the ideal wife and the perfect marriage? He proposed that a man's home would not and could not be complete unless his wife could achieve equality with him—a radical proposition for an early twentieth-century thinker and leader. But equality, marked by Alvarado and his cohorts, assigned women to gender-specific roles. For example, Alvarado professed that it was a husband's prerogative to look elsewhere if his home was not in order and if his wife did not stimulate him intellectually. Education was Alvarado's remedy. Education would improve a wife morally and intellectually for her husband and the nation. More important, the home was the first school for children; therefore, a mother must learn the rudiments of domestic economy. She would be responsible for sending into society sons who would make good citizens and countrymen.

This plea for women's education reduced women to only one space in the Revolution's new society: heterosexual marriage. Within that space she was free to embrace multiple identities: wife, mother, companion, sister, lover, mistress, friend, partner, and daughter to her husband. With so many possible mobile categoric identities, how could women request much more from the Revolution?

As Alvarado reiterated throughout his two volumes, "We will educate the woman, then, so she can rise to the level of her proper mission which is conferred by EMANCIPATION, INDEPENDENCE, AND CITIZEN-SHIP" (2: 115–16). Education, for Alvarado, might guarantee some civil rights for women, but heterosexual marriage, his nation's thread, would continue to weave specific gender roles at home.

Background on Education

When Governor Salvador Alvarado spoke at the Second Pedagogic Conference in Yucatán, he resolved to educate women. Educating women meant forcing them to break from the influence of the Catholic Church. It meant exposing them to rationalist ideas, ideas that promoted the Mexican Revolution. To the governor, women served a purpose. Both he and the Constitutionalist leader Venustiano Carranza agreed that women should be routed into teaching. The leaders sought to impress women with the Revolution's rhetoric. Then teachers would inculcate children in the classroom.[8] Reforms, before and during Alvarado's government, shaped teachers' lives in Yucatán. Did the education reforms improve women's lives? Did the rhetoric restrict women?

Throughout Mexico, before Alvarado's governorship in Yucatán, leaders and philosophers had already written their opinions and proposed plans about the education that best suited women. One such writer, Agustín Rivera y Sanroman, echoed the nation's sentiments when he asked, "What should women be taught?" Taking the question from a U.S. newspaper, he addressed the theme in an essay.[9]

Rivera described duties that bound women to the home. He noted, "First, give them a good solid elementary education, then show them how to sew, wash, iron, embroider, make dresses, and cook well." Economizing—that is, showing them how to spend less money—was a priority, he thought. After a woman mastered housework and cooking, she could devote herself to piano, painting, and the arts; these skills were only "secondary to her education" (1908, 1). He resolved that women needed instruction in hygiene, domestic medicine, and literary, intellectual, and moral education to provide them with "faith, hope, and charity." Rivera expounded that a woman must "dismiss vanity and hate lies" so that, "when it is time to marry, she will realize happiness is more important than the fortune or social position of her husband" (1).

In his writing, Rivera quoted European philosophers and prominent Latin American thinkers who were also influenced by Europeans.[10]

Rivera's ideas typified the era. These philosophers extolled motherhood and marriage while pointing out that education prepared women for these institutions. The bourgeois thinkers of Mexico restricted women to traditional roles, and Alvarado and Carranza were no exception. By encouraging women to become teachers, they coerced them into a gender-specific profession for the nationalist cause. It is fitting then, that the majority of women who attended the feminist congresses were, in fact, teachers.

Statistically, Yucatán had not fared well in training women to be teachers. In the Republic of Mexico over nine thousand women held jobs as primary school teachers.[11] The Porfiriato women had been routed into primary school education. The census reported that in Mérida 312 of the 470 public teachers were women, while only 158 were men.[12] These numbers differed from the state's average, where men outnumbered women, at least in primary schools. Also in 1910, the primary schools employed 257 men and 197 women in the entire state of Yucatán.[13]

Statistics also showed that in 1910, the state boasted 363 public schools, singling out 148 of those for girls. Private schools numbered only fifty-four, split evenly between those for girls and those for boys. Seven private schools were coeducational, a rarity in 1910. No coeducational schools existed in Yucatán from 1910 to 1915. Alvarado intended to change that. The public schools enrolled over eighteen thousand students, over seven thousand of whom were girls. In the private schools, over four thousand students were enrolled, and one-third of those were females.[14]

In 1913, the average income of a teacher in a public school was 720 pesos yearly. Rural teachers and evening school teachers earned considerably less, and instructors in small towns made only 360 pesos a year. According to the report by the General Treasury of Yucatán, women and men in teaching secured equal pay; women held fewer posts as administrators and directors, however. Directors earned 1,200 pesos yearly while assistant directors earned 960 pesos. At girls' schools, women were more likely to be the administrators; at boys' schools, mostly men held those posts. In the surrounding towns, directors averaged 480 pesos. One small town listed an income of 780 pesos for a male director and only 600 pesos for a female director assigned to similar tasks. Unequal wages between men and women clearly existed.[15] As a point of comparison, the governor of Yucatán in 1913, Nicolás Cámara Vales, took home 12,000 pesos each year he served as governor. His officials could earn as much as 2,100 pesos, twice the income of a public school administrator and more than twice what a teacher earned (*Estadistiea Escolar Primaria*, 1931, 13).

Alvarado's administration brought the most prominent changes in education since 1910. The census confirms the dramatic increase of women as educators. From 1910 to 1920, the number of female teachers in Yucatán's primary schools more than doubled, from 197 to 579. Male teachers nearly doubled, increasing from 257 to 474. In private schools, the numbers did not rise much at all;[16] these schools were most often Catholic and separated boys from girls in classrooms. Alvarado discouraged teachers from working at private schools not only because he criticized Catholicism, but also because he promoted coeducation in the classroom.[17]

One of his military commanders took advantage of the governor's stance when he prompted Alvarado to use a church under construction as a public school for girls because the one in the city required too much renovation.[18] The anticlerical governor readily consented. To demonstrate further the disapproval of private, Catholic education, from 1910 to 1920, the number of women teaching in Yucatán's private schools rose only from 31 to 56. This was considerably lower than the number of women pushed into public schools.

From 1910 to 1920, the number of public schools for boys decreased, but public schools for girls were eliminated. Instead, the number of coeducational public institutions rose from none to 421.[19] Governor Alvarado kept the promise he made at the Second Pedagogic Congress when he opened the doors to coeducation. The statistics firmly attest to his commitment, despite disgruntled parents frightened of permitting their girls and boys to learn in classrooms together. But the issues of coeducation, as well as sex education, became the controversy that challenged feminist Hermila Galindo at the feminist congresses, and it was the teachers from Yucatán who overwhelmingly disputed her position.

Hermila Galindo, "la Mujer Moderna"

Mexican feminist Hermila Galindo was exposed mostly to European feminists and sometimes to North American. Curiously, the title of her magazine, *La Mujer Moderna* (*The Modern Woman*), which published essays applauding vociferous feminists from these continents, echoed the title of Ignacio Gamboa's scathing essay about feminists.[20] Could she have been aware of Gamboa's essay? Was hers a refutation? Probably not, but the construction of the "modern woman" beckoned society's attention, and while Gamboa sketched stereotypes about feminists, Galindo was, in her own way, constructing the "modern woman's" feminism by publishing such a magazine. Before surveying the journal, more about Galindo must be disclosed.

Hermila Galindo was born in Durango. In 1911, she moved to Mexico City, where she joined a liberal club. The liberal clubs were organized strictly to oppose Porfirio Díaz. As her club's orator, Galindo delivered a welcoming speech to Venustiano Carranza when he arrived in the capital after General Victoriano Huerta's fall. Impressed with her oratorical skills, Carranza asked Galindo to join his constituents in Veracruz, where he stationed himself before solidifying his presidency in 1917. Galindo's career took an interesting turn. She became the private secretary and propagandist to the liberal, reform-minded Carranza. When she won his trust, she proceeded to lobby for the rights of Mexican women (Macías 1982, 33).

Before her involvement in both feminist congresses of 1916, Galindo's career with Carranza proved to be rewarding. With his assistance, she published her magazine, *La Mujer Moderna,* in 1915. The magazine's content ranged from literary essays to the latest Paris fashions. An essay on kissing hygiene appeared on the same page where the editors endorsed female suffrage, a politically volatile issue. The article exemplified Galindo's and other middle-class women's position on suffrage. The writer, Clarisa Pacheco de Torres, asserted that in the North American states where women could vote, they demanded and won legal reforms. With the vote, Mexican women could do the same. The magazine's collaborators were women who captivated an audience like themselves: literate, fashion-minded professionals who attended the opera, read Plato and Aristotle, and, most important, sought women's suffrage (Macías 1982, 14).

Galindo's convictions must have been known throughout Mexico when Carranza instructed state governors to subscribe to the magazine. The governors responded dutifully and requested fifty subscriptions for each of their respective states. Governors from the northern states of Sonora and Chihuahua to the coastal areas of Guerrero and Veracruz and throughout the interior of the country bought this magazine publishing essays promoting women's rights, especially their right to vote.[21] By this time, Galindo and Carranza had established a mutual understanding; a doubling of sorts was being negotiated.

The Feminist Congresses, 1916: The Gendered Subaltern

A year before the congresses in Yucatán, Professor María Martínez had declared to a Boston journalist while she studied in the United States that women in Mexico were not interested in pursuing the franchise for women; instead, they wanted to improve upon their education.[22] At the first and second feminist congresses, the women of Yucatán determined that some were prepared to demand voting rights for women, at least in local elections. Although interested in women's contribution to the country, Carranza's government was not prepared to recognize that contribution by granting them suffrage.

Governor Alvarado, on the other hand, a promoter of women's rights, called the feminist congresses in Mérida to provide women a stage to debate issues as controversial as the franchise. Alvarado intended to muster a population who would favor his reforms. He turned to the middle-class teachers of the region. Consequently, the governor ordered Professor Consuelo Zavala along with other female educators to organize the first congress in Mérida. Held 13–16 January, the conference attendance was restricted, at Alvarado's instructions, to literate women with a grade school education. Because illiterate women were not welcome, the attendance narrowed to middle-class teachers.

The governor also faced obstacles when he introduced socialist ideals such as rationalist schools to a middle-class population. The majority of women at the congresses disagreed with Alvarado's extreme proposals. Many held moderate beliefs, and some preferred conservative measures. The governor's discursive impositions only served to disappoint him later.[23]

Amid confusion, three political factions emerged at the First Feminist Congress. Hermila Galindo, though she did not attend, represented the most radical faction. Her controversial statement, read by one of Carranza's education administrators, Cesar González, recommended sex education for women, divorce, and anticlericalism, topics that pleased the governor. Galindo, perhaps explicating beyond the boundaries that Alvarado or other women dared to tread, interrogated the male double standard practiced in Mexican society for centuries. The feminist contested: "When a woman, mesmerized, surrenders herself to her lover, compelled by the ineluctable, sexual instinct, the man stands before society as a kind of daredevil. . . . But the wretched woman who has done no more than comply with one of the demands of her instinct, not denied to the lowest of females, is flung into society's scorn: her future cut off, she is tossed into the abyss of despair, misery, madness, or suicide" (Galindo 1915, 47).

The response was anything but favorable. A conservative group of women mobilized immediately to ban her speech from the congress records (Primer Congreso Feminista de Yucatán 1916, 96). Francisca García Ortiz, representing the conservatives, confronted Galindo's stance: "Let us pay slight attention to women's education, but a lot, a great deal of attention to the education of men, and above all to their enlightenment. . . . Let us never forget that the woman should always be the delight of the home, the gentle comrade of man; she may indeed overcome him through her love and sweetness. But let her not dominate him with her intellect nor with her learning" (96). Also a teacher, García Ortiz expressed a sentiment that the attending educators defended. Her political stance had its own rationale. She asked, "What social means should be employed to emancipate women from the yoke of tradition?" (96), and answered her own question, maintaining that twentieth-century women did not have to embrace nineteenth-century images: "That yoke is disappearing and we can make it vanish completely, by educating society" (96). Challenging the participants further, she asked, "Who forms society? Men. Well then, let us educate men" (96). And finally, she concluded that by educating men, women too would be educated because society would change (97). She also summoned men to accept a new enlightenment. "Today many men are afraid of the intellectual woman. Why? Because they understand that she improves herself every day; that each day her mind advances. Should men be afraid? No. Men should make sure they are not at a disadvantage. And to this a man must be more and more enlightened" (97).

How did García Ortiz intend to educate men? Like Antonio Manero, Carranza's administrator who idealized women as pillars of society, she also claimed mothers should educate children, beginning in the home. The professor proposed that the mother could most influence her son's education: "She will see to it that her sons respect women's advancement, that they look favorably on a woman's being intellectual" (97). A feminist blueprint, such as it was.

Not a mother herself, García Ortiz called upon the mothers at the convention to assist the "young idealist ladies," including herself. Finally, she ended, "May men become worthier and better men" (99). She hoped to educate women who, in turn, would educate men to improve society for women; an indirect means to equality, and perhaps a futile one.[24] Again, women are the social signifiers placed in binary opposition to men, yet representing for men the women men need. Woman is the sign that will construct "enlightened" man.

According to Anna Macías, Consuelo Zavala held a more moderate position than either García Ortíz's or Galindo's.[25] Zavala did not quarrel over ideological injustices; rather, she posed solutions to the inequalities women experienced in Yucatán. She was, in fact, a practitioner. She pushed for civil code reforms and property rights, tangible requests that the convention could take to the governor (Carranza 1917). Zavala did not overstep boundaries by demanding the vote (Primer Congreso Feminista de Yucatán 1916, 108). She took small steps, assured of what women could win.

The governor trusted Zavala; he appointed her to organize the January meetings at the Peón Contreras Theatre (42–48). To her credit, Zavala recruited 620 delegates to the first meeting. During the congressional debates, the teacher vowed to improve education for young women.[26] Women were visibly absent from professions in medicine, law, and engineering, for example; in 1910, less than 1 percent of the female population in Yucatán held jobs in such occupations.[27]

Zavala united the moderate and radical factions to reform the 1884 civil code. Articles in the code robbed women of their legal and property rights. According to Macías, the reform initiated President Carranza's Law of Family Relations in 1917. This new law allowed women to make contracts and file legal suits. They were also given the same rights that their husbands had over their children (Macias 1982, 75–76).

Perhaps the most extreme demand made at the congress was made by the radicals, who, unlike the conservatives or moderates, asked that women be allowed to vote in municipal and local elections. Despite protest from many women, a petition passed, pleasing Governor Alvarado, who called for a second congress (Primer Congreso Feminista de Yucatán 1916, 127). Alvarado, however, wanted women to vote in national elections. He aspired to be president of Mexico and therefore needed his female constituents (Alvarado [1919] 1980).[28]

The Second Feminist Congress, held from 23 November to 2 December, was not as well attended as the first. Consuelo Zavala failed to appear and Hermila Galindo again could not make her way from Mexico City.[29] The radical group took over the Second Congress, but unfortunately for Galindo, she was not present to lead the group with whom she most agreed.[30] She sent a representative to submit a statement entitled, "A Study by Hermila Galindo with Themes That Should Be Resolved at the Second Feminist Congress of Yucatán." The twenty-five-page essay was a rejoinder defending her first speech, "The Woman of the Future." Galindo asked: "My work is immoral? And how? Because I dare to expose the problems in our society . . . ? Is it immoral because as a perfectly intelligent and scientific woman, I have challenged men by demonstrating the intelligence of my sex, therefore showing that we too have equal rights with men?" (8). She insisted her studies reflected those of European philosophers August Bebel and Immanuel Kant, both of whom justified sex education as one of women's rights (7). She was not, therefore, the originator of such thoughts about women. That alone should have proven to her female audience that she was a "scientific woman" making rational assessments about the female gender.

Galindo recommended Carranza's revolution and she wrote almost as Governor Alvarado would have. We are only left to wonder what was left unsaid by Galindo herself. Her speeches at the feminist congresses demonstrate, once again, how the interior of Mexico attempted to administer every region of the country. Was this only revolution from above and not at all a grassroots movement? That the Yucatecan feminists denounced Galindo certainly shows a grassroots, insider response to outsiders. Moreover, this was not a national feminist congress.[31] Women mostly from Yucatán attended; a few came from Mexico City, but only those from Yucatán would decide what they would do for women of Yucatán. Even the radical faction at the Second Congress had its own issues to promote in the interest of Yucatecan women. But again, these predominantly middle-class women negotiated on behalf of themselves. Property rights, the right to legal suits, and education benefited a small group of elite women. The majority of the female population could not exercise such rights.

Yucatán was split between the wealthy and the poor. Alvarado's revolution hoped to create a larger middle-income group, especially after initiating agrarian reforms and nationalizing the henequen industry (Alvarado 1916). Perhaps Alvarado expected too much from such a small group of middle-class women. Given their circumstances, they did debate critical issues, but they failed to mention the Maya women blocked from the congresses, a marginalized subaltern who did not speak in this arena. There were no resolutions to address the needs of these exploited women, most of whom worked as domestic servants, some as prostitutes. In 1910, 57 percent of Yucatán's female population worked as domestics (Pérez 1993). They were neither present nor represented.

Hermila Galindo, an outsider like Alvarado, wanted to muster the congresses to reconceptualize equality between women and men—equality that reached into the classrooms to teach young girls the same subjects offered to boys, equality that gave women the franchise reserved for men, equality that defied sexual double standards. Galindo continued her career as a propagandist for President Carranza and even published a book in 1919 promoting a politician whose career was almost over in Mexico. She wrote *La doctrina Carranza* at a time when the leader's diplomatic relations with the United States were disintegrating. In the book she proclaimed that if Mexico was to be successful, it had to break its ties with its northern neighbor. Politically, she took a stand against the United States when she deconstructed the Monroe Doctrine to accuse the United States of racial arrogance for instituting a doctrine that only benefited the neighbor to the north (1919a, 19). Carranza's willingness to sever relations with the United States impressed Galindo, who argued that Carranza's "doctrine was the doctrine of the future, the one for humanity" (177). The Monroe Doctrine, on the one hand, represented the United States' neocolonial stranglehold on Mexico. A woman such as Galindo, familiar with politics since a young woman, was aware of Mexico's precarious relationship with the United States.

In her writings, Galindo expressed her confidence in Carranza's Constitution of 1917, which in itself promised social revolution only on paper. She wrote that suffrage was ineffective as long as workers and the bourgeoisie remained divided; for her, Porfirio Díaz's regime had made that grave mistake (1919a, 171). Galindo recognized that the vote alone would not free the people of Mexico. Like so many other Mexicans, she believed that Carranza would manifest the most revolutionary articles of the constitution, such as redistributing land to the peasants. Of course, he disappointed even his most avid advisors. By the time he escaped with the nation's treasury, only to be assassinated in his sleep by men he trusted, Carranza had quickly become the nemesis of the Revolution.

In 1919 Hermila Galindo published *Un Presidenciable* endorsing General Pablo González, Carranza's choice for president. When Alvaro Obregón was elected in 1920, not only had she promoted the wrong man, but the new administration had no use for her. She married in 1923 and was not heard from again (Macías 1982, 34). Her career in politics ended.[32]

Conclusion

Hermila Galindo, radical feminist for her era, became silent, unheard from again. She led the rest of her life without publicly voicing her political views. Surely, she was disillusioned with her country and its nationalist agenda, which in the end made limited inroads for women, whether middle class or poor. But Galindo's political interests found her backing a presidential candidate who was Carranza's chosen candidate. The corruption in Carranza's cabinet was already obvious to most. What could his candidate possibly have offered the gendered subaltern in their own country? Galindo, however, wrote a pamphlet endorsing Carranza's man, an essay that had little or no impact but was significant in that it was written by a woman who dared to go beyond traditional boundaries to steer politics usually reserved for male nationalists. Women, after all, could lecture about education for themselves and their children, but they could not decide who should be a political candidate for president, even if they might eventually win the franchise.

Hermila Galindo voiced her differences. She had lived in Mexico City most of her life and was genuinely interested in social change for women, though women of her class would benefit most from the reforms. Who was this subaltern voice who spoke between and among the elite, the middle classes, the socialist men, the counterrevolutionaries, and the Yucatecan feminists? Can we really know? Does it matter that we have only a few of her speeches and scant information about her life? It is unfair to characterize her as merely a *carrancista* with bourgeois ideals. She was incriminated at the feminist congresses for challenging a sexual double standard, but she was probably feared because she dared to throw sex into the discursive arena.

Galindo spoke out at a moment in the nation's history when few women were orators and few women wrote and published essays about their country's international policies. Her outsider/insider status in Yucatán placed enormous tension between the spokeswoman and the Yucatán feminists. Perhaps the Yucatecan women were annoyed that

Galindo did not show herself at either conference, instead sending a representative to read her position papers. Her stance was not so far removed from those of the Yucatecan feminists. She believed in women's education, but perhaps it was education for women that so disturbed the conservative faction, an education for women that did not emphasize their femininity nor their relegated roles as wives to the "nation," but instead was an education that finally probed women's sexual conditioning. However, three years later in *La doctrina Carranza*, she acquiesced that women were the moral guides of the nation destined to educate their children at home, echoing García Ortiz (1919a, 189–90). Perhaps Galindo tempered her earlier stance to recruit women to champion Carranza's doctrine. How much of his doctrine was her own? How much was she speaking, again, from and within an interstitial space?

The gendered subaltern's construction of a feminism-in-nationalism during the Mexican Revolution seemed to mimic the nationalist leaders' hegemonic discourse. What Carranza and Alvarado outlined was reiterated by Galindo and the teachers of the Yucatán congresses even when the factions disagreed. Only Galindo stands alone in the end, daring to invite sexuality into discourse. However, "the rhetoric of repetition or doubling" constructs the political discourse of feminism-in-nationalism. Although "things said" were a "sameness-in-difference," by whom these "things were said" makes some "difference" in retrospect (Bhabha 1994, 54). As Teresa de Lauretis points out, "the movement in and out of gender as ideological representation, which I propose characterizes the subject of feminism, is a movement back and forth between the representation of gender (in its male-centered frame of reference) and what that representation leaves out or more pointedly, makes unrepresentable. It is a movement between (the represented) discursive space of the positions made available by the hegemonic discourses" (1987, 26). In this instance, the feminist congresses were the spaces made available for women, "those other spaces both discursive and social that exist, since feminist practices have (re)constructed them, in the margins (or between the lines, or against the grain) of hegemonic discourses . . . [that] coexist concurrently and in contradiction" (26). No fusion, no integration.

Voices were seemingly identical, yet at odds. Alvarado's hegemonic narratives represented women in a particular way; feminists such as Galindo, García Ortiz, and Zavala (who did implement reforms) moved in and out of the male-defined representations, interstitially, congruently, yet often at variance with a seemingly identical discourse on women's rights. After all, women had something to gain if they voiced discrepancies from the margins, if only to disrupt hegemonic discourse interstitially. The nationalist agenda did not do much to improve or change women's social conditions. The changes, of course, were differential by degrees; but a forum was held, and the gendered subaltern voiced feminism-in-nationalism.

Notes

I would like to thank Anna Macías, Gil Joseph, John Hart, and Vicki Ruiz for reading early drafts of this essay. I also owe thanks to Homi Bhabha, a gracious teacher.

1   See Macías (1982, 16) for the English translation.

2   In her essay, "Can the Subaltern Speak?" Spivak's question seems to have ironic overtones, though perhaps not intentional. When or if the subaltern speaks, albeit interstitially to achieve agency, is my concern. See Spivak (1988, 271–313).

3   Homi K. Bhabha lectured engagingly and extensively on the "dialectics of doubling" in his six-week course at the School of Criticism and Theory, Dartmouth College, summer 1993. I am grateful to him for his insightful analysis. For more, refer to his eloquent essays on the postcolonial in Bhabha (1994). On pages 50, 52–57, 95, and 136–38, Bhabha defines his notion of "doubling."

4   Homi Bhabha, lectures, School of Criticism and Theory, Dartmouth College, summer 1993.

5   R. Radhakrishnan asks, "Why does the advent of nationalism lead to the subordination or the demise of women's politics?" as he calls for a new and different space for nationalisms. For me, history shows how women's politics may have been subordinated, but women as agents have always constructed their own spaces interstitially within nationalisms, that is, within male-centered nationalisms that miss the subtle interventions. See Radhakrishnan (1992).

6   See specifically the Latin American Subaltern Studies Group, "Founding Statement," (1993). Mallon was not a founding member but has written an excellent critique of subaltern studies for Latin Americanists. Founders include Chicana literary/cultural critics, Norma Alarcón and Clara Lomas, both of whom are in the "Founding Statement." Also refer to a special issue by members of the Latin American Subaltern Studies Group in *Dispositio/n* 19, 1994.

7   Two classic studies that ignited debates are Evelyn Stevens, "Marianismo:

The Other Face of Machismo in Latin America," in Pescatello (1973, 89–101); and Welter (1966). Welter, who coined "cult of true womanhood," argues that the domestic sphere robbed women of power, thus making them passive victims. Since then, many historians have disagreed with Welter. Silvia Arrom equates marianismo with the "cult of true womanhood," arguing that this Victorian idea from Europe and the United States greatly influenced Latin American women (1985, 259–68).

8   *Speech of General Alvarado, Governor of the State of Yucatán, at the Closing Session of the Second Pedagogic Congress, held at Mérida* (New York City, 1916), and *Carranza and Public Instruction in México: Sixty Mexican Teachers Are Commissioned to Study in Boston* (New York City, 1915).

9   Agustín Rivera y Sanroman's 1908 untitled pamphlet on the education of women in Mexico can be found in the Silvestre Terrazas Collection at the Bancroft Library, University of California, Berkeley.

10 Rivera referred to the sixteenth-century French essayist, Michel de Montaigne.

11 *Estadistica Escolar Primaria de la República Mexicana* (México, 1931). See tables.

12 México, Secretaría de Agricultura y Fomento, *Tercer censo de poblacion de los Estados Unidos verificados el 27 de octubre de 1910,* 2 vols. (México: Oficina Impresora de la Secretaría de Hacienda, 1918).

13 *Estadistica Escolar Primaria,* tables.

14 Ibid.

15 *Tesorería General del Estado de Yucatán, Mérida,* 1913, 41–46.

16 *Estadistica Escolar Primaria,* tables.

17 *Speech of General Salvador Alvarado at the Second Pedagogic Congress.*

18 Roberto Reyes Barriere to Governor Salvador Alvarado, 22 October 1915, Archivo General del Estado de Yucatán (AGEY).

19 *Estadistica Escolar Primaria,* tables.

20 *La Mujer Moderna,* 31 October 1915. The only surviving copy of Galindo's magazine known to me is housed at the Benson Latin American Collection, University of Texas at Austin. I searched through archives in Mexico City but have not encountered any other copies. I am hoping some may have survived in private collections.

21 Centro de Estudios de Historia de México Condumex, Carranza Collection, carpetas 107, 120, December 1916. I discovered at least twenty letters from state governors to Carranza showing their support for the magazine.

22 *Carranza and Public Instruction in Mexico,* 23.

23 Salvador Alvarado, *La Reconstucción de México* (México, 1919); *Speech of General Alvarado at the Second Pedagogic Congress; La Voz de la Revolución,* January, November, and December 1916. These issues of the newspaper report on the organizing of the congresses along with the proceedings.

24 García Ortiz's argument had been popular in the United States when progressive reformers decided that women could help clean up society through their participation in social agencies that would do "housecleaning."

25 In her chapter on "Yucatán and the Women's Movement, 1870–1920," Macías (1982) argues that the congresses were split ideologically into three camps: radical, moderate, and conservative. The proceedings do reflect this split. These categories should not be confused with contemporary notions of "radical" feminism, where "radical" can often imply "separatist" or "lesbian" politics.

26 *La Voz de la Revolución,* 10 January 1916, 1. Alvarado's newspaper kept the public informed about his activities in their state. The daily reported on the proceedings of both congresses. Unfortunately, the bound issues housed at the Hemeroteca Pino Suárez in Mérida are disintegrating because of humidity and age.

27 The census shows that only 1 woman was a dentist, 29 were midwives, none were doctors; 42 worked for the government in some capacity, and 5 were barbers. These were the nontraditional jobs, with the exception of midwives. Most other women worked in unskilled, ungainful employment (Secretaría de Agricultura y Fomento 1918).

28 In these volumes, Alvarado wrote about topics that might concern a presidential candidate. The volumes were originally published in 1919 after he left Yucatán.

29 *La Voz de la Revolución,* 24 November 1916, 1.

30 *La Voz de la Revolución,* 30 November 1916, 4–5.

31 Anna Macías argues that attendance from primarily Yucatecan women made it a regional congress. She also points out that the Mexican feminist writer, Artemisa Saénz Royo, falsely claimed that the congresses were international with women from Europe and Latin America (1982, 84, n. 79). Also see Saénz Royo (1954). The proceedings from the congresses defend Macías's argument.

32 She not only edited the journal, *La Mujer Moderna,* she also served as an honored faculty member with a doctorate at the Instituto Fiseotomologico Colombiano. See title page of *La doctrina Carranza.*

III

Transnational Subjects of Feminism:

Critical Interventions in an Era of Globalization

Multicultural Nationalism and the Poetics of Inauguration

Minoo Moallem and Iain A. Boal

> . . . not because empire, like capital, is abstract, but because empire messes with identity.
>
> —Gayatri Chakravorty Spivak,
> *Outside in the Teaching Machine*, 1993

The publication of *Systema Naturae* by Carl Linnaeus, the Swedish naturalist and physician, in the mid–eighteenth century was not only the founding act of modern biological science but a significant intervention in the sexual and racial politics of the emerging system of European nation-states. In his scandalous answer to what Thomas Huxley called "the question of all questions"—the place of humans in nature—Linnaeus coined the term "mammalia" in order to join *homo sapiens* to the animal kingdom. In choosing the breast (*mamma*) over other, more inclusive differentiating signifiers, he thereby struck a blow for republican motherhood and natalism by emphasizing how "natural" it was for bourgeois women to suckle their own infants rather than hire a wet nurse.[1] Linnaeus went on to encompass humanity within four quadrants of color—white, yellow, black, and red—systematically naturalizing northern European racism in his clockwise zoological taxonomy.[2] The embedding of race in scientific nomenclature continues to leave its traces in twentieth-century categories of U.S. immigration policy and quotas leading to citizenship. Carl Brigham's massively influential 1923 *Study of American Intelligence* deployed scientific data produced by the Eugenics Record Office to support both immigration restriction legislation and the preservation of segregation. He said that "we must face a possibility of racial admixture here that is infinitely worse than that faced by any European country today. . . . The really important steps are those looking toward the prevention of the continued propagation of defective strains in the present population. . . . This . . . will determine the future course of our national life" (quoted in Chase 1980, 272).

The Linnaean quadratic division was expanded in the course of the twentieth century to include a "brown" race. More recently, in the complex linkages between race and ethnicity, ethnocultural categories—African American, Asian American, Native American, Hispanic, and so on—have been mapped onto the old racial taxonomy.[3] This culturalizing of the officially acknowledged classification conforms to a multicultural logic that is open-ended; there is in principle no limit to the potential ethnocultural groupings that may compose the nation. The limit is in effect the ability of groups with a self-ascribed identity to mount successful appeals to the state, which manages such negotiations as part of the procedures of "official nationalism" with its various bureaucracies and state rituals such as the presidential inauguration.[4] Despite, or perhaps because of, the ethnicization of the taxonomy of national identification, the old rhetorics of a racialized biology are by no means dead. *The Bell Curve* is only the most recent malignant outgrowth.[5] Moreover, within the U.S. polity, Native American identity continues to be defined by the colonizers exclusively in racial/familial terms (as "tribes") (Perry 1995).[6]

Racialization remains a deep current in the politics of inequality. It has generated severe historical contradictions to the point of crisis for liberal nation-state formations, which must reconcile racial logic with the universalistic aspirations of Enlightenment ideology. Multiculturalism has emerged as an emblematic discursive site—a "corrective" to this crisis. It is a discourse that, in cobbling together elements from a number of political positions, attempts to square liberal notions of citizenship with a radical critique of the liberal subject. By this means it seeks to transcend modern racial formations in the shift from colonialism to postcolonial regimes of inclusion and exclusion. This fundamental contradiction produces symptomatic effects on the way in which the discourse of multiculturalism consistently evades engagement with three pressing issues: the enduring heritage of Eurocentrism, the question of justice, and the connections between national and global domains. With respect to the contingencies of Eurocentrism, "multiculturalism" has become a shibboleth that contrives to efface all historicity in its consumption of the present. It masks the legacy of racism and its systematic connection to dominant definitions of culture and civilization.[7] With respect to justice, modern law's disinterest is a sham. Equal legal rights inevitably presuppose the judgment of *some* particular collectivity; as a result, the expression of many collective forms of life is not even recognized. With respect to the process of globalization, multiculturalism has become an instrument of those economic and cultural forces working to perpetuate injustice and further intensify racial, ethnic, gender, and class divisions of labor by restructuring economies through deregulation and the recomposition of labor.

In this essay, we attempt to bring into sharper focus the question of multiculturalism's relation to the recent recoding of the American national imaginary, together with its legal and political implications. We see multiculturalism as a site where commodified global capitalism meshes with particular cultural and national formations. We draw on Berlant (1991) in the following discussion to locate multiculturalism at the meeting point of naturalization, normalization, and nationalization, the place where political estrangement and intimacy are linked. We examine in some detail the poetics of inauguration, when the state impresarios stage a significant, albeit banal, moment of convergence between the political regulation of the disembodied, abstract citizen and its popular reframing through the construction of a "national phantasy."[8] We argue that the making of a "multicultural nationalism" is an attempt by the liberal ideological apparatus to overcome the inadequacy of its existing institutions for the protection of freedom and cultural difference. Struggling with a crisis of legitimation—vide the 1992 Los Angeles insurrection—multicultural nationalism operates on the fault line between a universalism based on the notion of an abstract citizenship that at the same time systematically produces sexualized, gendered, and racialized bodies, and particularistic claims for recognition and justice by minoritized groups.

"Race," White Privilege, and U.S. National Identity

The national imaginary comes to be nourished by certain rituals and ceremonies through a historical process that Ranger and Hobsbawm (1983) have termed "the invention of tradition." Every four years the incoming president summons U.S. citizens to a fresh beginning, a new dawn. The post–cold war political context, the global expansion of communications media, and the crisis of the nation-state lent a certain significance to the inauguration of 1993. The transition from the Bush to the Clinton administration was notably marked by a politics of representation that offered a new image of national identity. The rhetoric of the successful campaign registered an emerging form of U.S. identity, one that we are calling "multicultural nationalism." The sense of distinctiveness has typically not been discussed in terms of "nation" and "nationalism," though expressions such as "American identity," "American ethnicity," and "racial formation" significantly correlate with notions of national identity, national character, and the ideological origins of U.S. identity.

U.S. identity was forged from its beginnings in the twin discourses of "nation" and "race." The ideological foundation of this nationality was a commitment to certain principles—liberty, equality, and governance on the basis of consent and identification with those principles. National identity was constructed in terms of a break from an English colonial past and, in the postrevolutionary period, the establishment of a unified government. Hobsbawm remarks, "What characterized the nation-people as seen from below was precisely that it represented the common interest against particular interests, the common good against privilege, as indeed is suggested by the term Americans used before 1800 to indicate nationhood while avoiding the word itself" (1990, 20). Whatever its representation, the nation was in fact predicated on the superiority of the "white Englishman," bearer of the values informing the new republic. There was a profound continuity in the cultural, political, and economic spheres, since white supremacist oppression in the United States was a mirror of, and had its roots in, English rule in Ireland.[9]

The organization of official nationalism has historically pivoted around establishment of racial boundaries within the framework of the nation-state. In this respect, U.S. national identity from the start has been formed and reformed in the discourse of race.[10] The later trajectory of official nationalist discourse, from the assimilatory politics of the melting pot through pleas for tolerance and respect for difference to the recent anti-immigrant backlash, has mediated between a unitary notion of U.S. identity and the quest for a hegemonic position at the onset of the postwar "American century."

Dream Logic: "On the Pulse of Morning"

At President Clinton's first inauguration, the poet Maya Angelou read her *vers d'occasion*, entitled "On the Pulse of Morning." By way of satellite relays and the new global communications media, Angelou's recital was heard by the largest poetry audience in history.[11] In American elementary and high schools, the poem achieved instant canonization, with vast sales in various editions. The poem rehearses stock themes—the "new dawn" motif, together with another quadrennial cliché, the rebirth of "the dream"—phantasies of infantile omnipotence and maternal fusion recently channeled through national networks with notorious success by Ronald Reagan.

The poem is, accordingly, constructed upon the old monument of state nationalism. Nevertheless, "On the Pulse of Morning" bears a reading not because of any poetic virtues, but because it inflects old tropes with the new discourse of multiculturalism. It officially registered, at a major ritual of state, the significant discursive shift from "melting pot" to "mosaic." Consider these verses:

There is a true yearning to respond to
The singing river and the wise Rock.
So say the Asian, the Hispanic, the Jew,
The African, the Native American, the Sioux,
The Catholic, the Muslim, the French, the Greek,
The Irish, the Rabbi, the Priest, the Sheikh,
The Gay, the Straight, the Preacher,
The privileged, the homeless, the Teacher . . .

Each of you, descendant of some passed
On traveller, has been paid for.
You, who gave me my first name, you
Pawnee, Apache, Seneca, you
Cherokee Nation, who rested with me, then
Forced on bloody feet, left me to the employment of
other seekers—desperate for gain,
Starving for gold.
You, the Turk, the Arab, the Swede, the German, the Eskimo,
   the Scot . . .
You the Ashanti, the Yoruba, the Kru, bought
Sold, stolen, arriving on a nightmare
praying for a dream.

The poem provokes questions about the implications of such a state-approved mutation in voice and subjectivity, one not readily imaginable at the Bush inauguration just four years before. Did this shift in political discourse—many years in the making—portend change in the direction of civil society? Does multiculturalism have much—or, indeed, anything—to do with redistribution of wealth and the social politics of equality? The "Western Culture" debate, the struggle over the "rainbow curriculum" in schools, and the "P.C. wars" are, to be sure, reflections of changed conditions. The narrative of American identity embodied in Western Civilization courses originated in a 1917 propaganda course at Columbia College. The aim was to turn student cadets, training for the trenches of Flanders, into "thinking bayonets." The triumphalist Eurocentric curriculum lay undisturbed in its essential Aryan features until the late 1960s, at which time the imperialist, racist, and sexist presuppositions could no longer remain tacit. The pedagogical crisis rumbles on—over textbooks, curricula, and affirmative hiring—of course without resolution.[12]

What are the structural causes of these changed conditions? What accounts for the polytonality refracted through those inaugural verses? First, the palpable presence of women and of ethnic and racial minorities in different spheres of American life—as well as the continuing challenge that minority social movements represent—have made it impossible for the establishment to maintain the old assimilationist discourse. The struggles of feminists as well as ethnic and racial minorities confront conventional notions of American national identity, exposing the different ways in which it has been shaped by sexism and racism. In response, an effort is underway within dominant institutions to recuperate the advances painfully gained during the civil rights and women's struggles and to preempt deeper change by a narrowly culturalist understanding of pluralism. Second, the current economic restructuring—namely, segmentation of the labor market and recomposition of the labor force nationally and internationally, the growth of ethnic economies, and the changing patterns of consumption—exploit ethnicity as a form of exotic "otherness." The neoimperialist cosmopolitan cultural appropriation and its potential for summoning authentic ethnicities in its masculinist nationalist reinvention more than ever creates pressure to recognize the "other" at the level of culture. Third, the growing number of ethnic and racial minorities, the demographic changes, and the effective disenfranchisement and exclusion of certain groups from civil society have had a significant impact on public policies and the electoral process.[13] Social movements and the changing demographics of postwar America have caused a number of revisions to official taxonomy, especially with respect to affirmative action. State logic is in this matter profoundly contradictory, incoherent even, since the classification is based on discrepant criteria, namely, "race," language, geography, and "country of origin."[14]

Reducing these divisions to the issue of diversity, therefore, can only work to mystify the underside of social reality. It also distracts from an engagement with the kind of pluralism that takes seriously the questions of discrimination, inequality, and social justice. Avery Gordon (1994) explores the paradox of the liberal antiracist attitude that coexists with support for racist outcomes; that is, there is a form of "liberal racism" governed by the law of an assimilationism that cannot do its work without diversity. Gordon notes the phenomenon of "diversity management," which characterizes liberal racism or neoracism; it is now a core component of the emerging "multicultural corporatism."[15]

At the same time, in a double movement, the logic of multiculturalism creates homogeneity within each culture or ethnicity, facilitating class alliances between whites and upper-class minorities to the neglect of internal complexities of identity as well as of their multiplicities (Grewal 1994). It deploys the myth of America as a nation of immigrants whose separateness can be mapped homogeneously onto their places of origin. Such a homogenized notion of community renders very problematic the matter of representation, authenticity, and exclusion. Who may speak in the name of whom? Spivak, in her discussion of this theme, notes, "Only the dominant self can be problematic; the self of the Other is authentic without a problem, naturally available to all kinds of complications. This is very frightening" (1990: 66).

Puritan Bearings: "The Gift Outright"

Notwithstanding the recuperation, it remains true that the voice of a "woman of color" at the presidential inauguration marked a sea change, not only in American political discourse but in political life. The poet's view of the "bruising darkness and wrenching pain" of American history and her inclusive vision of a nation embracing differences of ethnicity, "race," sexual preference, and religious faith signified a symbolic rupture at the level of political representation. The presence of Angelou, an African American woman, decked in a red ribbon of remembrance for those who have died of AIDS, and her multicultural America, broke from the dominant WASP ethnocentrism. Just how much of a break can be gauged by comparing "On the Pulse of Morning" with the poem read on an earlier such occasion—Robert Frost's "The Gift Outright," delivered in January 1961 at Kennedy's inauguration:

> The land was ours before we were the land's.
> She was our land more than a hundred years
> Before we were her people. She was ours
> In Massachusetts, in Virginia,
> But we were England's, still colonials,
> Possessing what we still were unpossessed by,
> Possessed by what we now no more possessed.
> Something we were withholding made us weak
> Until we found out it was ourselves
> We were withholding from our land of living,
> And forthwith found salvation in surrender.
> Such as we were we gave ourselves outright
> (The deed of gift was many deeds of war)
> To the land vaguely realizing westward,
> But still unstoried, artless, unenhanced,
> Such as she was, such as she would become.[16]

This New England poet's imagination conjured a land without people, inducing a national act of amnesia, a savage forgetting of several millennia of indigenous inhabitancy. Frost then smoothly composes possession of the land—in reality, its brutal dispossession.[17] The structure of memory in "The Gift Outright" mirrors the construction of "whiteness" in America and the creation of a "people without history" resident in a land likewise without history.

The idea of an empty wilderness, free of inhabitants, was, of course, a very congenial myth to the invading Puritans.[18] Some gift, indeed. The structure of the Puritan wilderness myth conforms to the logic of a dichotomized, gendered opposition between nature and civilization. It has continued to structure contemporary ideologies of, and attitudes toward, the natural.[19] For example, Carleton Watkins's 1860s photographs of Yosemite coached the modern imagination of wilderness by figuring the valley as a pristine garden of Eden. Indeed, it *was* a garden, thanks to the horticulture of the Miwok, whose home it had been until lethally expropriated just before Watkins made his images.[20] The transformation of the land "such as she was . . . unstoried, artless, and unenhanced" into the land "such as she would become" takes the usurpation for granted. A poem, after all, of Western conquest. And a poem of nation making by a hegemonic "we," who only become a "people" after blood sacrifice, spilt on the soil of the new creation at its foundation.

Frost's use of the landscape memorializes an imperialist, monocultural claim over territory; Angelou depicts a landscape at once primordial and teeming with peoples. What binds together her multicultural Whitmanesque catalogue of tired travelers is a biblical invocation of rock, river, and tree and the familiar Romantic nationalist trope—"Plant yourself"—purged this time of the condition of racial purity.

In the literature of nationalism there is always implicit a poetics of territory. Poems, national anthems, and novels, among other literary forms, have played their part in the hegemonization of national culture in the process of nation building. The entanglement of politics and literary practices produce what Doris Sommer (1991) has called an erotics of politics.[21] The history of poetry in the service of political powers constitutes, need one say, a dismal chapter. Most, perhaps all such effusions reproduce official consciousness. Indeed, Hans Magnus Enzensberger comes close to arguing that the only possible political poetry is one of irony and protest, because poetry cannot, without grotesque results, affirm any social power, whether of leader, party, or state. Yet much nationalist poetry has in its time been unofficial and oppositional. Often, its inspiration is the experience of place or the memory of it. It is certainly possible for such poetry to create a resonant symbolism by restructuring collective perceptions. By choosing an affective field that carries heavy, if uncrystallized, cultural freight, there remains the possibility of engagé poetry beyond mock epics or nationalist propaganda that rhymes.[22]

National Phantasy and Political Memory

Nationalism, albeit in multicultural dress, is at the heart of Angelou's poetical finessing of the dilemma of racial and ethnic harmony in America. No surprise here, really. One of the crucial missions of nationalism is the creation of a "unified community" that transcends gender, sex, "race," ethnic, and class divisions. A shared real or imagined past thus defines the present in the trajectory toward a common future. Indeed, Cornel West asserts that "America has always been a nation that looked to the future. It is a prospective nation. That is one of the reasons why we have such a limited sense of history, that we are a forward-looking nation rather than a backward-looking nation" (1993, 23). Not that there does not exist a countertradition of resistance to the national amnesia of dispossession, imperialism, and slavery; nor that the past — in the form of a fetishized constitution, the nation's ark of the covenant — is not endlessly deployed, often precisely to *foreclose* the future. The originary egalitarian mythos of the republic's foundation masks the continuity of the truly vast grants of land from the English crown. In 1700, for example, three-quarters of the territory of New York belonged to fewer than a dozen men (Parenti 1980, chap. 2).

The transcendent nature of nationalist discourse depends on a constant complementarity and reconciliation among groups with contradictory and even opposing interests and positions in society. The "unified community" of the nation requires unsleeping negotiation and renegotiation, construction and reconstruction, creation and re-creation. It works ceaselessly at the boundaries of inclusion and exclusion.[23] While Angelou's (1994) multicultural dream prompts a self-conscious awakening of America—

> But today, the Rock cries out to us, clearly, forcefully,
> come, you may stand upon my
> back and face your distant destiny,
> But seek no haven in my shadow.
> I will give you no hiding place down here

—its nationalism requires the reconstruction yet again of a transcending community, a "unity of contraries"—even, in the limiting case, as Angelou euphuistically has it, of "Midas" and the "mendicant." Underneath the romantic reconciliation of a community of brothers and sisters—

> Here on the pulse of this new day
> You may have the grace to look up and out
> and into your sister's eyes and into
> your brother's face

—dramatic class, racial/ethnic, and gender inequalities continue to determine different groups' destiny, undermining the hope of, this time, a "multicultural harmony."

The nation as an imagined community is a "cultural artefact" that keeps changing and taking new forms (Anderson 1983: 4). In the case of American nationalism, it is necessary to bear in mind the hegemonic global "posture" of the United States in the post–World War II context, and the tight linkage between national discourse and its positioning internationally. In the postwar period, American national identity was defined and structured strongly by a Manichean logic and a rhetoric of "anticommunism." Since 1989, the bipolar ideological axis of national-ist discourse has been unhinged. Now there is a new America, unique and monopolar in its representation as the only imaginable social order. This new dreamland—transfiguration of the Puritans' "shining city on the hill"—promises diversity, free will, and market democracy. The need for a redefinition of American identity is occasioned not only by the absence of a communist alter ego but also by the visible presence and political significance of women, minorities, and new immigrants from third world and non-European countries. The neoconservative response to the changed conditions has been a defensive recourse to a homesick-ness for the familiar and secure Anglo conformity of the melting pot. One result has been direct attacks on the poor and on immigrants.

Liberal reaction, by contrast, has sought ways to reconstruct Ameri-can identity by incorporating a certain discourse of pluralism and multi-culturalism. The new American discourse of "color awareness" portrays a fair society that is no longer "color-blind" but conscious of the im-pact of "race" in the everyday life of America. This "color awareness" is problematic less in its attempt to register the cultural politics of dif-ference vis-à-vis the historical construction of skin color as a signifier that condenses prior systems of marks into new categories, but rather in the comfortable "racialism" that accepts the ideological assumption that race is antecedent to racial differences.

This racialist form of color awareness conforms to a politics of in-clusion based on the model of a solid core surrounded by a periphery of the marginalized and the minoritized. It enables disidentification with those thus horizontally categorized, by creating boundary effects such that a homogeneous "we" reproduces itself through the constant fabrication of "them." This double movement has allowed conserva-tive intellectuals plausibly to claim that racism can be overcome while "race" is still in force.[24] In addition, it legitimizes anti-immigrant senti-ments among those "racialized" groups who have been categorized as "citizens." The mythos of America as a land of opportunity has thus been reconstituted—the promissory society now offers not material plenty, but rather a hospitable adoptive home for all kinds of "other-ness."[25]

America as "the land of diversity" imagines itself this time as tolerant of the "others," without, however, questioning the dynamic by which "othering" proceeds in American society. The recent deployment of the categories of documented/undocumented, a variant on the old alien/native division, is an example of this continuous process of hierarchical dichotomizing. A nationalized "land" mediates between the objective presence of the state and the subjective correlative of the nation. It represents both a context for action and a source of identity.[26] Multicultural nationality has a tense relation to the model of "consensual" citizenship, in which the nation is constructed through the intentionality of freely choosing subjects. The tension derives from the fact that "consensual" citizenship is in contradiction with "birthright" citizenship (traceable to English monarchical theory and a feudal system of "natural" allegiance), since the latter produces citizenship through blood and soil, in a conflation of *jus sanguinis* and *jus soli*.

Free choice and diversity—these are the contemporary shibboleths of the liberal discursive construction of "freedom," that lodestar of American nationalism, even as it facilitates the consolidation of the power structures of the state and its massive reliance on regimes of surveillance. The story, in fact, is one of continuing incorporation of new technologies that track citizens and noncitizens, together with corresponding redefinitions of privacy and personal freedoms (Grewal 1994). This redefinition is by no means confined to the state and its apparatuses; it is central to those modern institutions that constitute the regimes of control—drawing on wartime developments in cybernetics, computation, communications, and mass psychological warfare—now vital to the processes of capitalist production, distribution, and consumption.[27]

Cultural Pluralism and Diversity: Old Remedies, New Formulation

The American propagandists and psychological warriors of the 1940s used the postwar alliance between high-technology industry and the national security state to exploit the civil reconversion of military technics. They constructed a new field of "international communications," whose implicit strategy was to facilitate the export of progress—along with the capitalist cornucopia—to the rest of the world, via the apparatus of telecommunications. This diffusionist model operated under the rubrics of "modernization" and "development"; the new nations of the postcolonial world, playing catch-up, were to be on the receiving end of the global process of democratic homogenization. Domestically, the war produced a crisis of legitimacy within the segregated military. Mutinies and other forms of resistance resulted in de jure integration at the end of World War II. At the same time, the war—because it was a global conflict—had forced recognition of the plurality of cultures and languages worldwide. American postwar diplomacy, as well as industrial and commercial corporations, had to negotiate this polycultural world. In fact, appreciation of the complexity of intercultural communication by certain anthropologists could be more or less ignored in the first flush of American cold war hegemony. Nevertheless, by the mid-1950s it had become clear that assimilationist remedies were foundering both nationally and internationally, and that "holistic" management would be needed to regulate ethnic and national identities (Mattelart 1994, 211).

During the pluralist turn, which took place at the moment of convergence between anticolonial movements and ethnic insurgency in the United States, assimilation and acculturation were problematized and rejected. A new national imaginary had to be recreated through the naturalization and normalization of ethnicity. Given the evident persistence of "ethnicity," the social process of group formation based on culture and descent was dressed in theoretical garb by liberal pluralists and applied in policy at state and federal levels.[28]

The shift from cultural pluralism to multiculturalism has roots in the emergence of the racial minority oppositional movements of the 1960s. Indeed, it is necessary to see the ways in which the new multiculturalism is continuous with the earlier discourse of cultural pluralism in dealing with what Balibar calls the "theoretical racism" of liberal democracy. The mobilizing power—of multiculturalism and its mood—has met recuperation by the state. Multiculturalism within a logic of nationalism is bound to be recuperated, and has become an important factor in politics at the national level.[29] Recuperation proceeds by using the language of the polycultural to create strategies of "coping with differences" rather than taking steps toward a radical deepening of democracy. A recuperative multiculturalism dissimulates the reality of economic inequality, political and institutional discrimination, and cultural exclusion, which cuts across the basic social divisions of gender, "race," and class. The key discursive tactic is to denature and reduce exploitation, oppression, and domination to "respect for differences." She does Hanukkah, he does Kwanza; I like sushi, you like pizza.[30] Create "diversity" and then homogenize it.

Not that liberal pluralism escaped challenge from theorists who revealed the deep connection between ethnic pluralism and "race" relations (Blauner 1972), class and systematic inequalities (Steinberg 1981), and state regulatory mechanisms and "racial formation" (Omi and Winant 1994). These political theorists rejected institutional inclusion, equality, and universality as well as an ethnicity paradigm in favor of a radical theory of politics based on both the historicity of race and ethnic relations—conquest, slavery, exploitation—and on marginality, subjectivity, and difference. The interesting linkage of historicity, marginality, and subjectivity has been explored by radical women of color in their challenge to multiple layers of oppression, in the defetishization of "community" and a constant problematization of rigid boundaries (Anzaldúa 1987; Alarcón 1990; hooks 1990). La mestiza, or the new subject of the "borderland," develops a tolerance for contradictions and ambiguity and "learns to be an Indian in Mexican culture, to be Mexican from an Anglo point of view. She learns to juggle cultures. She has a plural personality, she operates in a pluralistic mode" (Anzaldúa 1987, 79). Still, as Alarcón notes, crossing ethnic or racial boundaries does not necessarily free the subaltern or marginal woman from "violence against herself" nor from hegemonic feminist constructions of sisterhood (1989: 87–88).

Multiculturalism, Oppositional Agency, and the Politics of "Difference"

The discourse of multiculturalism and its call for political and cultural recognition and inclusion *in the framework of a nationalist ideology* therefore has fundamental limitations. It does not address the question of cultural politics and its implications for ethnic and racial minorities. It is a discourse that homogenizes ethnic groups; it refuses specificity and particularity among and within groups, dismissing the question of hybridity. The discourse of multiculturalism finesses the historicity of constructed differences globally and locally. It ignores the relationship between the construction of ethnicities in a context of colonial and postcolonial social relations, and economic and cultural imperialism.[31] Reducing unequal power relations to "tolerating others" smothers the histories of colonialism and anti-imperialism (Bannerji 1993). The genealogy of domination as a global sociocultural formation is totally occluded, glossing over complexities and connections between the politics of recognition and the politics of redistribution, which do not necessarily complement each other. In fact, in many instances, they generate different logics with contradictory subliminal dynamics (Fraser 1995). For example, "race," "sexuality," and "gender" are sites of tension between the politics of recognition and the politics of redistribution. While recognizing social differences and group identifications based on those differences, the project of deconstruction of these marking systems and their historical contingency will remain at the heart of any process of social redistribution.

For many ethnic groups the politics of difference is an urgent matter of the relationships among culture, self-representation, and practice based on identity and subjectivity. The decentralization of politics—that is, the expansion of civil society and forms of nongovernmental control of groups' politics—cannot be reconciled with a caricatured version of ethnicity, which, even though supported by ethnic elites or state policies, is nonetheless recuperative in its interpretation of multiculturalism and cultural diversity. Official multiculturalism assumes that ethnic minority communities are homogeneous and somehow represent an authentic and unified culture. It trades on and reinforces the notion of cultures as static entities with fixed boundaries. Within such a framework, all transgression, singularity of experience, and multiplicity of identities are rendered "impure," even acts of betrayal.[32] It is a framework that effaces both the "hybrid" experience of many dislocated and diasporic populations, denying the ambiguity of belonging, and also what Homi Bhabha calls a "third space," which "displaces the histories that constitute it and sets up new structures of authority, new political initiatives" (1990b, 211). All ethnic and racial minorities are subsumed under one category, denying the significance of differentiated historical experiences—from slavery to immigration, from genocide of indigenous people, to exclusionary practices vis-à-vis new immigrants. This leads not only to a distorted view of the social relations of oppression, exploitation, and domination, which cut across as well as within different ethnic and racial minorities, but also to the assimilation of culture to "diversity," which takes for granted its universalist framework. In addition, feminist and lesbian theorists in ethnicized and racialized locations have lodged persistent reminders of the impossibility of community in its masculinist notions of culture based on the desire to control women's bodies and subjectivities.

Still, there is *something* about cultural differences that is not captured by the politics of recognition. The questions of identity and difference are particularly important at this political conjuncture where the basic concepts of social democracy are being challenged as exclusionary and assimilationist. The contradictions of culture, politics, and economy were at the root of the emergence of an abstract bourgeois liberal subject disconnected from difference and positionality. It is not easy, therefore, to see how multiculturalism—produced anyway by interpellation—can oppose an uncritical and commercialized notion of culture, which uses identity and ethnicity to create subjects incessantly being reformed within market-centered ideas of empowerment and endless choice-making capacities. In this sense, multiculturalism cannot be dissociated from issues related to the right of citizenship and the process of subject formation at national and global levels. After all, both nationhood and membership in a nation-state continue to be crucial sites in the production of legitimation and hegemony. Even "global man" is a national subject.

Disturbing Harmonies: A Final Refrain

How, then, might multiculturalism be construed so as to carry it beyond the politics of recognition?[33] For a start, one would have to retain and take very seriously the concept of "difference" at all levels—individually and collectively as well as within, between, and across the cultures.[34] At the same time, reflexivity is required in order to disturb the complacency of normalized social meanings and practices. But above all, it is necessary to refuse the fork of culture, politics, and economics. Only through such a refusal is it possible to grasp the way in which multiculturalism can be both a site of nationalism and at the same time a challenge to it. Culturalist effacement of the economy or economistic erasure of culture in a climate of depoliticization leaves multiculturalism resting too easily between culture and economy.

In any working-through of the question of multiculturalism, the issues of global racism, Eurocentrism, and orientalism must be tackled head-on.[35] It would necessarily take a deconstructive direction, recognizing oppositional agency and in the same breath destabilizing the very historical contingency that gave space to such agency. The complex regimes of knowledge, power, and desire associated with identity and subjectivity mean that the periphery is a place not only of domination but also of resistance, where one moves in solidarity to erase the category colonized/colonizer (hooks, 1990). To have to struggle by working strategically within vicious and oppressive categories that one is aiming to transcend—that is the tragedy of history. By not falling into the dissimulation of difference, it is possible to recognize the full range of lived experience as the ground of practical struggle and solidarity. It is rather in the impossibility of Angelou's dream—a multicultural happy nationalism—that a countervailing multiculturalism can take on life.

Oppositional agency is not only intimately connected to a strategic politics that simultaneously resists the assimilationist and homogenizing technologies of majority groups, but also struggles for more representative social institutions within and beyond the community. A differing multiculturalism could at least open up spaces in which identities, formed in the welter of political struggles, remain supple in repertoires, not frozen or cast in official molds. A politics of difference rooted in oppositional agency could retain the power to unsettle polarities and revoke assimilation. It might even inaugurate the disruption of all phantasies of cultural homogeneity and purity, not to say the truculent avowal of identities as relations, not things.

Notes

We would like to thank Caren Kaplan, Norma Alarcón, Ben Anderson, T. J. Clark, Inderpal Grewal, Richard Lewontin, and Richard Perry for their help at various stages in the writing of this essay.

1 We draw here on Londa Schiebinger's (1993) argument on the sexual politics of breastfeeding in the context of European nation building.

2 See George Stocking (1985) for a discussion of Linnaeus in relation to the ideological context of systematics and evolutionary biology.

3 See Hollinger (1995).

4 The founding inauguration, at which the incoming president addressed both houses of Congress in the Senate, was "consciously patterned" on Hanoverian England, where the king addressed both houses in the Lords' chamber. George Washington softened the monarchist cast of this state ritual by wearing a suit of brown broadcloth. See McDonald (1994, 215).

5 Harvard has been an especially congenial home to racist biologizing, as well as honorable dissent. Years before *The Bell Curve*, Herrnstein, the pigeon

behaviorist, taught a course on the biology of crime with James Q. Wilson. The history of biological determinism is critically examined in Kamin, Lewontin, and Rose (1984).

6   In 1990, George Bush signed the Indian Arts and Crafts Act, amending a law dating from 1935 that stated that "a person must be a member of an Indian tribe to be considered an Indian artist, or those who are not members must be certified as an Indian artisan by an Indian tribe" (cited in Walkingstick 1991: 20–21). For a general account, see Jaimes (1992).

7   Raymond Williams (1976) explores the nexus of the key terms "culture" and "civilization"; Martin Bernal (1987) excavates the historical construction of racist and Eurocentric theories of civilization. Edward Said (1978, 1993) reveals the connections between culture and domination, and Ashis Nandy (1983) illuminates the psychological dynamics of colonialism.

8   This is Lauren Berlant's phrase, deployed in her discussion of Hawthorne's comprehension of America, of how he adjudicates the "overlapping but differentially articulated positions: the official and the popular; the national and the local; the rule of law and the rule of men; the collective and the individual; the citizen as abstraction and the citizen as embodied, gendered; utopia and history; memory and amnesia" (1991, 5–6). But we use "phantasy" rather than "fantasy" to give a sense of the cathexis involved in the affective process of the individual's relation to an imagined community.

9   The case for the historical links between the racial oppression in Ireland and that in the United States is persuasively argued by Theodore Allen (1994). That "race" and "whiteness" are contingent is vividly exemplified in this study, since the Irish who emigrated as bitter opponents of racial oppression were transformed into white Americans who defended it.

10   Michael Rogin's (1996) examination of the founding films of Hollywood shows how they are centrally about race. See also Shohat and Stam (1994).

11   *San Francisco Chronicle*, 22 January 1992.

12   See Boal (1990) for a review essay on this topic in the light of Martin Bernal's excavation of the racist suppression of the Afro-Asiatic roots of the culture of classical Greece in *Black Athena*. See also the special issue of *Representations* (summer 1996) on affirmative action.

13   Among the most tragic aspects of exclusionary practices is the growing disaffection of a generation of young people from many different ethnic backgrounds and their involvement in ethnocentered peer groups (criminalized as "urban gangs") as an immediate means of access to a measure of social power.

14   For a brief overview of the contradictions involved in the state's classifying system, see Orlans (1989).

15   See Kaplan (1995).

16   Robert Frost had intended to recite a different poem at the inauguration, but

it was lost at the last minute. Instead, he recited from memory "The Gift Outright," which had originally been published in the spring 1942 issue of the *Virginia Quarterly Review.* That makes "The Gift Outright," composed as the United States was poised to take control of the Pacific, another kind of war poem.

17 One early seventeenth-century document on land asserts that "savages have no particular property in any part or parcel of that country, but only a general residency there, as wild beasts have in the forests" (Miller, cited in Steinberg 1981, 14–15).

18 This is indeed a structuring discourse of imperialism in general. Pratt's (1992) study of travel and exploration literature is rich in examples of the space of colonial encounters. Bloom (1993) examines in detail the construction of "empty" Arctic space in the popular scientific mind in early twentieth-century writings; they become a form of national colonial discourse by articulating imperial phantasy, masculinist nationalism, and scientific imagination.

19 For a discussion of the political iconology of landscape, see Boal (1996).

20 The story of Yosemite and the genocide of the Miwok is recounted in Solnit (1994) and Hecht and Cockburn (1989).

21 Sommer (1991) discloses the relations between various Latin American romantic novels and patriotic historiography, directly linking this genre of writing to the history of nation building.

22 Tom Paulin (1981) recently attempted to fashion new cultural symbolism out of the ordinary experience of Irish landscape and the "green springy resistance" of the juniper: "For no one knows/if nature allowed it to grow tall/what proud grace/the juniper tree might show/that flared, once, like fire/along the hills./On this coast/it is the only/tree of freedom/to be found."

23 Even the largest nations imagine their own limits. No nation imagines itself coextensive with humankind but having boundaries with *other* nations. The whole process is not a matter of genuineness versus falsity, but of invention and reinvention (Anderson 1983). Danielle Juteau (1996) elaborates on this process; she speaks of the constituting of a *double frontière,* both external and internal.

24 Multicultural curricula have been grossly misrepresented as a threat to white cultural values by several conservatives. D'Souza's (1991) book on the politics of race and sex is a striking example.

25 Social reality, for example, institutional racism, homophobia, and economic exclusionary practices, belies the mythos. Consider, as examples, Haitian immigration policy, the barriers to gay parenting, and police harassment in the ghettoes.

26 The concept of "place," and its importance for social identities, has been

theorized by, among others, Jackson and Penrose (1993); see especially the introduction. They take note of John Agnew's observations on the mediating role of place, both in the substantive sense of a mediation between state and society and, methodologically, in bringing together geographical and sociological imaginations (Agnew & Duncan 1989).

27 See Beniger (1986) for a history of the relations among control technologies, production/consumption, and the bureaucracies of modernity; see also Boal (1995).

28 See, among others, Glazer and Moynihan (1975).

29 In Canada, for example, where it has a longer history, a series of challenges to the liberal discourse of multiculturalism has been emerging. In the Canadian context, multiculturalism as a discourse broke through both liberal individualist (in reality, Anglo-conformist) and Anglo/French "two-nation" biculturalism. Multiculturalism as official state policy was adopted by Trudeau's government in 1971, first vis-à-vis cultural and linguistic expression, though later it was given an economic rationale. From the beginning, the policy was criticized by some as the old assimilationism in ethnic dress; the question of multiculturalism only became explicitly tied to immigration policies during the debate in 1989 over the bill to create a new Department of Multiculturalism and Citizenship. The right-wing Reform Party, for example, attacked multiculturalist policy by employing such terms as "multicultural zoo" and "mosaic madness," arguing that multiculturalism lowers national standards (Abu-Laban and Stasiulis 1992). Clearly, the current backlash against multiculturalism reflects both internal demographic changes (in particular, the growth of immigration from non-European countries) and the rising temperature throughout the capitalist northern core over issues of race and immigration. It is true that the new rhetoric of multicultural nationalism—with its organizing imagery of "mosaic," "quilt," and "rainbow"—abandons the trope of the "melting pot" and the hitherto dominant discourse of assimilationist nationalism in the United States. The culturalist distancing from Bush's WASP party by the New Democrats—who in their economic and foreign policies were indistinguishable from, or worse than, their predecessors—was an important factor in Clinton's election. Gays, lesbians, women, and minorities mobilized on his behalf.

30 Liberal capitalism takes advantage of such discourses of diversity to compete in international markets. Bannerji (1993) gives the example of agriculture in Canada.

31 Theodore Allen has noted that the hallmark of the racial oppression of the Irish, the Africans, and the American Indians in its colonial origins was the reduction of "all members of the oppressed group to one undifferentiated social status, a status beneath that of any member of any social class within the colonizing population" (1994, 32).

32 For an interesting discussion of the production of "otherness-machines" in the postcolonial context, see Appiah (1992, chap. 7).

33 For an extensive discussion of multiculturalism and the politics of recognition, see Charles Taylor, in Guttman (1994).

34 A number of scholars have invoked a "critical multiculturalism" as a promising alternative; see Chicago Cultural Studies Group (1992); Hollinger (1995); McLaren (1995); and Shohat (forthcoming).

35 Shohat and Stam in their recent contribution to the debate, defetishize any appropriation of multiculturalism to a nationalist teleology, cautioning that "Virtually all countries and regions are multicultural. Egypt melds Pharaonic, Arab, Muslim, Jewish, Christian/Coptic, and Mediterranean influences; India is riotously plural in language and religion; and Mexico's 'cosmic race' mingles at least three major constellations of cultures. Nor is North American multiculturalism of recent date. 'America' began as polyglot and multicultural, speaking a myriad of languages: European, African, and Native American" (1994, 5).

"Chicana! Rican? No, Chicana Riqueña!"

Refashioning the Transnational Connection

Angie Chabram-Dernersesian

> Yo soy tu hij[a]
> de una migración . . .
> ahora regreso, Puerto Rico . . .
> por uno de tus
> muchos callejones.
>
> [I am your daughter
> of a migration . . .
> now I return, Puerto Rico . . .
> through one of your
> many passageways.][1]

Following in the tradition of alternative ethnographies that self-consciously reference situated knowledges, global travels, and the reflexive commentary of a socially constructed author-coproducer, I begin by explaining why I chose to speak about transnational identities within Chicana/o discourse in the manner described in the title. In reality, I must admit that the explanation became the essay, that this essay displaced another one referencing a transnational connection with Mexico. While it could be stated that I willfully entered into a forbidden space by seriously interrogating *why* I was expending my intellectual and physical labor in a particular manner when academia leaves one so little room for doing so, I had no way of knowing that once I elaborated the rationale, I would enter another forbidden space: an unsanctioned transnational migration within Chicana/o discourse.

I am referring to a transnational migration: Chicana Riqueña, which intersects with Mexico, which crisscrosses Chicana/os in the contemporary world order, and which should be engaged, at least considered, if the Eurocentric bent of multicultural paradigms is to be newly challenged. From within the field of Chicana/o studies, this type of interrogation is timely because Chicana/os are assuming their founding discourses in a critical fashion, as discourses that have "not only liberated us, but also gagged and disempowered many of us," to extend the language of Anzaldúa (1990, xv–xxviii). This endeavor is also relevant for a feminist theory that is deconstructive in character and "seeks to destabilize—challenge, subvert, reverse, overturn—some of the hierarchical binary oppositions . . . of western culture" (Barrett and Phillips 1992, 1) along the lines of the "local, the specific, the particular."

It is important to note that these thoughts on transnational identities[2] coalesced as I prepared to visit Los Angeles, an urban space known for its "third world" extensions, glimpse of the future, and irreverent cultural and ethnic border crossings.[3] For me, the trip to "Our Lady of" Los Angeles offers more than a delicious and much awaited escape from the heart of agribusiness and the grip of the ivory tower *al norte* (to the North)—this trip offers a connection to my past, my family, and to a strategic body/*cuerpo* foregrounded in the area: Chicana/o studies. Not surprisingly, what is examined in this entrance into the field is a particular claim to representation, for it is within this slippery territory that I labor along with many others, refashioning fractured identities and community linkages, retracing critical histories, and reconfiguring social and political geographies. Given this context, it should not come as a surprise that the autobiographical should be foregrounded within this consciously assumed inquiry turned essay, because to a large extent that's what Chicana/o studies claims to be: a self-representation, a conscious and strategic doubling of oneself and each other, a way of affecting not only the content but also the relations and politics of representation (Hall 1992, 252–59).

In this essay, I choose to register my own autobiographical impulses, the ones that complicate earlier schemes of Chicana/o identity, the ones that prefigure the kinds of transnational multicultural linkages anticipated in Chicana/o Latina/o, a problematic, yet forward-looking attempt to forge semantic linkages between the peoples and cultures of the Americas—"here and there."[4] The event that propelled me to register these autobiographical impulses was a conversation that I had while on a postdoctoral fellowship at the Chicana/o Research Center at UCLA. Shortly after having made the acquaintance of a colleague and after delivering to him the familiar Chicana/o salutation (a mode of opening up discourse around a narrative of one's origins), the colleague remarked to me, "Chicana! Riqueña? You aren't a Puerto Rican, you're a Chicana!" To be sure, this bothered me, for I had voiced my plurality as a way of formulating a connection, not a disruption. Implicit in his statement was the idea that I had to be one or the other, a Chicana or a Puerto Rican, but not both, certainly not a hybrid—hybrids aren't authentic, they have no claim to an ethnic identity (here, a fixed insular ethnicity). Implicit in the statement was the idea that I might pass for a Puerto Rican in appearance, but that no one could seriously mistake me for a Puerto Rican. At least no one who knew Puerto Ricans, no one who could really distinguish between Latina/os, no one who could identify specific Latina/o roots.

I didn't talk like a Puerto Rican, I had never lived in New York or on the Island, *everything* about me spoke Chicana! That is, a particular rendering, refashioning of Chicana/os along singular Mexican/American lines. The fact that I was raised single-handedly by a Chicana from El Paso, Texas, grew up in La Puente, California, lived in Occupied Mexico and not Occupied Boriquen; the fact that I had reconstituted myself through strategic Chicana revisions of the 1990s; the fact that I taught Chicana/o studies at Davis: all of this only served to reframe my identity within this unitary mode of Chicana/o.

Since by this I was made akin to a card-carrying Chicana, there was no question of my Chicana*ness*, no dispute about this being a problem, about being on the *inside* of that representation; hence the exclamation point. The problem was with the selected ethnic equation, the particular framing of Chicana: the Rican that intersected her, the Rican that spoke to a continuity and a difference simultaneously, the Rican that interrupted the socially acceptable polarity as well as the mode of writing Chicana/o history, experiencing Chicana subjectivity, and drawing "American" relations. In retrospect, I know I was being challenged, as other Chicanas know they are being challenged when they are called *pochas* (half-breeds) and not Mexicanas, *marxistas y feministas* and not Chicanas, and inhabitants of the *United States* of America instead of inhabitants of the other America. The one José Martí termed "Nuestra América"/"Our America" in order to retain the plural character of this geopolitical space.

Yes, I had been administered the acid test that would confirm a particular claim to authenticity, and in all honesty, this type of ethnic containment was commonplace. However, I wasn't about to masquerade as a Puerto Rican national or a Nuyorican, to engage in the business of putting on a ready-made identity the way nationalists did when they celebrated a glorious Aztec past with questionable relations to the present but neglected to map vital relations to contemporary *indígenas* or other local underrepresented ethnic groups. I was after all a Chicana Riqueña, a particular type of Chicana Riqueña, a West Coast one with a Chicana Mexicana foundation. I did not have a patent on the identity or the multiple ways of assuming this identity delivered by histories, social experiences, and human subjects. And to be fair, I wasn't being singled out; it was not as if I hadn't heard similar things about being Mexican—that I wasn't really a Mexican either because I was a second-generation Chicana, because my mother was born in El Paso, Texas, as a result of the violence associated with the Mexican Revolution.

For years I had witnessed Central Americans, Latina/os, even Spaniards/*españoles* joining the ranks of the Chicana/o movement, consciously assuming a Chicano political identity and strategically glossing over their ethnic and cultural distinctions, and being expected to do so for a chance to join in to forge an alliance—*una relación con la causa chicana/* a relationship with the Chicana/o cause. But they were not alone in this endeavor; there was already a blueprint for containing ethnic differences engraved in important documents such as in the epic poem *I am Joaquín/ yo soy joaquín*, where the speaking subject infers that la raza—mexicanos, españoles, latinos, hispanos, and Chicanos; Yaquis, Tarahumaras, Chamulas, Zapotecs, mestizos (Gonzales 1972, 39), and *indios*—are all the same because of *his* authenticating discourse of the universal Chicano (98). This masculine construction, around whose body, social location, and ideological purview these particular multiethnic constructions converge and are diluted, can be read as a "Chicano" rendition of pluralism even though it is framed within a nationalist perspective that opposes assimilation and white melting-pot-ism. Artistic representations of mestizaje, in which the Chicano/male/mestizo is framed on the one side by the conquistador and the other by the indígena, also furnished a way of containing ethnic pluralities within selected brown masculinities.

Even today this model of mestizaje presupposes a confluence, based on equal mixtures, with the Chicano as the confluence and the other two, the Indians and the españoles, as the tributaries. This type of mestizaje is the age-old political embodiment of the Mexican national who has traditionally occupied this central space and is the subject of contention by many indígenas for whom mestizaje means inequality, a concerted dilution of Indianness, and partnership with the Mexican state. Yet, this "native" multiculturalism has been widely circulated among writers of Mexican descent. As Rosaura Sánchez points out, "Writers such as Octavio Paz and Carlos Fuentes have made a fetish of mestizaje, attributing to this notion essentialist monocausality to explain Mexican identity and history." She explains:

> "From this we are to understand that the struggle between warring Spanish conquistadores and hermetic, stoic Indians is ongoing in the blood of all Mexicans, a mixture that explains not only the contradictory national character but even problems in socio-economic development. Mestizaje then serves all too conveniently to explain away a multitude of economic, political, and social sins. The manipulation of essentialist discourses like mestizaje is thus another hegemonic strategy which we need to disarticulate and reject, just as in the U.S., notions such as the "meltingpot" of American culture need to be debunked. (Sanchez, forthcoming, 17)

Far from rejecting these ideas around mestizaje, many Chicana/o writers have privileged these ideas within essentialist discourses, "unwittingly perhaps repeating Mexican hegemonic discourses which have become, to a degree at least, part of the dominant political rhetoric there [Mexico] and served to distort and obfuscate the oppression and exploitation of thousands of Mexican Indians."[5]

For those seeking to reference the contemporary social realities and new ethnicities that mark a fully transculturated context, this type of native multiculturalism has little to offer. Given the ethnic absolutism that marked so much of the early thinking around issues of Chicano identity and subjectivity, it is not surprising that aside from the unsatisfactory discourse of la raza, there were so few possibilities for referencing the kind of "local" transnational plurality I was reckoning with at UCLA within an already constituted body of Chicano discourse.[6] In its authoritative renditions, this discourse is largely fashioned around Mexican American limits that are generally subverted within other cultural productions registering Latino "metanarratives," that is, border movements in other geographical directions within the Americas. However, these movements often maintain the interpellated ethnicities at a comfortable distance from one another at the level of lived experience.[7] Within dominant productions, the situation is worse, since these groups are either artificially polarized or else blended into an unrecognizable "Hispanic" mass.

It is ironic that, although we live in a period that prizes the multiplicity of identities and charts border crossings with borderless critics, there should be such a marked silence around the kinds of divergent ethnic pluralities that cross gender and classed subjects within the semantic orbit of Chicana/o. So powerful is the hegemonic reach of dominant culture that fixed categories of race and ethnicity continue to shape the production of social identities within the alternative sector. Few are those who have cut through the nationalist or pluralist registers that promote an all-or-nothing approach to writing the intersections between underrepresented transnational ethnic groups and their heterogeneous social movements toward one another.

I am the first to admit that to modify this scenario in ways that do not signal complicity with the nullifying gestures of the dominant culture is to enter a territory where strategic maneuvers are required at every turn, especially given the different kinds of multicultural scenarios that are present within the transnational context and that implicate Chicana/os in contradictory ways. Yet the cost of not confronting the new ethnicities that frame Chicana/o in 1998 is very high, for it is to accept what is seemingly unacceptable from a Chicana/o studies viewpoint: that we are not only unable, but also *unwilling* to engage the social panorama, the community, the *reason* for Chicana/o representation. For even though an academic Chicano discourse may lag far behind the continual refurbishing of global transnational identities, social reality has not. It is speeding ahead as the geopolitical boundaries of this territory extend north and south in an unrelenting march toward the twenty-first century. Los Angeles has led the way in this regard. There, if anywhere, the binary structure that manages distinct cultural and ethnic groups is destabilized within the social formation by series of mixed racial and ethnic identities that speak to the wide range of possibilities that frame Chicana/o: Chicana/o African American; Chicana/o Asian American; Chicana/o Native American; Chicana/o Central American; Chicana/o Latin American; Chicana/o white; Chicana/o Middle Eastern; and the list goes on, breaking down the familiar blocks that follow the term, Chicana/o here, expanding beyond them with such configurations as Chicana/o Ukrainian, Chicana/o Armenian, Chicana/o Indian.[8]

I am referring here to our relatives, our forebears, ourselves (*a nos otros*[9]), and to the *unacknowledged* generations of the past that were silenced by the ethnic absolutism of the Mexican American binary.

Can we afford to keep us/them within an ethnic closet? How will we/they write our/their herstories and histories and draw a connection to the past? To an alternative tradition of resistance and contestation? It seems to me that we/they have no choice: we/they must break out of the prisonhouse of nationalism if we/they are to engage our/their social intersected ethnicities "on the inside." This type of dialogue about the new ethnicities within Chicana/o identities must also interrogate the very notion of ethnicity, because historically this notion does not address any number of other pluralities at work in the formation of socially constructed identities. Instead, this notion of ethnicity tends to subsume them into an essentialist frame that promotes a notion of Americanness that survives by an imaginary notion of the nation as a unified cultural community, by marginalizing, dispossessing, displacing, and forgetting other ethnicities.[10]

I do not recall this context as a way of reinscribing racialized ethnic categories as primary or as a way of reinventing the primacy of race through an acknowledgment of another hybridity: Chicana Riqueña. Neither do I seek to expand the circumference of an oppressive nationalistic mode of writing Chicana/o identity by unproblematically adding Caribbean or Central American or Latin American linkages to it or by making the fatal move into an unmarked collectivity.

This Chicana Riqueña frame is a social identity constructed through any number of experiences and discursive practices that extend beyond what is illustrated here by way of an introduction. As it is articulated here, this frame intersects with Chicana/o in any number of ways, implicating not only race and ethnicity but also gender and class. Thus, it is susceptible to competing modes of interpretation, themselves intersected. Rather than inscribing monocausality, a one-dimensional view of oppression, this construction forecasts an articulation of other intersected and overlapping categories.

I appeal to this framing of social identity as a way of opening up a discussion around "the diversity of identities within ourselves and our communities" (Sanchez), and as a way of acknowledging the transnational perspectives that must be figured into a more "diverse concept of ethnicity." I am referring to a concept of ethnicity that "is theorized through differences: the relations among and between different social groups," and that *does* recognize the role that an alternative reframing of the discourses of national origin can play in contesting the dominant notion of ethnicity, which has coupled itself "with nationalism, imperialism, racism, and the state."[11] Instead of seeking recognition of Chicana Riqueña identity through a logic of exceptionalism that targets the unique struggles for self-determination that unite Chicana/os and Puerto Ricans into an important political convergence, I appeal to the Chicana Riqueña modality because of its significance for an alternative mode of writing social identities and agencies within the larger context in which we live as we approach the year 2000 within full purview of the so-called new world order.

Within this fully transculturated reality, where newspapers forecast an unprecedented browning of specific regions (according to the U.S. Census Bureau, 36 percent of the ten million immigrants estimated in California in the next quarter-century will be Latino)[12] there is little doubt that the subordinated ethnic pluralities to which we are being partnered in daily life will be here in unprecedented numbers.[13] Nor is there doubt that these socially constructed identities will be worked out in ways that beg for a rethinking of the politics of one's location and a response/ *una respuesta*, perhaps even a refashioning of a new critical language to reference alongside, between, and throughout Chicana/o.[14] Compared to the current scenario, the largely simplified Mexican American dilemma that was the staple of a nationalist ideology that combated Anglo-Saxon purism might seem manageable enough, easily referenced and consumed, and not at all like the complex relations inscribed through the Chicana/o compounds above. However, that is only until we begin to deconstruct a state-generated *Mexican* identity; claim its absented presences: the underrepresented multiethnic communities in Mexico; voice the other intersected ethnic pluralities that link us to the *American of the Americas;* and forge our complex historical relationships to both sides of the deconstructed binary.

In my own case, I was motivated along this line of thinking not only by the heterogeneous social panorama and my unspoken circumstance, but also by the children, the ones who are well on their way to adulthood and to forging cultural and political identities. I am referring to those who live well out of the limits proscribed by early Chicana/o discourse and its traditional notions of mestizaje. In particular, I am motivated by my nieces and nephews, the sons and daughters of my brothers and sister,[15] who, like me, have counterparts with Mexican–

Puerto Rican linkages. This situation is not all that unique, it may well be the norm. While these types of social identities have not occupied a strategic place within Chicana/o discourse, there is no reason why they should not.

Given this context, there is no reason why the Puerto Rican, for instance, should be othered as *another* within this space, where historic social and ethnic intersections have been prominent at least at the symbolic level and where even the Spanish and Yankee colonizers have earned recognition. Within Chicana/o discourse, assuming a claim to representation means staking out a territory based on historical and political entitlements. This claim involves a strategy of reversal commonly activated by Chicana/os who contest exclusion within mainstream and alternative sectors. From this vantage point, the counterposition Chicana Riqueña is a response to those who would silence the pluralities marking alternative subject positions and histories. It is a counterposition to those who would suggest that the intersected Riqueña (and by extension, the intersected African American, Native American, or Asian American) was/were not there (*aquí*/here), and to the idea that their/our intersected herstories and histories—local or global—should not be written within, throughout, or across Chicana/o.

This position involves a passionate form of "talking back"—*es lanzar la palabra,* it is to throw the word back as you would throw a rock. This speech intersects with a tradition of defiance that extends beyond the dualistic limits of resistance inscribed by the ballad of the border hero which negotiates a political boundary between Mexico and the United States, and thus it incorporates an interrogation of identity formations that do not script the relations among underrepresented ethnic groups. To throw the word back in this particular case (Chicana Riqueña) can be construed as a response to the original ethnic dislocation and absolutism contained in the violent phrase: "You're not a Puerto Rican!"[16] In this particular instance, I throw the word back with an alternative mapping of an ethnic ancestry, one that I refashion here on the basis of a partial life story rendered in the tradition of the *testimonio*/testimony with the *contestación* (here, a question, answer, and contestation): "Who?"

Who has the right to deny me this ethnicity, a particular history mediated by the contemporary experiences of rupture, conquest, migration, and divorce? Who dare tell me that my first and most formative experiences with collectivity do not constitute a cultural identity

worthy of a presence and a place within a Chicana/o genealogy of difference? Who can dispute the fact that my *abuelos*/grandfathers, the
one who cut lawns in El Paso and the one who taught women on the
island, weren't both my abuelos? Who can dispute the fact that María,
who migrated from Arecibo, Puerto Rico, to Monterey, California, and
back to Arecibo, and Chavela, who migrated from Chihuahua to El
Paso, Texas, would not anticipate a kind of transnational migration that
their grandchildren would consciously assume generations later as a
way of tracing different ethnic ancestries and cultural identities denied
to them through the state-sanctioned borders of television and public
education? Those identities that complicate the Chicana Riqueña frame
many times over from other compounded spaces and transnational migrations through occupied territories that share an uneven distribution
of the wealth of the globe.

Who would erase my *tía*, my wonderful Puerto Rican aunt turned
Chicana Riqueña in the 1970s, she who modeled a Chicana/o studies
identity for me and provided a much needed path from literature to Chi-
cana/o studies? Who would censor the life histories of all those Central
Americans, Puerto Ricans, and Latina/os who are in Chicana/o studies
classes, calling themselves Chicana/os in the tradition of my tía? Those
students who live a strategic connection between different histories and
peoples, a connection that is often relegated to the private realm or the
back burner as ready-made notions of Chicana/o are rapidly consumed
within the academy.

Will these transnational migrations through Chicana/o be written?
Or will they be perceived as ripping away at the core of Chicano studies,
a domain that is being contested under the deconstructive insights of
gender and cultural studies, and where the glue that is generally accepted as "holding it all together in spite of it all" is often a specific
notion of race or ethnicity? Will the tensions that mediate political alliances and/or ruptures between Chicanas and Chicanos, Chicanas and
Chicanas, Chicana/os and Mexicana/os, Chicana/os and other Central
Americans, Latin Americans, and Caribbean groups be silenced within
the age-old multicultural discourse of Chicanos? Will we disseminate
the impression that the inherited notion of mestizaje is a "natural"
biological phenomenon and not a discourse? That this framing of the
mixture is always desirable—that it should not give way to others—
because of the existence of histories referencing shared experiences of

colonialism and imperialism, histories that also inscribe other no less important ruptures (internal divisions and unique characteristics) that are often repressed by native multiculturalisms?

Will we insist that this type of native multiculturalism is enough to usher away the tensions between "Chicana/os" "Latinos" and "Hispanos"? That it is enough to silence the tensions, between, for example, Chicana/os and those Latinos who arbitrarily dispense with this group and other groups (such as Puerto Ricans) because of their links to colonized territories and tribes and the working poor—and because the Chicana/o denomination deliberately strays from the "Hispanic" ethnic flock by attaching specific political conditions and ideological sequences to the notion of ethnic identity? Even at the cultural and linguistic levels, these groups are repeatedly impugned for their already historic "bilingual" expressions and for the fact that their particular code of Spanish is not reaccentuated by the dominant form of linguistic capital within institutions that promote the class and racial interests of a well-funded Spanish-speaking elite.

Native forms of multiculturalism often reinscribe a brown smorgasbord, and this is risky business not only when Central Americans, Latinos, Latin Americans, and Cubanos are arbitrarily mixed into the political equation that both houses and contains an unruly pan-ethnicity; multiple tensions also surface when Chicana/os are arbitrarily partnered with Mexicans along an essentialist transnational route, without consideration for the disruptive influences of history, class, race, and gender. As Rosaura Sánchez points out, "representation on the basis of national origin alone continues . . . to be unidimensional and to bracket other forms of oppression and exploitation in society." She continues: "There is an excellent antidote to this essentialist discourse, a practice that shatters all notions of collectivity or identity purely on the basis of national origin. And that practice is interactional, requiring only that one come in contact with upper-class Mexicans. It is then that the myth of a shared cultural identity goes up in smoke for Chicanos, who at that moment experience the same class-based rejection to which they are subject in the U.S." (forthcoming, 16).

By invoking these examples, I do not wish to undermine the importance of the histories of those Mexicans, Central Americans, Puerto Ricans, and Latina/os whose life histories, social conditions, and political desires converge strategically with Chicana/os, and who bring important lessons of resistance that are often ignored by nationalists who walk a more separatist and exclusionary path even while appealing to global notions of la raza. I offer these examples as a way of demonstrating the complex relations that are to be negotiated among those people that government documents loosely refer to as Hispanic, Spanish, or Latino, as if they all shared the same social, cultural, and ethnic characteristics and social interests, and as if they all sought natural coalitions with one another.

All too often, predominant multicultural paradigms sin by virtue of casting these social constituencies as homogeneous elements that encounter difference only when relating to other groups in the United States (dominant or subordinate) that are not "Spanish-speaking." This kind of faulty thinking has important repercussions because, without accounting for their differences, it is impossible to comprehend, for instance, why some Chicana Riqueña coalitions are desirable within an alternative subject position recording intersected Chicana/o political agencies while others are not. The same holds true for other Chicana/o Latina/o, Latina/o Chicana/o connections.

Marking these types of positionalities within identities is not entirely new to Chicana/o discourse, where from the very beginning lines were drawn between Chicana/os and those Mexican Americans who claimed the subordinated ethnicity and the benefits to be reaped from Chicana/o struggles and Chicana/o sufferings, but not the politics inscribed in this controversial mode of self-naming which continues to raise eyebrows. The difference is that native multiculturalisms have rarely been scrutinized, thus these amorphous essentialist constructions of race and ethnicity prevail.

If it is true that the differences among and between Chicana/os and Latina/os are commonly factored out of predominant multicultural paradigms; it is also true that within these paradigms, different ethnic groups are often cut off from the transnational context so that crucial relations among competing nation-states are factored out of the social panorama of identity formation. The result is that these groups are deprived of the vital connections that make diverse ethnic communities part of a local culture as well as globalized cultures in contact. Forging the connections outside of the proscribed limits of national culture (at home and abroad) offers the possibility of apprehending transnational and multicultural linkages that have generally gone unexplored. This approach also promises to shed light on the complexity of the unconventional narrative of ethnic ancestry contained in Paul Gilroy's eye-catching title "It Ain't Where You're From, It's Where You're At" (1991). As I see it, "where you're at" involves a necessary and oftentimes continuous reconfiguration of "where you've been."

In the case of Chicana/os, Mexicana/os, and Puerto Ricans, for instance, this is particularly relevant, especially because the nation— "where you've been"—is itself disputed. Forging viable transnational linkages within this type of social context not only involves navigating across physical, intellectual, and political borders and joining multiethnic communities over there/here—Mexico, Puerto Rico, and the other Mexico, Aztlán. This type of recovery also involves contending with the realities of conquest; with having state-sanctioned borders being crossed over you and your ancestors; with being labeled a legal or an illegal alien; and with fighting to maintain an area studies that lacks cultural capital. It also involves retaining a viable memory of another type of political geography, one that is sustained through strategic multicultural and multiethnic linkages that often go unrecognized and that must be newly articulated in order to respond to contemporary social realities.

Forging transnational linkages that operate in a dynamic manner also involves acknowledging the various forms of multiculturalism that coexist within a global culture, outside of the U.S. national context, and addressing a series of competing notions of what constitutes multiculturalism. Most multicultural readers offer little insight into these "other worlds," and even within ethnic studies there is a tendency to focus on how multiethnic populations here experience their dislocations and their strategic relocations, instead of focusing on how these human movements are also inscribed at the point of origin: the local communities, nation-states, and unofficial territories from where migration takes place. Within Chicana/o studies, a much-needed project involves looking at how different Mexican and indigenous communities have incorporated Chicana/o political agencies and modes of writing culture and reviewing how multiculturalism takes place through a transnational Mexican register that also "talks back" to Chicana/os through a Mexicana/o Chicana/o, Chicana/o Mexicana/o dialogue.

Recently, an important novel, *Paletitas de Guayaba, Guayaba Popsicles,* by Erlinda Gonzales-Berry (1991) staged some of these complexities around a female protagonist who repatriates herself to Mexico City through memory, journey, and sexual desire. She travels as a way of reclaiming her connection to her past and making sense of her present.

Rather than encountering the ready-made, unproblematic, mimetic identities furnished by movement narratives, her identity is contested at every turn. She struggles with the *pocha* or *pochita* (a female half-breed/outsider and its diminutive form, "little") stigma, activated by Mexican males who would deny her partnership with a Mexican national identity; she struggles with the *manita* stigma, activated by Chicano nationalists who interrogate her Chicananess because of regionalism, her New Mexican affiliation; and she challenges received notions of New Mexican identity for being Spanish-centered and for ignoring the necessary Mexican Chicana/o working-class connection.

In addition, she explores the sexual nuances that are attached to any number of these terms by competing masculinities (white, Mexicano, Chicano) who would rob her of her agency and reify her as a sex object. Assuming social relations within a world fractured by split identities means that she negotiates her relations with others through different subject positions, acquiring power over discourse through extensive monologues and definitions that must be rendered as a kind of pedagogy of resistance in light of the rampant ignorance about her mode of living out a Chicana/o Mexicana/o transnational experience. This also involves reformulating a number of heterosexual displacements, moving from their space into her own space, and connecting to other Mexicana subjects and icons.

Though the novel does threaten to inscribe various forms of essentialism and at times rearticulates dated notions of Chicano identity, it reverses the strategy of multicultural paradigms that speak to a Mexican ancestry only as a way of figuring a distant past from the position of the United States. In fact, all too often, the Mexican disappears quickly once the Chicana/o emerges within the annals of history. This does not occur in *Paletitas*, for the scene of the multicultural encounter is in Mexico, and the protagonist does not leave her baggage behind once she arrives—she does not instantaneously receive a new fictitious identity, and it isn't presumed that she'll be nourished in spirit automatically. She negotiates from the *inside* of a Chicana representation, and these negotiations are often painful, ironic, sarcastic, and humorous. She travels through layers of contestation, and this means responding to national dynamics, to regional dynamics, to gender dynamics, to racial dynamics, to sexual dynamics, and to the politics of the movement. Finally, it means confronting the discourse of the brown female other, the pochita, at the point of origin.

A point where one is susceptible to insult, a point where one is disrupting another hegemonic construction of national identity, from the inside, as someone who carries different traces of Mexicanness that are foreign to accepted notions of mestizaje—this is a radically different location than what is offered to Joaquín in the movement poem "I am Joaquín," for his immersion is an adaptation of a ready-made epic of Mexico's official history—it does not offer the possibility of a Mexican rejection, of someone else (otro Mexicano, for instance) talking back to him as he claims a Mexican space through various levels of mestizaje. Nor does this poem entertain the possibility of another Mexican offering a rampant distortion of who Joaquín is. This poem lacks the kinds of tension involved in making coalitions that we see in Paletitas because Joaquín's act of poetic self-constitution involves identifying with the conquerors and the conquered, and he is spared the kind of gender objectification experienced by Chicanas and Mexicanas within a national space that is notorious for its masculinist orientation. By relocating the Chicana/o subject positions into Mexico, Paletitas offers a kind of a forum, the possibility of another type of multicultural paradigm that seeks to be participatory at many levels, at least to talk back, and where speaking across difference does involve risks, contradictory processes of reterritorization, and the creation of strategic coalitions.

Gonzales-Berry's novel offers us a glimpse of the types of transnational complexity that can mark a Chicana/o Mexicana/o border crossing, and yet this is only one location from which such a transnational connection can be made. Multiple border crossings are possible outside of this kind of cultural production in everyday life, where local transnational migrations from Chicana/o to Mexicana/o and back again take place all over the Southwest, in Michigan, Chicago, and other places as well. In the Greater Sacramento area, for example, it is common to see Mexican farmworkers from specific regions in Mexico settled in Chicana/o communities, marking out separate as well as shared terrains of coexistence, of difference and similarity. The kinds of transnational linkages that they refashion in daily life in the factories, in the fields, in the barrios, and in the schools are rich, but they are far from the epic narratives that are commonplace within the founding authoritative Chicana/o discourses. Suffice it to say that these local connections rarely make their way into highly idealized native multicultural paradigms even when Mexican linkages are actively sought across transnational lines. It is even rarer to encounter alternative narratives of ethnic ancestry in Chicana/o discourse that charts transnational migrations toward multiple geopolitical sites.

The transnational migration through *Paletitas* offers an example of how one aspect of a transculturated connection can be written through an international register that reverses the terms of the old-style multiculturalism. An admittedly partial and highly interpretative glimpse of my own transnational connection to Puerto Rico offers a different example, a local example, of how another side of these connections can be articulated through a narrative of ethnic ancestry that intentionally deviates from quantifiable bilingual constructs that pretend to measure "how much one is one thing and not another" and that naïvely assume that hybrid identities necessarily operate from stable or equal mixtures of two ethnic blocs.

Drawing partially on Kobena Mercer's reinterpretation of Walter Benjamin's phrase, "I seek not so much to rearticulate the past the way it really was," but "to seize hold of a memory as it flashes up at a moment of danger."[17] I do so at this moment in which Chicana/os are being interpellated by hegemonic discourses urging them to reject immigrants (their families), at this moment in which defensive nationalistic frameworks and unsatisfactory multiculturalisms reemerge in the alternative sector as a way of countering the twin effects of capitalism and racism. However, in contrast to Mercer's account, this memory that I "seize hold of" is woven through a family history, one of the many starting points for a critical elaboration of our imagined communities and for rethinking the terms of the counterhegemonic struggles that prevail within Chicana/o.

I newly assume—take—"the word" (*retomo la palabra*) in the manner familiarized in the Chicana/o oral tradition, by stating that, in my childhood, I crossed the border many times, but not only the border to Mexico. I never traveled to Puerto Rico, but it was there, *here*, it was all around me although he, the Puerto Rican national, my father, he was not there/here. I experienced Puerto Rico from a Chicana-centered household on Eldon Street, from a working-class Chicana/o barrio of household, domestic, factory, and service workers, many of whom commuted to Los Angeles and "made ends meet" to send their children to the local Catholic school.[18] At home, the connection was there in our *pláticas* (conversation) as we revisited the historical and economic junctures that brought our parents together that fateful day in the *parque* in El Paso, Texas, and later at Fort Bliss; the connection was there as we rotated *frijoles* with *habichuelas, arroz blanco con sopa de arroz, sofrito* with *salsa mexicana,* and the connection was there as we listened to Javier Solís sing "En mi viejo San Juan" ("In My Old San Juan"). Through his tunes, he transported us once again from Mexicanness to Puerto-Ricanness with somber, passionate verses and the nostalgic desire of the immigrant who has gone to "a strange nation" but dreams of the return, of the day he will search for his love and dream once again there, in his "Old San Juan."[19]

Solís's refashioning of an island, vibrant in memory, is nourished by a contradictory *despedida* (*me voy, adiós, adiós*) and a return (*pero algún día volveré,* but one day I'll return), one that I experienced not as a Puerto Rican immigrant, but as a member of an extended family of Chicana/o Mexicana/o and Puerto Rican im/migrants. For me the song was a return, a way of contending with historical, geographical, and emotional displacements—the song was a way of making Puerto Rico present. And it *was* present beyond the nostalgia of the song, but it was present in an unusual form. It was there, coexisting, at times interrupting and intermingling, and it was spoken from the interstices of Chicana/o, irreverently recreating itself through a family narrative of Chicana/o discourse that would do for me what the Chicano movement discourse had not done and would not do.

The Puerto Rican and the Chicana were partnered in the contrasting narratives of how my parents negotiated their ethnic and political differences, in spoken memories of how the linguistic imaginations of a first-generation bilingual Chicana and a Puerto Rican migrant, whose tongue was primarily Spanish, converged, many times only to diverge.[20] The Chicana and the Riqueña were partnered in the rest home where *mis abuelos/* grandparents worked in La Puente. There grandpa, Rafael Chabrán, gave *mi hermano* by the same name, his first lessons *en literatura* by recounting the necessary *declamaciones y repeticiones,* all the while smoking his *puro cubano* and *saboreando* (tasting) the day he would return to Puerto Rico. Grandpa got his wish; he returned to Arecibo, but not before instilling in us grandchildren the desire to teach, something that we would instill in other Chicana/o subjects.

And the Chicana Riqueña narrative was reinscribed again, indelibly marked on my imagination through the narratives of divorce, the ones that are rarely talked about even as the gates of sexuality are opened wider and rupture is now preferred to continuity. I am referring to the narratives around *la ruptura/*the rupture and *la sobrevivencia/*survival, around how we would pull together and how the *vecinos*/neighbors were an integral part of the process.[21] And I am referring to all of the *mujer*-centered theories that were born at home about what this meant for a mother of four in the early 1960s, a mother who was indisputably on her own and the first in her family to bravely assume the Texas–California migration by then already in full swing in order to make her own life work on her own terms before there was a socially acceptable feminism to legitimate her path. Through her cluster of narratives, she anticipated poststructuralist dynamics, carefully marking the absence/presence dynamic, a movement of continuity and discontinuity, which marked complex negotiations with this gendered Puerto Rican ethnicity. She did so through her narrative that framed *her* cry "*Si se puede*" ("It can be done") within a Chicana Tejana imaginary that insisted it was *necessary* for women to work outside of the home, that one need not be married to survive, that one (women) could do without men if that's what one wanted to do, and that the children of divorced parents need not be juvenile delinquents, as was commonly assumed in those days.[22]

My first lesson in Chicana resistance, the most important lesson in self-fashioning, was framed around a dialogue between a Chicana and a Puerto Rican body, a body that encapsulated an individual and a collective. There she framed the contested identity with her own self-styled positioning, offering a daring and forward-looking conscious assumption of masculine and feminine roles and rendering an account of those aspects of Puerto-Ricanness that she would pass to her children. There the working-class origins, her unforgettable heroic struggle for survival, and her historic entrance into the labor force as a factory worker were counterposed with another Puerto Rican's ascending middle-class lifestyle and masculine heterosexual privilege. Yes, class and gender are definitely a part of this ethnic equation, an inescapable part of this transnational ethnic connection, and this is, of course, not the only way of encountering them within a Chicana Riqueña frame.

It does not cease to amaze me that it was *she* who nurtured a sense of Puerto-Ricanness in me—she who had all the right to be a nationalist following the purist dictates associated with this politics, for she was a Chicana without a compound, she was not mixed in my way with the Riqueña.[23] In retrospect, it occurs to me that what she presented me with throughout one of the trajectories of our lives as mother and daughter was a Chicana pedagogy: a way of knowing Puerto Rico from the inside of Chicana/o, of speaking across fractured ethnicities, and of initiating a dialogue among and between different groups.[24] As an astute community theorist, she furnished a way of giving Puerto Rico and Mexico another decisive connection, another border crossing beyond those that are naturally assumed when ethnic and cultural identities are automatically derived from the contexts of rapidly diminishing two-parent households, where both intersected ethnicities are believed to be equally represented within the immediate geopolitical space and are believed to exist outside of the socioeconomic constraints of gender. While this narrative of ethnic ancestry cannot begin to approach the kinds of political negotiations that are required when these intersections (the compound terms) are marked by political identities incorporating collective histories, specific programs for social change, and the diverse subject positions enlisted in such programs, this narrative reveals the irreverent ways in which people disrupt prevailing ethnic absolutisms and stray from the chauvinistic gateways of racial and ethnic dominance, the ones Chicana/o discourse is theoretically committed to eradicating for ourselves and for others.

If it is true, as Stuart Hall has suggested, that we live in a period of a new cultural politics that engages rather than suppresses difference and depends, in part, on the construction of new ethnic identities, then writing the repressed within Chicana/o discourse in terms that far exceed the bordered ethnicity described here by means of an illustration is entirely appropriate at this time. A contemporary refashioning of subordinated and underrepresented transnational subjects from the inside of another politics of Chicana/o offers the opportunity to renegotiate the other pluralities silenced by the Mexican American binary; to begin to really acknowledge the heterogeneous Indian communities that are contained by the PRI's[25] ideology of mestizo nationalism; to offer another ideological contestation to the state-generated metaphysics of Americaness; and to activate dynamic ways of speaking across subordinated groups, particularly African Americans, Asian Americans, Native Americans, and their subgroups—the ones that cannot be so easily avoided now that they are on the inside of representation (on the right and on the left), and not divided by walls separating the major ethnic studies departments. These walls are there to remind us that if we really engage each other, we'll be fused together and all will lose. Unfortunately, all too often the warning is unheeded: it is not uncommon that individual ethnic studies programs have more to say to Spanish, English, political science, history, or sociology departments than they do to each other.

Encountering the new ethnicities that frame Chicana/o can also be border crossings in the positive sense. Now that these ethnicities are intersecting Chicana/os in a variety of ways, we have the opportunity to reconfigure *una relación* with our *América, desde adentro/*from the inside, *desde afuera/* from the outside, *de otra manera/*in a different way, and we have the opportunity to problematize the pan-ethnic Latino essentialist identity that proposes an undifferentiated collectivity. This configuration stresses the Latin and not the indigenous identities, and nonchalantly fuses the political claim of Chicana/os by constructing it along a singular ethnic axis. Without a linguistic path to guide the strategic relations with Latino and to articulate a much-needed changing transnational project of Chicana/o, this configuration, Latino, can offer little more than a dose of brown brotherhood, and this is a highly questionable effect.

However, by examining specific intersections we can begin to answer crucial questions, such as how Chicana/o Latino expresses itself in relation to particular social, political, and historical movements and identities. Engaging in this form of multiculturalism not only involves naming a collectivity, but marking its strategic interrelations and further marking a connection with our América, that is, with our heterogeneous Chicana/o Latina/o herstories/histories, and with other histories of the Americas. At times, these histories accompany one another, at times they intersect and mix with one another, and at times they separate from one another for everyone's good.

In encouraging the refashioning of unregistered transnational migrations through Chicana/o, I appeal to the idea of *un movimiento* (a movement) because the idea is central to Chicana/o practices of resistance, which effect a number of strategic relocations through contested territories that are coded in the word Chicana/o. However, unlike many of my predecessors who are embraced as cultural gurus, I dispute the claim that we can be anywhere or anyone we want to be, that we can speak for anyone, acritically usurp anyone's position, because our ancestors traveled transnationally. We cross the border with Mexico in both directions; and we cross the border internally in any number of ways and with any number of cultural and ethnic groups. To admit that our bodies are actually crossed with multiple histories of domination that are not restricted to an original indigenous-Spanish or a Mexican-Anglo clash is positive,[26] because, after all, there are many historical and political contexts that mark our borders; there are international borders at every corner, and the corner has moved down to Central America.

The question is, how do we encounter these ethnicities within Chicana/o discourse? It is doubtful that we can encounter the new socially constructed ethnicities that intersect with Chicana/o from the founding narratives of Chicano or Latino, which tend to be universal in scope and shadow a privileged selection. It is more likely that these identities will be encountered from particular social and historical interventions, from situated knowledges, ethnographic experiences of rupture and continuity, and a complex web of political negotiations with which people inscribe their sociohistorical experiences and deliver their self-styled counternarratives. I do not think that we need to celebrate the transnational movement for its own sake. Just having a transnational identity is not something to be romanticized, or something that only we have: *everyone* in the world has one, thanks to the global culture of communications and the far-reaching grip of capitalist formations.

So the crucial question is: Whose transnational movements will we narrate in Chicana/o discourse and why? When reflecting on this question it is useful to remember what happened with NAFTA, to remember how the border was crossed by two dominant cultures without regard for many on both sides. Maybe, upon further reflecting on the symbolic value of how NAFTA was countered by the indígena women who got their own informal economy going by using the Zapatista movement to sell their own wares (thus evading the U.S. corporate move to usurp most of the benefits by displacing Japan), it will be possible to gain insight into the kinds of limits and possibilities that can be afforded by transnational movements and identities. We might begin to see that, yes, transnational movements function along contrary axes of resistance and subordination, and thus choose a path of transnational resistance that is destined to fortify us, not disempower us. For after all, like many other theorists who walk a public path among our borders, we are within range of forging a contemporary counterdiscourse.

I am referring to a counterdiscourse that is capable of contesting *many* dominant cultures, including the ones that are supported by conservative, upper-class Hispanos, Mexican Americans and Latin(o) Americans—the ones who resist being interpellated by Chicana/os and the new ethnicities they partner; who actively contest being made to share in the linguistic, social, and economic plight of *campesinos, in-*

documentados, factory workers, and their children; and who abhor the presence of a newly merged Chicana/o Latina/o and its forecasting of solidarity and more equitable gender relations. Until Latino is intersected by a political mediation inscribing particular forms of resistance, it will continue to promote confusion and unexpected border disputes and it will deprive Puerto Ricans, Central Americans, Latin Americans, and Chicana/os of a much-needed social agency that interrogates relations of power within systems that breed oppression at home and abroad through a number of social and economic intersections.

Insofar as Chicana/o studies is concerned, this is *not* to suggest that we abandon the idea of having a Chicana/o discourse or area of study, even when it appears that the job is too big and too complex and even when it is now common knowledge that Chicana/o studies can never be a home to us in the same old unproblematic mimetic way that many naïvely once thought it was when it was written "Chicano." However, Chicana/o studies must be interrogated; it cannot remain the same. Chicana/o studies has unwittingly reinforced an insular attitude by constructing its object of analysis, Chicana/os, on the basis of differences between a dominant and a subordinate group, with little in the way of mapping the vital relations to other subordinated ethnic communities. It goes without saying that this is an artificial rendition of Chicana/o subjects; in reality, people don't live in these types of compartment.

To be sure, these trends in Chicana/o studies are part of an overall strategic reaction to the way dominant culture has simultaneously diluted ethnic, racial, and political differences and privileged particular social, ethnic identities, overlooking others in the construction of national episodes and historical events that inscribe the national body or community. For a recent example of this we can turn to representations of the Los Angeles riots which continue to be constructed through a black/white overdetermination that suggests that this difference is the difference that counts, even when the visual images revealed something else.

The academic context has also had its impact on this particular construction of Chicana/o subjects. Historically, Chicana/o studies programs have been intentionally subverted by watered-down ethnic studies requirements, garden-variety multicultural programs, mainstream "Spanish for Native Speakers Programs" that edit the voices of the natives to suit the tastes of their colonial masters, and even postmodern frameworks that divorce Chicana/o studies of its political content as well as its relationship to lived Chicana/o Latina/o communities. In the worst of cases, this procedure has led to tokenism or to editing out the Chicano subject altogether in favor of a Hispanic construction with the assistance of Spanish-speaking groups vying for institutional power from the position of economic privilege and a brown rendition of whiteness.[27]

Here the promise of plurality has been revealed to be the reality not of difference, but of absence, invisibility, and repeated marginality. While the effort to reinscribe a racial, ethnic opposition to dominant culture along nationalist lines may be constructed as an act of resistance to hegemonic discourse, this is destined to fail, since this approach doesn't apprehend the nature of the pluralities that frame Chicana/o. In fact, this approach assumes that you need to confront a plurality, them, the dominant culture, with a singularity, us.[28] If the Chicana/o movement has taught us anything, it is that this is just not the case.[29] We should also be "wary of any attempt to reduce us to one identity," because as Rosaura Sánchez astutely points out, "no single subject position defines us" (Sanchez, forthcoming, 29).

Within Chicana/o studies, it is not uncommon to hear that one of the greatest threats to this area of study and praxis comes from *their* brand of multiculturalism, the one that circulates within the institutions of dominant culture. If this is true, then there is no doubt that a political refashioning of our own viable pluralities "on the inside and next door" is one of the most valuable and most important endeavors that can be undertaken. For what we would be doing is none other than providing the basis for a counterhegemonic mode of plurality and difference, one that doesn't cancel us out, one that engages us from every corner, and one can settle the score with those who would deprive us of a global representation.

One of the premises behind multiculturalism is that this configuration involves a mixture on the outside of us, that it is something that is not inside. Therefore, it is not uncommon to hear university administrators counterpose their culturally dominant multiculturalism with particular ethnic studies programs and even to assume an attitude while doing so, an attitude that signals a desire for an expanse of territory. The territory of these programs is claimed under the erroneous assumption that because they don't have the plural inside them, and because they won't relinquish their singular underrepresented ethnic identity, then they need someone else to come in and do it for them, to forge global relations that look like the world does: intersected and not polarized.[30]

This line of thinking is plagued with faulty assumptions, although the maneuvers are skillful and this U.S. construction of multicultural-ism does target weak spots. To begin with, Chicana/o does engage plu-ralities, it engages them at the very core within the social formation, even though this worldliness has never been able to fully acquire its potential as a counterhegemonic force within Chicana/o discourse and successfully expose and destabilize the real subtext of the hegemonic multicultural discourse. I am referring to the subtext that says that "we are all the same" so it doesn't matter if we are fused into "them." In-scribing an alternative form of transnational multiculturalism within the core of Chicana/o studies means fortifying these sites of study and practice in ways that are unusual, for it means further extending the scope of one's analysis, countering our presumed singularity with our historically verifiable pluralities, the ones that are intersected and do engage positions from diverse fields of contestation.

And, as I pointed out earlier, this counterhegemonic multiculturalism won't be encountered readily, nor in a vacuum, but will develop from the heterogeneous social, political, and historical contexts in which we live, and from the diverse subject positions and linguistic markers that we have developed in our progressive movement toward self-representa-tion and social reform.[31] This not only entails looking forward to an ethnically transformed region/America, but looking backward, too.

Seeing what happened to the ethnic pluralities within Chicana/o dis-course, asking whether the Mexican American binary really ever had the power to make our/their other social identities fully disappear, and armed with the belief that they hadn't, I returned to early Chicano texts and found many references to other subordinated ethnic groups, even among the most nationalistic of documents.[32] Other social groups were there, but they were canceled out through a language of difference that stressed racial, cultural, and ethnic similarities among Chicanos and differences between this group and all others. There was no way to cross this "unbridgeable binary."[33] Within such a structure, how could we encounter the differences among Chicana/os and the similarities they shared with other subordinate groups whose lives they would affect? It was impossible to do so.

This is why the project of critical cultural studies must be complemented with a timely and much needed rearticulation of the varied social relations that produce these heterogeneous social identities. These relations give way to new intersections between Chicana/os and other groups that can be apprehended through competing social registers and different historical epochs. This endeavor is not marginal or secondary to Chicana/o studies, it is fundamental to the survival of this area studies, for at this particular juncture, Chicana/o studies need not be bound by fixed categories or histories, the fictitious categories of oneself and others, the limits of traditional disciplines and multicultural frameworks. Chicana/o studies need not be bound by unchanging intellectual and political requirements or the logic of capitalist, patriarchal, and heterosexist reproduction.

As many of us see it, Chicana/o studies breaks with the equivalence between the discipline and the nation-state, especially insofar as its draws its object of analysis from competing geopolitical sites and unofficial territories. Chicana/o studies views shifting social and ethnic borders as being central to its mode of apprehending the divergent communities that refurbish and frame Chicana/o populations. Chicana/o studies can be a border crossing between Chicana/o and other underrepresented groups, a way of speaking critically about the internal and transnational connections between Chicana/os and other peoples of the Americas.

Arriving at this type of an approach involves a significant complication of the current attempts to recognize the plurality and diversity of actors and identities at play in contemporary politics in a period in which many of our cultural studies practitioners are also working against what Kobena Mercer calls "the race, class and gender mantra" (Mercer 1992, 425–26). According to Mercer, this line of thinking posits that "serial acknowledgment of various sources of identity" is "sufficient for an understanding of how different identities get articulated into a common project or don't" (442).

We also face the effective limitations of the current rhetorical strategies in which identities are articulated and the challenge "to go beyond the atomistic and essentialist logic of 'identity politics' in which differences are dealt with only one-at-a-time." This logic ignores "the conflicts and contradictions that arise in the relations *within* and *between* the various movements, agents, and actors in the contemporary forms of democratic antagonism" (Mercer 1992, 425). However partial our responses are to this incredible challenge at this time, we also count on a powerful legacy that inscribes a notion of dramatic change and intellectual growth, community linkages that are fashioning paths where academic and nationalistic roadblocks still prevail, and an area studies that has blossomed and yet managed to retain the notion of intellectual growth premised on collaborative perspectives.

At this time, it is ludicrous to imagine that these challenges will be met only by Chicana/o studies—that our transnational identities won't also be refashioned through women's studies, Native American studies, Latin American studies, Latina/o studies, Puerto Rican studies, cultural studies, Asian American studies, gay and lesbian studies, and/or other geopolitical sites outside the academy where alternative knowledges have emerged and promise to emerge. Considering the impact that the cultural and ethnic discourses of Chicana/o studies have had on the politics of Chicana/o representation, considering the rhetorical and practical frames that have relimited many of the grassroots struggles for Chicana/o studies departments and programs, and considering the way Mexicans are now being targeted by a conservative agenda, this is a strategic location from which to refashion a transnational connection to ourselves and one another and from which to widen imagined communities and spheres of contestation.

It is in this vein that I posit that by expanding the horizons, Chicana/o studies can subvert the question mark after the Rican and replace it with an exclamation point—a marker signaling how it is possible to struggle *beyond* the quandary of biculturalism, *beyond* the crossroads of two discordant cultures, and how it is possible to arrive at "yet another border generation and a different pattern of migration and settlement,"[34] to the point of the repressed: the silenced and the discarded we's that we are.

Juan Flores suggests that Puerto Rican culture today is a culture of commuting, a back-and-forth transfer. Chicana Riqueña is then a refashioning of a transnational connection. It takes us from the Mexican to the Chicana/o, from the Puerto Rican to the Nuyorican to the Los Angeles Rican back again through other sites of "mutually intruding differences" (J. Flores 1992, 201), to those sites that are occupied by people whose lives hang on the hooks of the question marks ¿allá, acá? there? here?[35] This is but a rearticulation of the other territories that are there to reclaim, for these are spaces between us, from where we draw borders, from where we speak to one another and struggle, and from where we migrate, commuting across transnational and multiethnic communities and cultural frameworks, refashioning a connection to our/nuestra América from this side of the political spectrum.

Notes

A mi mamá, Angelina "Lita" Gonzalez Chabram, otherwise known as Angie, á quien se lo debo todo.

1   This was inspired in "Nuyorican," by Tato Laviera, AmeRícan, and quoted by Juan Flores in "Cortijo's Revenge: New Mappings of Puerto Rican Culture," *On Edge* edited George Yúdice, Jean Franco, and Juan Flores.

2   Cultural studies critics have called for "transnational perspectives" from different contexts and intellectual traditions. See Mercer (1992) for an example of the usage of this concept in the black context; Yúdice, Franco, and Flores (1992) for the Latin American context; and a forthcoming version of Rosaura Sánchez's pivotal essay, "The Politics of Representation in Chicana/o Literature."

3   I would like to thank Raymond Rocco for offering me the opportunity to present these ideas at UCLA.

4   A critical examination of these kinds of transnational linkages can destabilize traditional multicultural constructions that revisit melting pot theories of assimilation in an effort to ward off a presumed "tribalism" or that apprehend ethnic difference through simplified relations between dominant and subordinate groups without accounting for the differences between them or for the complex ways they negotiate these differences in daily life.

5   Sánchez posits this in relation to the essentialist discourse that prevails around mestizaje: "It is the discourse of mestizaje that is fetishistic because it posits the existence of a particular identity, a particular human nature based as much on blood lines as on posited cultural practices of past modes of production. Blood is posited as a carrier of cultural material which allows one to view the world in a particular way." But she also posits that "self-representation on the basis of mestizaje and language, if viewed historically and dialectically rather than in an essentialist fashion, can undoubtedly play a counter-hegemonic role in a country where the discourse of color and origin have been instrumental in our oppression and exploitation" (forthcoming, 17–18). Unfortunately, this dialectical view of mestizaje is rare in Chicana/o discourse, where revisionist notions of José Vasconcelos's *La Raza Cósmica* predominate.

6   It is important to note that other types of transnational perspectives, other than the ones examined here, inscribed resistance through a political contestation aimed at curbing the effects of capitalism and racism. I am re-

ferring to the grassroots movements that incorporated Fidel Castro, Frantz Fanon, and Che Guevara in an effort to formulate alliances with third world liberation movements. This political current in Chicana/o representation did break away from the ethnic absolutism of nationalism but it did not emerge as the authoritative discourse. This current rarely incorporated issues of gender although there were third world feminist movements that did. Finally, these movements often undermined the reality of local ethnic intersections in Aztlan (other than the cases examined here).

7   One of the few journals that initiated a move against this grain and to popularize the Chicano Riqueña connection was *Revista Chicano Riqueña,* which offered an important comparative approach, fashioning a transnational objective across "Latino" borders. The journal offered "a cross section of opinion through poetry, prose, and graphics of Latinos throughout the country who proclaim their cultural heritage, examine their lives in the cities and towns where they reside, and further enliven the telling of our historical presence." In an important issue, the editors clarify that the journal looks at the United States "from the perspective of the literature of the Latino minorities," taking positions "on our status in the U.S.A." They explicitly mentioned the heterogeneous populations affected by this circumstance, populations such as Chicanos, Mexicanos, Puerto Ricans, Cubans, Dominicans, and other Latinos living in the United States (Kanellos and Dávila 1971, 1–2).

As a response to mainstream celebrations of the bicentennial, the editors elaborate that the *Revista Chicano Riqueña* serve as a forum "for clarifying the historical past, for proclaiming our cultural heritage," in a context where "our ancestors experienced the loss of their lands and patrimony, the invasion of their islands, massive forced migrations and even the flagrant imposition of colonial rule" (1).

While *Revista Chicano Riqueña* anticipated an important transnational coalition that disrupts Mexican American limits and offered a forum where a cross-cultural dialogue can be forged by bringing Chicanos and Puerto Ricans together, this type of an articulation necessarily inscribes the types of hybrid identities examined here that count with a number of "internal" mixtures. These identities are intersected not only by histories of colonialism, but also by the dictates of gender and work in the so-called new world order.

8   It is not my intention to furnish a comprehensive list of the mixtures or to suggest that all of these mixtures will be equally represented in a contested Chicana/o Latina/o identity formation that counters the hegemonic practices of dominant culture. Undoubtedly, the diverse social, historical, and geographical contexts in which these identities are produced will deter-

mine how these new ethnicities are refashioned across different social registers. However, it is important to call attention to the problematic nature of these intersected identities as they are commonly scripted through the denominations Chicana/o Asian American, Chicana/o Latin American, Chicana/o African American, according to the familiar groupings. As Hollinger (1992) has argued elsewhere, this move threatens to reinscribe an essentialist frame in that it refers to blocks of people and these blocks erase the diversity among the subgroups that comprise the block. By appealing to the Chicana Riqueña frame in this paper, I am targeting an internal diversity, offering a breakdown of the block. Hollinger (1992) offers a conservative approach to the topic.

9   In Spanish, the first-person plural, but here it is deliberately scripted as "us others."

10   I have elaborated my critique on the basis of the insights delivered by Stuart Hall (1992), Rosaura Sánchez (forthcoming), and Paul Gilroy (1992). Hall explains: "I am familiar with all of the dangers of 'ethnicity' as a concept and have written myself about the fact that ethnicity, in the form of a culturally constructed sense of Englishness and a particularly closed, exclusive and regressive form of English national identity, is one of the core characteristics of British racism today" (47). Sánchez points out that "the discourse of ethnicity may in some cases be a way of sidestepping the more problematic discourses of race and class since the term is all-encompassing, used now as much to refer to European immigrant groups as to all underrepresented minorities" (16). Gilroy adds another viewpoint by discussing how certain absolutist notions of ethnicity mask racism: "We increasingly face a racism which avoids being recognized as such because it is able to link 'race' with nationhood, patriotism and nationalism, a racism which has taken a necessary distance from crude ideas of biological inferiority and superiority and now seeks to present an imaginary definition of the nation as a unified cultural community" (53).

Notwithstanding his critique, Hall calls for a new contestation over the term ethnicity, a contestation that involves a retheorizing of difference, a more diverse concept of ethnicity—an ethnicity of the margins, of the periphery, which is not doomed to survive by marginalizing. He advocates splitting away from the dominant notion, which connects it to nation and race (257–58). Sánchez responds to this second characterization with: "Hall suggests contestation on the basis of ethnicity, devoid of its connections to race and nation and linked to the concept of marginality or peripheralization, a discourse that would build on diversity and difference. Hall's proposal then for 'freeing' ethnicity of its of its racial and third world connotations fits in well with other models . . . which advocate positing constructs of difference, otherness, diversity and pluralism as the basis for the creation of counterhegemonic affinity groups. My problem with these proposals is that they displace exploitation and cleverly conceal class stratification. In fact these spatial models of periphery and marginality do not really constitute a threat to hegemonic discourses or to the dominant social and political structures of society" (20–21). Sánchez's discussion of Hall deserves further attention than what can be rendered here, and it is not limited to a critique of this notion of ethnicity.

11 I have revised Stuart Hall (1992) here according to the conditions of the context in which I work.

12 "Increasing Diversity in California," *Sacramento Bee*, 20 April 1994, B4.

13 In response to the projected increase in Latino immigration, the governor of California launched Proposition 187, which sharply curtailed immigrant rights. Recently, he supported Proposition 227, a measure that won and effectively ends bilingual education in California schools. On the heels of this victory his key backers also supported a movement to "review" ethnic studies programs at the University of California.

14 Raymond Rocco's description of the communities surrounding the urban core of Los Angeles is in this sense instructive:

In the area immediately surrounding the urban core . . . to the west, only a few blocks from the financial district, the Pico-Union area has been completely transformed into a Central American environment. Further to the south, around Figueroa and Martin Luther King Boulevards, neighborhoods have entire blocks populated by Mexican and Central American families. To the southeast are the cities of Huntington Park and South Gate, which went from being 4 percent Latino in 1960 to 90 percent in 1990. And of course to the east is the oldest and largest barrio of East Los Angeles, and to the northeast the Lincoln Heights and Highland Park areas are over 70 percent Latino. Colombian communities have been established in neighborhoods around the corners of Third Street and Vermont Avenue, as well as in South Gate, Long Beach, Huntington Park, Glendale. Cubans, Puerto Ricans, and Colombians have established a sizable presence in the Echo Park and Silverlake area, as well as immediately adjacent to Pico-Union. (1990, 324)

15 You know who you are, Missy, Rhonda, Marissa, Rafael, Paco, and Gabriel.

16 I am very well aware that many Nuyoricans hear this upon returning to the island.

17 Mercer (1992, 427) quotes Walter Benjamin's phrase [1940].

18 This is my interpretation of the order of things and it is but one of my interpretations. My account does not pretend to be mimetic and it does not necessarily apply to anyone else. I do not pretend to speak for any other

family members, in recognition of the fact that they have their own memories of our imagined communities and their own rich ways of giving these communities style within discourse.

19 Javier Solís, "En mi viejo San Juan," on *Sombras,* audiotape, Caytonics, CBS Int'l, n.d. The song was written by Noel Estrada.

20 Such as the times my mamá would say "Hi there" to her male friends and my papa would hear "Hi dear."

21 I take this opportunity to thank these neighbors on Eldon Street for their support.

22 This page was discussed with her, but this is my construction and any economic gain that comes from this essay will go to her. There are many twists to this narrative that I will keep to ourselves, in the tradition of Rigoberta.

23 It was as much a question of solidarity with my mother as it was the constraints of Chicano discourse that delayed my arrival to this type of a Chicana Riqueña intervention. But she taught me that I could transgress that particular ethnic border, that I could encounter a collective not bound by the same decisive ruptures, and that to do so was not a betrayal of my Mexicanness, my Chicananess, but rather an affirmation of their permeable borders. And at age sixty-five-plus, she paved the way for me, when she finally boarded a plane and reclaimed *her* Puerto Rican relatives, met the extended family, and gave her received memories of Puerto Rico definitive forms, visual images. She even began her own self-styled migration to Puerto Rico. Without my mother's historic revisions, my own subsequent trips to Puerto Rico would have been something quite different from what they turned out to be: part of a culturally decisive experience.

24 Certainly this is not the only way to dialogue across ethnic borders, and I do not mean to suggest that it is the way for all of us.

25 The Partido Revolucionario Institucional, Mexico's dominant political party.

26 *Encontronazo* is a term that contests the friendly multicultural encounter that is often used to describe Columbus and his conquest.

27 Kobena Mercer's proposal that "cultural difference was used as a means of fragmenting the emergence of a collective black identity" is valid for Chicana/os even today. It is not uncommon for university administrators to deconstruct nationalist paradigms as a way of collapsing these programs and underfunding them.

28 By grouping all members of this racial and ethnic opposition under the term "us" I wish to point out the contradiction in this line of thinking.

29 It is common knowledge that it was the pluralities that gave the struggle its power—the strategically placed alliances with other political movements, third world liberation movements, the black civil rights movements, the coalitions among Mexicans, and the feminist movement, for example. How-

ever, the "pluralities" within Chicana/o bodies were often repressed, as race took precedence over class and gender and Chicana/os were constructed according to masculine collectives.

30 The *encargado*/one in charge is generally someone who proposes to create an identity, a mode of multiculturalism, that no one can identify as being uniquely anyone's.

31 I have taken this idea of what I see as a critical genealogy from Mercer's retrospective discussion of 1968.

32 See, for example, Armando Rendon's *The Chicano Manifesto* (1972). I discuss this topic in an essay entitled, "Out of the Labyrinth, Into the Race," which will appear in an issue of *Cultural Studies* entitled "Chicana/o Cultural Studies: Transnational and Transdisciplinary Possibilities."

33 For a discussion of how these binaries are constructed through the black context, see Mercer (1992).

34 I am rephrasing and revising a point made by Juan Flores (1992, 201) in order to accommodate this third space of ethnic identification.

35 This is a point quoted by Juan Flores from Luis Rafael Flores's "Air Bus," in Yúdice, Franco, and Flores (1992, 201).

Fabricating Masculinity:

Gender, Race, and Nation in a Transnational Frame

Dorinne Kondo

Concerns with the national and the transnational have been refrains in Japan of late, taking the form in the 1980s of a preoccupation with "Japanese identity" and "internationalization." Japan's historical positioning fostered assertions of a new Japanese confidence and a burgeoning nationalism commensurate with Japan's status as an economic superpower, a "Japan that can say no" (Ishihara 1991). In the Japanese case, the popularity of so-called *kokusaika* (internationalization) ideology in the 1980s is arguably of a piece with the rise of neonationalism. Preoccupations with internationalization, in fact, often simultaneously reinscribed the discourse called *Nihonjinron*, "the master narrative celebrating Japanese uniqueness" (Yoshimoto 1989, 22), in which an ineffable Japanese essence inaccessible to foreigners ultimately grounds claims to Japanese economic and political superiority. Here, as is often the case, nationalism and transnationalism can operate dialectically, as mutually interdependent discourses.

This essay examines the complex intersections of nationalism/transnationalism with the forces of gender and class, through what might initially seem an unlikely site for the articulation of geopolitical concerns: an ad campaign mounted by Comme des Garçons, an internationally successful, critically acclaimed avant-gardist high-fashion house, for their domestic line of menswear called "the Japanese Suit." The campaign intricately, boldly interweaves history, nationhood, and masculinity through its invocation of a *Japanese* aesthetic sensibility, a *Japanese* masculine body, and Japan's present historical position in the world, culminating in the need for Comme des Garçons's especially "Japanese" suit. These ads directly confront geopolitical histories of defeat and "inferiority" vis-à-vis "the West," symbolized by the "demasculinization" and de-eroticizing of Japanese men, and they skillfully elide histories of Japan's militarization and evoke nostalgia for both British and Japanese empire. The Japanese Suit eloquently writes the complexity of Japan's positioning at a transitional historical moment, as a first world, capitalist power with an imperialist history and thinly veiled neoimperial fantasies, that is nonetheless racially marked and orientalized.

Comme des Garçons mobilizes and amplifies the circulating discourses of Nihonjinron,[1] Orientalism, internationalism, and neonationalism, inescapably foregrounding these constitutive contradictions animating Japanese identity. Given a history of penetration by the West, ongoing racism in Japan-U.S. interactions, and the continued circulation of orientalist tropes, the problematic invocation of Nihonjinron also becomes an appropriation of orientalist discourse to combat racial marking—for thoroughly commodified ends. In so doing, the ads deploy strategies that are premised on the creation of consumer-subjects, the provocation of neoimperialist and nationalist fantasies, the gendering of abjection as feminine, elitist class distinctions, and the reinscription of highly problematic, even dangerous essentialisms.

Further contradictions emerge when we consider multiple contexts of reception, for given an Asian American subject position, the ad copy can also stir deep feelings about Asian American/Asian bodies, highlighting the importance of clothing as a medium for fashioning gendered, raced identities. In its skillful mobilization of history, politics, and the geopolitical histories of specific bodies, the Japanese Suit campaign serves as a point of entry into gender, race, nation, and the transnational, in which the tensions between nationalism and transnationalism are materially embodied in its figuration of masculine subjects.

Consuming Subjects

Within our regime of commodity capitalism, it is hardly surprising to find powerful articulations of identity in advertising, the domain whose business is the creation of idealized objects of desire. Designed specifically to promote identification and provoke object lust, consciously deploying techniques to pull on issues resonant for their audience, advertisements—and particularly fashion advertisements—become privileged sites for the examination of subject formation.[2]

It is equally fitting that the imbrications of masculinity with nationalism, race, and class would be so eloquently elaborated in a campaign for men's suits. Suits have a long history of fabricating class-inflected masculinities in the West. For example, Anne Hollander outlines their development in Britain and France, arguing that suits articulated idealized masculine images represented most strikingly in the model of the classic Greek nude. Garments became sites where social transformations appeared in material form; for example, at the turn of the nineteenth century, men's garments and the masculine ideal shifted from "courtly refinement to natural simplicity" (1994, 90), as they changed from aristocratic decoration to a more sober silhouette, incorporating motifs from multiple sources variously marked with respect to class, including the garments of the French sans-culottes and the wardrobe of English country gentlemen. Hollander vividly details the complexities of subject formation revealed in the suit:

> The modern masculine image was thus virtually in place by 1820, and it has been only slightly modified since. The modern suit has provided so perfect a visualization of modern male pride that it has so far not needed replacement, and it has gradually provided the standard costume of civil leadership for the whole world. The masculine suit now suggests probity and restraint, prudence and detachment; but under these enlightened virtues also seethe its hunting, laboring, and revolutionary origins; and therefore the suit still remains sexually potent and more than a little menacing . . . they remain one true mirror of modern male self-esteem. (55)

Clearly, then, suits provide an exemplary site for our examination of the interweavings of aesthetics, politics, class, nation, sexuality, and masculinity.[3]

Comme des Garçons, Homme Deux, and "the Japanese Suit"

To comprehend more fully the arresting character of the Japanese Suit campaign requires an understanding of Comme des Garçons' location in the landscape of Japanese and international high fashion. In the early 1980s, Comme des Garçons created a sensation with the showings of their first Paris collections. Head designer Rei Kawakubo, along with Yohji Yamamoto and Issey Miyake, are the Japanese designers who did much to set the global fashion aesthetic of this period: loose cuts, asymmetry, the predominance of black. These three tend to be grouped together under the sign of national essence and are generally considered in the industry to be "experimental," architectural, artistic, avant-garde. For example, commentators often trace the origins of their design principles to "traditional" Japanese aesthetics and simultaneously note their penchant for the latest in technological innovation, particularly in terms of experimenting with innovative fabrics. Here, two orientalist tropes—the Orient as aesthetic and Orient as high-tech virtuoso—come together. Each design house has its own particular emphasis, however. Miyake is known for his otherworldly museum pieces and artistic creations, as well as a recent emphasis on pleats, in the style of Fortuny.[4] Yamamoto, the son of a dressmaker, is perhaps the most attuned to tailoring of the three, and consequently, some of his cuts could be labeled the most conventionally elegant. He aspires to create nouvelle couture, a new kind of made-to-order clothing. Comme des Garçons' Rei Kawakubo is the sole woman, and she is both chief designer and head of the company. Her work is striking for its uncompromising use of asymmetry, unusual fabrication, and "deconstructive" elements: a suit jacket for women consisting only of lapels, for example, or dresses that possess multiple openings through which the wearer could put her head or her arms, thus changing the configuration of the dress. All three designers could be said to have provided different possibilities for figuring gender, especially in the early 1980s (see Kondo 1997). Within the limited and elitist domain of high fashion, the work of Comme des Garçons and the other Japanese designers made significant interventions, blurring the boundaries between fashion and architecture, fashion and sculpture; refiguring class-inflected gender in garments clearly made for someone other than the soignée woman of classic elegance; challenging clothing conventions and forcing a reconsideration of what counts as clothing. Their challenge, moreover, is inevitably a racialized one, given a racialized reception in the West. Their garments tend to accommodate different kinds of racialized bodies, beginning with shape, fabric, and concept rather than with (Western) ideals of the feminine form or feminine beauty. Indeed, Kawakubo averred to me in an interview that the notion of "a woman's beauty" had never once crossed her mind.

Furthermore, it is also true that the Japanese designers are aware of, and must play on, a field that is not "theirs," a reality that its designation in Japanese makes indisputably clear: *yofuku*, Western clothing, as opposed to *wafuku*, Japanese clothing. Comme des Garçons' very name—

the adoption of a French term—itself eloquently testifies to a certain colonization of consciousness and a desire to strive for parity on someone else's ground. In fact, most Japanese design firms either adopt Western (usually French, English, or Italian) names, such as Novespazio or Oxford Quincy, or use the designer's name, but in the Western alphabet rather than with Japanese characters, and in Western word order rather than the Japanese order that gives the family name first. Indeed, having attended the Tokyo collections, it is apparent to me that by and large, the Japanese domestic fashion industry is primarily "just clothes," indistinguishable from what you might see in any Western country. Perhaps this represents appropriation and/or mimesis. In either case, the marks of a colonization of consciousness are unmistakable, in which Western models, Western clothing, Western aesthetic ideals are still enshrined.

The avant-garde, deconstructive thrust in the work of the Japanese designers, the larger political and economic context of shifting Japanese positioning, and a history of Western penetration of the national body and the colonization of consciousness delineate the field within which Comme des Garçons mounts its startling Homme Deux/ Japanese Suit campaign. The Homme Deux line is aimed at a tough, competitive domestic market for business suits that would seem to be initially resistant to inroads from high-fashion companies. It is one of many Comme des Garçons lines (e.g., Robe de Chambre, Tricot, the bridge line Comme des Garçons Comme des Garçons) that are ancillary to the central Comme des Garçons women's collections and Homme Plus for men. Homme Deux possesses several distinctive features. It combines a conservative look with elements that are unconventional in a Japanese work setting stereotypically known for its single-breasted navy blue suits and white shirts. To a Western eye, they are not recognizably high style. Aside from a slightly looser fit, a soft shoulder, and no back vents, they are not visibly different from any other tasteful, nicely tailored, rather conservative business suit. However, the lone photograph of a suit in the campaign, featured in an in-house brochure, shows a double-breasted rather than single-breasted jacket: a challenge to convention, for double-breasted jackets are not quite comme il faut in a Japanese corporate setting.[5] Second, Homme Deux is aimed at an older, more conservative market than is Homme Plus; alternatively, it can be worn by Homme Plus devotees of any age who might need to dress more conservatively at the workplace but who still want the Comme des Garçons cachet. And third, the Homme Deux advertising campaign is unprecedented in Comme des Garçons history both in terms of placement of the ads and the design of the ads themselves: the extensive use of text[6] and the adroit, aggressive use of the thematics of gender, race, and nation. The campaigns clearly aim for name recognition and market share in this untapped market for high style.

How different is this campaign from the Comme des Garçons approach to its primary lines? The firm rarely advertises its high-fashion lines in fashion magazines. If ads are placed at all, they might appear in *Artforum* or *BAM*, but almost never in *Vogue*. Each season, the boutiques in Tokyo and New York become part art gallery, displaying the work of a featured artist, including, recently, Cindy Sherman. Direct-mail postcards to Comme des Garçons customers feature this artwork and constitute another form of advertising. In 1988 Comme des Garçons developed an "image book" distributed to the fashion press and to customers, a practice shared by other "artistic" design houses such as Yohji Yamamoto and Romeo Gigli. Here, the emphasis on the allusive and the oblique is pushed to an extreme. Beautifully produced in large format, these magazines are collections of specially commissioned photographs from some of the world's best-known fashion and art photographers, foregrounding image over (absent) text. The photos are often playful visual rhymes, urban scenes, abstract compositions that often have no obvious connection to clothing as such. "Art" rather than "mere advertising," the image books encode the message that Comme des Garçons is about more than just clothes.

In contrast, the Homme Deux campaign is striking in its direct approach. Comme des Garçons has targeted its market and advertises in the equivalents of the *Wall Street Journal*, *Business Week*, and *Fortune* (e.g., *Nihon Keizai Shimbun*, *Nikkei Business*). Even more fascinating, they developed a strategy to direct advertising at women, capitalizing on the tendency of women to buy clothing for their husbands and sons. Ad copy shows well-known women as commentators on men's style, and these ads appear in the venerable *Katei Gaho*, a glossy, large-format women's magazine that represents the epitome of upscale feminine respectability.

In choosing to enter the highly competitive domestic market for men's suits, Comme des Garçons is faced with the problem of convincing Japanese men to attend more carefully to the aesthetics of appearance at the workplace. Thus, the thematics of the campaign are crucial. Having strategically targeted the venues that will reach businessmen, what better way for Comme des Garçons to pique their interest than to link clothing choice to the resonant, weighty matters of nationalism, politics, history—and masculinity?

And they do so striking fashion. I first came across the ads for the Japanese Suit as a relatively minor part of my study on Japanese designers. Looking through clippings at the Comme des Garçons office one muggy August afternoon in Tokyo, I came across an arresting page, bold black characters arrayed on stark white. Reading it, I was stunned, both seduced and compelled to read on.

THE JAPANESE SUIT
COMME DES GARÇONS HOMME DEUX IS CLOTHING FOR THE
JAPANESE BUSINESSMAN OF THE FUTURE.
IT IS THE CLOTHING FOR THE SPIRITUAL ELITE, WHO LIVE AS
PART OF A HARMONIOUS WHOLE, YET STILL POSSESS A
CLEARLY DEFINED INDIVIDUALITY BASED ON INNER
REFINEMENT.

WAKON YOSAI (JAPANESE SPIRIT AND WESTERN KNOWLEDGE)[7] expressed the Meiji man's way of life.[8] It means living by the Japanese spirit while flexibly assimilating Western civilization. Created in 1978, Comme des Garçons Homme is clothing designed to keep alive the Meiji spirit and aesthetic sensibility, carrying it into the present. This clothing appealed to the young who have no inferiority complex vis à vis the West. Since the Industrial Revolution of the 19th century, THE WORLD OF MEN'S CLOTHING possesses a history in which the world's economic and cultural leader sets world style. Isn't the timing right for Japan, now said to be a world economic power, to set forth its own distinctive style of menswear? Now, what might be the basis for this uniquely Japanese aesthetic awareness and Japanese way of living?

THE AESTHETIC SENSE OF SHIBUI (tasteful, quiet elegance) is the answer. Like the stylish flair of a man wearing a pongee kimono. This sensibility is sustained by a fundamentally Japanese aesthetic awareness and feeling for life that downplays surface showiness, concealing and refining individuality deeply within. The notion of "*bankara*" (rustic, unconventional dress) that once thrived among the students of the old high school system, is one of these expressions of *shibui*.

JAPAN is now moving and shaking IN THE WORLD. It is squarely facing numerous problems: the recession caused by the appreciation of the yen, the growth of domestic demand, the opening of markets, the limitation of exports. Perhaps there has never before been a time when we have felt so strongly that, through economics, we live as individuals within a larger world, in a Japan that is globally interconnected. What is needed in this new world are the sense of judgment and the decision-making power to clearly set forth your point of view by choosing wisely from the flood of available information.

COMME DES GARÇONS HOMME DEUX is businesswear for this historical era. Clothing that is easy to wear, tastefully elegant, not restrictive to the body. As "preppie" clothing represented the Ivy Leaguer of the American East Coast, this is the new businesswear based on the aesthetic sensibility of Japan's business elite.

The suit here becomes a site for the play of geopolitical relations between Japan and the West. The ad copy conjures a history of the suit as a material emblem of Japanese conformity and racial inferiority. Derisive jokes both within and outside Japan about Organization Men in their stodgy navy blue jackets pointedly satirize the restrictive conventions of the male business world. Historically, suits have resonated deeply with the feelings of discomfort some Japanese have felt vis-à-vis Europe and the United States. One recalls Natsume Soseki, the celebrated Meiji-period author, who writes of his sojourn in London with considerable pathos. His feelings of inferiority were embodied in his sense of looking out of place and ill at ease in Western clothing. In a searing anecdote, Soseki tells us that as he walked down the street in a frock coat and top hat, two working men derisively called out "A handsome Jap!"[9] Here, the attempt to fit into British society through adopting the proper outward accoutrements of Westernness—the frock coat and top hat—cannot disguise Soseki's racial markings.

Comme des Garçons skillfully plays upon this history of conformity, discomfort, and inferiority. Of course, the conditions for perceived "inferiority" have undergone major transformations since the Meiji period. The Japan of the 1980s was economically powerful, increasingly confident, and in many quarters, increasingly exasperated at U.S. assertions of dominance in arenas such as the ongoing trade negotiations. The dilemma of the 1980s was not one of playing catch-up, since in many economic fields Japan had assumed a position of eminence, if not preeminence. Rather, it involved combating racism and perceived unfairness, attempts to deal with the anger that American and European assumptions of superiority provoked. The ads write this dilemma: How should Japan address a complex situation of historical inferiority, shifting economic and geopolitical balances, domestic confidence, and U.S./European fear, racism, and condescension? In writing this problem, they also propose the means for its resolution: the Japanese Suit.

The campaign's catchphrase *Nihon no sebiro* engages the complexities of the changing dynamic between Japan and the West. Forgoing the more contemporary word *sutsu*, Comme des Garçons selects the nostalgic term *sebiro*, from the English Saville Row, a testament to British hegemony as world power and world trendsetter in the late nineteenth century. But it is not just any *sebiro* Comme des Garçons invokes, it is a Japanese *sebiro*. Japan has appropriated and made its own a genre of clothing originally defined as quintessentially British. Clad in such a suit, no longer will Japanese men feel out of place or inferior. The ad copy allows readers and consumers to participate in a nostalgia for the glories of empire, both British and Japanese, giving implicit license to neoimperial fantasies in which Japan displaces Britain. Indeed, say the ads, style is set by world powers, and Japan has finally joined those ranks, suggesting that Japan is Britain's proper heir.

Further, the ads deploy script styles and word choice as essentializing practices that write an ambivalent and complexly positioned Japanese identity. Take, for example, the use of loan words. It is no accident that they are primarily from English, given a constitutive history of penetration and occupation. The use of loan words indexes that relationship of historical inferiority and defeat. On the other hand, English terms have been appropriated in ways that render them Japanese. Significantly, the Saville Row of *sebiro* is written in characters that mean "back" and "broad." More common for foreign loan words is the use of the *katakana* syllabary that marks the terms as foreign; the many other English loan words sprinkled throughout the ad are rendered in the usual *katakana: bizinesuea* (business wear), *toraddo* (trad, or preppie), *bodeishieipu* (body shape), *apiru* (appeal). And of course there is the Japanicized French of the company name itself, indexing the history of French dominance in the fashion world. The liberal use of loan words endows the piece with cosmopolitan cachet, as it both gestures toward the West as center and indexes the Japanese appropriation of the West.[10] Yet, the piece carefully retains the essence of Japanese identity in its invocation of *shibui* (adjective) or of *shibusa* (noun) in Japanese characters, allowing subtle understatement to remain the distinctive feature of Japanese culture and aesthetics. Thus, the use of script and effective choice of terms gives us a Japan flexible enough to assimilate and appropriate the West, in a resynthesized identity that asserts an essential Japaneseness based in the culture of *shibusa*—a term that itself possesses eloquent double meanings. Among younger people, *shibui* signifies "hip," "cool."[11] Consequently, *shibui* as the essence of Japanese identity temporarily resolves the tradition/modernity binary, evoking both a history of subtle aestheticism *and* the vibrantly contemporary.

The subject position created here, then, is at one level oppositional to certain kinds of orientalist discourses. In combating the orientalist stereotype of the businessman as the corporate drone as well as domestic critiques of the conservatism and lack of creativity of the Organization Man, the campaign asserts a creative assimilation of the West that contests narratives of Western preeminence or Japanese imitativeness and, arguably, undermines the East/West binary. Indeed, the ad challenges stereotypes of Japanese conformity by invoking a particularly *Japanese* individuality imbued with *shibusa*. Both refined and hip, the businessman who will wear *Nihon no sebiro* is his own man. He is neither a conformist in a cheap navy blue suit and white shirt nor a wild radical incapable of getting along with others in society. His personality, his unique dispositions, are ineffably present but visible only in elegant, tasteful—yet contemporary—form. The foundation for this unique synthesis is located in the cultural essence of *shibusa*. Thus, at one level, the ads take on orientalist stereotypes while at another level engaging a self-orientalizing that reinscribes a nationalist essence based in racial difference.

The contradictions of Japanese identity at this transitional historical juncture thus permeate the text: racially marked and orientalized on the one hand, a first world power with neoimperialist ambitions on the other. The campaign highlights subtextually a history of various forms of domination by the West—the opening and penetration of Japan by Commodore Perry, defeat in World War II and the subsequent occupation and foreign intrusion into the national body, and the continuing dominance of American and European popular culture. The businessman is located within this history. The would-be consumer of *Nihon no sebiro* is a cosmopolitan man of erudition, as the frequent use of loan words would suggest. The ad also writes the potential consumer as the class equivalent of an Ivy Leaguer, possessing both the financial and cultural capital to be part of the business and government power elites in Japan. But he is also someone of a vintage who must remember the humiliations of the war and who yearns to be free of feelings of inferiority toward the West. The Japanese Suit promises to fulfill this yearning, giving the consumer the material means by which he can assume leadership on a par with the men of Meiji and the confidence of today's cosmopolitan young people. The ad campaign writes a particular subject of desire who can satisfy that desire and create a satisfying Japanese masculinity by purchasing a Japanese Suit.

The Homme Deux ads weave a compelling, skillfully constructed narrative that is, simultaneously, profoundly gendered. Japan's history of defeat and the orientalizing and racializing of the body are implicitly associated with femininity. Feminized and orientalized in his relations to the West, the businessman is given an opportunity to construct a fully masculine identity that would necessarily involve righting former geopolitical imbalances, embracing a masculinity based on strength, leadership, individuality, and intelligence. This masculinity becomes the figure defined against the ground of a passive femininity defined as defeat and penetration and subjection to domination. Becoming fully a man, then, will require dominance—a dominance attainable in a Japanese Suit.

Precisely at this point the fissures in this stirring narrative reveal themselves. Invoking the Meiji period highlights a revolutionary period of nation building in Japan, a massive mobilization in response to Western challenges. But along with nation-state formation came imperialist ambitions, and the advertisements' focus on Meiji nation building elides other imperial and colonial histories, including the "successes" of the Sino-Japanese and Russo-Japanese wars, the colonization of Korea and Taiwan, and the processes of militarization that brought Japan to the Pacific War. In the ads, parity is conceived only in terms of Japan's relation to the West. But the tacit message is that dominance equally calls up fantasies of Japanese empire as Japan takes over Britain's imperial mantle. The man who wears a Japanese Suit then will truly stand as Britain's heir.

In making such bold appeals to gendered nationalisms, Comme des Garçons attempts to address the daunting task of differentiating its product within a highly competitive market. Three different phases of the campaign illustrate three related strategies the company pursues in order to capitalize on its high-fashion cachet for a diffident, conservative consumer who may consider fashion a trivial female concern.

"Real" Men Consume Fashion

One series of ads involves testimonials from well-known critics, authors, and technological experts who thematize the links between a satisfying Japanese male identity and the world of style. Not only is it permissible for men to care about clothing, but such care is synonymous with masculinity and worldly success. One critic tells a sad tale of going to America in the immediate post–World War II period, where he suffered discrimination as a Japanese. Defeat and poverty left him poorly dressed, and he suffered further humiliation for his out-of-date garments. The vignette ends with his acquisition of a fashionable American suit, which he wears home to Japan in a triumphant return. A second writes about managerial dress, emphasizing the ways clothing reflects corporate identity: the histories, personalities, and identities of both the managers and the companies themselves. An art critic discusses East/West exchange in art, especially the popularity of Japonaiserie among the fin de siècle Impressionists and post-Impressionists. He suggests that the Japanese artists who had gone to Paris and returned to Japan at the turn of the century were fundamentally changed by the experience; they also brought Paris back with them. He ties this East/West exchange and the blurring of East/West distinctions to clothing and to the need for a suit reflecting this "blend culture." An engineer and computer specialist talks about technological innovations in the fashion industry, forecasting future developments. Fashion, these ads tell us, is for "real men."

Muramatsu Yugen, a writer and novelist, offers an especially telling vignette thematizing style as a marker of national, racial, and gender identities. In a quirky, humorous, breezy testimonial, he says:

> Now for a Japanese, the suit . . . well, this is alien territory. The Japanese were originally pros at wearing kimono, but in the span of just a hundred years, wearing Western clothes has become our common sense. Should we comment on how quickly the Japanese can transform themselves? Find it amazing to change so much in the space of a hundred years? In any case, it's indisputable that a lifestyle of European haircuts, beef, and Western clothing has firmly taken hold since Meiji.
>
> From that moment, the importation of a "Western sensibility" began. The men [of Meiji] who had been at fashion's cutting edge suc-

cessfully adapted their bodies to the demands of Western clothing. In this era these men achieved the same success with their economic endeavors. Now, if you look at their photographs—men who had only a short history of acquaintance with Western dress—you immediately notice their surprisingly fresh, stylish way of wearing the clothes. It's a strange shock to see that these Japanese men whose inner spirit was far from tranquil, whose spirit led them to do things like commit *seppuku*, were far more stylish than the men of today, who wear Western fashions in a Western way.

Maybe there's an important hint here for the men who live in today's so-called fashion era. If you think about body type [of the Japanese], I sense the possibility of a style that reaches a good compromise, in a suit that's a touch different from a Westerner's. The suit envelops the Japanese soul. [*Sebiro ga Nihonjin no tamashi o tsutsunde iru.*] This is the promise for the future, this is the secret ingredient of a Japanese suit that transforms a former minus into a plus, a world of the Japanese suit that transcends the original.

As in other vignettes, the preoccupation here is with preserving some sense of "Japanese" identity in the face of internationalization/globalization/transnationalism. Again the historical referent is the Meiji period, citing a moment of national mobilization and success in imperial endeavors. The play of inner and outer is thematized through intertwining racialized masculinities and nationalisms: the Meiji men who wore Western suits as though they weren't really Western suits looked better than present-day Japanese men, who are more thoroughly acquainted with Western dress, presumably because the Meiji men were preserving something "Japanese" in their bearing. It implies that the Meiji men were more *manly* because of their untamed, martial, truly Japanese spirit. Here, the invocations of *seppuku*, though comic and somewhat fearful, are eloquent. The stylish attractiveness of these men who lived by the samurai codes far surpasses that of today's domesticated—dare I say feminized?—imitators of Western style. Muramatsu thereby writes a gendered, raced body distinctive in its stature, skin color, physical movements, and gestures, and this distinctiveness becomes the essence of Japanese identity. One could wear a Western suit while retaining such an essence, but even better would be a suit designed especially to express this essence, "the Japanese soul." The transcendent, inspirational ring of that phrase echoes historically with powerful nationalist sentiment, from the relatively innocuous to the right-wing and jingoistic. For example, it raises the specter of *Yamato damashi*, the Japanese spirit linked to *bushido*, the way of the warrior, a key component of the ideologies and nationalisms of the Sino-Japanese War and World War II. The citation is, quite frankly, stunning in its baldness. This Japanese spirit animates the Japanese Suit in a refigured world in which the Japanese have taken a foreign object, appropriated it, and made it their own. Indeed, *Nihon no sebiro* surpasses in style, quality, and appropriateness a "real" British suit tailored on Saville Row. Conversely, a suit is far more than frivolous adornment; it protects and expresses the Japanese soul. Style, gender, nationalism, are all inextricably linked. If you buy the Japanese Suit, you too can become a Japanese Man imbued with an essence of Japanese masculinity, who wears the suit made for *his* distinctive spirit and *his* distinctive body, a man who is no longer a feminized, orientalized, domesticated subject vis-à-vis the West. Far from being an exclusively feminine preoccupation, Comme des Garçons tells us that fashion can be mobilized as the idealized expression of Japanese masculinity.

Ad(d)ing History

A third phase of the campaign picks up these themes, invoking even more explicitly the parallels between the 1980s and the Meiji era. Contemporary commentary evoking the Golden Age of Meiji gives way here to a more direct deployment of gendered masculinity and nationalism in the persons of historical figures—many from the Meiji period—who played key roles in the "internationalization" of Japan. It features photographs of prominent writers and political figures, with accompanying text that ties their accomplishments to geopolitics and to style. This series narrates the need for a Japanese Suit appropriate for this historical moment when Japan has taken its place as a world economic power. The suit here reflects personal character, national identity, and international prominence.[12] The vignettes mobilize a nostalgia for a Golden Age when Japan was able to respond to the "threat" of the West through the efforts of "great men." Rearticulating 1980s concerns with *kokusaika* (internationalization) and with the continued global success of Japanese business, these ads construct a Japanese masculinity that is successful in challenging Western hegemony, where masculinity means dominance in the worldly domains of the political and economic, implicitly defined against the passive, orientalized femininity of Japan's opening to the West and its defeat in World War II.

One ad features a full-page photograph of Goto Shinpei, a leading government administrator in the Meiji (1868–1912) and Taisho (1912–1926) periods. The text reads as follows:

> Born in the home of poor aristocrats in Mizusawa, Goto Shinpei was an impoverished student, dressed in "ragged *hakama* and mismatched *geta*," the forerunner of "*bankara*" [the rustic, unconventional style of students of this era]. A practitioner of medicine, student in Germany, President of the Manchurian Railroad, Home Minister, a count, he lived through the Meiji era as one of its great politicians. In that period, *bankara* became *haikara* [stylish dandy], and he continued to create a persona that could take any garment and wear it with his refined, personalized sense of style. In another sense, isn't *bankara* perhaps like Japan's punk, the explosion of youthful energy? Goto Shinpei was a person who throughout his life possessed the spirit of the avant-garde.

This is the most obvious case of a discursively produced history that asserts a dubious historical equivalence. It enshrines Goto in a particular way: as someone who could be stylish in any situation—indeed, poverty is encoded as simple style in this text. Power, internationalism, and the force to shape history are linked to fashion; being a great politician and being in vogue are presented as coextensive. Leadership means a position at the cutting edge of history and at the cutting edge of style. The final logical link, the comparison of *bankara*, the unconventional look of poor students, to punk, an English working-class phenomenon in its origins, posits them as historical equivalent explosions of "youthful energy," eliding the vast cultural and historical specificities separating the two. This move exemplifies the tendency of the fashion industry to reduce historical and political difference to consumable elements of style. But perhaps the most disturbing aspect of the ad is the aestheticizing of politics. Walter Benjamin links this tendency to processes of objectification and self-alienation that enable "mankind" to "experience its own destruction as an aesthetic pleasure of the first order" (1969, 242). In Benjamin's case, this meant a celebration of the beauties of war thematized in fascist ideologies. Though the contemporary historical situation in Japan does not immediately recall the burgeoning militarism of the 1930s, certainly there is cause for disturbance in the encoding of class and poverty as mere ingredients of style. Finally, the ads erase and even implicitly celebrate an entire history of Japanese expansionism and imperialism, in which Goto was centrally implicated as a party to the annexation of Manchuria. In fact, this complicity is recuperated as avant-gardism.

Selectively stressing the ways Meiji leaders such as Goto responded to the Western challenge, the ad copy erases imperialist histories and creates subject positions for readers that allow the transfer of desired qualities to the consumer through the purchase of the product. In this case, the Japanese Suit positions the buyer within a masculinized, nationalist legacy embodied in the personae of Great Men such as Goto Shinpei. Clad in such a suit, the Homme Deux man can aspire to a similar position of greatness, defined through key masculine attributes: powerful leadership, a vanguard spirit, resourcefulness. Here, power and style are coextensive.

Specular Women

A final campaign puts another distinctive spin on these themes. If Goto Shinpei and other Meiji leaders embody a masculinity based on political power and resourceful response to the West, if Muramatsu constructed a masculine essence based on an indomitable, ineffably Japanese spirit that resexualizes the male body, this campaign introduces heterosexuality as the necessary next step for the full construction of Japanese masculinity. It features similar prominent historical figures in full-page head shots, but the commentary this time comes from contemporary women, followed by the copywriter's text. Aimed at female consumers who purchase attire for their husbands and sons, these campaigns appear in the very proper women's magazine, *Katei Gaho*.[13] If in the other phases of the campaign, femininity serves as the ground for the figure of active masculinity, here "woman" emerges as the necessary opposite for the existence of "man": his audience, his mirror, his guarantor of heterosexuality. Fully reinscribing the gender binary, the ads invoke the female gaze as indispensable to the full performance of masculinity.

A particularly striking example features Nobel prize–winning novelist Kawabata Yasunari as seen through the eyes of actress Kishi Keiko, who narrates their relationship as the classic pairing of the naïve, young ingenue and the worldly, seductive, dangerous older man. Kishi Keiko, well-known actress, celebrity, and long-time Parisian resident, embodies cosmopolitan grace; Catherine Deneuve and Grace Kelly come to mind as cross-national parallels. One of Kishi's best-known roles was as Komako, the provincial geisha in the film version of Kawabata's novel *Snow Country*. In the following ad campaign copy, she alludes to this experience and to her first interaction with Kawabata, who at one point dissolves into an image of Shimamura, Komako's lover in *Snow Country*:

> The first time these penetrating, quiet eyes, burning with passion, gazed at me, I was in high school. I stood transfixed. . . . Sensei, who that day had come to see me play the role of Komako, stood there cutting a romantic figure in a suit, framed by the snow-capped mountain in the evening light behind him. For an instant, I felt dizzy, as though sensei and Shimamura had become one. The night of my wedding reception in Paris, when sensei had done us the honor of acting as go-between, he gracefully picked up with his slender fingers a spear of asparagus that had appeared on the dinner table and elegantly ate it, the way French connoisseurs might. I've never met another tuxedo-clad Japanese man who could eat asparagus with such style. Even now, the fiery eyes of Kawabata Yasunari sensei, who could wear both kimono and Western suits with breezy nonchalance and a uniquely refined sensitivity and aesthetic sensibility, live on within me (Kishi Keiko, actress).
>
> Through Kawabata Yasunari's works, brimming with beauty and acute insight, we are taught about the existence of the aesthetic consciousness at the foundations of the Japanese heart and mind. Beginning with his Nobel Prize lecture, and continuing with "Japanese Culture and Beauty," "The Existence and Discovery of Beauty," these works continued to take this message abroad. Beauty is the world's common language. Is it not the work of the next generation to continue to translate this message into concrete forms and theoretical structures and impart it to the world?

In this passage, we find the copywriter engage a self-orientalizing that deploys tropes of Japan as the land of the aesthetic, suggesting that aesthetics can ground claims to Japanese uniqueness, excellence, and moral superiority. Indeed, Japan can assimilate the best of the West while teaching the West about "real" beauty. Skillfully, Comme des Garçons places the *Nihon no sebiro* directly in line with the works of Nobel prize–winning Kawabata, as heir to his legacy of creative genius and international acclaim. Taking on Kawabata's mission of imparting the Japanese aesthetic sensibility to the world, *Nihon no sebiro* takes the necessary next step required of "our" generation by translating this Japanese aesthetic into material forms such as clothing. The suit thus becomes the concrete embodiment of an essentially Japanese cultural superiority.

Kishi's testimonial completes the performance of racialized, nationalist masculinity; it is a brilliant gesture. Known for her cosmopolitan elegance, Kishi acts as idealized "other," judge, mirror, and appreciative audience. Under her refined and knowledgeable gaze, Kawabata becomes a "real" man: sexually appealing but slightly dangerous, an older man of the world much like his character Shimamura from *Snow Country*. Such a man is at ease even in the most rarefied European circles, possessed not only of the savoir faire to navigate the customs and manners of the French elite, but the confidence to break with those customs. The gendered subject created here is cosmopolitan, acutely intelligent, passionate, elegant. He is unafraid of being his own man, sufficiently self-possessed to wear both Western and Japanese clothing with easy panache. An alluring image indeed.

Thus, the ad takes the construction of a satisfying Japanese masculinity to the next necessary level, heterosexualizing the subject. Muramatsu used the indomitable, implicitly martial spirit as an essence of masculinity; Meiji political figures attest to the linkage of style with masculinity as political leadership. But the full (hetero)sexualization of the Japanese man can be fully realized only through the reinscription of the gender binary, wherein men and women are created as mutually defining opposites. Kawabata is troped as the attractive, dangerous, famous older man, Kishi as young, nervous, naïve. Yet Kishi is also the intended audience for the construction of maleness, the mirror through which heterosexual masculinity can be performed and seen. Although women are by definition in the position of relative subordination, they also are given the power to adjudicate and mirror who counts as a "real man."

Thus, gender, race, sexuality, class, nation, and the transnational intersect in this picture of *Nihon no sebiro* and the man who wears it. He is both subject of masculinity and object of (female) desire. These advertisements construct a gendered "Japanese" identity, creating a subject of desire and fulfilling that desire through the product they offer. The text recreates a sense of inferiority to the West—an inferiority implicitly gendered as feminine—and offers a means for transcending the very discomfort it has discursively produced and amplified, one with its own complex history in the realm of geopolitics. Against a history of penetration, occupation, and cultural domination by the West and a historical situation positioning Japan as economically preeminent, they create a masculine dominance that refigures penetration as creative assimilation, constructing a raced, heterosexualized body that will be able to resist further penetration by the West. This body can articulate the anger of having been racialized and denigrated; it is a body that can perform Japan's global economic power. It is also a body implicated in imperial histories and continuing neocolonial projects. These colonizing imperatives are elided on the one hand through a focus on Meiji as a period of nation building that sought parity with the West, suppressing the traces of militarism and expansionist aggression that accompanied the building of the nation-state. On the other, the suit as *sebiro* invokes Britain's class elitisms and the British imperial project, tacitly placing Japan in the role of Britain's heir. All these complexities of subject formation can be condensed in a startlingly simple act: buying a Japanese Suit.

Contradictions animate the politics of reception in no less striking form when one removes the campaign from its domestic context. Lata Mani (1990) has written eloquently about the multiply mediated agendas at play when one writes for multiple and perhaps discrepant audiences. Analogously, the campaign takes on unexpected shades of meaning when we place the Japanese Suit within a sedimented history of U.S.-Japan relations and the history of Japanese Americans and of raced Asian American bodies. Despite the urgently necessary problematizing of Japanese rivalry with U.S. dominance and the uncritical celebration of nationalisms and imperialisms in the ad campaign, the Japanese Suit can produce unexpected readings when positioned in an Asian American politics and history. For example, given a Japanese American history of incarceration, Japan-bashing discourses, and the recirculation of insidious racial tropes as a result of the trade wars, the construction of gender in the Homme Deux campaign can be seductive. The businessman is probably the most familiar contemporary stereotype of Japanese masculinity. The bespectacled, camera-carrying, bucktoothed, asexual, emotionless automaton, the corporate soldier who threatens to invade the American economy, is here recuperated as a vehicle for ethnic and racial pride in a historical situation when anti-Asian racism continues unabated.[14] In such a climate, even an *ad campaign* reclaiming the businessman in a positive way can be compelling at one level. Asian and Asian American men single out emasculation and desexualization as their distinctive oppressions, and certainly that emasculation is countered deftly here in the construction of a Japanese masculinity that is (hetero)sexualized and powerful in the world. On this plane, the advertisements skillfully and seductively mobilize counterorientalist discourses in the service of commodification and the provocation of consumer desire.

Equally seductive is its use of the materiality of clothing to refigure normative identities. In industrialized societies, clothing in standard sizes acts as a vehicle for the production of standard human beings, materially constructing who is normatively human. One of the innovations of the Japanese avant-garde was to make clothing in only one size, which is then adapted to different body shapes, as are kimono. For example, in the United States, accoutrements of authority in the academy and corporate worlds—lecterns, desks, chairs, first-class plane seats—are obviously not constructed with many Asian American women in mind. The size and scale of objects constitute seemingly trivial but profoundly telling practices of marginalization. From this perspective, the notion of garments made especially for one's size and body type is deeply satisfying. As a strategically essentialist deployment of identity, as an intervention in orientalist discourses, the Japanese Suit campaign mobilizes issues that could be profoundly significant, both for its intended Japanese audience and within a racialized U.S. context. The seduction seems all the more insidious and poignant when we note that a raced body worthy of pride appears in an advertisement deployed in the service of capitalist accumulation. Given advertising's raison d'être, this surely indicates the skillfulness of the ads in pulling on issues that deeply compel its potential consumers.

The campaign's seductive and problematic resonances lead me to ask what is at stake—not only for the producers/creators and for the consumers, but what is our stake, and what are our interests as analysts? Here, the use of an unlikely object—an ad campaign—as a locus for the production of problematically alluring identities also leads me to interrogate further those arenas often presumed to be beyond commodification: art, for example, or the academy.

Conventional discourse posits the relationship of the academy to the fashion world as one of depth to surface, the monastic conceit of pure, profound intellectual pursuit invidiously contrasted with the mindless celebration of shallow trends and superficial decoration. Subverting the surface/depth binary is a compelling challenge in light of the moralizing fashion provokes, with its obvious enmeshment in processes of commodification and objectification. I hope to have suggested in this essay and in other work that matters are much more multiply nuanced, and that limited contestatory moves—always riven with contradiction —can occur even in this world of surfaces.

Subverting the surface/depth binary thus becomes a way of interrogating our own sites of privilege, for we in the academy can hardly claim to inhabit a pristine space apart from the forces of commodification, commercialization, or the pursuit of marketable difference. We all participate in a capitalist publishing industry; some chase crossover dreams (sell-out, accessibility, or both?) with trade books and lucrative contracts. The persistence of the myth of originary genius and the enshrining of the author (despite his "death") feeds the need, in commodity capitalism, for the marketable difference that makes individual careers, even as "new" ideas develop and extend a larger conceptual vocabulary and reflect transformations in the world. The "star" phenomenon is certainly another aspect of our regime of consumer capitalism, where the discourse of originary genius intertwines with those of celebrity and the hunger of the market for the "new" and the "hot."

By making such arguments, I am not attempting to imply that I somehow speak from a pristine space outside these forces. This is precisely *not* an argument for a right-wing anti-intellectualism or an unproblematized empiricism that sees cultural studies or theoretically vigorous work as merely trendy. The lives of all academics and all denizens of consumer capitalist societies are inextricable from the forces of commodification. The question is not how one can transcend it—as though one could—but how, *within it,* one can make interventions that matter. At some level, like the authors of the Japanese Suit campaign, we who write are out to sell our writing, our theorizing, our political challenges. This does not necessarily negate our efforts to be contestatory. Rather, perhaps this is the most realistic appraisal of one kind of inevitably complicitous intervention in such a commodified world as ours.[15] Our enmeshment in capitalism and the contradictions enacted when we seek to make moves that are purely contestatory emerge as themes in both the ad campaign and in our academic interventions. Academia and fashion are not exactly the same, nor are the challenges to orientalism and racism made by the ad campaign entirely parallel to the theoretical/political challenges that could be mounted from the academy. Nonetheless, precisely because we presuppose a radical disjuncture between these worlds, there might be fruitful cause for reflection in holding them together for a moment. The Japanese Suit shows us how consumption might work when it pulls on issues compelling to the people who are its prospective consumers, offering wish-images that, at the very least, articulate our deep desires and fears even as it does so in obvious service of capitalist accumulation. These complexities also appear in the domain of the academy, pointing us toward the contradictions that animate our own enterprise. Both the academic conceit of disinterested scholarship and the progressive conceit of liberatory intervention fail to take account of the complexities of cultural politics, where interventions at one level can reinscribe other power relations at another. Yet these contradictions should not immobilize our attempts to intervene. They might lead us instead toward a scrutiny of our own sites of enunciation, what Kamala Visweswaran calls "homework," an explicit recognition that the battles one chooses to fight and the positions from which we mount our arguments matter, and matter crucially. In the end, the Japanese Suit, in all its multiple and contradictory figurations of nationalism, transnationalism, race, gender, class, imperialism, and sexuality, provokes reflection on the equally complex contradictions of cultural politics. The advertisements and their complex contradictions of production and reception return us to the politics of location and to the questions Where are we positioned? And what is at stake?

Notes

This is a substantially revised version of a chapter in my book *About Face: Performing "Race" in Fashion and Theater.* I want to express appreciation to Routledge for permission to include it in this volume. The fieldwork on which the article is based occurred from 1989 to 1992. My thanks to designer Rei Kawakubo and the press departments at Comme des Garçons in Tokyo and Paris and to Marion Greenberg Associates in New York for their time and assistance with my research during that period. Acknowledgments as well to the Research Committee at Pomona College and to funds from my MacArthur Chair that enabled the trip to Japan on which this article is based. For their careful readings and suggestions, my appreciation goes to Lynne Miyake, Clyde Nishimoto, Lisa Rofel, Miriam Silverberg, and to the editors of this volume.

1   See, e.g., Befu (1993).

2 Numerous works have dealt with advertising, the articulation of subjects, and the provocation of consumer desire from a variety of theoretical standpoints. For some well-known formulations, see Stuart Ewen (1988); Wolfgang Haug (1986); Judith Williamson (1978); Michael Schudson (1984). For Japan specifically, see Marilyn Ivy (1995).

3 For other analytic work on fashion and men's clothing, see, e.g., Valerie Steele and Claudia Kidwell (1989); Elizabeth Wilson (1988); Richard Martin and Harold Koda (1989).

4 Venetian designer who worked from the turn of the century until the 1950s. His best-known designs were on classic Greek costume, including gowns that were simple columns of fabric permanently pleated in small, irregular pleats.

5 Thanks to Emiko Ohnuki-Tierney and Sumiko Iwao for pointing this out.

6 The campaign won a design award for advertising from a Japanese fashion industry trade paper. In *Marie Claire Japon*, editor Akiko Kozasu, a longtime Comme des Garçons supporter, quotes industry experts who pointed to the tension and the exemplary use of Japanese typography in the ads.

7 A political slogan from the Meiji Restoration and a response to Western penetration.

8 The Meiji Restoration covers the period 1868–1912, when Commodore Perry "opened" Japan to the West.

9 Quoted in Miyoshi 1974, 57.

10 See, e.g., Ivy (1988) and Stanlaw (1992) on the semiotics of the use of loan words and different scripts in Japanese. The latter account centers on this issue but fails to link it adequately to a constitutive political history of occupation and "opening" by the United States.

11 At a joint Comme des Garçons/Yohji Yamamoto men's show, I overheard this example of the use of *shibui*. During the Yohji half of the proceedings, a black man with sunglasses and dreads, dressed in black leather, appeared on the runway. As he posed in front of us, I heard some young Japanese women behind me gasp loudly, "Shibui!"

12 One ad, with leading postwar politician, longtime conservative Prime Minister Yoshida Shigeru, again trumpets the theme of world powers setting world style. Since Meiji, the ad asserts, there have been just a handful of men who could take that quintessentially British object, the suit, and make it distinctively theirs. The text constructs a narrator who claims a desire to possess a *Nihon no sebiro* appropriate for the public position or "face" of Japan at this moment, when Japan has become an international player.

13 One ad, for example, features Shiga Naoya, author of *A Dark Night's Passing* and the founder of the White Birch literary group. Commenting on his work is the author Mori, who is married to an Englishman. She writes with lively humor of her husband's reaction to Shiga's photograph. There is some-

thing recognizable in Shiga's contemplative expression, she says, that made her English husband sit bolt upright. This ineffable Japaneseness is linked to a gentlemanly, tastefully elegant style that transcends cultures—a style so distinctively Japanese and so compelling that an Englishman is forced to do a double take.

14   See, for example, the final chapter of Kondo (1997), which deals in part with Michael Crichton's *Rising Sun.*

15   Elliott Shore in *Talkin' Socialism* (1988) writes eloquently of the dilemmas of socialist journalists at the turn of the century. How does one put one's message across? Does one adopt strategies used by more mainstream, even popular culture venues, in order to attract readers? Does one accept advertising? Or implicitly condone labor practices associated with capitalist firms?

Transnationalism, Feminism, and Fundamentalism

Minoo Moallem

In the past few decades, with the expansion of new forms of print and visual media, with globalization, and with the erosion of the nation-state, societies, social groups, and individuals have suffered a "crisis of identity." This crisis of identity is correlated with the expansion of a global culture and the forces opposing it in the aftermath of decolonization (S. Hall, 1992). The outcome has been a war of representation and position between dominant and dominated ethnicities as well as hegemonic masculinities and emphasized femininities.[1] These crises have generated a series of questions of varying range and scale concerning group identifications and individual selves, from globalism to nativism, from center to periphery, and conversely. Typical questions might be: Who are we?[2] What is our relationship with others? How do we relate to our own selves? What is particular about us? Has anyone the authority to control us? If so, in the name of what and for whom?

In this crisis, the dimension of gender is central. Gender issues and gender identities are at the heart of shifting cultural and economic meaning systems. The massive intrusion of women into labor markets, the shift of power relations between women and men, the visible presence of women in the institutions of knowledge and especially their access to print, scripture, and visual media have brought gender to center stage. The possibility of storing, organizing, and transmitting meaning by means of writing and images via transnational networks and institutions is as fundamental as the production and storage of wealth.[3] These changes have left unresolved such issues as the separation between the private and public realms, between domestic and nondomestic production, and between an ethic of care based on the invisible emotional labor of women and the ethic of responsibility based on the notion of abstract, rational citizenship. Such changes have intensified gender identification across class, race, and ethnic lines, and contribute to the significance of identity politics.

Feminisms and fundamentalisms are among those growing forces that attempt to deal with both individual and communal identities in global and local conditions. A war of position between advocates of fundamentalist and feminist worldviews is being waged in the cultural sphere at both local and global levels. Feminisms and fundamentalisms are now competing global forces, both attempting to find means to control the mechanisms of cultural representation. Both feminism and fundamentalism are major factors responsible for and responding to the "crisis of rationality" as well as the crisis of "masculinity" and "femininity." Both arose inside the problematic of modernity as it deals with relations between men and women with respect to the universal and the particular, public and private, family and state, and individual and community.

While global and local encounters are marked by the presence of both feminism and fundamentalism in various geopolitical locations, cultural contexts, and religious traditions, Islamic fundamentalism and what may be called Western egalitarian feminism have become important sites of the construction of new forms of global oppositions perpetuating old colonial divisions between a barbaric, oppressive, and patriarchal Muslim world versus a civilized, tolerant, and liberated West.

Here I pass over a number of different and sometimes antagonistic strands of feminism to address one particular category of Western egalitarian feminism that emerged within the context of Euro-American modernity, even though generated in various places and containing a range of positions on women's social subordination. In my treatment of Islamic fundamentalism I address the particular interpretation of Shi'a Islam prevalent in the pre- and post-1979 revolutionary era in Iran. At the same time, I deconstruct the dichotomization of Western egalitarian feminism and Islamic fundamentalism as unitary transhistorical formations representing good and evil, freedom and unfreedom, civilization and fanaticism, modernity and tradition. This will allow me to look at three sociological matters: first, the contemporary ground upon which both feminist and fundamentalist discourses encounter one another; second, the cognate issues that both feminist and fundamentalist discourses address; and third, the discursive spaces where feminism and fundamentalism find themselves radically at odds.

Islamic Fundamentalism and the Transnational Politics of Representation

The case of Islamic fundamentalism in Iran points to the profound significance of discursive and visual forms in the transnational sphere of representation and gender relations. The publication of *Satanic Verses* in 1988 and the Islamic fundamentalist offensive against Salman Rushdie was a turning point in the transnationalist politics of representation not only as it intersects with movements of capital and labor in a multinational world, but also as it comes into contact with theoretical and critical allegories of the liberal political subject (Alarcón, 1996).[4] The controversy was seen by certain Euro-American commentators as merely another chapter in a struggle between Western freedom and Oriental despotism and unfreedom, thereby reinforcing the conventional dichotomous pairings—West/East, Occident/Orient, good/bad. Each side, attributing to itself the love of a sacred or a profane god, refused to acknowledge the book's subject, namely, the experience of hybridity, impurity, and change-by-fusion in the lives of not only large numbers of migrants but of those metropolitans who are no longer able to achieve an ontological sense of security in a postmodern era (see Rushdie 1991, 394). This has blocked any serious examination of fundamentalism in its religious or secular forms and in its geopolitical specificity. Moreover, a persistent fundamentalist reading perpetuates discursive formations that are closed to the cycles of hermeneutic and everyday forms of resistance.

The representation of Islamic fundamentalism in the West is greatly influenced by the general racialization of Muslims in a neoracist discourse rooted in cultural essentialism and a conventional Eurocentric notion of "people without history."[5] Islamic fundamentalism has become a generic signifier used constantly to single out the Muslim other, in its irrational, morally inferior, and barbaric masculinity and its passive, victimized, and submissive femininity.[6] New forms of Orientalist discourse not only legitimize Western intervention and the protection of Western economic and political interests in the Middle East,[7] but also justify discrimination and the exclusion of Middle Eastern and Muslim immigrants in diasporic locations (see Kadi 1994). Such a discourse reduces all Muslims to fundamentalists, and all fundamentalists to fanatical antimodern traditionalists and terrorists,[8] even as it attributes a culturally aggressive and oppressive nature to all fundamentalist men, and a passive, ignorant, and submissive nature to all fundamentalist women.[9]

The putative line of demarcation separating fundamentalism from modernity has played a crucial role in the identity formation of fundamentalism in recent years. If fundamentalism has been characterized as the negation of modernity, democracy, progress, and development and as an orientation toward the past, then the posited antitheses between fundamentalism and modernity are constitutive not only of Muslim identity but of its ontological status, its raison d'être. The dualistic and demonizing representation of fundamentalism as a site of absolute evil has induced resistance to the term among some scholars, who accordingly either avoid the concept completely, or replace it with some other term, such as political Islam, Islamic militancy, communalism or orthodoxy.[10]

In this context, I intend to situate fundamentalism as a modern discursive formation (no less modern than "progress" or "development") with a genealogy and a history of representation. Fundamentalism may be defined as follows: a regime of truth based on discourses identified with, or ordained by, God (taken metaphorically or literally) and binding its observants. This definition of fundamentalism is, I know, problematic to the extent that it remains tied to religion, and to the history of Christianity in particular. Not surprisingly, the analytic application of fundamentalism to non-Christian contexts has been the subject of much controversy. I believe, therefore, that any religion-based construal of fundamentalism must be challenged and replaced by an analytical definition that enables critical intervention in both religious and secularist forms of fundamentalism.

As a regime of truth, fundamentalism is not premodern. Indeed, it is a by-product of the process of modernization and in dialogue with modernity. In one sense, fundamentalism's impulse is to *counter* modernity. Yet as a moment of modernity, fundamentalism is discontinuous with related premodern discourses. Moreover, it also opposes cultural "difference" associated with postmodernity by claiming cultural unity and homogeneity.[11] Furthermore, it is a useful comparative concept with important implications for women's movements, because as a site of unfreedom, it is not only used to disperse the gendered crisis in the order of modernity (especially the belief in rationalism and progress), but has also become a site of the paradoxical desire for the expression of the freedom to be "unfree." Finally, it is also an important place for the systematic production of discursive enclosures as it defines women's othering and legitimizes day-to-day oppressive gender practices.[12]

Global Cultural Encounters of Feminism and Fundamentalism

Moving beyond the dichotomization of feminism and fundamentalism as two separate and antagonistic positions, I define both Western egalitarian feminism and Islamic fundamentalism as regimes of truth with consistencies and inconsistencies in their desire for change and closure. I argue that on both sides of the equation, a desire to question what is intolerable in modernity merges with a desire to construct new absolutes, postponing the emergence of any notion of ethical responsibility in relation to a notion of interdependence and autonomy. I am arguing that feminism and fundamentalism are neither uniquely secular nor religious phenomena.[13] They include a plurality of discourses and practices. However, while Western egalitarian feminism emerged claiming a subject position within the pervasive masculinism of liberal discourse and its paradigm of equality, Islamic fundamentalism opposes the assimilatory forces of modernity, modernization, and Westernization to claim cultural uniqueness and difference. Thus, the equality/difference pairing of modernity becomes indeterminate in both feminist and fundamentalist discourses.

Neither feminism nor fundamentalism is located exclusively in the West or in the Middle East.[14] Feminism and fundamentalism are opposing transnational worldviews, located in the "West" and the "East." Both are located within and beyond the borders of the nation-state. Both have found a place within different religious meaning systems and their secularist counterparts.[15] Both are matrices within which a constant process of subject formation is taking place.

Feminism and fundamentalism have cross-fertilized to create hybrids, that is, feminism with fundamentalist elements and fundamentalism with feminist elements. Indeed, even though for some critics any interpenetration between feminism and fundamentalism is a conceptual scandal, in reality both hybrid varieties exist. Many fundamentalist women have started to negotiate and renegotiate their place in society within fundamentalist discourse, by using mainstream feminist concepts and ideas such as patriarchy and male chauvinism.[16] In the case of feminists, certain culturalist positions, by depending on a form of essentialized nurturing femininity associated with women's nature and the construction of a glorious matriarchal past, thereby import fundamentalist components into feminism. Consider, for example, the notion of "goddess" worship as "a symbol of the affirmation of the legitimacy and beauty of female control" (Christ, 1980, 278), "Womanspirit" (Christ and Plaskow, 1979), "mother-child love" as "passionate, sensual and personal love" (Starhawk, 1979, 264), and the need for a holistic worldview. For both feminism of this kind and for fundamentalism, a nonnegotiable fictive past determines the vision of the future. Certain white feminists' notion of the category "woman" deploys an essentialism that leads to a rigidification of gender categories.[17] Both feminist fundamentalists and fundamentalist feminists are constrained in the negotiation of women's issues and are complicit in perpetuating power relations, either by sustaining the boundaries of a totalistic ideology (in the case of fundamentalist feminists), or by creating restricted boundaries through a replacement of patriarchy by matriarchy, or by limiting women's issues to only one set of social relations, and thus putting an end to any constructive sociological discussion.[18]

In this context, I want to problematize not only fundamentalism for—among other things—the construction of a false totality, but also feminism for its potential to construct rigidified categories.

The Paradoxes Haunting Feminism and Fundamentalism

In their attempts to address contemporary crises of identity, both Western egalitarian feminism and Islamic fundamentalism begin from similar premises. Both are critical of a global, rationalist, and universalistic order;[19] both question the sexual objectification and commodification of women in a modernized global patriarchy; both assert the repossession of women's bodies; both renounce the separation between private and public in creating a direct relation between individuals and political community; both claim transnationalism in their attempt to reach people beyond the boundaries of the nation-state; and both call particularly for women's subjectivity and participation.

Accordingly, because both feminism and fundamentalism are implicated in this nexus of issues, I wish to explore the paradoxical, ambiguous nature of their relationship and to show how they sometimes function as rivals and antagonists, sometimes as complicit forces in the spheres of social, political, and cultural representations.

With respect to the sphere of production, both feminists and fundamentalists insist upon the value of the domestic and emotional work of women, yet come to very different conclusions. Fundamentalists, on the one hand, base their arguments on the inevitability and naturalness of the role of women as the main providers of such work in society, and see it as a space for social respectability and women's virtues in their complementary role in the institution of heterosexuality. Feminists, on the other hand, problematize the social forces acting to produce such sexual division of labor. They question the discourse and practice of domestic work and caregiving in heterosexual intimacy and challenge the institution of domesticity that contains it.[20]

Both feminists and fundamentalists claim access, on behalf of both sexes, to the institutions of knowledge, but paradoxically the desire to know is influenced by the will to power and the construction of knowledge. Feminists' access to the institutions of knowledge has created new sites of interpretation and reinterpretation. Fundamentalists also endorse access to knowledge for all individuals—men and women—but minimize the possibility of interpretation.

Both feminism and fundamentalism challenge the modern dichotomies—material/spiritual, natural/cultural, secular/religious, public/private—to come to a holistic reading of gender relations. While fundamentalist challenges to modern dichotomies find expression in the notion of an essentialized woman as universal particular, feminist claims to particular universals via such notions as "global sisterhood" become a site of struggle against a universalized patriarchy. In creating an abstract and all-encompassing notion of "woman" or "women," both feminists and fundamentalists are complicit in constructing a discursive site of the solidification of either universals or particulars.

Both feminists and fundamentalists are concerned about the body as a bearer of culture, religion, values, and morality.[21] They criticize the sexual objectification of women's bodies by a global, rationalist, patriarchal order. Fundamentalists reappropriate women's bodies and impose on them a particular form of femininity that dictates their communal duties and responsibilities while offering them gratification in return. Maternity and motherhood become an important site of social gratification. Egalitarian feminists' notion of an abstract and universal female body—biologically determined and through its reproductive capacities made vulnerable to social subordination—converges with the fundamentalist position, yet differs in its quest to overcome such restrictions via new technologies or changes in the social restraints. While fundamentalists call for the repossession of women's bodies and their natural capacities, feminists question the patriarchal construction of the female body in order to dismantle the machinery that turns a female body into a feminine one.[22] If for fundamentalists the body is a secure site of gender identity, for feminists the body is a site of femaleness opposing the patriarchal construction of femininity. If egalitarian feminists' idea of the body as a site of true femaleness or maleness converges with its fundamentalist counterpart, nevertheless feminism's concern for the patriarchal construction of normative femininity provides space for a rethinking of gendered bodies. Both feminists and fundamentalists draw on historical memory, theological texts, legal practices, cultural spaces, and body symbolism to control, define, and negotiate sexualized and gendered bodies and to create discursive sites around motherhood, sexual identity, femininity, and masculinity. Fundamentalists deploy historical memory to reinforce the sovereignty of the binary opposition and naturalness of heterosexism in the face of the anomalies of homosexuality, bisexuality, and transsexuality; feminists use it to trace the social disciplinary practices involved in the symbolic and material marking of bodies in the process of genderization and sexualization. In terms of motherhood, female bodies are particularly important in both feminist and fundamentalist discourses in relation to the control of reproductive forces. Fundamentalist and nationalist ideologies in defense of a "right to life," by speaking of the "fetus as a human being" or "threats against the nation," turn the female body into an incubator for children and a site of collective surveillance. Western equality feminists advocate technological innovation or ideological equalization to facilitate women's control of their bodies.[23]

As both feminism and fundamentalism move beyond the boundaries of the nation-state, they envision two radically opposed notions of transnationalism. Feminists embrace the idea of a global oppositional discourse of all women against patriarchy. In this view, women are the other of the nation—an "otherness" within the "we-ness"—seeking solidarity under the sign of this otherness. Fundamentalist transnationalism, although it, too, moves beyond the political boundaries of the nation-state, invokes a particularistic form of community, namely, "the community of God." In this sense, fundamentalist transnationalism fails to break with nationalism vis-à-vis the control of women. Nationalist fundamentalists regard women as an important force in the creation of group cohesion and continuity, making sure that women transmit group values to their children. Thus, a group can share its identity through the conduit of women's bodies and women's powers of social reproduction.[24]

The nation-state, that important site of modernity, has been at the core of legal constructions of what is permitted and prohibited. Both feminism and fundamentalism contribute to the crisis of legitimation, to what Bhabha (1994, 149) calls "the unbearable ordeal of the collapse of certainty" at this historical juncture. For both feminists and fundamentalists, citizenship is related to how individuals stand not only before the law, but before the good, the moral, and the ethical. While egalitarian feminists have sided with the absolutist universalism of modernity, this universalistic impulse has been questioned by fundamentalists who assert a relativism of values as the condition of the perception of the intolerable and hence immoral action.[25] Such action is, however, predicated on a particularistic absolutism, despite the fact that the fundamentalist critique of modern universalist absolutism is pertinent. An ethic of responsibility, together with an ethic of care, are no sooner articulated than at once surrendered to God-given categories. Egalitarian feminists criticize the modern universalistic discourse of human rights in their exclusion of women, yet hegemonize women under the same rubric at the exclusion of geopolitical and cultural differences. Both egalitarian feminists and Islamic fundamentalists become complicit with modernity when they uphold absolute values and generate a transcendental ethic in a social world that produces moral subjects by forming, wrapping, and protecting them.

Both feminism and fundamentalism claim ethical issues as political. Fundamentalists root ethical standards in moral authority and agency devoted to a faith demanding self-sacrifice. They assert, therefore, the priority of morality over politics. Feminist consciousness, on the contrary, has been marked by the experience of ethical ambiguity and a form of moral agency based on historical distinctiveness, singularity, alienation, and reflexivity.[26] There is nevertheless a convergence between fundamentalist and feminist responses to the contemporary crisis of morality, in that both attempt to address moral questions around "caring activities."[27] For both feminists and fundamentalists, the modern subordination of the private sphere and the family to the public sphere and the state is intolerable. But even though fundamentalism integrates the public and the private within the same frame of reference, it becomes complicit with modernity in its prevention of the emergence of an ethic of responsibility for women corresponding to an ethic of care for men, because it divides gender roles and gender ideologies. It justifies caring as the essentialized, God-given role of motherhood and wifehood, leaving masculinity unchallenged. Men stand outside the sphere of caring, while women's citizenship becomes domesticated. Fundamentalists work to revitalize "women's morality" by insisting on the primacy of morality over politics; feminists prioritize politics over morality in their elaboration of an "ethic of care" and the private as the domain of "political life."

Finally, both feminism and fundamentalism are concerned with women's subjectivity and participation. While feminism valorizes women's subjectivity and participation as individuals in a liberatory process of change and uncertainty, the fundamentalist understanding of subjectivity is tied to a sense of how a woman is perceived and what she knows how to do, as narrowly prescribed by a faith that offers certainty. Fundamentalists and feminists share impulses characteristic of modernity—the invention of man as participant in the political community, its categories of consciousness, agency, responsibility, and choice, and the inclusion of women as equal participants. In this sense, both grapple with problems of modernity, one by attempting to create absolute values and the other by trying to resolve the tension between equality and difference.

In the next section, using the case of Islamic fundamentalism in Iran as illustration, and drawing on my participant-observation data and the discourse of some Iranian fundamentalist leaders, both men and women, I elaborate on these theoretical claims by focusing on the transnational discourse of fundamentalism as it challenges modernity yet creates an important site of gendered agency, and as it encounters the Western egalitarian feminism in a cultural war of representation.

"Veil" and "Blood" in the Community of God

"My sister, your veil is more assertive than my blood." This was one of the most popular slogans of Islamic fundamentalist groups in Iran. I used to see it repeatedly on the walls of Teheran, on banners in fundamentalist demonstrations, during and after the revolution of 1979. At the time, it tickled my sociological curiosity and filled my feminist consciousness with much anxiety about this alliance between veil and blood, this bonding between veiled sister and warrior brother.[28]

These two metaphors—"blood" and "veil"—signify the reconstruction of a hegemonic masculinity and an emphasized femininity in a community of brothers and sisters. Both tropes refer to Muslim men and women particularly committed to their community and to its militancy against local and global *taroute* (idolatry).[29]

In 1979, the revolutionary challenge to the social order disrupted hegemonic gender identities, including Westernized and modernized models of femininity and masculinity based on a racialized notion of a pre-Islamic Persian superiority, Islam's "otherness," proximity to the West and the heterosexist class culture of a modernized local elite. Such dominant notions were countered by various forms of oppositional and politicized gender and class identifications from Islamic to marxist and socialist.[30] As Najmabadi notes, "the *gharbzadeh* woman came to embody at once all social ills: she was a super-consumer of imperialist/dependent–capitalist/foreign goods; she was a propagator of the corrupt culture of the West; she was undermining the moral fabric of society; she was a parasite, beyond any type of redemption" (1991, 65).[31] Models of emphasized femininity with their sexual objectification of women were rejected and replaced by a "combative model of femininity" in the discourses of the various oppositional groups. Counterhegemonic feminine performativity constituted by different political ideologies became an important site of identification and resistance. Each group according to its political ideologies defined a particular appearance code for women. For example, women identifying with leftist urban guerrilla groups wore trousers and long shirts and sport shoes; Islamic guerrillas wore scarves to distinguish themselves from fundamentalist women who wore a long black chador. Long before the revolution and under the surveillance of the dictatorship, certain of these women activists became secret heroines for many young Iranian women. Asharaf-e-Dehghani's (a leading figure of the leftist guerrilla group) torture, imprisonment, and successful escape from one of the most heavily guarded of the shah's prisons and her omnipresence in dangerous urban spaces, became one of the most important prerevolutionary urban legends mobilizing and politicizing hundreds of young Iranian women.[32]

Islamic fundamentalist discourse in Iran also used particular notions of masculinity and femininity to oppose the ancien régime and its Western allies and to construct gendered citizenship in the postrevolutionary establishment of an Islamic republic. Throughout the pre- and postrevolutionary period, gendered performance tropes remained an important site of everyday forms of boundary constructions. While the main obligation of both men and women became *jihad-e-nafs* (worldly asceticism), different but complementary gender identities were established to create a national and transnational homogenized community. Through the new signification of a God-based community, warrior brother and veiled sister emerged, evoking persistent militancy, political awareness, and ethnoreligious pride.

The warrior brother, by sacrificing his life to the community and showing his commitment and responsibility, remasculinizes the Muslim man.[33] For men, as it is put by Hadi Gafari, a fundamentalist leader, dependence on material trappings, such as wealth, family, women, and children, had to be rejected in order to regain humanity (1979, 34). Martyrdom as a process of "remasculinization" entered into the symbolic language of gender identity to reestablish a community that was both gender-divided and complementary. Public spaces (the streets, avenues, and alleys) in every city and town were reappropriated by the names and memories of *shohada* (martyrs). In this way, men martyred for religion took back the public sphere once dominated by the ancien régime (the shah's dictatorship). Their pictures, visible and omnipresent in the urban spaces of contemporary Iran as symbolic models of masculinity, have recaptured the sphere of representation and citizenship. This hegemonic masculinity was complemented by an emphasized femininity symbolized by "the veiled woman." This does not mean that fundamentalist women do not give their blood, but blood does not symbolize the women's contribution. While devotion to the political community of God is essential in the construction of a will to peoplehood, the representation of "blood" and "veil" as the main sites of subjection assigns radically different yet complementary positions to men and women. Indeed, during the revolutionary period, the will to die for the revolution was neither uniquely gendered nor did it require an adherence to Islamic religion, but was a revolutionary site of oppositional subjectivity for both men and women, Muslim or non-Muslim. For example, on Black Friday (Sharivar of 1978), a turning point in the revolution when the shah's troops fired upon a crowd in Zhaleh Square in Tehran, a spectacular number of women, some heavily pregnant, were martyred.[34] In postrevolutionary Iran and during the Iran-Iraq war, the transformation of Islamic fundamentalism from an oppositional movement to state power and the marginalization and suppression of

social movements of diverse political ideologies brought a sharper gender division on the question of militancy and war. While the taking up
of arms by urban women during the revolution remained in the sphere
of representation and popular social memory and influenced women's
notions of political participation, the Islamic state officially institutionalized the role of warrior for men, who were supposed to fight on the
battlefield. Women were expected to perform a variety of tasks: raising
future martyrs, nursing, cooking, and cleaning "behind the battlefield"
(posht-e-jebheh). In this case, even though women continued to undergo
military training, the attribution of "offense" to men and "defense"
to women displaced gender-neutral revolutionary notions such as the
"people's army" and established a gender division of labor within institutions such as the Guardians of the Revolution.

Discursively, both blood and the black chador carried symbolic local
and global meaning.[35] Locally, it transcended all differences of class,
religion, and ethnonational origin among women; globally, it created a
transnational Muslim femininity and masculinity that stood in opposition to the West in complicity with the ummat (community of believers). In a cultural war of representation, it was the responsibility of the
woman to cover herself in a black chador. The black chador became
a "weapon," in the idiom of Rahnavard (a fundamentalist woman and
a leader and scholar; 1992, 9), symbolizing belonging to the ethnoreligious community of Allah which stood in opposition to the Westernized
local elite as well as to a global order.[36] The veil also signified an Islamic
femininity that patrolled feminine bodily comportment and generated
a restricted spatiality. The violation of the body, its opening to veiling
and death, was eroticized through the complementarity of an Islamic
femininity to a discernible masculinity.

In this scenario, through martyrdom, by transgressing the boundary
between life and death, the man gained an ultimate subject position
to become ghalb-e-tarigh (here, I am referring to another popular slogan: "Martyrs are the heart of history"). On the other hand, it was
through the maintenance of the body's boundaries in veiling that the
woman—according to Rahnavard—"could transcend her physical and
sensual attributes to become the divine's essence of womanhood, an
essence which endows her with the power to be a mother, a sister and
the sweetheart of her husband" (1990, 9). Women and men entered the
sphere of cultural representation, intervening in the symbolic realm by

way of competing masculinities and femininities, in constant conflict over power, self-realization, and self-expression. The cultural imagination of an emerging Islamic ummat not only created space for the interpellation of new gendered subject positions, but also facilitated social intervention in the revolutionary moment to reorder the chaos resulting from the breakdown of the prerevolutionary national imaginary.

These symbols also spoke to individuals, reminding them of their responsibility and commitment to the Islamic ummat, calling them to give up their individuality to the communal will and the laws of political citizenship in the sacred community of God. It is a mistake to read fundamentalist encouragement of the wearing of the black chador either as a sign of passivity or as a sign of religiosity. It is rather a gendered invitation to participation in political activity and a sign of membership, belonging, and complicity.[37]

From the Community of Man to the Community of God

> Mais je ne suis pas d'accord avec qui dirait: "inutile de vous soulever, ce sera toujours la meme chose." On ne fait pas la loi a qui risque sa vie devant un pouvoir. A-t-on raison ou non de se revolter? Laissons la question ouverte. On ne souleve, c'est un fait; et c'est par la que la subjectivité (pas celle des grandes hommes mais celle de n'importe qui) introduit dans l'histoire et lui donne son souffle.
>
> —Michel Foucault, Inutile de soulever? *Le monde*
> (May 1979, 1–2)

In the revolutionary period, multiple forms of political ideologies were represented in different demonstrations. Thousands of the inhabitants of urban spaces, from the working, lower middle, and middle classes, intentionally or spontaneously participated in daily political action against dictatorship. To the hegemonic leadership of Khomeini, an anti-Western, anti-imperialist, and antidictatorship movement was associated with a particular notion of an Islamic republic that radically distinguished itself from nationalist, radical democratic, marxist, and socialist visions of politics. This shift in the postrevolutionary era is characterized by the slogan "Neither West, nor East, the Islamic Republic." "East" was used as a signifier of marxist, socialist, communist modernities representing those oppositional groups who were defend-ing such notions as People's Democratic Republic (*Jomhouri democratic Khalq*).

Ayatollah Khomeini's successful articulation of the notions of indi-vidual and ummat, with reference to a particular reading of Islamic reli-gion in general and Shiism in particular, not only reconciled Islam with the nation-state but also expanded it to include a transnational commu-nity. These two very modern constructs are related to a concept of sov-ereignty based on the idea of God as the ultimate and absolute sovereign of all creation. God, in this sense, is owner and master vis-à-vis the um-mat in which each individual is a participant. In his writings, Ayatollah Khomeini, for example, makes constant reference to this idea, empha-sizing that the entire religion must be totally in the service of the indi-vidual and the individual totally in the service of religion (1980, 76–78).

There are five interconnected elements that work to create an Islamic community contained within modernity's order of time and space. Entry into the normative time of modernity is predicated on a particular historicity and a bounded spatiality that, in the context of postmodernity and the recent erosion of the nation-state (owing in part to the expansion of mass media, to migration flows, and to the inten-sified displacement of capital and labor), can no longer be exclusively defined by a recourse to national territoriality.[38]

The first notion is the appeal to a common and historicized past. The cyclic time of myth becomes the linear time of social and historical struggles (Shayegan, 1989, 139). In the reconstruction of the past within the framework of Shiism, two episodes in the history of Shi'a Islam becomes especially important: the usurpation of power by illegitimate Caliphs, and the *karbala* uprising.[39]

The second notion is a specific idea of "territory." On the basis of this idea, Khomeini refers to an Islamic space defined in a metaphoric loca-tion between the West and East.

The third notion is a reference to the cultural cohesion of Islam as *tassavor* (vision), realizable through an Islamic revolution and a com-mitment to collectivity. This vision recalls *Jahiliyya*, an age of igno-rance located in the past, and *taghut* (idol), its contemporary manifes-tation, where man rules over man, and opposes it to a society where God dispenses equality and justice for believers through the realization of an Islamic praxis. The real significance of Islam, according to this schema, is not subjective religious experience but acceptance of the collective Islamic life and individual devotion to the cause. Certain ideas and concepts related to significant historical events can be singled out and applied to the contemporary situation. Islamic culture is used to unify and empower the marginalized majority, the poor, the disadvantaged, the dispossessed, the weak ("the Mostasaf"), against the rich, the powerful, the superior ("the Mostakbar"). The fundamentalist version of revivalism hopes to protect itself from the criticism that it concerns only the "privileged few."

The fourth notion is the polarization of Allah (God) and taghut and the constant reference to jihad (holy war). Fundamentalist discourse, like nationalist discourse, is dependent on "otherness" to organize an ideological "we." Here the subject emerges in its Hegelian sense to recognize an unhappy consciousness resulting from subordination and finds his maleness in an ethical world of responsibility.[40] In contrast to the modern Cartesian self (which denies splitting in exchange for a rational self), the subject of the Islamic fundamentalist discourse recognizes such inner splitting and connects it to an outer form of splitting. An awareness of such inner and outer splitting of self and its regulation makes possible a subject position that challenges dominant regimes of subjectification. In the fundamentalist view, jihad is not only a revolt against the ruler but also against oneself (*jahad-e-nafs* "worldly asceticism"). Ayatollah Khomeini refers to these two forms of jihad as *jihad-e-akbar* (major jihad) and *jihad-e-asghar* (minor jihad) or holy war against taghut/idolatry (1980, 52). The reference to jihad-e-nafs as akbar underscores the importance and difficulty of a holy war waged against one's individual needs; the self is sacrificed to the will of Allah. The polarization of Allah and taghut in the jihad-e-nafs opens the way to an enduring cultural and psychological rejection of non-Islamic values and to the internalization of Islamic values. To become a member of Allah's community, one must reject the taghut before proclaiming a new adherence to Allah. Hadi Gafari, a fundamentalist leader, refers extensively to the inner/outer dynamism of such a dichotomy (1979, 19–30).

The fifth element is the reference to a common present. The Islamic ummat had to be constructed as material, historical, and actual. In this sense, the ummat contains the idea of progress and a turn toward the future. None of the various versions of Islamic fundamentalism reject the idea of progress. In fact, all of them assert the compatibility of progress and Islam. In this sense, *harekat* and *tagiir* (movement and change) are placed in an evolutionary schema of progress (Gafari, 1979, 15, 17).

The fundamentalist ummat as a fictive entity is a site of contradiction and tension, since it contains both those who are the subjects of the legitimation of the power of the nation-state's sovereignty—a desacralized community—by definition, and those subordinated to power—subjects within a sacred community. Here a double process of sacralization/desacralization is at work in the legitimation of power by the force of a nonnegotiable God and the notion of community as a collection of atomized individuals as source of legitimation and subordination. So any claim to a sovereign nation-state prompts the question of who has the right to rule, engendering a crisis of legitimation. In fundamentalism, the individuals making up the fictive "people" cede sovereignty to God and become its source of legitimation. Such legitimacy is precisely contradictory to and inconsistent with any particular people's attempt (a particular lived community) to incarnate this impossible entity.

Fundamentalist communalization constructs a direct relation between God and individual. Like his modern counterpart, I argue, fundamentalist man emerges into a self-conscious identity through a process of remasculinization and becomes a legitimate citizen of the local and global community. This does not apply, however, in the case of women, because of their domestication through their voluntary submission to the community of God.

The Voice of Martyrs: Death, Feminization, and Remasculinization

Death and its representation are central to Islamic fundamentalist ideology in Iran. Indeed, awakening consciousness of the body as an "instrument of power" is part of an effort to reconstruct and remap the body in a counterhegemonic movement. Martyrdom provides a sense that death makes the human will and power both possible and impossible. Martyrdom is a site of representation where death is given not only a voice but also a life. Bonyade-Shahid (The Martyrs' Foundation) is one of the most important state-regulated institutions in Iran.[41] Being the mother of a martyr confers high status in the new fundamentalist state. Martyrdom is constantly used in the media, directed to both global and local audiences. Death takes on a meaning suffused with "masculinity" because death, power, and political representation are closely intertwined.⁴² While death has always been an important motif, in the context of political oppression it becomes a dramatized scene of subjectivity and empowerment. The boundaries between life and death, between past and present, between living and dead bodies are blurred and reproduced in the reconstruction of social memory through mythical concepts and forms, moving constantly from semiology to ideology.⁴³

Through the symbolic order of martyrdom, men's bodies are constructed as omnipotent and transcendental. In the case of women, however, even as veiling constructs an Islamic femininity beyond geographical and temporal location, it binds them to a transhistorical and biological female body. Through this process of martyrdom, the body is rejected for higher values. Nevertheless, through veiling, the body becomes at the same time desired yet objectified, forbidden, and alienated. But it is through the "otherness" of femininity and its domestication that men gain subjectivity and agency in the scene of martyrdom. There are at least three places where women's domestication precludes the exchange of objectification and submission for individuation and subjectivity: first, their representation in the reconstruction of the past; second, their domesticated role in the drama of martyrdom; and third, the veiling and reterritorialization of women's bodies. Shiite myths have a great deal of influence in the daily life of Iranians; they are of great importance not only to the understanding of such forms of communalization, but also to the way women enter history.⁴⁴ In the "Karbala Parable," the martyrdom of the third imam, Mohammed's grandson, Hussein, stands with his family against the oppressive tyranny and corruption of the Umayyid caliph, who for Shiites is usurper of the legitimate leadership of Islamic ummat and destroyer of its promise of social justice. Watching the existential tragedy of the war between good and evil and the victory of the forces of evil over the forces of good, played by local performers in the month of Moharam, the audience learns to identify with the extreme pain and suffering that Hussein and his family experienced in Karbala. Karbala is not only a key episode in Shiite history, but also a symbol of self-sacrifice and resistance. Women and men in Karbala are brave, but in different ways: men are the warriors and women the guardians of family ties and kinship. Women are, therefore, the main agents of social continuity; in this sense, mothers, sisters, wives, and daughters are role models for the community. The double embrace of this world and the other world in Karbala has been effectively used to mobilize the disempowered Muslim masses. *Shehadat* (martyrdom) becomes a core element and the culmination of the realization of the impossible. Women enter the fundamentalist reconstruction of the past always in the form of wives, mothers, and daughters, not as individuals. The imposition of veiling contributes significantly to the domestication of their martyrdom.

Surveyors and Surveyed: Women in the Drama of Martyrdom

The veil then is highly pertinent to our understanding of the relationship between subjectivity and objectification in fundamentalist discourse. Both martyrdom and veiling, indeed, have an enormous capacity for retelling. In the case of martyrdom, two elements are used to domesticate the experience of women. One is the fact that women enter the sphere of martyrdom as family members. They are either sisters, mothers, or daughters; no woman can join the scene of martyrdom as an individual. As women enter into the picture, their predetermined social roles constitute their relationship to God. The fundamentalist position on unmediated individual-God relations is nullified in the case of women. Indeed, women have to become dependent on men and community before becoming independent individuals before God. Any sense of agency depends on the acknowledgment and validation of such social roles and their inclusion in the community. The work of mothers, sisters, wives, and daughters is validated and encouraged. Women in this sense are reskilled and given an identity, but their sense of subjectivity and agency is based on domestication. Even at such a radical site of subjectivity where it is impossible to die for the other (in the sense of "to die in his place" [Derrida 1990, 25]), martyrdom cannot create agency for women because of the mediation of domesticity. Death becomes a site of subjectivity and cultural identification. Indeed, death is always culturally contextualized.[45]

Veiling plays an important part in this domestication, racialization, and genderization in fundamentalist ideology. It racializes women by establishing a sense of inclusion/exclusion, genderizes and sexualizes them as a sign of femininity, and creates a particular sense of subjectivity by casting them as both surveyor and surveyed, as objects of others' gaze and subjects of their own submission. Veiling, as a system of symbolic and material marking, disciplines and homogenizes women in a single category. It distinguishes Muslims from non-Muslims and renders invisible local, national, ethnic, class, and age differences as well as all the ways of being a Muslim woman. It thereby consolidates a unified notion of Muslim femininity. In this case, Islamic womanhood becomes a site of transnationality, feminine subjectivity, and citizenship in the community of God by calling on a participatory process of becoming that is guaranteed by deepening knowledge of Islamic traditions and laws.[46]

Conclusion

> I would say that the future of a philosophy that is no longer anti-feminist is being performed somewhere in the direction of Brechtian drama, which . . . produces unfinished plays which always have a missing act and are consequently left wide open to history.
>
> —Michele Le Doeuff (1977, 8)

Western egalitarian feminism and Islamic fundamentalism are not unmediated discursive spaces. They are haunted by the phantoms and monsters of modernity. They both have their own horizons and contradictions. Feminism and fundamentalism are ideologically positioned discourses, both of which serve to destabilize modernity and at the same time contain and make manageable the chaotic situation arising from the basic contradictions of the same modernity. Within the spectrum of equality, "difference" emerges to put feminism in crisis; within the fundamentalist spectrum of difference, "equality" emerges to create a crisis.[47]

While both reject a feminine ideal characterized by passivity and powerlessness, Western egalitarian feminism and Islamic fundamentalism adopt diametrically different views of women's subjectivity. Fundamentalism invites women to adopt a sense of identity and calls on them to enter a predetermined realm of identification, whereas Western egalitarian feminists have a notion of subjectivity based on an understanding of women as free, rational, and self-determining subjects. Both invite women to get intentionally involved in the transformation of a happy consciousness. In feminism, this involves a process of becoming an individual; in fundamentalism, membership in a God-given community. Feminist and fundamentalist views of subjectivity are complicit with modern Western epistemological notions of subjectivity in postponing

the emergence of a "joyous consciousness" that is not only a consciousness, that turns a "fact" into a "contradiction" (Bartky, 1990) but that also
becomes aware of its own contradictory social location, as both victim
and victimizer.[48] While Islamic fundamentalists offer women a subject
position as devoted agents in the consolidation of a God-given community, egalitarian feminists affirm individuality as a site of subjectivity. In
this play of mirrors reflecting gendered notions of modernity, a transnational notion of an Islamic womanhood underpinned by religious community emerges to join the egalitarian feminist notions of global sisterhood. However, a transnational womanhood with a logic of equality (in
feminism) or difference (in fundamentalism) lacks an understanding of
the very discourses in which such subject positions are constructed.
In the past decade, Western hegemonic feminism has been challenged
by the critical writing of antiracist, anti-imperialist, postcolonial, and
postmodernist feminisms. The constant effort to deconstruct "woman"
as a category by underlining "white Western" women's complicity in
the formation of an ethnocentric and imperialist order is part of the contemporary feminist identity crisis.[49] In the case of fundamentalism, the
transition of Islamic fundamentalism from an oppositional social movement to hegemonic state ideology in Iran has created fragmentation and
contradictions in fundamentalist transnationalism. In the case of Iran,
in the past few years, Islamic fundamentalists have had serious difficulty reconciling their transnationalist claims of Islamic particularity
and unity with the demands of a class- and gender-based nation-state.

    Feminism and fundamentalism cannot avoid mirroring each other. A
separation between the ontological as a site of fundamentalist recognition of the feminine self and the epistemological as a site of feminist
consciousness has culminated in exclusive forms of subjectivity.[50] A
conscious effort in feminism to resist domesticity has become a site of
subjectivity in fundamentalism. Feminists' challenge to women's subjection to gendered citizenship has created a site of gender desirability
in fundamentalism and the promise of a new pleasure in motherhood
and domesticity. In this sense, fundamentalism has become contagious
to its feminist counterpart because it takes pleasure in what is prohibited to feminism. But while the "signifiers" of domesticity are at the
center of both feminist and fundamentalist conscious discourses and
practices, the meanings of such signifiers in the symbolic unconscious
are left undisturbed. The subordinated masculinity of fundamentalist

discourse attempts to seize the meaning from the hegemonic masculinity of modernity by making female subjectivity disappear, and so overcoming the challenge of equality from the feminist subject position. However, the "speaking subject" of feminism cannot escape the attributes of the unconscious mechanisms of culture, nation, class, and sexuality, its momentary relation to the socioeconomic conditions, or its concomitant effects in lived experience. The "speaking subject" of feminism facing the inequality of modernity can be harmonized with fundamentalism while trying to line up a fixed subject position for every single situation. Obviously, feminism is haunted by subject positions that are components of the radical singularity of a lived life in the symbolic unconscious. Here I am not talking about the unconscious as a repertoire of repressed content that can simply be manipulated and regulated by a rationalized subject, but the complex relation between the subject/individual and its own sociohistorical constitution and epistemological instability, a subject position that is always conflictual, complicit, and contradictory. I want to call for transnational feminist theories and practices that are based on historicity, subjectivity, and the linkage between a macro- and micropolitical and relational articulation of nation, race, gender, class, and sexuality. I find what Layoun (1991, 413–14) calls "narratological (theoretical) competence" a useful concept. Layoun explains that "narratives are internally and externally conflictual whatever their medium. There are no foregone and conclusive master narratives though there are, clearly, dominant or hegemonic narratives. . . . Internally, narratives attempt to contain their constituent elements—actors, actions, story past, and present, narrative space—within 'an orderly' and 'naturally' self-justifying framework. But they are also spoken or written or played out from multiple perspectives, not all of which are equal, or equally convincing" (1994, 412). She adds, "The workings of narrative and narralogical competence are learned, socially shaped, and always partial; they are interjected, articulated, and acted out or practiced in various ways. The competence in question is not simply chosen and 'performed' individually from an unlimited array of possibilities but is discursively and practically constructed—and theorized—in speaking, thinking, and acting" (414).

The identitarian claims of fundamentalism and feminism do not necessarily disrupt the logic of capital or the nation-state and its exclusionary notions of citizenship as long as the subject does not come to discern its own complicity in its suppression of alterity, its own non-contradictoriness. Such a subject position remains imprisoned and self-contained because it is cut off from the historical and the geopolitical.[51]

The survival of fundamentalism is conditional upon a communitarianism based on the exclusion of women as individuals and their inclusion as "selfless others." I believe that the survival of feminism, on the contrary, will depend on our embracing a transnationalism rooted in the recognition of the various intersecting social relations of nation, "race," ethnicity, class, gender, and sexuality and the positionality of the self. Both an Islamic particularistic fundamentalism and a Western universalizing feminism are undercut by multiple forms of transnational subjectivities and resistance to the new forms of subjugation. The fetishization of the unitary individual and the universalization and rigidification of totalizing categories potentially lead feminism to a fundamentalist politics of closure and a simple inversion of moral superiority, thereby leaving space for a fundamentalist hegemonic community to rule. Rethinking subjectivity, difference, and political community is therefore especially important for feminism. In this global war of representation, in order for feminism to subvert fundamentalism, it has to recognize, understand, criticize, and disrupt complicitous sites where it is itself liable to fundamentalist rigidification.

Notes

I am grateful to Norma Alarcón, Iain Boal, Inderpal Grewal, Arlie Hoch-schild, and Caren Kaplan for their thoughtful and helpful suggestions on various versions of this essay.

1   I have borrowed this formulation from Connell (1987). He refers to "hegemonic masculinity" and "emphasized femininity" in distinguishing various forms of gender hierarchies and power relations. The politics of masculinity and femininity is a core feature of current forms of globalism, nationalism, and fundamentalism (Enloe, 1989, 1993) and an integral part of modern social formations.

2   The question Who are we? is an important one in ethnic and national movements. These movements are all similar in questioning technical, scientific, and administrative forms of power.

3   An attempt to give a feminist interpretation of sacred texts in different religious traditions and their distribution as printed material is an interesting example of recent changes in power/knowledge relations. This process has

facilitated desacralization and is resisted by a fundamentalist resacralization.

4   I am referring to what Alarcón (1996, 138) calls a transnational geopolitics with a concomitant production of "new" subjects of history who come into contact with theoretical and critical allegories of the liberal political subject.

5   Guillaumin, referring to the great variety of essentialisms applied to races, peoples, and cultures, writes: "Sans doute la notion de race, sous sa forme simple et réduite au terme lui-même, n'est elle plus aujourdhui d'une unité première dans le système de pensée raciste. Un tel essentialisme de couleur génétique-corporelle peut s'accommoder de bien d'autres termes ou catégories. Autrefois, l'usage du terme ethnie, supposé éviter les pièges de la pensée raciste, l'avait rapidement réintegré. Actuellement le terme culture semble suivre une trajectoire analogue. . . . Le même syncrétisme est désigné par l'autre pôle perceptif: non plus le physique mais le mental, non plus le concret mais le symbolique" (1985, 218–19).

6   With the collapse of communism, new regimes of "otherness" have been set in place to leave undisturbed the political discourses of liberal democracies. In this regard, Jeliça Šumič-Riha's (1996) discussion of the discourse of democracy in relation to its constitutive outside (through which it achieves its closure) is very interesting.

7   Cold war "security" metaphors have been retooled to construct an Islamic fundamentalist global threat in the West (Esposito 1993; Pieterse 1994). Fundamentalism has served to distinguish between Western allies and its enemies in the Middle East, South Asia, and North Africa. The U.S. media's reflex attribution of the Oklahoma City bombing to Muslim fundamentalists is an example.

8   Along these lines, some theorists have gone so far as to talk about a worldwide rivalry based on the civilizational "faultlines separating the West and Islam." Huntington's (1993) "The Clash of Civilisations?" and his outlook on future global conflicts between Islam and the West is an excellent example.

9   Such totalizing discourses not only deny the presence of dissenting social movements in the region, but also dissimulate the existence of various forms of negotiation over the meaning and interpretation of Islam in many different Muslim countries, perpetuating what Said (1978) identified as Orientalism.

10   Abrahamian (1991); Ayubi (1991); Jansen (1980); L. Ahmed (1992); Esposito (1993).

11   In my forthcoming book, *Between Warrior Brother and Veiled Sister: Islamic Fundamentalism and the Cultural Politics of Patriarchy*, I take up at length the questions of fundamentalism, modernity, and postmodernity.

12   An essentialized notion of "womanhood" justifies collective legal and po-
     litical control of women's bodies and sexualities in a number of fundamen-
     talist discourses. See, for example, Mazumdar (1992); Honig-Parnass (1994);
     Hawley (1994); Yuval-Davis and Sahgal (1992); Afshar (1994); and Diamond
     (1995).

13   The male subject of various religious and secular discourses has been chal-
     lenged by feminist claims of equality. In the case of religious discourses,
     feminist challenges include both a reconstruction from within different
     religious traditions and a secularist rejection of patriarchal religious prac-
     tices. Within the framework of Islam, both of these forms of feminist chal-
     lenge are lively and present. See, among others, Leila Ahmed (1986), Fatima
     Mernissi (1992), and Nawal El Saadawi (1988).

14   In the case of feminism, Eurocentric notions of Western feminists that con-
     ceive of the women's liberation movement as a purely Western European
     and North American phenomenon have been seriously challenged by post-
     colonial and poststructuralist feminists, "critical feminists of color," and
     "third world feminists." See Anzaldúa (1987); hooks (1984); Grewal and Kap-
     lan (1994); Trinh (1989); Mohanty (1991); and Spivak (1978). In the case of
     fundamentalism, recent comparative studies of religious fundamentalism
     have challenged monolithic notions of fundamentalism as uniquely related
     to Islam; see Moghadam (1994); Yuval-Davis and Sahgal (1992); and Hawley
     (1994).

15   Grewal and Kaplan's (1994) suggestion of a transnational mode of analysis
     that insists on the importance of geopolitical forces is very useful.

16   In Iran since 1980, the celebration of the 8th of March (Women's Day) has
     been replaced by the celebration of the birthday of Fatemeh Zahra, the
     prophet's daughter (Adelkhah, 1991). Debates in fundamentalist women's
     journals such as *Puyandegan-e-rah-Zenab, Payam-e-Hajar,* and *Mahjoobeh*
     also represent such a convergence. Klatch (1987, 152) reports that laissez
     faire conservative women share a measure of the feminist vision vis-à-vis
     the construction of gender and the existence of sexual inequality. In her
     book on newly orthodox Jewish women, Kaufman (1991) argues that despite
     the distrust of feminism by "born-again" women, their focus on raising
     women's status, promoting female interests, and altering gender roles reso-
     nates with issues long of concern to feminists.

17   Sandoval's (1990) critique sheds light on the rigidification induced by the
     tendency of white feminism to freeze understanding of power by reducing
     to a binary opposition the signifying "nodules" in the currents of power as
     they flow within the United States.

18   In her discussion of feminist fundamentalism, Wilson (1993, 27) argues that
     certain secular fundamentalist methods have been used by feminists in
     antipornography campaigns in the United States. Also, the desire to create

a safe niche, especially with the institutionalization of feminism, has been identified in the theoretical work of "women of color"; see Anzaldúa (1990).

19 A number of feminist critiques have exposed the rationalist ideal of man as a neurotic denial of the chaos, decomposition, and death associated with femininity and otherness. This ideal leaves masculinity as an imagined zone of safety encircled by the feminine "other."

20 Major issues are raised in feminist literature vis-à-vis the sexual division of labor in general and domestic work in particular. An important part of this literature looks at domestic work as a site of social and economic activity, where a political economy based on the sex/gender division of labor made it possible for both patriarchy and capitalism to take advantage of women's unpaid and unrecognized work. Several important sites of women's activities in the family are identified as significant to the understanding of women's position in society: (1) childbearing and child rearing, (2) domestic services, (3) sexual services, and (4) emotional labor and caretaking services. See, among others, Delphy (1976); Hochschild (1989); Guillaumin (1978); Juteau and Laurin (1988); Hartmann (1987); Smith (1992); and Walby (1988).

21 In the case of Christianity, Castelli suggests that "from the earliest Christian texts and practices, the human body functioned as both a site of religious activities and a source of religious meanings" (1991, 29). In the case of Islam, according to El Sabbah (1984), the female body is a field of sacred writing.

22 This critique in social constructionist feminists and feminists of difference become a site of theorizing. Foucault's (1979) notion of disciplinary practices producing "docile bodies" has flourished in feminist literature, especially the notion of "gendered embodiment."

23 As Renate Salecl puts it in the case of "the socialist moral majority" in Slovenia and Croatia, "a fetus is also a Croat" (1992, 59).

24 Several essays in Moghadam's (1994) anthology elaborate on this issue in Jewish, Christian, Hindu, and Muslim fundamentalisms. Controlling women's bodies through their reproductive powers resonates with certain claims of the U.S. religious right. However, it is very important to distinguish among the particular sociohistorical and geopolitical contexts of such discourses in the United States, the Middle East, and elsewhere.

25 In Iran since the Islamic regime, certain civil codes—especially those affecting women—have been replaced by the Islamic Rule of Ethics (the *Shari'a*) interpreted by Iranian Shia clergy. See Tohidi (1991).

26 A great deal of feminist writing has been concerned with the question of feminist consciousness and morality. The range of issues varies from questioning "feminine" virtues in a liberal feminist framework, to abortion and reproductive technologies in radical feminist perspectives, as well as a so-

cialist feminist theory of the alienation of women and, in poststructuralist feminisms, the notions of gaze, double consciousness, and divided self.

27 A number of feminist scholars draw a direct connection between women's maternalism and the emergence of welfare states (e.g., Koven and Michel, 1993).

28 With the postrevolutionary authoritarian imposition of *hijab* (modesty in general and Muslim women's dress code in particular) on all women, more punitive slogans such as *Ya ru sari ya tu sari* emerged to discipline women. As a result, many women were punished, discriminated against, and excluded from political, social, and economic spheres because of their uncompromising conduct vis-à-vis such rules and regulations. For further details see Tabari and Yeganeh (1982); Afshar (1987); and Adelkhah (1991).

29 Sometimes similar signifiers such as *hijab* and black chador are used to refer to veiling.

30 For more information, see Tohidi (1990).

31 *Gharbzadeh* is a portmanteau word that might be translated "westoxicated." The concept of *gharbzadegi* ("westoxication") was articulated in a 1962 book of the same name by Jalal-e Al-e Ahmad, an Iranian writer and cultural critic. It was popularized and very widely used by secular and religious oppositional movements to describe the colonizing effects of Westernization.

32 Ashraf-e-Dehghani wrote a short autobiographical prison memoir in which she described her resistance to different forms of torture, including rape. Her memoir was published as a *samizdat* and recited on the resistance radio stations.

33 I add *remasculinization* to the social phenomenon that includes the construction of masculinity and the process of emasculation. I have argued elsewhere (Moallem 1992) that one of the core components of the colonial civilizing mission in Middle Eastern countries has been the construction of gender identities as they relate to the global construction of race relations. Historically, both Eurocentrism and Orientalism, in their construction of a Muslim and Arab otherness, have used masculinity and femininity to legitimize power for Eurocentric subject positions (see Shohat and Stam 1995). This process has led to the emasculinization of Muslim men via their subordination to the Eurocentric and hegemonic models of masculinity. It also invented competing models of femininity for women. This process is still at work in the construction of the "Muslim other" in the new Euro-American racist discourses.

34 For more information on women's participation in the Iranian Revolution of 1979, see Azari (1983).

35 While an Orientalist and Eurocentric view constructs veiling as the ultimate form of Muslim women's victimization and oppression by a backward

and barbaric patriarchal order, this can only be related to what Fanon (1983) calls the "historic dynamism of the veil." While meanings assigned to dress are fully implicated in power relations, veiling in particular has been defined and manipulated within a range of historically, culturally, politically, and socially variable discourses and practices. In the modern epoch—spanning the period from colonialism and post–neocolonialism to the emergence of nationalism, fundamentalism, and feminism—veiling, unveiling, and reveiling have become an important metaphoric site of hegemonic politics and subject formation. A number of prominent Middle Eastern feminist scholars have consistently been engaged in an effort to demystify and decenter the monolithic dominant Eurocentric and Orientalist notions of veiling, see Abu-Lughod (1986), Ahmed (1992), Hoodfar (1992), Lazreg (1994), Mernissi (1992), and Milani (1991). In tracing the cultural basis and effects of imperialism, Grewal (1996) contextualizes the use of veiling in the colonial discourses of female incarceration shaping relational nationalist constructs of "home" and "harem."

36 In promoting Islamic *hijab*, Rahnavard writes, "And what of the unrestrained style of the colonialist, capitalist or imperialist systems, which expose you to lustful gazes, abuse you for the stupefaction of minds, and the rejection of superior values?" (1992, 9)

37 The underworld of women's responses to the demands of the Islamic ummat remains to be excavated.

38 The growing transnational movements of capital and labor, issues of migration, and the compression of time and space in the cultural flows of globalization demand careful examination—beyond the scope of this essay—with respect to both nationalization and transnationalization.

39 As emphasized by Cole and Keddie (1986, 2) Shi'ism is not now and never has been a monolithic movement, nor have either the *ulama* (religious scholars) or the followers of this branch of Islam always been activists or united in their views. For a multidimensional reading of the Karbala paradigm in its Shiite inflections in Iran, see Fischer and Abedi (1990).

40 In *The Phenomenology of Spirit,* in the section on "Lordship and Bondage," Hegel elaborates on the unhappy consciousness, which is based on the bondsman's recognition of enslavement.

41 The bureaucratization of the revolution and the Iran-Iraq war led to the institutionalization of martyrdom in the Islamic Republic.

42 An analysis of Muslim fundamentalist discourse must go beyond the notion of "reality testing," as argued by Gordon (1997). She refutes the Freudian restriction of the haunted field, arguing that "it is precisely the experience of being haunted in the 'world of common reality,' and the unexpected appearance of ghosts, wolves and uncanny images, that hampers or even destroys our ability to distinguish reality and fiction, magic and science, savage and

civilized, self and other, and in those ways lend reality a different color-
ation."

43   Barthes's ([1957] 1972) notion of myth as a mode of signification is very
useful for an understanding of death and martyrdom in fundamentalism.

44   In these local performances, women's roles are exclusively played by men
who dress up in women's clothing.

45   Death has been an important site of philosophical reflection. There are
a number of genealogical and sociological studies of death, e.g., Foucault
(1978); Derrida (1992); Bronfen (1992); and Kristeva (1980).

46   In addition to mainstream women's magazines such as *Zan-e-Rouz* and
Zanan, a number of specifically fundamentalist women's magazines and
journals are published in Iran. Examples such as *Mahjubah, Payam-e Ha-
jar, Mahjubah,* and the *Islamic Magazine for Women,* which is published in
English in Iran and distributed internationally, represent a variety of issues
that interest women, from women's rights in Islam to Islamic fundamentalist women's achievements worldwide.

47   Spivak speaks of a crisis as "the moment at which you feel that your presuppositions of an enterprise are disproved by the enterprise itself" (1990,
139).

48   Many philosophers have written about ambiguity and mystification as
prominent features of modern social life (Hegel, Marx, Heidegger, Marcuse,
and Sartre, among them).

49   Grewal's (1996) study of how the discursive colonial encounters shaped and
linked distinct constructs of gender and nation provides an excellent theoretical framework for the examination of the conditions of possibility of
feminist subject positions in historically contextualized locations.

50   Elspeth Probyn's (1993) effort to break through such a dichotomy is a contribution to feminism and fertile ground for further reflection.

51   Using The Body Shop as a case study, Caren Kaplan (1995) explores the complicities and resistances to transnational capital in some Euro-American
feminist discourses and practices. The signifiers of fundamentalist discourse have been adopted and used in advertisement and marketing. Within
the framework of the Islamic dress code, Islamic dress in the Iranian fashion industry has been reinvented in a variety of ways. Iran's new Sarah doll
shadows the Barbie marketing concept (but not its clothing).

Transnational Feminist Cultural Studies: Beyond the

Marxism/Poststructuralism/Feminism Divides

Caren Kaplan and Inderpal Grewal

Transnational feminism is neither revolutionary tourism, nor mere celebration of testimony. It is rather through the route of feminism that economic theories of social choice and philosophical theories of ethical preference can be complicated by cultural material.

—Gayatri Chakravorty Spivak,
Outside in the Teaching Machine, 1993

Why do we need a theory of transnational feminist practices?[1] After the 1993 annual Modern Language Association meetings, the question presents itself with a new urgency. That year's program contained many references to "gender," "geography," and "nation," yet we were powerfully struck by the fact that there was very little theorization of the relationships among these historically grounded terms. In the apparent quest to reorganize and expand the canon, recourse to geographical difference seems to be emulating the prior territory of sexual difference. In this happy pluralism, the conflicts and dependencies that structure a multinational world of neo- and postcolonialisms are erased or managed. Such management of diversity is not in and of itself new, nor is the role of feminism in this process of containment a recent development. Yet, in the effort to deconstruct the present positions of subjects within postmodernity, the tensions between liberal and more progressive forms of feminism are not being confronted.

In the midst of liberal versions of feminism that celebrate "multiculturalism" in order to manage diversity, we argue for the emergence of what could be called "transnational feminist cultural studies." Rather than maintaining and reproducing the divides between marxism, post-structuralism, and feminism, transnational feminist cultural studies would bring these approaches and tensions to bear on each other. Our purpose is not only to argue for the necessity of such a methodology but also to point out the consequences of maintaining the old divides. We see these consequences in the retrenchment of masculinist theories that consolidate traditional class analyses under the category of marxism, as well as in the recuperation of patriarchal representational practices within theorizations of contemporary transnational proletarian or subaltern movements (the so-called new social movements) (Mercer 1992, 440; Escobar 1992, 20–56; Escobar and Alvarez 1992). Feminist thought remains an important way to deconstruct such retrenchments and recuperations as long as it does not effect similar consolidations around the category of gender.

The reception of a feminist theorist such as Gayatri Chakravorty Spivak most compellingly illustrates the hegemonic force of the masculinist recuperation of marxism as it defines itself over and against both poststructuralism and feminism. Spivak's contributions to the theorization of the production of academic knowledge have been fundamental. In focusing on the interconnections among theories, institutions, and representations, Spivak's work mediates between marxism and feminism via poststructuralism. Her ambivalent reception by contemporary marxist theorists illustrates not only the strained dynamics among these methodologies and sets of interests but also the extent of patriarchal reassertions of authority in postmodern contexts. In this essay, we address these tensions among fields from a transnational feminist cultural studies perspective. First, we examine briefly the relation between marxism and Anglo-American feminism in order to map several points of conflict. Next we consider Spivak's erasure in recent masculinist marxist practices as a reassertion of patriarchy within modernist and postmodernist contexts. Finally, we propose transnational feminist cultural studies as a practice of resistance and critique that transforms the traditional divides in ways that are crucial to ongoing and emergent cultural theories and politics.

Old Divides for New Subjects: The Relationship between
Marxism and Anglo-American Feminism

In many instances, marxist thought refuses the possibility of theoretical and material alliance with poststructuralism, deconstruction, and theories of cultural representation. Rigid notions of what counts as marxism often lead to unexamined subject positions and an inability to account for the material conditions of theoretical production.[2]

Yet the modes of analysis rejected by masculinist marxist theorists have integrated and made at least partial use of marxist thought. For example, transnational feminist cultural studies relies on such terms as division of labor, class, capital, commodification, and production, among others, in order to analyze conditions of postmodernity just as much as it requires poststructuralist methodologies. In particular, the Gramscian notion of hegemony, Althussarian revisions of ideology, Williams's theorization of the role of literature and writing in society, Fanon and Cesaire's analysis of colonization and decolonization have all been crucial for our work and, indeed, for an entire generation of feminists such as Chandra Mohanty, Maria Mies, KumKum Sangari, Mary Layoun, Uma Chakravorty, Norma Alarcón, Gloria Anzaldúa, Ella Shohat, Cynthia Enloe, Donna Haraway, Nelly Richard, Aihwa Ong, Catherine Hall, Vron Ware, and Hazel Carby (to name just a few).

Historically, the link, or "marriage," between marxism and feminism has been termed an unhappy one (Hartmann 1979). Yet the relationship between marxist feminist and poststructuralist feminist methods has not been particularly friendly. Marxist feminist conventions posit gender as a class. Thus, many feminists who identify themselves as marxist view all women as belonging to a unified class with a homogeneous class consciousness. The Eurocentric and class-bound nature of this analysis is reflected in the theorization of the family as the primary site of oppression. Third world feminists and feminists of color have objected to a hegemonic approach that demonizes non-Western families as more oppressive than their first world counterparts. Valerie Amos and Pratibha Parmar's groundbreaking critique of such forms of feminist cultural hegemony, "Challenging Imperial Feminism," has been joined by more recent work, such as the essays collected in *Third World Women and the Politics of Feminism*, constituting a complex field of feminist engagement with marxist terms and the legacy of colonialism

(Amos and Parmar 1984; Mohanty, Russo, and Torres 1991). Conventional marxist feminist analyses are directed only at relations between men and women, not among women of various classes and races. As Hazel Carby has argued, such an analysis excludes nationalism as a condition of possibility for various forms of feminism and, therefore, ignores the context of imperialism and decolonization (1982, 212–35). This mode of analysis has been utilized beyond obviously marxist feminist projects, appearing in theories of cultural production that posit a singular or global notion of gender.[3]

On the other hand, recent approaches to global capital tend to ignore several decades of feminist research. Topics such as a gendered division of labor, sex tourism, critiques of Western development, and women and nationalism have an extensive bibliography that is rarely, if ever, referred to by the major marxist theorists. For example, Fredric Jameson has never rigorously engaged with or performed close readings of gendered issues or texts. His homogenizing focus on a "third world" that does not differentiate between elite or subaltern and male or female subject positions can be viewed as Eurocentric as well as masculinist. Such analyses that do not question the patriarchal construction of culture or cultural difference will recuperate another form of patriarchy, this time deployed by the status and prestige of the U.S. academic left. But Jameson is hardly unique in this regard. Just in passing, we can note the proliferation of such patriarchal critical formations in the supposedly oppositional practices of Terry Eagleton, Immanuel Wallerstein, Etienne Balibar, Perry Anderson, Franco Moretti, and Stanley Aronowitz. On the other hand, the work of Cornel West and Stuart Hall, to name only two important theorists, does incorporate marxist insights into gendered and racialized analyses of contemporary social formations. Without overgeneralizing, we argue that it is the critics who energetically question the doctrinaire paradigms of their received traditions along the lines of critiques of race, gender, and sexuality who have made some breakthroughs in articulating questions of agency and subjectivity against homogenizing theories.

The number of feminist scholars engaged in working with notions of class, ideology, and the division of labor in regard to the female body is legion, yet the lack of attention given to such a large and significant field of interdisciplinary work continues at many different levels. This refusal to engage scholarship on gender reproduces institutional patriarchies through academic "gatekeeping" rather than encouraging affiliation and exchange. The denial or rejection of gender as a crucial category of analysis refuses attention to the subject positions of people who fall under the category of "subaltern"; the proletariat as a universal category ignore the uneven divisions between men and women, as well as between first and third world constructions of class as inflected by race. Even though some feminist approaches to development, as well as global feminist approaches, have been seriously critiqued by Chandra Mohanty, Aihwa Ong, Trinh Minh-ha, Norma Alarcón, Gloria Anzaldúa, and Gayatri Spivak, we argue that such debates are worthy of rigorous scholarly attention for *all* those who seek to understand the role of gender within economic/cultural criticism. This history of controversy and debate is not parochial or simply local to Anglo-American feminism but is essential to any analysis of social movements.

Of course, earlier scholarship is always being changed, corrected, and critiqued, testifying to the institutionalizing as well as the viability of feminist academic practices. Yet these interested institutional divisions persist in part because they serve the purpose of demarcating professionalized boundaries of theories, disciplines, and canons. Thus, part of the emergence of interdisciplinary area studies was because of resistance against such rigid demarcations and institutional gatekeeping. At the present moment, interdisciplinary studies need to be reconfigured in light of new scholarship and altered social conditions. For instance, social theory has begun to examine the new social movements such as gay liberation in the United States and Europe, indigenous rights in the Americas, and transnational environmental activism. While some of this scholarship is attentive to understanding subject positions constructed by multiple and contingent social divisions, we also observe masculinist marxism reasserting itself by absorbing and appropriating the terms of social critique.

The tensions among the methodologies and locations of social critique have implications far beyond their academic manifestations since intellectual contestations over culture impact powerfully though differentially across and between public spheres. Therefore, it is not surprising that a theorist such as Spivak who continues to theorize these tensions is often erased or at best treated ambivalently by those who have a stake in consolidating new traditions of state and institutional power.

Situating Spivak: Reading *The Post-Colonial Critic*

Despite Spivak's ongoing contributions (it is not too extreme to say that she single-handedly cleared the ground for what we now call the field of postcolonial feminist studies), a backlash that includes the complete erasure or suppression of her work can be discerned in certain contexts. For instance, Aijaz Ahmad's influential and controversial study of the relationship of contemporary marxism and poststructuralist theory, *In Theory*, does not even list Spivak in the index. In *Public Culture*'s recent roundtable response to the publication of *In Theory*, several respondents noted the absence of any discussion of Spivak's work in the context of the marxism/poststructuralism divide. For example, Vivek Dhareshwar points out Spivak's work has been far more influential than either Rushdie's *Shame* or Jameson's piece on third world literature. As we will discuss in more depth, Spivak has made possible crucial negotiations among marxism, feminism, and poststructuralism. Yet, as Dhareshwar notes, Spivak plays no role in Ahmad's lengthy discussion of these very topics. Therefore, Dhareshwar goes on to argue, Ahmad's book enacts "a male agon, so common once among certain Marxist intellectuals." To include women would "change the character and intensity of that agon" (Dhareshwar 1993, 45).

We argue, however, that this "male agon" is not a phenomenon of the past but continues almost without interruption throughout the production of marxist cultural theory. *In Theory* enacts a particular kind of retrenchment in the face of poststructuralist critiques of historical narrativization and subject construction. Calling for more political accountability, Ahmad actually erases the evidence of concrete political emergences. Making only cursory and vague reference to feminist scholarship, Ahmad crafts an entire chapter on gender in Rushdie's work. He pays no attention to his own location as constructed by gender, just as he gives no appearance of acknowledging the transnational inequities in cultural production that pertain to gender. In this context, Ahmad's erasure of Spivak's central contribution to the topic of his book raises questions that move beyond the idiosyncrasies of individual choice and authorial intention. That is, as Ahmad the critic is reduced in a historically specific culture of marxism, his textual gestures can be read in a broader vein.

In Theory and the debates the text has engendered instigate questions about what gets to count as marxism and who is considered a marxist theorist. Part of the cultural debate in the aftermath of the book's publication includes a masculinist identity politics around marxism: who is or is not a "real" marxist, and so on.[4] Such discussions call upon discourses of authenticity: Which Marx is the authentic Marx? Which interpretation, which utilization overpowers others to be advanced as the singular or most valid version?[5] Which critiques are embraced as timely and valuable, and which are dismissed or suppressed? In the face of such efforts to contain the subject of marxism, it must be pointed out that the very history of marxist thought includes the proliferation of numerous "marxisms."[6] As Spivak points out, marxist texts are polyvocal: "The immense energy in transforming this to a univocal narrative has its own political history" (1990, 162). Efforts to purify the field through moralizing judgments about contaminated practices simply call into question institutional politics as they intersect with patriarchal practices. The question becomes then: What is being consolidated, and who is being served through such retrenchments? Such poststructuralist questions of marxism provide insight into the institutional locations of the cosmopolitan masculine subject.

If masculinist marxists leave Spivak out of the loop, Anglo-American feminism has displayed an, at best, ambivalent regard toward Spivak. For instance, in feminist film and literary studies, where psychoanalytic paradigms are dominant, Homi Bhabha's work may be more easily assimilable (Modleski 1991; Penley 1989; Doane 1991). Even in recent work on nationalism and feminism, bypassing Spivak (usually on the grounds of the impenetrability of the theoretical language) is quite common.[7] The continual misreading of the essay "Can the Subaltern Speak?" points to the readiness with which Anglo-American feminism rejects problematizing the metaphysics of voice and experience, particularly in relation to the representation of nonmetropolitan or poor women in diverse locations.[8] Thus, when U.S. feminists interpret Spivak as suggesting that the subaltern cannot speak, they devise a humanist take on an antihumanist political project. The intensity of the desire to extract authentic information and testimony from what is perceived to be peripheral or "other" suggests that what is necessary for an Anglo-American feminism is a misrecognition of complicity in colonial and neocolonial discursive formations. While Spivak asks us to analyze this desire and its linkages to first world consolidation of power, this mis-reading refuses such a linkage in favor of narrowly conceived metro-politan feminist concerns.

By bringing together marxism, poststructuralism, and feminist per-spectives within a comparative study of the first and third worlds, Spivak radically rewrites the paradigms of modernity and postmoder-nity (Young 1990, 157–75). Rather than follow the path of retrenchment and consolidation, Spivak has used moments of crisis and contradic-tion to theorize the relationships between cultural and economic value systems. The concept of crisis management is, therefore, key to her cri-tique of recuperative ideologies; in fact, it functions as a metaphor for deconstructive practice. By "crisis" she means the point at which "the presuppositions of an entire enterprise are disproved by the enterprise itself" (1990, 138–39). Thus, for Spivak, crisis can be the point of both opposition and recuperation. In particular, what Spivak describes as "negotiating the structures of violence" demonstrates a critical practice whereby one comes to understand one's location in the world. Under-standing violence in this sense does not give the theorist making the critique a pure space from which to speak. Thus, one's subject position, as Spivak would call it, is constituted through links among thoroughly unequal social forces. For instance, feminism must negotiate with the structures of phallocentrism, because "that is what enables us" (147). There is no space outside this configuration of power. As a theoretical concept, negotiation bypasses conventional binary divisions between positive and negative judgments in order to articulate a relationship be-tween the subject and the world.

Another powerful example of Spivak's methodology is visible in her sustained interrogation of value. In her analysis of the "materialist predication of the subject as labor power," Spivak utilizes the marx-ian notion that the worker is the producer of capital and, therefore, the source of value (1990, 97). Here Spivak combines marxism with deconstruction, reading surplus value as *différance*—that is, as the understanding of social injustice through interrogations of value (Chow 1993b). Unlike many other marxist critics, Spivak shifts her discussion of value to questions of global inequities within the context of cultural as well as economic imperialism, arguing that the third world pro-duces not only the material wealth but the "possibility of the cultural self-representation of the 'First World,'" continuing what she calls the idealist and the materialist predication of the subject (1990, 96). Thus, beyond Derrida *or* Althusser, Spivak's understanding of value and *différance* emerges from her practice as a postcolonial critic.

Such a practice leads Spivak to theorize imperialism and gender as keys to the texts of modern Europe and the culture of late capital. This theorization enables an understanding of the relations between culture and capital, not only within asymmetrical global relations but also as they are manifested in existing disciplinary and institutional formations. For example, in Spivak's critical practice, third world texts and contexts enter the Anglo-American cultural sphere not as marginal, minority, or multicultural objects but as materials central to first world subject formation. She performs this critique through her notion of "worlding," where the Anglo-American individualist's subject position is constructed by means of the exclusion of the "native woman" (1985, 262–80). Spivak critiques the project of the female individualist's subject constitution as part of the discursive field of "imperialist" ideology. She argues for feminist deconstruction of both subject constitution and sexual reproduction in the struggle to understand women's negotiation with hegemonic structures. In reading the great narratives of nationalism, internationalism, secularism, and culturalism as linked, Spivak's critical project illuminates the "epistemic violence" of both colonization and decolonization.

Therefore, Spivak's work illustrates the methodological imperative that brings together gender, political economy, the international division of labor, and, crucially because of where we are located, a critical understanding of the role of academic institutional production. This methodology can lead to what we have termed transnational feminist practices—that is, an attention to the linkages and travels of forms of representation as they intersect with movements of labor and capital in a multinational world. The institutional location of such a practice could be viewed in terms of an emergent field, cultural studies. We argue, however, that this field is easily appropriated for the very kinds of retrenchment and recuperation that have occurred within marxism (and some kinds of feminism) unless an international frame that addresses asymmetries of power and complex constructions of agency is rigorously engaged.

Toward Transnational Feminist Cultural Studies

Working in the interlocking fields of postcolonial discourse, international feminist theory, and literary/cultural production, we believe that the situation today requires a feminist analysis that refuses to choose among economic, cultural, and political concerns. What we need are critical practices that link our understanding of postmodernity, global economic structures, problematics of nationalism, issues of race and imperialism, critiques of global feminism, and emergent patriarchies. In particular, we are interested in how patriarchies are recast in diasporic conditions of postmodernity—how we ourselves are complicit in these relations, as well as how we negotiate with them and develop strategies of resistance. Theories of opposition that rely on unified subjects of difference and metaphysics of presence and voice cannot create alliances across differences and conflicts within a context of imperialism and decolonization. Transnational feminist cultural studies recognize that practices are always negotiated in both a connected and a specific field of conflict and contradiction and that feminist agendas must be viewed as a formulation and reformulation that is contingent on historically specific conditions.

We do not view this emergent set of practices as postfeminist. We adopt the term feminist in our critiques of masculinist social theory as well as in our attention to the scattered hegemonies that mark women's lives in postmodernity. As poststructuralists, we recognize the power relations that are a part of representational practices. Thus, gender must be viewed as intersected by numerous interests, including class, race, and sexuality. Our major departure from the standpoint epistemology school of thought within feminist studies stems from the interpellation of feminism and its discourses within modern social relations.[9] Instead of positing a humanist individual subject as the basis for a feminist standpoint, we utilize a notion of feminist practices (as historically specific instances, not as transhistorical doctrine) as a means to focus on gendered forms of cultural hegemony at diverse levels in societies. Simultaneously, we focus on the travels of feminist discourse as it is produced and disseminated through the cultural divides that mark global inequalities. Such a notion of travel marks asymmetries of power rather than a global cosmopolitanism.[10] Feminism remains an important political project that incorporates difference and hegemony as crucial to the study of women's lives in various societies.

Our points of affiliation with Spivak's project, therefore, reside most clearly in muddying the pure positions of institutional divides rather than in consolidating anything pristine or authentic. For purposes of praxis, it is more useful to work with Spivak's concept of "negotiating the structures of violence" than opting for some form of third world nostalgia, since the supposedly international concept of three worlds often masks a masculinist, unalienated notion of culture.[11] Where we differ may be in moving away from what we have seen as Spivak's internationalism (for example, in her essay "French Feminism Revisited") as well as her utilization of notions of strategic essentialism. Her internationalism can also be read in certain instances as a form of Eurocentrism; for example, Spivak's endorsement of Marie Aimée Hélie-Lucas's positing of an "indigenous" global feminism seems inadequate for an analysis of transnational movements of power and capital as well as national hegemonies (Spivak 1993, 141–71). Yet, despite these moments of disagreement with some aspects of Spivak's argument, it is Spivak's own methodologies that enable us to question any emphasis on similarities, universalisms, or essentialisms in favor of articulating *links* among the diverse, unequal, and uneven relations of historically constituted subjects.[12] Within humanist paradigms, similarities imply bonding between full subjects. Linkages suggest networks of economic and social relations that occur within postmodernity vis-à-vis global capital and its effects. Linkage does not require reciprocity or sameness or commonality. It can and must acknowledge differentials of power and participation in cultural production, but it also can and must trace the connections among seemingly disparate elements such as various religious fundamentalisms, patriarchies, and nationalisms.

Clearly, Spivak's response to institutional and political affiliations, as well as to the problems of dealing with coexisting modernisms and postmodernisms, is to accept both the limitations and the insights of marxism. We find that her complex methodological innovations never rest in easily categorizable locations. In fact, in more recent work, Spivak seems to depart from her earlier internationalism and its use of essentialism and homogenizing categories, turning to terms such as "transnational cultural studies" to describe her particular nexus of practices. In the final essay in her most recent book, *Outside in the Teaching Ma-*

chine, Spivak clearly addresses a new theoretical field, writing that her current work "concerns itself much more intensely with the U.S. scene and transnationality" (1993, 255). Spivak's new concern meets our interests not only in theorizing linkages rather than similarities but in practicing solidarity and coalition work in resistance to these linkages. As Spivak suggests, misrecognition of transnational links is an important political agenda in the service of reactionary interests: "There is interest, often unperceived by us, in not allowing transnational complicities to be perceived" (256). The task for transnational feminist cultural studies, therefore, is "to negotiate between the national, the global, and the historical, as well as the contemporary diasporic" (278).

In "Scattered Speculations on the Question of Cultural Studies," Spivak argues that questions of value and subject formation within an international frame would be central in any institutional formation of transnational cultural studies. Such a site for cultural studies would necessitate a politics of the classroom that moves "outside," linking subjects to the world. Without such questions, and without transnational feminist studies, cultural studies would be mere management of diversity or a trendy popular culture field. Unfortunately, such a danger is imminent in the United States since subject constitution, regionalized narrowly, can recuperate forms of ethnic nationalism.

From its earliest instance in the Birmingham context, cultural studies has incorporated important feminist critiques that address the intersections of race, class, gender, and ethnicity in Britain (Centre for Contemporary Cultural Studies 1992). However, a transnational frame did not emerge at that moment, leading to a narrowly defined idea of resistance that was limited to concerns that were British but by no means monolithic. In the United States, as programs and curricula come under the rubric of cultural studies, a narrow conception of feminism is more easily accommodated than are issues of class, race, and imperialism. Inasmuch as Eurocentrism predominates in these institutional locations, the likelihood of transnational critical practices diminishes. In fact, the demarcation made between postcolonial cultural studies and cultural studies suggests that in the United States, what was central in the Birmingham context is being separated out of a dominant cultural studies paradigm. Thus, U.S. postcolonial studies seems to erase considerations of neocolonialism within the constraints of its disciplinary formation. Further, focus on multiculturalism and on cultural nationalism recuperates problematics of ethnicity and race that are narrowly conceived, thereby erasing examinations of relationships between the United States and the rest of the world (Gilroy 1992, 187–98). Such a move is counter both to the Birmingham version of cultural studies, where the target was a racist state, and to transnational feminist cultural studies, where the target is those transnational complicities that recast national and cosmopolitan patriarchies.[13]

Given the state of these institutional, political, cultural, and economic developments, the reduction of the critical debate to an assumed divide between marxism and poststructuralism strikes us as regressive and pointless. Rather than balkanizing fields around micrologics—universalizing periodization, parochial nostalgias, and masculinist ideologies—we require affiliative projects based on synchretic methodologies. Turning away from internecine squabbles, we need to pay more attention to complex and linked inequalities and to the emergence of new ideologies and retrenchments.

Even a theorist such as Ahmad recognizes that contemporary struggles need to be "global and universal in character" to respond to transnational conditions (1992, 316).[14] Thus, even a masculinist marxist thinker must acknowledge that the stakes in what happens in metropolitan institutions as well as in upcoming struggles to represent emerging proletarian movements are now somewhat different. In this context, our struggle (and we believe we join Spivak at this juncture) is to utilize gender as an analytic category and to acknowledge transnational patriarchal links of culture and capital as important reactionary interests. If contemporary marxist theorists try to recuperate this terrain through a suppression or erasure of gender, forthcoming analyses of gendered subaltern subjects will misrepresent the nature of the struggle and cultural politics will remain patriarchal.

Notes

1 We began this discussion in the introduction to our edited collection *Scattered Hegemonies: Postmodernity and Transnational Feminist Practices* (Kaplan and Grewal 1994).

2 We want to be careful not to overgeneralize here, but it is fair to say that the marxist thinkers we are referring to are those who engage in poststructuralist ideas, participating in debates about the relationship between culture and political economy, even as they resist accounting for their gendered subject positions. Among those who fall into this category, we would

include Fredric Jameson, Terry Eagleton, Aijaz Ahmad, Stanley Aronowitz, and Frank Lentricchia.

3 In an interesting way, then, "radical cultural feminism" in the United States shares many characteristics with its supposed opposite, marxist feminism (particularly through globalizing gender). For a representative articulation of "global feminism," see Robin Morgan (1984).

4 Feminist scholars consolidate other kinds of authoritative subject positions. We should also note that "masculinist" gestures are frequently performed by female agents.

5 The roundtable response in *Public Culture* to *In Theory* provides a good example of this gesture; see Partha Chatterjee's essay "The Need to Dissemble" (1993b) and Aijaz Ahmad's response (1992) on which marxism is most representative of "Indian" nationalist interests, the "Calcutta" or the "Delhi" variety.

6 A complex and rigorous study of the travels of marxist ideas and practices in transnational reception remains to be written.

7 In a groundbreaking book such as *Third World Women and the Politics of Feminism*, the only critic to engage Spivak's work at any length is Rey Chow. For an extended discussion of Spivak's theory of value, see Chow (1993b).

8 At recent feminist conferences, we have noticed the prevalence of an almost obligatory attack on Spivak, based in part on the alleged opaqueness of her prose and in part on her supposed insistence on the silence of inaccessibility of "subaltern" speech. These readings of Spivak always center on a defense of the project of recovering "authentic" subject positions that can be discovered and self-articulated through "speech." In this scenario, Spivak plays the villain who would keep well-meaning first world inquiring minds and third world native informants apart.

9 For full critiques of "standpoint epistemology," see Alarcón (1990), and Grewal (1994).

10 We acknowledge a strong debt to both Edward Said (1983) and James Clifford (1992) in this notion of travel, even as we differ in important respects from their employment of the term (Kaplan 1996).

11 The cultural productions of feminists of color in North America and Europe in particular, as well as antiracist and anti-imperialist feminist practices in general, are often erased in such third worldism.

12 For a critique of strategic essentialism, see Dhareshwar (1989, 152). We argue that Spivak resorts, at times, to the very binaries that her work deconstructs. Marnia Lazreg points out that Spivak reads Devi's story "Dopti" as "documenting the villainous acts of Indian men and the victimization of Indian women." Lazreg's reading of Spivak's reading, then, illustrates Spivak's construction rather than deconstruction of a gendered binary, thereby losing

the opportunity to bring more attention to the complex subject positions of Senanayak and Arjan Singh, as well as Dopti (Lazreg 1988, 81–107).

13 Kobena Mercer (1992) points out that even in Britain, the "Rushdie affair" highlighted fissures in "Black Britain" that require a different kind of cultural studies.

14 For a discussion of this aspect of Ahmad's analysis and an in-depth examination of the "Ahmad controversy," see Lazarus (1993). At the heart of these discussions lies a debate over analyses of diasporic formations. We are arguing that the theories of this diaspora, which are emergent and conflicted, are being attacked by Ahmad for not being "rigorously marxist" (i.e., not conforming to masculinist notions of marxist practice).

Works Cited

Abdo, Nahlo. 1994. "Nationalism and Feminism: Palestinian Women and the Intifada—No Going Back?" In *Gender and National Identity*, edited by Valentine M. Moghadam, 148–70. London: Zed Books.

Abdo, Nahlo, and Nira Yuval-Davis. 1995. "Palestine, Israel and the Zionist Settler Project." In *Unsettling Settler Societies: Articulations of Gender, Race, Ethnicity and Class*, edited by Daiva Stasiulis and Nira Yuval-Davis, 291–322. London: Sage.

Abrahamian, Ervand. 1991. "Khomeini's Populism." *New Left Review* 186 (March–April): 102–19.

Abu-Laban, Yasmeen, and Daiva Stasiulis. 1992. "Ethnic Pluralism under Siege: Popular and Partisan Opposition to Multiculturalism." *Canadian Public Policy* 18, no. 4: 365–86.

Abu-Lughod, Lila. 1986. *Veiled Sentiments: Honor and Poetry in a Bedouin Society*. Berkeley: University of California Press.

Acuña, Rodolfo. 1981. *Occupied America: A History of Chicanos*. New York: Harper & Row. Published in 1972 as *Occupied America: The Chicano's Struggle Toward Liberation*. San Francisco: Canfield Press.

Adelkhah, Fariba. 1991. *La revolution sous le voil: Femmes islamiques d'Iran*. Paris: Karthala.

Adorno, Theodor. 1973. *Negative Dialectics*. New York: Seabury Press.

Afshar, Haleh. 1987. *Women, State, and Ideology: Studies from Africa and Asia*. Albany: State University of New York Press.

———. 1994. "Women and the Politics of Fundamentalism in Iran." *Women Against Fundamentalism* 5, no. 1: 15–20.

Agnew, John, and James Duncan, eds. 1989. *The Power of Place and Politics: Bringing Together Geographical and Sociological Imaginations*. Boston: Unwin Hyman.

Agnew, Vijay. 1996. *Resisting Discrimination: Women from Asia, Africa, and the Caribbean and the Women's Movement in Canada*. Toronto: University of Toronto Press.

Ahmad, Aijaz. 1992. *In Theory: Classes, Nations, Literatures*. London: Verso.

Ahmed, Leila. 1986. "Women and the Advent of Islam." *Signs* 11, no. 4: 665–91.

———. 1992. *Women and Gender in Islam*. New Haven: Yale University Press.

Alarcón, Norma. 1989. "Traddutora, Traditora: A Paradigmatic Figure of Chicana Feminism." *Cultural Critique* 13 (fall): 57–87.

———. 1990. "The Theoretical Subject(s) in *This Bridge Called My Back* and Anglo-American Feminism." In *Making Face, Making Soul/Haciendo Caras*, edited by Gloria Anzaldúa, 356–69. San Francisco: Spinsters/Aunt Lute.

———. 1996. "Conjugating Subjects in the Age of Multiculturalism." In *Mapping Multiculturalism*, edited by Avery Gordon and Chris Newfield, 127–48. Minneapolis: University of Minnesota Press.

Al-e-Ahmad, Jalal. 1962. *Gharbzadegi*. Tehran: Ketap.

Alfred, Gerald. 1995. *Heeding the Voices of Our Ancestors*. Toronto: Oxford University Press.

Allen, Paula Gunn. 1988. "Who Is Your Mother? Red Roots of White Feminism." In *Multicultural Literacy: Graywolf Annual Five*, edited by Rick Simonson and Scott Walker, 13–27. Saint Paul: Graywolf Press.

Allen, Theodore. 1994. *The Invention of the White Race*. London: Verso.

Allor, Martin. 1993. "Cultural Métissage: National Formations and Productive Discourses in Québec Cinema and Television." *Screen* 34, no. 1: 65–70.

Allor, Martin, and Michèle Gagnon. 1994. *L'état de la culture: Généalogie discursive des politiques culturelles québécoises*. Montréal: GRECC.

Alvarado, Salvador. 1916a. *Breves apuntes acerca de la administración del General Salvador Alvarado, como Gobernador de Yucatán, con simple expresión de hechos y sus consecuencias*. Mérida, Yucatán: Imprenta del Gobierno Constitucionalista.

———. 1916b. *Speech of General Alvarado, Governor of the State of Yucatán, at the Closing Session of the Second Pedagogic Congress, held at Mérida*. New York City.

———. [1919] 1980. *La reconstrucción de México: Un mensaje a los pueblos de America*, 3 vols. México: Ediciones del Gobierno de Yucatán.

Amos, Valerie, and Pratibha Parmar. 1984. "Challenging Imperial Feminism." *Feminist Review* 17: 3–19.

Anaya, Rudolfo A., and Francisco Lomelí, eds. 1989. *Aztlán: Essays on the Chicano Homeland*. Albuquerque: Academia El Norte Publications.

Anderson, Benedict. 1983. *Imagined Communities: Reflections on the Origin and Spread of Nationalism*. London: Verso.

Angelou, Maya. 1994. *The Complete Collected Poems of Maya Angelou*. New York: Random House.

Anthias, Floya, and Nira Yuval-Davis. 1989. Introduction to *Woman-Nation-State*, edited by Nira Yuval-Davis and Floya Anthias, 1–15. London: Macmillan.

———. 1992. *Racialized Boundaries: Race, Nation, Gender, Color, and Class and the Anti-Racist Struggle*. London: Routledge.

Anzaldúa, Gloria. 1987. *Borderlands La Frontera: The New Mestiza*. San Francisco: Spinsters/Aunt Lute.

———, ed. 1990. *Making Face, Making Soul/Haciendo Caras*. San Francisco: Spinsters/Aunt Lute.

Appiah, Anthony Kwame. 1992. *My Father's House*. Oxford: Oxford University Press.

Armas, José. 1975. "On the Journey to Octavio Paz." *De Colors* 2, no. 2: 4–10.

Armstrong, Sally. 1996. "Qui ou Non? What Do the Women of Québec Really Want?" *Homemaker's Magazine* (January–February): 16–27.

Arrieta, Rose. 1994. "Outside Looking In." *San Francisco Bay Guardian*, 3 August.

Arrom, Silvia. 1985. *The Women of Mexico City, 1790–1857*. Stanford: Stanford University Press.

Arteaga, Alfred, ed. 1994. *An Other Tongue: Nation and Ethnicity in the Linguistic Borderlands*. Durham, NC: Duke University Press.

Aubry, Jack. 1995. "Quebecers Less Sympathetic to Native Issues than Other Canadians: Poll." *Montréal Gazette*, 28 September.

Authier, P. 1995. "Landry Leaves Immigration Portfolio after Charges of Racism." *Ottawa Citizen*, 4 November.

Azari, Farah, ed. 1983. *Women of Iran: The Conflict with Fundamentalist Islam*. London: Ithaca Press.

Aztlán: Chicano Journal of the Social Sciences and the Arts. 1970. Los Angeles: Chicano Studies Center, University of California.

Ayubi, Nazih N. M. 1991. *Political Islam: Religion and Politics in the Arab World*. London: Routledge.

Badets, Jane. 1994. "Canada's Immigrants: Recent Trends." *Canadian Social Trends* 2: 27–30.

Bakan, Abigail B., and Daiva Stasiulis. 1995. "Making the Match: Domestic Placement Agencies and the Racialization of Women's Household Work." *Signs* 29, no. 2: 1–33.

Balibar, Etienne. 1991. "The Nation Form: History and Ideology." In *Race, Nation, Class*, edited by Etienne Balibar and Immanuel Wallerstein, 86–106, London: Verso.

———. 1994. *Masses, Classes, Ideas: Studies on Politics and Philosophy before and after Marx*. New York: Routledge.

Balibar, Etienne, and Immanuel Wallerstein, eds. 1991. *Race, Nation, Class: Ambiguous Identities*. London: Verso Press.

Balthazar, Louis. 1994. "Les nombreux visage du nationalisme au Québec." In *Québec: Etat et societé*, edited by A. G. Gagnon, 82–95. Montréal: Editions Québec/Amérique.

Bambara, Toni Cade. 1980. *The Salt Eaters*. New York: Random House.

Bannerji, Himani, ed. 1993. *Returning the Gaze: Essays on Racism, Feminism and Politics*. Toronto: Sister Vision Press.

Bannerji, Himani, et al., eds. 1991. *Unsettling Relations: The University as a Site of Feminist Struggles*. Toronto: Women's Press.

Barak, Gregg, ed. 1991. *Crimes by the Capitalist State*. New York: State University of New York Press.

Barrera, Mario, et al. 1972. "The Barrio as Internal Colony." In *People and Politics in Urban Society*, edited by Harlan Hahn, 465–98. Los Angeles: Sage.

Barrett, Michèle. 1991. *The Politics of Truth*. Stanford: Stanford University Press.

Barrett, Michèle, and Anne Phillips. 1992. *Destabilizing Theory*. Cambridge: Polity Press.

Barthes, Roland. [1957] 1972. *Mythologies*. New York: Noonday Press.

Bartky, Sandra Lee. 1990. *Femininity and Domination*. New York: Routledge.

Bateson, Gregory. 1972. *Steps Towards an Ecology of Mind*. San Francisco: Chandler Publishing.

Baudrillard, Jean. 1979. *Seduction*. Translated by Brian Singer. New York: St. Martins Press.

Befu, Harumi, ed. 1993. *Cultural Nationalism in East Asia: Representation and Identity*. Berkeley: Institute of East Asian Studies.

Beniger, James. 1986. *The Control Revolution: Technological and Economic Origins of the Information Society*. Cambridge, MA: Harvard University Press.

Benjamin, Walter. 1969. *Illuminations*. New York: Schocken Books.

Berlant, Lauren. 1991. *The Anatomy of National Fantasy: Hawthorne, Utopia, and Everyday Life*. Chicago: University of Chicago Press.

Bernal, Martin. 1987. *Black Athena: The Afroasiatic Roots of Classical Civilization*. New Brunswick, NJ: Rutgers University Press.

Bessmer, Sue. 1976. *The Laws of Rape*. New York: Praeger.

Bhabha, Homi K. 1990a. *Nation and Narration*. London: Routledge.

———. 1990b. "The Third Space: Interview with Homi Bhahba." In *Identity: Community, Culture, Difference*, edited by Jonathan Rutherford, 207–21. London: Lawrence & Wishart.

———. 1994. *The Location of Culture*. New York: Routledge.

Bisson, Sylvie. 1994. "Francophones et anglophones ont des vues opposés sur les autochtones." *Les Presses*, 11 March.

Bizjak, Tony. 1994. "Nearly 50 Million Californians Predicted in 2020." *The Sacramento Bee*, 20 April.

Blanco, Iris, and Rosalía Solórzano. 1994. "O te aclimatas o te aclimueres: aspectos de la emigración en la frontera con California." *fem* 34 (June–July): 20–22.

Blauner, Bob. 1972. *Racial Oppression in America*. New York: Harper & Row.

Block, Ian. 1995. "Quebecers at Heart: Province Launches $1.2 Million Ad Campaign to Right Against Intolerance of New Immigrants." *Gazette*, 9 May, Montréal ed.

Bloom, Lisa. 1993. *Gender on Ice: American Ideologies of Polar Expeditions.* Minneapolis: University of Minnesota Press.

Boal, Iain A. 1989. "Facing the Past." *Before Columbus Review* (spring–summer): 7–31.

———. 1995. "The Rhetoric of Risk." *Psychoculture* 1, no. 1: 6–8.

———. 1996. "Marjorie Nicolson and the Aesthetics of Nature." *Antipode* 28, no. 3: 304–15.

Boase, Joan Price. 1994. "Constitutional Change as a Political Issue." In *Canadian Politics*, edited by James P. Bickerton and Alain G. Gagnon, 389–405. Peterborough: Broadview Press.

Bonacich, Edna, ed. 1994. *Global Production: The Apparel Industry in the Pacific Rim.* Philadelphia: Temple University Press.

Borowy, Jan, Shelley Gordon, and Gayle Lebans. 1993. "Are These Clothes Clean? The Campaign for Fair Wages and Working Conditions for Homeworkers." In *And Still We Rise: Feminist Political Mobilizing In Contemporary Canada*, edited by Linda Carty, 299–330. Toronto: Women's Press.

Bourdieu, Pierre. 1977. *Outline of a Theory of Practice.* Trans. by Richard Nice. Cambridge: Cambridge University Press.

Brah, Avtar. 1991. "Difference, Diversity, Differentiation." *International Review of Sociology* 2: 53–72.

Breton, Raymond. 1974. "Types of Ethnic Diversity in Canadian Society." Paper read at the Eighth World Congress of Sociology, Toronto.

Brigham, Carl. 1923. *A Study of American Intelligence.* Princeton: Princeton University Press.

Bronfen, Elizabeth. 1992. *Over Her Dead Body: Death, Femininity and the Aesthetic.* New York: Routledge.

Brown, Elsa Barkley. 1995. "What Has Happened Here: The Politics of Difference in Women's History and Feminist Politics." In *We Specialize in the Wholly Impossible: A Reader in Black Women's History*, edited by Darlene Clark Hine, Wilma King, and Linda Reed, 39–54. Brooklyn: Carlson Publishing.

Buell, Frederick. 1994. *National Culture and the New Global System.* Baltimore: Johns Hopkins University Press.

Burnham, Margaret. 1987. "An Impossible Marriage: Slave Law and Family Law." *Law and Inequality* 5: 215.

Butler, Judith. 1990. *Gender Trouble: Feminism and the Subversion of Identity.* New York: Routledge.

———. 1993. *Bodies That Matter: On the Discursive Limits of "Sex."* New York: Routledge.

———. 1997. "Against Proper Objects." In *Feminism Meets Queer Theory*, edited by Elizabeth Weed and Naomi Schor, 1–26. Bloomington: Indiana University Press.

Cairns, Alan C. 1995. *Reconfigurations: Canadian Citizenship and Constitutional Change.* Toronto: McClelland and Stewart.

Cambron, Micheline. 1989. *Une société, un récit: Discours culturel au Québec.* Montréal: l'Hexagone.

Capirotada. 1997. Chicano Studies Program, University of Texas at El Paso. Spring.

Carby, Hazel. 1982. "White Women Listen! Black Feminism and the Boundaries of Sisterhood." In *The Empire Strikes Back,* edited by Centre for Contemporary Cultural Studies, University of Birmingham, 212–35. London: Hutchinson.

———. 1987. *Reconstructing Womanhood: The Emergence of the Afro-American Woman Novelist.* New York: Oxford University Press.

Cardinal, Linda. 1995. "Making a Difference: The Theory and Practice of Francophone Women's Groups, 1969–82." In *A Diversity of Women: Ontario, 1945–1980,* edited by Joy Parr. Toronto: University of Toronto Press.

Carens, Joseph H., ed. 1995. *Is Québec Nationalism Just? Perspectives from Anglophone Canada.* Montréal: McGill-Queen's University Press.

Carranza, Venustiano. 1915. *Carranza and Public Instruction in México: Sixty Mexican Teachers Are Commissioned to Study in Boston.* New York: n.p.

———. 1917. *Ley sobre relaciones familiares.* Mexico: Imprenta del Gobierno.

Castellano, Marlene Brant, and Janice Hill. 1995. "First Nations Women: Reclaiming Our Responsibilities." In *A Diversity of Women: Ontario, 1945–1980,* edited by Joy Parr, 232–51. Toronto: University of Toronto Press.

Castellano, Olivia. 1990. "Canto, locura y poesía: The Teacher as Agent-Provocateur." *The Women's Review of Books* 8, no. 5: 18–20.

Castelli, Elizabeth. 1991. "'I Will Make Mary Male': Pieties of the Body and Gender Transformation of Christian Women in Late Antiquity." In *Body Guards: The Cultural Politics of Gender Ambiguity,* edited by Julia Epstein and Kristina Straub, 29–49. London: Routledge.

Centre for Contemporary Cultural Studies, University of Birmingham, eds. 1992. *The Empire Strikes Back.* London: Hutchinson.

Certeau, Michel de. 1984. *The Practice of Everyday Life.* Trans. Steve Rendall. Berkeley: University of California Press.

Chabram-Dernersesian, Angie. 1992. "I Throw Punches for My Race, but I Don't Want to Be a Man: Writing Us—Chica-nos (Girl/Us)/Chicanas—into the Movement Script." In *Cultural Studies,* edited by Lawrence Grossberg, Cary Nelson, and Paula Treichler, 81–95. New York: Routledge.

Chacón, Leona Ruth. 1977. "Nací mujer." *Capirotada* (spring): 13.

Chase, Allan. 1980. *The Legacy of Malthus: The Social Costs of the New Scientific Racism.* Urbana: University of Illinois Press.

Chatterjee, Partha. 1993a. *The Nation and Its Fragments: Colonial and Postcolonial Histories.* Princeton: Princeton University Press.

———. 1993b. "The Need to Dissemble." *Public Culture* 6, no. 1: 55–64.

Chestnut, Mary Boykin. [1905] 1949. *A Diary from Dixie,* edited by Ben Ames Williams. Boston: Houghton Mifflin Company.

Chicago Cultural Studies Group. 1992. "Critical Multiculturalism." *Critical Inquiry* 18 (spring): 530–55.

Chow, Rey. 1991. *Woman and Chinese Modernity: The Politics of Reading Between West and East.* Minneapolis: University of Minnesota Press.

———. 1993a. *Writing Diaspora: Tactics of Intervention in Contemporary Cultural Studies.* Bloomington: Indiana University Press.

———. 1993b. "Ethics after Idealism." *Diacritic* 23, no. 1 (spring): 3–22.

Christ, Carol. 1980. *Diving Deep and Surfacing: Women Writers on Spiritual Quest.* Boston: Beacon Press.

Christ, Carol, and Judith Plaskow, eds. 1979. *Womanspirit Rising: A Feminist Reader in Religion.* San Francisco: Harper & Row.

Clifford, James. 1992. "Traveling Cultures." In *Cultural Studies,* edited by Lawrence Grossberg, Cary Nelson, and Paula Treichler, 96–117. New York: Routledge.

Cobb, Thomas. 1858. *Inquiry into the Law of Negro Slavery.* Philadelphia: T. J. W. Johnson.

Cobo-Hanlon, Liela. 1994. "Another Side of the 'Crazy Life.'" *Los Angeles Times,* 21 July.

Cole, Douglas L. 1971. "The Problem of 'Nationalism' and 'Imperialism' in British Settlement Colonies." *The Journal of British Studies* 10, no. 2: 160–82.

Cole, R. I. Juan, and Nikki Keddie, eds. 1986. *Shi'ism and Social Protest.* New Haven: Yale University Press.

Colombo, John Robert. 1996. "Canada Is the Only Constitution Without a Country." *Globe and Mail,* 13 September.

Come, Matthew Coon. 1995. "A Message Regarding the Rights of the Crees and Other Aboriginal Peoples in Canada." In *Sovereign Injustice: Forcible Inclusion of the James Bay Crees and Cree Territory into a Sovereign Québec.* Grand Council of the Crees. Nemaska, *Eeyou Astchee* (Québec).

Conlogue, Ray. 1996. "The Misleading Question of Québec Racism." *Globe and Mail,* 26 March. Toronto ed.

Connell, R. W. 1987. *Gender and Power.* Stanford: Stanford University Press.

Córdoba, Arnaldo. 1973. *La ideología de la Revolución Mexicana.* Mexico City: Ediciones Era.

Córdova, Teresa, et al., eds. 1986. *Chicana Voices: Intersections of Class, Race, and Gender.* Austin, TX: Center for Mexican American Studies.

Cornford, Adam, et al. 1987. "Political Poetry and Formalist Avant-gardes." In

City Lights Review 1, edited by Lawrence Ferlinghetti and Nancy J. Peters, 129–47. San Francisco: City Lights Books.

Cotera, Martha P. 1976. *Diosa y Hembra: The History and Heritage of Chicanas in the U.S.* Austin, TX: Information Systems Development.

———. 1980. "Feminism: The Chicana and Anglo Versions, a Historical Analysis." In *Twice a Minority: Mexican American Women*, edited by Margarita B. Melville, 217–34. St. Louis, MO: Mosby.

CrossRoads: Contemporary Political Analysis & Left Dialogue. 1993. "A Salute to Latinas in the Arts," no. 31 (May).

Daes, Erica Irene. 1993. "Some Considerations on the Right of Indigenous Peoples to Self-Determination." *Transnational Law and Contemporary Problems* 1: oo–oo.

Darwish, Mahmud. "Here We Are Near There." In *Dahāyā al-kharīta/Victims of a Map.* London: al-Saqi, 1984.

Dehghani, Ashraf. 1978. *Torture and Resistance in Iran: Memoirs of the Woman Guerilla.* New Delhi: Iran Committee.

de Lauretis, Teresa. 1986. *Feminist Studies/Critical Studies.* Bloomington: Indiana University Press.

———. 1987. *Technologies of Gender: Essays on Theory, Film, and Fiction.* Bloomington: Indiana University Press.

———. 1988. "Sexual Indifference and Lesbian Representation." *Theater Journal* 40, no. 2: 151–77.

Deleuze, Gilles. 1994. "Désir et plaisir." *Magazine littéraire* 325 (October): 59–65.

del Fuego, Laura. 1989. *Maravilla.* Encino, CA: Floricanto Press.

Delphy, Christine. 1983. "Agriculture et travail domestique: La réponse de la bergère à Engels." *Nouvelles questions féministes* 5 (spring): 3–17.

———. 1984. "Les femmes et l'état." *Nouvelles questions féministes* 6, no. 7 (spring): 5–19.

Derrida, Jacques. 1982. *Margins of Philosophy.* Translated by Alan Bass. Chicago: University of Chicago Press.

———. 1993. *Aporias.* Translated by Thomas Dutoit. Stanford: Stanford University Press.

———. 1995. *The Gift of Death.* Translated by David Wills. Chicago: University of Chicago Press.

De Seve, Micheline. 1992a. "The Perspectives of Québec Feminists." In *Challenging Times: The Women's Movement in Canada and the United States*, edited by Constance Backhouse and David H. Flaherty, 110–16. Montréal: McGill-Queen's University Press.

———. 1992b. "Women, Political Action, and Identity." In *Culture and Social Change: Social Movements in Québec and Ontario*, edited by Colin Leys and Marguerite Mendell, 128–39. Montréal: Black Rose Books.

Dhareshwar, Vivek. 1989. "Towards a Narrative Epistemology of the Postcolonial Predicament." *Inscriptions* 5: 135–58.

———. 1993. "Marxisms, Location Politics, and the Possibility of Critique." *Public Culture* 6, no. 1: 41–54.

Diamond, Sarah. 1995. *Roads to Dominion: Right-Wing Movements and Political Power in the United States.* New York: Guilford Press.

Dirlik, Arif. 1994. "The Postcolonial Aura: Third World Criticism in the Age of Global Capitalism." *Critical Inquiry* 20: 328–56.

Doane, Mary Anne. 1991. *Femmes Fatales: Feminism, Film Theory, Psychoanalysis.* New York: Routledge.

Douglass, Ann. 1977. *The Feminization of American Culture.* New York: Avon Books.

Dowell, Pat. 1994. "Poor Creatures." *In These Times,* August 8.

D'Souza, Dinesh. 1991. *Illiberal Education: The Politics of Race and Sex on Campus.* New York: Free Press.

Duclos, Nitya. 1993. "Disappearing Women: Racial Minority Women in Human Rights Cases." *Canadian Journal of Women and the Law* 6: 25–51.

Dumont, Micheline. 1992. "The Origins of the Women's Movement in Québec." In *Challenging Times: The Women's Movement in Canada and the United States,* edited by Constance Backhouse and David H. Flaherty, 72–89. Montréal: McGill-Queen's.

Edwards, Susan M. 1981. *Female Sexuality and the Law.* Oxford: Oxford University Press.

Egan, Carolyn, and Linda Gardner. 1994. "Race, Class and Reproductive Freedom: Women Must Have Real Choices!" *Canadian Woman's Studies* 14, no. 2: 95–99.

Eisenstein, Zillah. 1988. *The Female Body and the Law.* Berkeley: University of California Press.

El Saadawi, Nawal. 1988. *The Fall of the Imama.* London: Minerva.

Enloe, Cynthia. 1989. *Bananas, Beaches and Bases. Making Feminist Sense of International Politics.* Berkeley: University of California Press.

Enzensberger, Hans Magnus. 1982. "Poetry and Politics." In *Critical Essays,* edited by Reinhold Grumm and Bruce Armstrong, 15–34. New York: Continuum Books.

Escobar, Arturo. 1992. "Imagining a Post-Development Era? Critical Thought, Development, and Social Movements." *Social Text* 31–32: 20–56.

Escobar, Arturo, and Sonia Alvarez, eds. 1992. *The Making of Social Movements in Latin America: Identity, Strategy, and Democracy.* Boulder, CO: Westview.

Esposito, John L. 1993. *The Islamic Threat: Myth or Reality?* New York: Oxford University Press.

Estadistica Escolar Primaria de la República Mexicana. 1931. Mexico City: N.p.

Estrich, Susan. 1986. "Rape." *Yale Law Journal* 95, no. 6: 1087–1184.

———. 1987. *Real Rape.* Cambridge: Harvard University Press.

Ewen, Stuart. 1988. *All Consuming Images: The Politics of Style in Contemporary Culture.* New York: Basic Books.

Fanon, Frantz. 1967a. *Black Skin, White Masks.* New York: Grove Press.

———. 1967b. *A Dying Colonialism.* New York: Grove Press.

Fédération des femmes du Québec. 1990. "Memoire." Paper presented at Commission Sur L'Avenir Politique Et Constitutionnel du Québec, November.

Fischer, Michael M. J., and Mehdi Abedi. 1990. *Debating Muslims: Cultural Dialogues in Postmodernity and Tradition.* Madison: University of Wisconsin Press.

Fiske, Jo-Anne. 1995. "Political Status of Native Indian Women: Contradictory Implications of Canadian State Policy." *American and Indian Culture and Research Journal* 19, no. 2: 1–30.

Fitzhugh, George. 1971. *Cannibals All! Or Slaves Without Masters.* Cambridge: Belknap Press of Harvard University.

Flores, Francisca. 1971a. "Conference on Mexican American Women: Un Remolino." *Regeneración* 1, no. 1 (January): 1–5.

———. 1971b. Editorial. *Regeneración* 1, no. 10: n.p.

Flores, Juan. 1992. "Cortijo's Revenge: New Mappings of Puerto Rican Culture." In *On Edge,* edited by George Yúdice, Jean Franco, and Juan Flores, 187–205. Minneapolis: University of Minnesota Press.

Forrester, John. 1990. *The Seduction of Psychoanalysis.* Cambridge: Cambridge University Press.

Forum pour un Québec féminin pluriel. 1994. *Pour changer le monde.* Montréal: Les Éditions Écosociéte.

Foucault, Michel. 1970. *The Order of Things: The Archaeology of Human Sciences.* New York: Random House.

———. 1972. *The Archeology of Knowledge.* New York: Pantheon Books.

———. 1978. *The History of Sexuality.* Vol. 1. New York: Pantheon.

———. 1979a. *Discipline and Punish.* New York: Vintage Books.

———. 1979b. "L'Esprit d'un monde sans esprit." In *Iran: La revolution au nom de dieu,* edited by Claire Briere and Pierre Blanchet, 227–41. Paris: Editions du Seuil.

———. 1989. "La gouvernementalité." *Magazine littéraire* 269: 97–103.

———. [1954] 1994. "Introduction to *Le Rêve et l'Existence* by Ludwig Binswanger." Paris: Desclée de Brouwer. Reprinted in *Dits et écrits,* 1: 65–119. Paris: Gallimard.

———. 1994. "Distance, aspect, origine." In *Dits et écrits,* 1: 272–85. Paris: Gallimard.

———. [1979] 1994. "Inutile de Soulever?" Reprinted in *Dits et écrits*, 3: 790–94. Paris: Gallimard.

Fox-Genovese, Elizabeth. 1988. *Within the Plantation Household: Black and White Women of the Old South.* Chapel Hill: University of North Carolina Press.

Frager, Ruth A. 1992. *Sweatshop Strife: Class, Ethnicity, and Gender in the Jewish Labour Movement of Toronto, 1900–1939.* Toronto: University of Toronto Press.

Franco, Jean. 1988. "Beyond Ethnocentrism: Gender, Power and the Third-World Intelligentsia." In *Marxism and the Interpretation of Culture,* edited by Cary Nelson and Lawrence Grossberg, 503–15. Urbana: University of Illinois Press.

Frankenberg, Ruth, and Lata Mani. 1993. "Crosscurrents, Crosstalk: Race, 'Postcoloniality' and the Politics of Location." *Cultural Studies* 7: 292–310.

Fraser, Nancy. 1991. *Unruly Practices.* Minneapolis: University of Minnesota Press.

———. 1994. "Rethinking the Public Sphere." *Social Text* 25–26: 56–90.

———. 1995. "From Redistribution to Recognition? Dilemmas of Justice in a 'Post-Socialist' Age." *New Left Review* 21, no. 2 (July–August): 68–93.

Fregoso, Rosa Linda. 1992. "Chicana Film Practices: Confronting the 'Many-Headed Demon of Oppression.'" In *Chicanos and Film: Representation and Resistance,* edited by Chon Noriega, 189–204. Minneapolis: University of Minnesota Press.

———. 1993. *The Bronze Screen: Chicana and Chicano Film Culture.* Minneapolis: University of Minnesota Press.

———. 1995. "Hanging the Homegirls: *Mi Vida Loca,* Alison Anders." *Cineaste* 21, no. 2: 36–37.

Fregoso, Rosa Linda, and Angie Chabram, eds. 1990. "Chicana/o Cultural Representations: Reframing Alternative and Critical Discourses." *Cultural Studies* 4, no. 3: 203–341.

Frideres, James. 1993. *Native Peoples in Canada: Contemporary Conflicts.* Scarborough, Ontario: Prentice-Hall.

Friedman, Susan. 1995. "Beyond White and Other: Relationality and Narratives of Race in Feminist Discourse." *Signs: Journal of Women in Culture and Society* 21, no. 1: 1–49.

Frost, Robert. 1995. *Collected Poems, Prose, and Plays.* New York: Library of America.

Gabriel, Christie. 1996. "One of the Other? 'Race,' Gender and the Limits of Official Multiculturalism." In *Women and Canadian Public Policy,* edited by Janine Brodie, 173–95. Toronto: Harcourt, Brace and Company.

Gafari, Hadi. 1979. *Hamd Mi Amouzad.* Tehran: Bessat.

Galindo, Hermila. 1915. *La mujer en el porvenir.* Mérida, Yucatán: Imprenta y Litografía de "La Voz de la Revolución."

———. 1916. *Estudio de la Señorita Hermila Galindo con motivo de los temas que han de absolverse en el Segundo Congreso Feminista de Yucatán.* Mérida, Yucatán: Imprenta del Gobierno Constitucionalista.

———. 1919a. *La doctrina Carranza y el acercamiento indolatino.* Mexico: N.p.

———. 1919b. *Un Presidenciable.* Mexico, D.F.: Imprenta Nacional.

Gamboa, Ignacio. 1906. *La Mujer Moderna.* Mérida, Yucatán: Imprenta Gamboa Guzman.

García, Alma M. 1989. "The Development of Chicana Feminist Discourse: 1970–1980." *Gender and Society* 3: 418–31.

García, Mario T. 1989. *Mexican Americans: Leadership, Ideology and Identity, 1930–1960.* New Haven: Yale University Press.

George, Alexander, ed. 1991. *Western State Terrorism.* New York: Routledge.

Getman, Karen. 1984. "Sexual Control in the Slaveholding South: The Implementation and Maintenance of a Racial Caste System." *Harvard Women's Law Journal,* 7: 115–52.

Gilroy, Paul. 1987. *There Ain't No Black in the Union Jack: The Cultural Politics of Race and Nation.* London: Hutchinson.

———. 1991. "It Ain't Where You're From . . . It's Where You're At . . . The Dialectics of Diasporic Identification." *Third Text* 13: 3–16.

———. 1992a. "Cultural Studies and Ethnic Absolutism." In *Cultural Studies,* edited by Lawrence Grossberg, Cary Nelson, and Paula Treichler, 187–98. New York: Routledge.

———. 1992b. "The End of Antiracism." In *"Race," Culture and Difference,* edited by James Donald and Ali Rattansi, 49–61. London: Sage/The Open University.

Giménez, Martha. 1989. "The Political Construction of the Hispanic." In *Estudios Chicanos and the Politics of Community,* edited by Mary Romero and Cordelia Candelaria, 66–85. Boulder: National Association for Chicano Studies.

Glazer, Nathan, and Daniel P. Moynihan. 1975. *Ethnicity: Theory and Experience.* Cambridge, MA: Harvard University Press.

Goldberg, David Theo, ed. 1994. *Multiculturalism: A Critical Reader.* Oxford: Basil Blackwell.

González, Rodolfo. 1972. *I am Joaquín.* New York: Bantam.

González, Sylvia Alicia. 1974. *La Chicana Piensa: The Social Cultural Consciousness of a Mexican-American Woman.* N.p: n.p.

Gonzales-Berry, Erlinda. 1991. *Paletitas de Guayaba.* Albuquerque: El Norte.

Goodell, William. [1853] 1968. *The American Slave Code.* New York: Johnson Reprint Corporation.

Goodleaf, Donna K. 1993. " 'Under Military Occupation': Indigenous Women,

State Violence and Community Resistance." In *And Still We Rise: Feminist Political Mobilizing in Contemporary Canada*, edited by Linda Carty, 225–42. Toronto: Women's Press.

Gordon, Avery F. 1997. *Ghostly Matters: Haunting and the Sociological Imagination*. Minneapolis: University of Minnesota Press.

Gordon, Avery F., and Christopher Newfield, eds. 1996. *Mapping Multiculturalism*. Minneapolis: University of Minnesota Press.

Gramsci, Antonio. 1971. *The Prison Notebooks*, edited and translated by Quintin Hoare and Geoffrey Nowell-Smith. New York: International Publishers.

Grand Council of the Crees. 1995. *Sovereign Injustice: Forcible Inclusion of the James Bay Crees and Cree Territory into a Sovereign Québec*. Grand Council of the Crees. Nemaska, *Eeyou Astchee* (Québec).

Gray, John. 1995. "English-Speaking Montrealers Cry Foul over Hospital Closings." *Globe and Mail*, 11 November. Ottawa ed.

Grewal, Inderpal. 1993. "Reading and Writing the South Asian Diaspora: Feminism and Nationalism in North America." In *Our Feet Walk the Sky: Women of the South Asian Diaspora*, edited by The Women of South Asian Descent Collective, 226–36. San Francisco: Aunt Lute Books.

———. 1994. "Autobiographic Subjects and Diasporic Locations: *Meatless Days and Borderlands*." In *Scattered Hegemonies*, edited by Inderpal Grewal and Caren Kaplan, 231–54. Minneapolis: University of Minnesota Press.

———. 1996. *Home and Harem: Nationalism, Imperialism, and the Culture of Travel*. Durham, NC: Duke University Press.

Grewal, Inderpal, and Caren Kaplan, eds. 1994. *Scattered Hegemonies: Postmodernity and Transnational Feminist Practices*. Minneapolis: University of Minnesota Press.

Griswold del Castillo, Richard, Teresa McKenna, and Yvonne Yarbro-Bejarano, eds. 1990. *Chicano Art: Resistance and Affirmation, 1965–1985 / CARA*. Los Angeles: Wight Art Gallery, University of California.

Grossberg, Lawrence, Cary Nelson, and Paula Treichler, eds. 1992. *Cultural Studies*. New York: Routledge.

Guillaumin, Colette. 1977. "Race et nature: Système des marques, idée de groupe naturel et rapports sociaux." *Pluriel* 11: 39–55.

———. 1978a. "Pratique du pouvoir et idée de Nature (1): L'appropriation des femmes." *Questions féministes* 2: 5–30.

———. 1978b. "The Practice of Power and Belief in Nature, Part 1: The Appropriation of Women." *Feminist Issues* 1, no. 2: 3–28.

———. 1985. "Avec ou sans race." *Le genre Humain* 11: 215–22.

———. 1995. *Racism, Sexism, Power and Ideology*. New York: Routledge.

Gutiérrez, Natividad. 1995. "Miscegenation as Nation-Building: Indian and Immigrant Women in Mexico." In *Unsettling Settler Societies: Articulations of Gender, Race, Ethnicity and Class,* edited by Daiva Stasiulis and Nira Yuval-Davis, 161–87. London: Sage.

Gutmann, Amy, ed. 1994. *Multiculturalism.* Princeton: Princeton University Press.

Habermas, Jürgen. 1973. *Legitimation Crisis.* Boston: Beacon Press.

Hall, Catherine. 1993. "Gender, Nationalisms and National Identities: Bellagio Symposium, July 1992." *Feminist Review* 44 (summer): 97–103.

Hall, Stuart. 1986. "Gramsci's Relevance for the Study of Race and Ethnicity." *Journal of Communication Theory* 10, no. 2: 5–27.

———. 1989. "Cultural Identity and Cinematic Representation." *Framework* 36: 68–81.

———. 1990. "Cultural Identity and Diaspora." In *Identity, Community, Culture, Difference,* edited by Jonathan Rutherford, 222–37. London: Lawrence & Wishart.

———. 1991. "The Local and the Global: Globalization and Ethnicity." In *Culture, Globalization and the World System,* edited by Anthony King, 19–40. Binghamton: State University of New York Press.

———. 1992. "New Ethnicities." In *"Race," Culture, and Difference,* edited by James Donald and Ali Rattansi, 49–61. London: Sage Publications/Open University.

Hall, Stuart, et al., eds. 1996. *Modernity: An Introduction to Modern Societies.* Oxford: Blackwell Publishers.

Hamilton, Sylvia. 1993. "The Women at the Well: African Baptist Women Organize." In *And Still We Rise: Feminist Political Mobilizing In Contemporary Canada,* edited by Linda Carty, 189–206. Toronto: Women's Press.

Harris, Mary. 1994. "Cholas, Mexican-American Girls, and Gangs." *Sex Roles* 30, nos. 3–4: 284–301.

Hart, John Mason. 1987. *Revolutionary Mexico: The Coming and Process of the Mexican Revolution.* Berkeley: University of California.

Hartmann, Heidi. 1979a. "The Unhappy Marriage of Marxism and Feminism: Towards a More Progressive Union." *Capital and Class* 8 (summer): 1–33.

———. 1979b. "Capitalism, Patriarchy and Job Segregation by Sex." In *Capitalism, Patriarchy, and the Case for Socialist Feminism,* edited by Zillah Eisenstein, 206–47. New York: Monthly Review Press.

Harvey, David. 1996. *Justice, Nature and the Geography of Difference.* Cambridge, MA: Blackwell Publishers.

———. 1989. *The Condition of Postmodernity.* Oxford: Basil Blackwell.

Haug, Wolfgang. 1986. *A Critique of Commodity Aesthetics: Appearance, Sexuality, and Advertising in Capitalist Society.* Minneapolis: University of Minnesota Press.

Hawley, John Stratton, ed. 1994. *Fundamentalism and Gender.* New York: Oxford University Press.

Hecht, Susanna, and Alexander Cockburn. 1989. *The Fate of the Forest: Destroyers, Developers and Defenders of the Amazon*, 2d ed. London: Verso.

Hegel, G. W. F. 1977. *The Phenomenology of Spirit*. Trans. by A. V. Miller. Oxford: Oxford University Press.

Hélie-Lucas, Marie-Aimée. 1987. "Bound and Gagged by the Family Code." In *Third World/Second Sex: Women's Struggles and National Liberation*, edited by Miranda Davies, 3–15. London: Zed Books.

Henry, Keith S. 1981. *Black Politics in Toronto Since World War I.* Toronto: Multicultural History Society.

Hernández, Deluvina. 1970. "La Raza Satellite System." *Aztlán: Journal of the Social Sciences and the Arts* 1, no. 1 (spring): 13–36.

Herrnstein, Richard, and Charles Murray. 1994. *The Bell Curve: Intelligence and Class Structure in American Life*. New York: Free Press.

Higginbotham, A. Leon. 1989. "Race, Sex, Education and Missouri Jurisprudence: *Shelley v. Kraemer* in a Historical Perspective." *Washington University Law Quarterly* 67: 673–708.

Hindess, Barry, and Paul Hirst. 1975. *Pre-Capitalist Modes of Production*. London: Routledge and Kegan Paul.

Hobsbawm, Eric J. 1990. *Nations and Nationalism Since 1789*. Cambridge: Cambridge University Press.

Hochschild, Arlie Russell. 1989. *The Second Shift: Working Parents and the Revolution at Home*. New York: Viking-Penguin.

Hollander, Anne. 1994. *Sex and Suits*. New York: Kodansha International.

Hollinger, David A. 1992. "Postethnic America." *Contention* 2, no. 1: 79–96.

———. 1995. *Postethnic America: Beyond Multiculturalism*. New York: Basic Books.

Honig-Parnass, Tivka. 1994. "Jewish Fundamentalism and Oppression of Women as Inherent in the Jewish-Zionist State." *Women Against Fundamentalism* 1, no. 5: 21–24.

Hoodfar, Homa. 1991. "Return to Veil: Personal Strategy and Public Participation in Egypt." In *Working Women: International Perspectives on Labour and Gender Ideology*, edited by Nanneke Redclift and M. Thea Sinclair, 104–24. London: New York: Routledge.

hooks, bell. 1981. *Ain't I a Woman? Black Women and Feminism*. Boston: South End Press.

———. 1984. *Feminist Theory: From Margin to Center*. Boston: South End Press.

———. 1990. *Yearning: Race, Gender, and Cultural Politics*. Boston: South End Press.

Huntington, S. P. 1993. "The Clash of Civilisations?" *Foreign Affairs* 72, no. 3 (summer): 22–49.

Hurtado, Aída. 1989. "Relating to Privilege: Seduction and Rejection in the Subordination of White Women and Women of Color." *Signs* 14, no. 4: 833–55.

Huyssen, Andreas. 1986. *After the Great Divide: Modernism, Mass Culture, Postmodernism.* Bloomington: Indiana University Press.

Ignatieff, Michael. 1993. *Blood and Belonging: Journeys into the New Nationalism.* Toronto: Viking.

Irigaray, Luce. 1985. *This Sex Which Is Not One.* Ithaca, NY: Cornell University Press.

Ishihara, Shintaro. 1991. *The Japan That Can Say No.* New York: Simon & Schuster.

Ivy, Marilyn. 1988. "Tradition and 'Difference' in the Japanese Mass Media." *Public Culture* 1, no. 1 (fall): 21–29.

———. 1995. *Discourses of the Vanishing: Modernity, Phantasm, Japan.* Chicago: University of Chicago Press.

Jackson, Peter, and Jan Penrose, eds. 1993. *Constructions of Race, Place and Nation.* London: UCL Press.

Jaimes, M. Annette, ed. 1992. *The State of Native America: Genocide, Colonization and Resistance.* Boston: South End Press.

Jameson, Fredric. 1983. "Euphorias of Substitution: Hubert Acquin and the Political Novel in Québec." *Yale French Studies* 65: 214–23.

———. 1991. *Postmodernism, or, the Cultural Logic of Late Capitalism.* Durham, NC: Duke University Press.

Jansen, Godfrey H. 1980. *Militant Islam.* New York: Harper & Row.

Jardine, Alice A. 1985. *Gynesis: Configurations of Woman and Modernity.* Ithaca, NY: Cornell University Press.

Jefferson, Thomas. [1801] 1982. *Notes on the State of Virginia.* New York: Norton.

Jhappan, Radha. 1993. "Inherency, Three Nations and Collective Rights: The Evolution of Aboriginal Constitutional Discourse from 1982 to the Charlottetown Accord." *International Journal of Canadian Studies* 7–8 (spring–fall): 226–59.

———. 1996. "Post-Modern Essentialism or a Post-Mortem of Scholarship." *Studies in Political Economy* 51 (fall): 15–64.

Jordan, Winthrop. 1968. *White Over Black: American Attitudes Toward the Negro, 1550–1812.* New York: Norton.

Joseph, Gilbert M. 1982. *Revolution from Without: Yucatán, México and the United States, 1880–1924.* London: Cambridge University Press.

Joseph, Gilbert M., and Daniel Nugent, eds. 1994. *Everyday Forms of State Formation: Revolution and the Negotiation of Rule in Modern Mexico.* Durham, NC: Duke University Press.

Joseph, Suad. 1977. "Zaynab: An Urban Working Class Lebanese Woman." In *Middle Eastern Muslim Women Speak,* edited by Elizabeth W. Fernea and Basima Q. Bezirgan, 359–71. Austin: University of Texas Press.

———. 1978. "Women and the Neighborhood Street in Borj Hammoud, Lebanon." In *Women in the Muslim World*, edited by Lois Beck and Nikki Keddie, 541–57. Cambridge, MA: Harvard University Press.

———. 1983. "Working Class Women's Networks in a Sectarian State: A Political Paradox." *American Ethnologist* 10, no. 1: 1–22.

Juteau-Lee, Danielle. 1979. "La sociologie des frontières ethniques en devenir." In *Frontières ethniques en devenir/Emerging Ethnic Boundaries*, edited by Danielle Juteau, with the collaboration of Lorne Laforge, 3–21. Ottawa: Editions de l'Université d'Ottawa.

———. 1983. "La production de l'ethnicité ou la part réelle de l'idéel." *Sociologie et sociétés* 15, no. 2: 33–47.

Juteau, Danielle. 1992. "The Sociology of Ethno-National Relations in Québec." In *Deconstructing a Nation: Immigration, Multiculturalism & Racism in '90s Canada*, edited by Vic Satzewich, 323–42. Halifax: Fernwood.

———. 1993. "The Production of the Québécois Nation." *Humbolt Journal of Social Relations* 19, no. 2: 79–101.

———. 1996. "L'ethnicité comme rapport social." Paper presented at the conference *Etat, Nation, Multiculturalism et Citoyenté*, CEETUM, Montréal, 30 May–2 June.

Juteau, Danielle, and Nicole Laurin. 1989a. "La sécularisation et l'étatisation du secteur hospitalier au Québec de 1960 à 1966." In *Jean Lesage et l'éveil d'une nation*, edited by Robert Comeau, 155–67. Montréal: Les Presses de l'Université du Québec.

———. 1989b. "From Nuns to Surrogate Mothers: Evolution of the Forms of the Appropriation of Women." *Feminist Issues* 9, no. 1: 13–40.

———. 1997. Un métier et une vocation: *Le travail des religieuses du Québec, de 1901 à 1971*. Montréal: Les Presses de l'université de Montréal.

Juteau, Danielle, and Marie McAndrew. 1992. "Project national, immigration et integration dans un Québec soverain." In *Les attributs d'un Québec soverain*, edited by Commission d'etude du Québec a la souveraineté, 161–80. Québec: Bibliothèque nationale du Québec.

Kadi, Joanna, ed. 1994. *Food for Our Grandmothers: Writings by Arab American and Arab Canadian Feminists*. Boston: South End Press.

Kamin, Leon, Richard C. Lewontin, and Steven Rose, eds. 1984. *Not in Our Genes: Biology, Ideology and Human Nature*. Harmondsworth: Penguin.

Kandiyoti, Deniz. 1991. *Women, Islam, and the State*. Philadelphia: Temple University Press.

Kanellos, Nicolás, and Luis Dávila. 1971. Introduction. *Revista Chicano Riqueña* 4, no. 4: 1–2.

Kaplan, Caren. 1995. "'A World Without Boundaries': The Body Shop's Trans/National Geographies." *Social Text* 43 (fall): 45–66.

———. 1996. *Questions of Travel: Postmodern Discourses of Displacement*. Durham, NC: Duke University Press.

Kauffman, Linda A. 1990. "The Anti-Politics of Identity." *Socialist Review* 1: 67–80.

Kauffman, Renee Debra. 1991. *Rachel's Daughters: Newly Orthodox Jewish Women.* New Brunswick, NJ: Rutgers University Press.

Kawabata, Yasunari. 1957. *Snow Country.* Translated by Edward G. Seidensticker. New York: Perigee.

Kaye, Mary. 1990. "In the Spirit of the Family." *Canadian Living* 13 (October): 1–138.

Kemble, Fanny. 1984. *Journal of a Residence on a Georgia Plantation in 1838–1839,* edited by John A. Scott. Athens: University of Georgia Press.

Khomeini, Sayyid Ruhullah Musavi. 1980. *Selected Messages and Speeches of Imam Khomeini.* Tehran: Ministry of National Guidance.

———. 1981. *Islam and Revolution: Writings and Declarations of Imam Khomeini.* Translated by Hamid Algar. Berkeley, CA: Mizan Press.

———. 1986. *Simay-e Zan dar Kalam-e Imam Khomeini.* Tehran: Vezarat-Ershad-e Islami.

———. 1989. *Hukumat-e Islami: Velayat-eFaqih.* Tehran: Amir Kabir.

Klatch, Rebecca E. 1987. *Women of the New Right.* Philadelphia: Temple University Press.

Kondo, Dorinne. 1997. *About Face: Performing "Race" in Fashion and Theater.* New York: Routledge.

Korac, Maja. 1996. "Understanding Ethnic-National Identity and Its Meaning: Questions from a Woman's Experience." *Women's Studies International Forum* 19, nos. 1–2: 133–43.

Kort, Michele. 1994. "Filmmaker Alison Anders: Her Crazy Life." *Ms.* May–June: 80–83.

Koven, Seth, and Sonya Michel. 1993. *Mothers of a New World: Maternalist Politics and the Origin of Welfare States.* New York: Routledge.

Kozasu, Akiko. 1989. "Rei Kawakubo and Her Stylish Atmosphere." *Marie Claire Japon* 3 (March): 159–74.

Kristeva, Julia. 1982a. *The Powers of Horror: An Essay on Abjection.* Translated by Leon S. Roudiez. New York: Columbia University Press.

———. 1982b. *Pouvoirs de l'horreur.* Paris: Editions du Seuil.

———. 1993. *Nations Without Nationalism.* New York: Columbia University Press.

Kroker, Arthur. 1984. *Technology and the Canadian Mind: Innis/McLuhan/Grant.* Montréal: New World Perspectives.

Krosenbrink-Gelissen, Lilianne Ernestine. 1993. "The Native Women's Association of Canada." In *Native Peoples in Canada: Contemporary Conflicts,* 4th ed., edited by James Frideres, 335–64. Scarborough, Ontario: Prentice-Hall.

Kymlicka, Will. 1995. *Multicultural Citizenship.* Oxford: Clarendon Press.

Labelle, Michelle. 1990. "Immigration, culture et question nationale." *Cahiers de recherché sociologique* 14: 143–51.

Laczko, Leslie. 1995. *Pluralism and Inequality in Québec.* Toronto: University of Toronto Press.

Larner, Wendy. 1995. "Theorizing 'Difference' in Aotearoa/New Zealand." *Gender, Place and Culture* 2, no. 2: 177–90.

Larner, Wendy, and Paul Spoonley. 1995. "Post-Colonial Politics in Aotearoa/New Zealand." In *Unsettling Settler Societies: Articulations of Gender, Race, Ethnicity and Class,* edited by Daiva Stasiulis and Nira Yuval-Davis, 39–64. London: Sage.

Latin American Subaltern Studies Group. 1993. "Founding Statement." *boundary 2* 20 (fall): 110–21.

Laurin, Nicole, Danielle Juteau, and Lorraine Duchesne. 1991. *Les communautés religieuses de femmes, de 1900 à 1970: A la recherché d'un monde oublié.* Montréal: Éditions du Jour.

Laurin-Frenette, Nicole. 1978. *Production de l'état et formes de la nation.* Montréal: Nouvelle Optique.

Lavigne, Marie, Yolande Pinard, and J. Stoddart. 1979. "The Féderation Nationale Saint-Jean-Baptise and the Women's Movement in Québec." In *A Not Unreasonable Claim: Women and Reform in Canada, 1880s–1920s,* edited by Linda Kealey, 71–88. Toronto: Women's Press.

Layoun, Mary. 1991. "Telling Spaces: Palestinian Women and the Engendering of National Narratives." In *Nationalisms and Sexualities,* edited by Andrew Parker et al., 407–23. New York: Routledge, 1991.

Lazarus, Neil. 1993. "Postcolonialism and the Dilemma of Nationalism: Aijaz Ahmad's Critique of Third-Worldism." *Diaspora* 2 (winter): 373–400.

Lazreg, Marnia. 1988. "Feminism and Difference: The Perils of Writing as a Woman on Women in Algeria." *Feminist Studies* 14 (spring): 81–107.

———. 1994. *The Eloquence of Silence: Algerian Women in Question.* New York: Routledge.

Leah, R. 1989. "Linking the Struggles: Racism, Feminism and the Union Movement." In *Race, Class, Gender: Bonds and Barriers,* edited by Jesse Vorst, 169–200. Toronto: Between the Lines.

Le Doeuff, Michele. 1977. "Women and Philosophy." *Radical Philosophy* 17 (summer): 2–11.

Li, Peter S. 1988. *The Chinese in Canada.* Toronto: Oxford University Press.

Linnaeus, Carl. 1758. *Systema naturae,* 10th ed. Stockholm: Salvius.

Longuaez y Vásquez, Evangelina. 1975. "The Women of La Raza." *Regeneración* 2, no. 4: 34–36.

López, Yolanda M. 1978. *Yolanda López. Works: 1975-1978.* San Diego, CA: Mandeville Center for the Arts Exhibition Catalog, La Jolla, California, December.

Lorde, Audre. 1984. *Sister/Outsider.* Trumansburg, NY: Crossing Press.

Lowe, Lisa. 1996. *Immigrant Acts: On Asian American Cultural Politics.* Durham, NC: Duke University Press.

Lubiano, Wahneema. 1991. "Shuckin' Off the African-American Native Other: What's 'Po-Mo' Got to Do with It?" *Cultural Critique* 18: 149–86.

———. 1992. "Multiculturalism: Negotiating Politics and Knowledge." *Concerns* 2, no. 3: 11–21.

Lyotard, Jean-François. 1988. *The Differend: Phrases in Dispute.* Translated by Georges Van den Abbeele. Minneapolis: University of Minnesota Press.

Macías, Anna. 1982. *Against All Odds: The Feminist Movement in Mexico to 1940.* Westport, CT: Greenwood Press.

MacKinnon, Catherine A. 1983. "Feminism, Marxism, Method and the State." *Signs* 8, no. 4 (summer): 635–58.

Mallon, Florencia E. 1994. "The Promise and Dilemma of Subaltern Studies: Perspectives from Latin American History." *American Historical Review* 99 (December): 1491–515.

Manero, Antonio. 1915. *The Meaning of the Mexican Revolution.* Mexico City: n.p.

Mani, Lata. 1990. "Multiple Mediations: Feminist Scholarship in the Age of Multinational Reception." *Feminist Review* 35 (summer): 24–41.

Maroney, Heather J. 1992. "'Who Has the Baby?' Nationalism, Pronatalism and the Construction of a 'Demographic Crisis' in Québec, 1960–1988." *Studies in Political Economy* 39 (autumn): 7–36.

Marquis, Louise-Marie. 1987. *Analyse comparative de la main-d'oeuvre féminine religieuse et laique, 1931 à 1961.* Master's thesis, Université de Montréal, Canada.

Martin, Richard, and Harold Koda. 1989. *Jocks and Nerds: Men's Style in the Twentieth Century.* New York: Rizzoli.

Martínez, Elizabeth. 1992. *500 Años del Pueblo Chicano / 500 Years of Chicano History in Pictures.* New Mexico: Southwest Organizing Project.

Masiello, Francine. 1992. *Between Civilization and Barbarism: Women, Nation, and Literary Culture in Modern Argentina.* Lincoln: University of Nebraska Press.

Massey, Doreen. 1994. *Space, Place, and Gender.* Minneapolis: University of Minnesota Press.

Mattelart, Armand. 1983. *Transnationals and the Third World: The Struggle for Culture.* South Hadley, MA: Bergin and Garvey.

———. 1994. *Mapping World Communication: War, Progress, Culture.* Minneapolis: Minnesota University Press.

Mawani, Nurjehan. 1994. "Violations of the Rights of Women in the Refugee Context." *Human Rights Research and Education Bulletin* 26 (September): 1–8.

Mazumdar, Sucheta. 1992. "Women, Culture and Politics: Engendering the Hindu Nation." *South Asia Bulletin* 12, no. 2 (fall): 1–24.

Mbembe, Achille. 1992. "The Banality of Power and the Aesthetics of Vulgarity in the Postcolony." *Public Culture* 4, no. 2: 1–30.

McClaurin, Melton. 1991. *Celia, A Slave.* New York: Avon Books.

McClintock, Anne. 1992. "The Angel of Progress: Pitfalls of the Term 'Post-Colonialism.'" *Social Text* 31–32: 84–98.

———. 1995. *Imperial Leather: Race, Gender and Sexuality in the Colonial Contest.* New York: Routledge.

McDonald, Forest. 1994. *The American Presidency.* Lawrence: University of Kansas Press.

McLaren, Peter. 1995. *Critical Pedagogy and Predatory Culture: Oppositional Politics in a Postmodern Era.* New York: Routledge.

McLaughlin, Andrée Nicola. 1990. "Black Women, Identity, and the Quest for Humanhood and Wholeness: Wild Women in the Whirlwind." In *Wild Women in the Whirlwind,* edited by Joanne M. Braxton and Andrée N. McLaughlin, 147–80. New Brunswick, NJ: Rutgers University Press.

Meléndez Hayes, Therese. 1977. Editorial comments. *Capirotada* (spring): 3.

Melville, Margarita, ed. 1980. *Twice a Minority: Mexican American Women.* St. Louis, MO: C. V. Mosby.

Mendieta Alatorre, Angeles. 1961. *La Mujer en la Revolución Mexicana.* México: Talleres Gráficos de la Nación.

Mercer, Kobena. 1992. "'1968': Periodizing Politics and Identity." In *Cultural Studies,* edited by Lawrence Grossberg, Cary Nelson, and Paula Treichler, 424–49. New York: Routledge.

Mercredi, Ovide, and Mary Ellen Turpel. 1993. *In the Rapids: Navigating the Future of First Nations.* Toronto: Viking.

Mernissi, Fatima. 1991. *The Veil and the Male Elite: A Feminist Interpretation of Women's Rights in Islam.* Reading, MA: Addison-Wesley.

———. 1992. *Islam and Democracy: Fear of the Modern World.* Reading, MA: Addison-Wesley.

Mies, Maria, et al., eds. 1989. *Women: The Last Colony.* London: Zed.

Milani, Farzaneh. 1992. *Veils and Words.* Syracuse: Syracuse University Press.

Miles, Robert. 1982. *Racism and Migrant Labour.* London: Routledge.

———. 1993. *Racism after "Race Relations."* London: Routledge.

Miller, John. 1974. *This New Man.* New York: MacGraw-Hill.

Miyoshi, Masao. 1974. *Accomplices of Silence: The Modern Japanese Novel.* Berkeley: University of California Press.

———. 1993. "A Borderless World? From Colonialism to Transnationalism and the Decline of the Nation-State." *Critical Inquiry* 19: 726–51.

Moallem, Minoo. 1989. *La pluralité des rapports sociaux: Similarité et diffé-*

rence. Le cas des Iraniennes et Iraniens au Québec. Doctoral thesis, Université de Montréal, Canada.

———. 1992. "The Ethnicity of Islam: The Case of Iran." *South Asia Bulletin* 12, no. 2 (fall): 25–34.

Modleski, Tania. 1991. *Feminism Without Women: Culture and Criticism in a "Post-Feminist" Age.* New York: Routledge.

Moghaddam, Fathali M., ed. 1994. *Identity Politics and Women: Cultural Reassertions and Feminisms in International Perspective.* Boulder, CO: Westview Press.

Moghaddam, Fathali M., et al. 1994. "The Warped Looking Glass: How Minorities Perceive Themselves, Believe They Are Perceived, and Are Actually Perceived by Majority Group Members in Québec, Canada." *Canadian Ethnic Studies* 26, no. 2: 112–23.

Mohanty, Chandra Talpade. 1987. "Feminist Encounters: Locating the Politics of Experience." *Copyright* 1: 30–44.

———. 1991. "Cartographies of Struggle: Third World Women and the Politics of Feminism." In *Third World Women and the Politics of Feminism,* edited by Chandra Talpade Mohanty, Ann Russo, and Lourdes Torres, 1–47. Bloomington: Indiana University Press, 1991.

Mohanty, Chandra Talpade, Ann Russo, and Lourdes Torres, eds. 1991. *Third World Women and the Politics of Feminism.* Bloomington: Indiana University Press.

Molina de Pick, Gracia. 1972. "Reflexiones sobre el femenismo y la Raza." *La Luz* (August). Reprinted in *Regeneración* 2, no. 4 (1975): 33–34.

Molyneux, Maxine. 1985. "Mobilization without Emancipation: Women's Interests, the State, and Revolution in Nicaragua." *Feminist Studies* 11, no. 2: 227–54.

Mongardini, Carlo. 1993. "Towards a European Sociology." In *Sociology in Europe: In Search of Identity,* edited by Brigitta Nedelmann and Piotr Sztompka, 67–71. New York: Walter de Gruyter.

Montour, Pierre. 1994. "*Miséricorde.* Tout a commencé au Café Cherrier . . ." *TV Hebdo* 35, no. 45: 14–15.

Monture-Angus, Patricia. 1995. *Thunder in My Soul: A Mohawk Woman Speaks.* Halifax: Fernwood Press.

Monture-Okanee, Patricia A. 1992. "The Violence We Women Do: A First Nation's View." In *Challenging Times: The Women's Movement in Canada and the United States,* edited by Constance Backhouse and David H. Flaherty, 72–89. Montréal: McGill-Queen's University Press.

Moore, Joan W. 1991. *Going Down to Barrio: Homeboys and Homegirls in Change.* Philadelphia: Temple University Press.

Mora, Magdalena, and Adelaine R. del Castillo, eds. 1980. *Mexican Women in the*

United States: Struggles Past and Present. Los Angeles: Chicano Studies Research Center, University of California.

Moraga, Cherríe, and Gloria Anzaldúa, eds. 1981. *This Bridge Called My Back: Writings by Radical Women of Color.* Watertown, MA: Persephone Press.

Morgan, Edmund. 1979. *American Slavery, American Freedom.* New York: Norton.

Morgan, Robin. 1984. *Sisterhood Is Global: The International Women's Movement Anthology.* New York: Anchor.

Morley, David, and Kevin Robins. 1995. *Spaces of Identity: Global Media, Electronic Landscapes and Cultural Boundaries.* London: Routledge.

Morokvasic, Mirjana. 1983. "Women in Migration: Beyond the Reductionist Outlook." In *One Way Ticket: Migration and Female Labor,* edited by Annie Phizacklea, 13–32. London: Routledge.

Morris, Meaghan. 1992. "On the Beach." In *Cultural Studies,* edited by Lawrence Grossberg, Cary Nelson, and Paula Treichler, 450–78. New York: Routledge.

La Mujer Moderna. 31 October 1915. Periodical, Mexico City. Benson Latin American Collection, University of Texas at Austin.

Muñoz, Carlos Jr. 1989. *Youth, Identity, and Power: The Chicano Movement.* London: Verso.

Najmabadi, Afsaneh. 1991. "Hazards of Modernity and Morality: Women, State and Ideology in Contemporary Iran." In *Women, Islam and the State,* edited by Deniz Kandiyoti, 48–76. Philadelphia: Temple University Press.

Nandy, Ashis. 1983. *The Intimate Enemy: Loss and Recovery of Self under Colonialism.* New York: Oxford University Press.

Nietzsche, Friederich. 1972. "On Truth and Falsity in Their Extramural Sense." In *Essays on Metaphor,* edited by Warren Shibles, 1–14. Madison: The Language Press.

Noriega, Chon, ed. 1992. *Chicanos and Film: Representation and Resistance.* Minneapolis: University of Minnesota Press.

Okigbo, Christopher. 1971. "Lament of the Silent Sisters III." In *Labyrinths.* London: Heinemann.

Olivárez, Elizabeth. 1975. "Women's Rights and the Mexican American Woman." *Regeneración* 2, no. 4: 40–42.

Omi, Michael, and Howard Winant. 1994. *Racial Formation in the United States: From the 1960s to the 1990s.* New York: Routledge.

Ong, Aihwa. 1987. *Spirits of Resistance and Capitalist Discipline: Factory Women in Malaysia.* Albany: State University of New York Press.

Orlans, Harold. 1989. "The Politics of Minority Statistics." *Society* 26, no. 4: 24–25.

Palmer, Howard. 1982. *Patterns of Prejudice: A History of Nativism in Alberta.* Toronto: McClelland and Stewart.

Parenti, Michael. 1980. *Democracy for the Few*. New York: St. Martin's Press.

Pateman, Carole. 1988. *The Sexual Contract*. Stanford: Stanford University Press.

Patterson, Orlando. 1982. *Slavery and Social Death*. Cambridge, MA: Harvard University Press.

Paulin, Tom. 1981. *The Book of Juniper*. Newcastle upon Tyne: Bloodaxe Books.

Penley, Constance. 1989. *The Future of an Illusion: Film, Feminism, and Psychoanalysis*. Minneapolis: University of Minnesota Press.

Pérez, Emma. 1993. "'She Has Served Others in More Intimate Ways': The Domestic Servant Reform in Yucatán, 1915–18." *Aztlan* 20, nos. 1–2: 11–33.

Perry, Richard. 1995. "The Logic of the Modern Nation-State and the Legal Construction of Native American Tribal Identities." *Indiana Law Review* 28, no. 3: 547–74.

Pieterse, Jan Nederveen. 1994. "Fundamentalism Discourses: Enemy Images." *Women Against Fundamentalism* 1, no. 5: 2–4.

"El Plan Espiritual de Aztlán." 1989. In *Aztlán: Essays on the Chicano Homeland*, edited by Rudolfo A. Anaya and Francisco A. Lomelí, 1–5. Albuquerque: Academia/El Norte Publications.

Platiel, René. 1996. "Native Life Improved, Statistics Show." *Globe and Mail*, 11 March, Ottawa ed.

Ponce, Mary Helen. 1989. *The Wedding*. Houston: Arte Público Press.

Pratt, Mary Louise. 1992. *Imperial Eyes: Travel Writing and Transculturation*. New York: Routledge.

Prentice, Alison, et al. 1988. *Canadian Women: A History*. Toronto: Harcourt Brace Jovanovich.

Primer Congreso Feminista de Yucatán. 1916. *Anales de esa Memorable Asamblea*. Mérida, Yucatán: Talleres Tipográficos del "Atenco Peninsular."

Probyn, Elspeth. 1987. "Bodies and Anti-Bodies: Feminism and the Post Modern." *Cultural Studies* 1, no. 3: 349–59.

———. 1993. *Sexing the Self: Gendered Positions in Cultural Studies*. London: Routledge.

———. 1996. *Outside Belongings*. New York: Routledge.

Québec, Ministère des communautés culturelles et immigration. 1990. *Let's Build Québec Together: A Policy Statement on Immigration and Integration*. Montréal: Direction des communications.

———. 1991. *Integrating Immigrants and Québecquers from the cultural communities: Background and Strategy Paper*. Montréal: Direction des communications.

Radhakrishnan, Rajagopalan. 1992. "Nationalism, Gender, and the Narrative of Identity." In *Nationalisms and Sexualities*, edited by Andrew Parker et al., 77–95. New York: Routledge.

Rahnavard, Zahra. 1990. *The Message of Hijab*. London: Al Hoda.

———. n.d. *Toloueh Zaneh Mosalman*. Tehran: Mahboubeh.

Ranger, Terence, and Eric J. Hobsbawm. 1983. *The Invention of Tradition.* Cambridge: Cambridge University Press.

Rendon, Armando. 1972. *Chicano Manifesto.* New York: Macmillan.

Rich, B. Ruby. 1994. "Babes in Gangland." *Elle* no. 109 (September): 42.

———. 1995. "Slugging It Out for Survival." *Sight and Sound* (April): 14–17.

Richardson, Boyce. 1993. *People of Terra Nullius: Betrayal and Rebirth in Aboriginal Canada.* Vancouver: Douglas and McIntyre.

Rincón, Bernice. 1975. "La Chicana, Her Role in the Past and Her Search for a New Role in the Future." *Regeneración* 2, no. 4: 36–37.

Rivera y Sanromán, Agustín. 1908. Untitled pamphlet, Mexico. Bancroft Library, University of California at Berkeley.

Roberts, Barbara. 1979. " 'A Work of Empire': Canadian Reformers and British Female Immigration." In *A Not Unreasonable Claim: Women and Reform in Canada, 1880s–1920s,* edited by Linda Kealey, 185–201. Toronto: Women's Press.

Rocco, Raymond. 1990. "The Theoretical Construction of the 'Other' in Postmodernist Thought: Latinos in the New Urban Political Economy." *Cultural Studies* 4, no. 3: 321–31.

Rogin, Michael. 1996. *Blackface, White Noise: Jewish Immigrants in the Hollywood Melting Pot.* Berkeley: University of California Press.

Rojas, Guillermo. 1989. "Social Amnesia and Epistemology in Chicano Studies." In *Estudios Chicanos and the Politics of Community,* edited by Mary Romero and Cordelia Candelaria, 54–65. Boulder, CO: National Association for Chicano Studies.

Rose, Nikolas, and Peter Miller. 1992. "Political Power Beyond the State: Problematics of Government." *BJS* 43, no. 2: 173–205.

Rouse, Roger. 1995. "Thinking Through Transnationalism: Notes on the Cultural Politics of Class Relations in the Contemporary United States." *Public Culture* 7, no. 2: 353–402.

Ruiz, Vicki L., and Susan Tiano, eds. 1987. *Women on the US-Mexican Border: Responses to Change.* Winchester, MA: Allen & Unwin.

Rushdie, Salman. 1991. *Imaginary Homelands.* London: Granta Books.

Sabbah, Fatna A. 1984. *Women in the Muslim Unconscious.* New York: Pergamon Press.

Sadowski, Yahya. 1993. "The New Orientalism and the Democracy Debate." *Middle East Reports* 183, nos. 23–24: 14–26.

Saénz Royo, Artemisa. 1954. *Historia política-social-cultural del movimiento femenino en México.* México: M. León Sánchez.

Said, Edward. 1978. *Orientalism.* New York: Pantheon.

———. 1983. *The World, the Text, and the Critic.* Cambridge, MA: Harvard University Press.

———. 1993. *Culture and Imperialism.* New York: Knopf.

Saint Jacques, Denis, and Roger de la Garde, eds. 1992. *Les pratiques culturelles de grande consommation.* Québec: Nuit Blanche.

Salas, Abel. 1994. "Alison Anders Discusses *Mi Vida Loca.*" *Latin Style* (August): 67.

Saldívar, José David. 1991. *The Dialectics of Our America.* Durham, NC: Duke University Press.

Salecl, Renate. 1992. "Nationalism, Anti-Semitism, and Anti-Feminism in Eastern Europe." *New German Critique* 57 (fall): 51–65.

Salee, Daniel. n.d. "La mondialisation et la construction de l'identité au Québec. École des affaires publiques et communautaires, Université Concordia." N.p.: n.p.

Sánchez, Rosaura. Forthcoming. "The Politics of Representation in Chicano Literature." In *Chicana/o Cultural Studies: New Directions,* edited by Mario García and Ellen McCracken.

Sandoval, Chela. 1990. "Feminism and Racism: A Report on the 1981 National Women's Studies Association Conference." In *Making Face, Making Soul/ Haciendo Caras,* edited by Gloria Anzaldúa, 55–71. San Francisco: Aunt Lute.

Sangari, Kum-Kum, and Sudesh Vaid, eds. 1990. *Recasting Women: Essays in Indian Colonial History.* New Brunswick, NJ: Rutgers University Press.

Sangster, Joan. 1985. "The Communist Party and the Woman Question, 1922–1929." *Labour/Le Travail* 15 (spring): 25–57.

Sarup, Madan. 1988. *An Introductory Guide to Post-structuralism and Postmodernism.* Toronto: Harvester Wheatsheaf.

Scarry, Elaine. 1985. *The Body in Pain.* New York: Oxford University Press.

Schafer, Judith. Forthcoming. *Slavery, the Civil Law, and the Supreme Court of Louisiana.* Baton Rouge: Louisiana State University Press.

Schein, Louisa. 1994. "The Consumption of Color and the Politics of White Skin in Post-Mao China." *Social Text* 41: 141–64.

Schiebinger, Londa. 1993. *Nature's Body: Gender in the Making of Modern Science.* Boston: Beacon Press.

Schudson, Michael. 1984. *Advertising, the Uneasy Persuasion: Its Dubious Impact on American Society.* New York: Basic Books.

Schwartzwald, Robert. 1991. "Fear of Federasty: Québec's Inverted Fictions." In *Comparative American Identities: Race, Sex and Nationality in the Modern Text,* edited by Hortense J. Spillers, 175–95. New York: Routledge.

Secretaría de Agricultura y Fomento. 1918. *Tercer censo de población de los Estados Unidos verificados el 27 de octubre de 1910.* México: Oficina Impresora de la Secretaría de Hacienda.

Sedgwick, Eve Kosofsky. 1988. "Nationalisms and Sexualities in the Age of Wilde." In *Nationalisms and Sexualities,* edited by Andrew Parker et al., 235–45. New York: Routledge.

Sharara, Yolla Polity. 1995. "Citizenship and Difference." Paper presented at the University of California, Davis, February.

Sharer, Jill. 1994. "Gang Girls on Attitude, Reality, and *Mi Vida Loca.*" *LA Weekly*, 22–28 July.

Shayegan, Daryush. 1989. *Le regard mutilé: Shizophrenie culturelle, pays traditionels face á la modernité.* Paris: Albin Michel.

Shohat, Ella. 1991. "Gender and the Culture of Empire: Toward a Feminist Ethnography of the Cinema." *Quarterly Review of Film and Video* 13, nos. 1–3: 45–84.

———. 1992. "Notes on the 'Post-Colonial.'" *Social Text* 31–32: 99–113.

———. Forthcoming. *Talking Visions: Multicultural Feminism in the Age of Globalization.* New York and Cambridge, MA: The New Museum of Contemporary Art and MIT Press.

Shohat, Ella, and Robert Stam. 1994. *Unthinking Eurocentrism: Multiculturalism and the Media.* New York: Routledge.

Shore, Elliot. 1988. *Talkin' Socialism.* Lawrence: University of Kansas Press.

Simon, Pierre-Jean. 1983. "Le sociologue et les minorités: Connaissance et idéologie." *Sociologie et sociétés* 15, no. 2: 9–21.

Smart, Carol. 1989. *Feminism and the Power of Law.* London: Routledge.

Smith, Anthony D. 1986. *The Ethnic Origins of Nations.* Oxford: Blackwell.

Smith, Pam. 1992. *The Emotional Labour of Nursing.* London: Macmillan.

Solnit, Rebecca. 1994. *Savage Dreams.* San Francisco: Sierra Club Books.

Sommer, Doris. 1991. *Foundational Fictions: The National Romances of Latin America.* Berkeley: University of California Press.

Sosa-Riddell, Adaljiza. 1974. "Chicanas and El Movimiento." *Aztlán: Chicano Journal of the Social Sciences and the Arts* 5, nos. 1–2 (spring–fall): 155–65.

Spillers, Hortense. 1987. "Mama's Baby, Papa's Maybe: An American Grammar Book." *Diacritics* (summer): 64–81.

Spivak, Gayatri Chakravorty. 1985. "Three Women's Texts and a Critique of Imperialism." In *"Race," Writing and Difference*, edited by Henry Louis Gates Jr., 262–80. Chicago: University of Chicago Press.

———. 1987. *In Other Worlds: Essays in Cultural Politics.* New York: Methuen.

———. 1988. "Can the Subaltern Speak?" In *Marxism and the Interpretation of Culture*, edited by Cary Nelson and Lawrence Grossberg, 271–313. Chicago: University of Illinois.

———. 1989. "The Political Economy of Women as Seen by a Literary Critic." In *Coming to Terms: Feminism, Theory, Politics*, edited by Elizabeth Weed, 218–29. New York: Routledge.

———. 1990. *The Post-Colonial Critic: Interviews, Strategies, Dialogues*, edited by Sarah Harasym. New York: Routledge.

———. 1993. *Outside in the Teaching Machine.* New York: Routledge.

———. 1996. "Diasporas Old and New: Women in the Transnational World." *Textual Practices* 10 (2): 245–69.

Stanlaw, James. 1992. " 'For Beautiful Human Life': The Use of English in Japan." In *Remade in Japan: Everyday Life and Consumer Taste in a Changing Society*, edited by Joseph J. Tobin, 58–76. New Haven: Yale University Press.

Starhawk. 1979. *The Spiral Dance: A Rebirth of the Ancient Religion of the Great Goddess*. San Francisco: Harper & Row.

Stasiulis, Daiva K. 1987. "Rainbow Feminism: Perspectives on Minority Women." *Resources for Feminist Research* 16, no. 2 (March): 5–9.

———. 1988. "The Symbolic Mosaic Reaffirmed: Multiculturalism Policy." In *How Ottawa Spends, 1988/89*, edited by Kath Graham, 81–111. Ottawa: Carleton University Press.

———. 1993. " 'Authentic Voice': Anti-Racist Politics in Canadian Feminist Publishing and Literary Production." In *Feminism and the Politics of Difference*, edited by Sneja Gunew and Anna Yeatman, 35–60. St. Leonards, New South Wales: Allen & Unwin.

Stasiulis, Daiva, and Radha Jhappan. 1995. "The Fractious Politics of a Settler Society: Canada." In *Unsettling Settler Societies: Articulations of Gender, Race, Ethnicity and Class*, edited by Daiva Stasiulis and Nira Yuval-Davis, 95–131. London: Sage.

Stasiulis, Daiva, and Nira Yuval-Davis, eds. 1995. *Unsettling Settler Societies: Articulations of Gender, Race, Ethnicity and Class*. London: Sage.

Steele, Valerie, and Claudia Kidwell. 1989. *Men and Women: Dressing the Part*. Washington, DC: Smithsonian Institution Press.

Stegemeyer, Anne. 1988. *Who's Who in Fashion*. New York: Fairchild Publications.

Steinberg, Stephen. 1981. *The Ethnic Myth: Race, Ethnicity and Class in America*. Boston: Beacon Press.

Stevens, Evelyn. 1973. "Marianismo: The Other Face of Machismo in Latin America." In *Female and Male in Latin America: Essays*, edited by Ann Pescatello, 89–101. Pittsburgh: University of Pittsburgh Press.

Stocking, George, ed. 1985. *Bodies and Behavior*. Madison: University of Wisconsin Press.

Šumič-Riha, Jeliça. 1996. "Post-Modern Democracy, Politics, and Collective Identities." Paper presented at *Etat, Nation, Multiculturalisme et Citoyenté* Conference, CEETUM, Montreal, 30 May–2 June.

Swyripa, Frances. 1993. *Wedded to the Cause: Ukrainian-Canadian Women and Ethnic Identity 1891–1991*. Toronto: University of Toronto Press.

Tabari, Azar, and Hahid Yeganeh, eds. 1982. *In the Shadow of Islam: The Women's Movement in Iran*. London: Zed.

Tafolla, Carmen. 1992. *Sonnets of Human Beings and Other Selected Works.* Santa Monica, CA: Lalo Press.

Thobani, Sunera. 1992. "Making the Links: South Asian Women and the Struggle for Reproductive Rights." *Resources for Feminist Research* 13, no. 1: 19–22.

Thomas, Kevin. 1994. "The Road to *Mi Vida Loca* 'Paved with Good Intentions.'" *Los Angeles Times,* 22 July.

Thompson, Robert Farris, ed. 1984. *African and Afro-American Art and Philosophy.* New York: Random House.

Tohidi, Nayereh. 1990. "'Masaleh-e Zan' va roshanfekran te-ye tahavolat-e akhir." *Nimeye Digar* 10 (winter): 51–95.

———. 1991. "Gender and Islamic Fundamentalism: Feminist Politics in Iran." In *Third World Women and the Politics of Feminism,* edited by Chandra Talpade Mohanty, Mary Russo, and Lourdes Torres, 251–65. Bloomington: Indiana University Press.

Tompkins, Jane. 1985. *Sensational Designs: The Cultural Work of American Fiction, 1790–1860.* New York: Oxford University Press.

Tong, Rosemary. 1984. *Women, Sex, and the Law.* Totowa, NJ: Rowman and Allanheld.

Trinh, Minh-ha T. 1989. *Woman/Native/Other.* Bloomington: Indiana University Press.

———. 1991. *When the Moon Waxes Red.* New York: Routledge.

Trujillo, Carla. 1998. "La Virgen de Guadeloupe and Her Reconstruction in Chicana Lesbian Desire." In *Living Chicana Theory,* edited by Carla Trujillo, 214–31. Berkeley: Third Woman Press.

———. ed. 1991. *Chicana Lesbians: The Girls Our Mothers Warned Us About.* Berkeley: Third Woman Press.

———. ed. 1998. *Living Chicana Theory.* Berkeley: Third Woman Press.

Tu Thanh Ha. 1995. "The PQ's Narrow Ethnic Vision." *Globe and Mail,* 11 November.

———. 1996a. "Angst in Montréal: To Go, or To Stay." *Globe and Mail,* 22 June.

———. 1996b. "Language War Flares in Québec." *Globe and Mail,* 15 August.

Turpel, Mary Ellen. 1992. "Does the Road to Québec Sovereignty Run Through Aboriginal Territory?" In *Negotiating with a Sovereign Québec,* edited by Daniel Drache and Roberto Perrin, 93–106. Toronto: James Lorimer & Co.

———. 1993. "Patriarchy and Paternalism: The Legacy of the Canadian State for First Nations Women." *Canadian Journal of Women and the Law* 6: 174–92.

Valverde, Marianne. 1991. *The Age of Light, Soap and Water: Moral Reform in English Canada, 1885–1925.* Toronto: University of Toronto Press.

———. 1992a. "'When the Mother of the Race Is Free': Race, Reproduction and

Sexuality in First-Wave Feminism." In *Gender Conflicts,* edited by Franca Iacovetta and Marianne Valverde, 3–26. Toronto: University of Toronto Press.

———. 1992b. "Racism and Anti-Racism in Feminist Teaching and Research." In *Challenging Times: The Women's Movement in Canada and the United States,* edited by Constance Backhouse and David H. Flaherty, 160–64. Montréal: McGill-Queen's University Press.

Vasconcelos, José. 1979. *La Raza Cósmica.* Translated by Didier T. Jaén. Pensamiento Mexicano 1, Los Angeles: Centro de Publicaciones.

Vásquez, Esperanza. 1977. *Agueda Martínez: Our People, Our Country.* 16 min., 35mm film. Produced by Moctesuma Esparza.

Vickers, Jill, Pauline Rankin, and Christine Appelle. 1993. *Politics As If Women Mattered: A Political Analysis of the National Action Committee on the Status of Women.* Toronto: University of Toronto Press.

Vincent, Ian. 1995. "Nation Won't Make It into 2000, a Third Believe." *Globe and Mail,* 18 December, Toronto ed.

Visweswaran, Kamala. 1994. *Fictions of Feminist Ethnography.* Minneapolis: University of Minnesota Press.

La Voz de la Revolución. 1916. Mérida, Yucatán.

Walby, Sylvia. 1986. *Patriarchy at Work: Patriarchal and Capitalist Relations in Employment.* Minneapolis: University of Minnesota Press.

———. 1990. *Theorizing Patriarchy.* Oxford: Blackwell.

Walkingstick, Kay. 1991. "Democracy, Inc." *Artforum* 30, no. 3: 24–26.

Wallerstein, Immanuel. 1974. *The Modern World-System: Capitalist Agriculture and the Origins of the European World-Economy in the Sixteenth Century.* New York: Academic Press.

———. 1980. *The Modern World-System II: Mercantilism and the Consolidation of the European World-Economy.* New York: Academic Press.

———. 1988. *The Modern World-System III: The Second Era of Great Expansion of the Capitalist World-Economy, 1730–1840.* San Diego, CA: Academic Press.

Warren, Scott. 1984. *The Emergence of Dialectical Theory: Philosophy and Political Inquiry.* Chicago: University of Chicago Press.

Weaver, Sally. 1993. "First Nations Women and Government Policy, 1970–92: Discrimination and Conflict." In *Changing Patterns: Women in Canada,* edited by Sandra Burt, Lorraine Code, and Lindsay Dorney, 92–150. Toronto: McClelland and Stewart.

Weber, Max. [1921] 1978. *Economy and Society.* Vol. 1. Translated by Ephraim Fischoff et al. Berkeley: University of California Press.

Welter, Barbara. 1966. "The Cult of True Womanhood: 1820–1860." *American Quarterly* 18 (summer): 151–74.

West, Cornel. 1993. *Beyond Eurocentrism and Multiculturalism.* Monroe, ME: Common Courage Press.

Whitaker, Reg. 1995. "Québec's Self-Determination and Aboriginal Self-Government: Conflict and Reconciliation?" In *Is Québec Nationalism Just? Perspectives from Anglophone Canada*, edited by Joseph H. Carens, 193–220. Montréal: McGill-Queen's University Press.

Whitla, Wendy. 1995. "A Chronology of Women in Canada." In *Feminist Issues: Race, Class, and Sexuality*, edited by Nancy Mandell, 315–49. Scarborough, Ontario: Prentice Hall.

Williams, Raymond. 1976. *Keywords: A Vocabulary of Culture and Society.* Oxford: Oxford University Press.

———. 1981. *Marxism and Literature.* Oxford: Oxford University Press.

Williamson, Judith. 1978. *Decoding Advertisements: Ideology and Meaning in Advertisements.* New York: Marion Boyars.

———. 1986. *Consuming Passions: The Dynamics of Popular Culture.* New York: Marion Boyars.

Wilson, Elizabeth. 1988. *Adorned in Dreams: Fashion and Modernity.* Berkeley: University of California Press.

———. 1992. "Feminist Fundamentalism: The Shifting Politics of Sex and Censorship." In *Sex Exposed: Sexuality and the Pornography Debate*, edited by Lynne Segal and Mary McIntosh, 15–28. New Brunswick, NJ: Rutgers University Press.

Wong, Sau-ling. 1995. "Denationalization Reconsidered: Asian American Cultural Criticism at a Theoretical Crossroads." *Amerasia Journal* 21: 1–27.

Yarbro-Bejarano, Yvonne. 1993. "Turning It Around." *CrossRoads* 31 (May): 15, 17.

———. 1995. "The Lesbian Body in Latina Cultural Production." In *¡Entiendas? Queer Readings, Hispanic Writings*, edited by Emilie L. Bergmann and Paul Julian Smith, 181–97. Durham, NC: Duke University Press.

Ybarra-Frausto, Tomás. 1990. "Rasquachismo: A Chicano Sensibility." In *Chicano Art: Resistance and Affirmation, 1965–1985/CARA*, edited by Richard Griswold del Castillo, Teresa McKenna, and Yvonne Yarbro-Bejarano, 155–62. Los Angeles: Wight Gallery of Art, University of California.

Yoshimoto, Mitsuhiro. 1989. "The Postmodern and Mass Images in Japan." *Public Culture* 1, no. 2: 8–25.

Young, Robert. 1990. *White Mythologies: Writing History and the West.* New York: Routledge.

Yúdice, George, Jean Franco, and Juan Flores, eds. 1992. *On Edge.* Minneapolis: University of Minnesota Press.

Yuval-Davis, Nira. 1995. "Citizenship and Difference." Paper presented at the University of California at Davis (February).

Yuval-Davis, Nira, and Gita Saghal. 1992. *Refusing Holy Orders: Women and Fundamentalism in Britain.* London: Virago Press.

Zavella, Patricia. 1984. *The Impact of "Sun Belt Industrialization" on Chicanas.* Palo Alto, CA. Stanford Center for Chicano Research working paper series 7, Stanford University.

———. 1987. *Women's Work and Chicano Families: Cannery Workers of Santa Clara Valley.* Ithaca, NY: Cornell University Press.

Žižek, Slavoj. 1989. *The Sublime Object of Ideology.* London: Verso.

———. 1990. "Beyond Discourse Analysis." In *New Reflections on the Revolution in Our Time,* edited by Ernesto Laclau, 49–60. London: Verso.

Zubaida, Sami. 1988. *Islam, the People, and the State.* London: Routledge.

Index

Acquin, Hubert, 51
Ahmad, Aijaz, 3, 354, 361
Alarcón, Norma, 7, 256
Alfred v. State, 117–18, 139 n.13
Alvarado, Salvador (Governor), 222–36
American Me (Olmos), 83–85
Amos, Valerie, 351
Anders, Alison, 85–89
Anderson, Benedict, 6, 8, 40–41 n.3,
    49, 55, 163
"And when I dream dreams" (Tafolla),
    79
Angelou, Maya, 246, 249–52, 259
Anthias, Floya, 142, 158 n.1
Anzaldúa, Gloria, 28, 38–39, 65, 67
Australia. *See* Nationalism
Aztlán, 25

Babel, August, 233
Balibar, Etienne, 1–2, 190–91, 194, 255
Baudrillard, Jean, 123
Benjamin, Walter, 279, 310
Berlant, Lauren, 13, 245, 260 n.8
Bhabha, Homi K., 5–11, 221, 257, 328,
    355
Biberman, Herbert, 85
Binaries: theory and practice, 4–5, 8,
    41 n.3; transnational circulations
    versus margin and center, 4–5; *Vir-
    gen de Guadalupe/La Malinche*, 78;
    Western freedom versus Oriental
    despotism, 322

Blanche (Cousture), 56, 58
Boal, Iain, 14
*Borderlands/La Frontera: The New
    Mestiza* (Anzaldúa), 38
Bouchard, Lucien, 188
Brah, Avtar, 194
Brigham, Carl, 243
Bronze Screen, The (Fregoso), 85
Buell, Frederick, 5
Butler, Judith, 7–9, 16, 157

Cámara Vales, Nicolás, 227–28
Cambron, Micheline, 50
Camp Trad, 165–66, 176–80
Canada: indigenous/settler schism,
    184; immigrants and immigra-
    tion, 185; nation building, 185–87,
    198–99; as "two founding nations,"
    186–87, 198–99, 262 n.29; women's/
    feminist movement, 199–212. *See
    also* Québec
Canadian Charter of Rights and Free-
    doms, 205
*Cannibals All! Or, Slaves Without
    Masters* (Fitzhugh), 124
"Can the Subaltern Speak?" (Spivak),
    355
Capirotada (Meléndez Hayes), 27–28
Carby, Hazel, 352
Carranza, Venustiano, 224–36
Castrellón, Clara Gloria, 27
Celia (slave), 111, 114, 119–20

Chabram-Dernersesian, Angie, 13
Chacón, Leona Ruth, 27–28
"Challenging Imperial Feminism"
 (Amos and Parmar), 351
Charlotte (slave), 118
Charlottetown Accord, 203–6
Chatterjee, Partha, 7, 8, 55, 163, 179–
 80
Chestnut, Mary Boykin, 121
Chicana: and Aztlán (nation/alism),
 19–26, 29, 38–39, 42–43 n.8; in
 cinema, 81–90; confinement to
 domesticity, 77–78; critique of
 heterosexual family, 26–27; cultural practices, 19–20, 41 n.5; femi-
 nist/feminisms, 22–39, 64, 70–71;
 lesbians and lesbian practices, 22,
 26–28, 38; literary and visual arts,
 26–39; and mestizaje, 25–26, 66, 68,
 267–68, 273; Mexican-Americans,
 21; movement, 22–26, 65; native
 woman, 66–68; as political class,
 63–64; Riqueña, 270–73, 291 n.7;
 and social identity/ethnicities, 22,
 26, 268–71, 278, studies, 265–66,
 269, 273, 276, 285–90; and transnational identities (Puerto Rican),
 265–69, 279–82; writers, 64–67.
 See also Ethnic Studies; Feminism;
 Pachuca/o
Clinton presidential inauguration
 (1993), 246, 249
Cobb, Thomas, 132–37
Colors (Hopper), 82–83
Comme de Garçons (high-fashion
 house), 296–312; advertising, 297,
 301–6, 311–15; and geopolitical
 histories of Japan, 296–97, 303;
 Homme Deux, 300–3, 306, 311, 314;
 Japan and U.S. relations, 314–15;
 and Japanese identity, 304–9, 313,

315; Japanese inferiority/Western
 superiority (East/West distinctions),
 303–5, 307, 313–14; "The Japanese
 Suit," 296–98, 306, 309, 314, 317;
 Meiji (1868–1912) and empire building, 303, 306, 308–11, 314; and
 subject formation, 297, 305. See
 also Fashion
Commodity/consumer capitalism,
 297; and the academy, 316–17
Cultural studies, 360–61

Da Crew (Oakland), 88
David, Françoise, 210–11
Dehghani, Asharaf-e-, 330
de Lauretis, Teresa, 236
del Fuego, Laura, 79
Delphy, Christine, 11
Derrida, Jacques, 5–7
De Seve, Micheline, 205
Dhareshwar, Vivek, 354
Díaz, Porfirio, 221, 229, 334
Dirlik, Arif, 3–4
Dumont, Micheline, 202

"El Plan Espiritual de Aztlán," 23, 25
Enzensberger, Hans Magnus, 251
"Eres Mujer Chicana" (Sandoval), 27
Ester, Mary, 73–74
Ethnic studies, 282–83. See also Chi-
 cana

Fashion, 296–317; female consumers
 and femininity, 311; and gender,
 299; and heterosexuality, 311–14;
 Japanese domestic markets, 301–
 3; kokusaika (internationalization),
 296, 309–10; and masculinity, 298,
 302, 306–9; and national/ism, 296–
 97, 302; Orientalism, 297, 299; and
 racialized bodies, 299, 311; yofuku

(Western clothing) and *wafuku* (Japanese clothing), 299–300. *See also* Comme de Garçons

Fédération des femmes du Québec (FFQ), 202–5, 208, 210

Fédération Nationale Saint-Jean-Baptiste, 202

Femininities and masculinities, 144–46; and chador (veil), 332–33; and gendered identities (blood and veil; warrior brother and veiled sister), 330–33

Feminism: global feminism, 7, 12–15, 321, 326, 340; "indigenous," 359; liberal versions, 349; Marxist, 351–52; in nationalist movements, 182–83, 219–37; post-structuralist, 351; and Spivak, 355; and standpoint epistemology, 358; transnational, 12–16; transnational feminist cultural studies, 350, 358. *See also* Chicana; Feminisms and fundamentalisms; Feminist practices; Québec

Feminisms and fundamentalisms: the body, 326–27; and citizenship, 328; and consciousness, 339–40; and ethical issues as political, 328–29; as hybrids, 324–25; and institutions of knowledge, 326; martyrdom and veiling, 336–39; and modernity, 324, 329, 339; and modern dichotomies, 326; as regimes of truth, 323–24; and transnationalism, 327; and women's subjectivity and participation, 329; as worldviews, 321, 324. *See also* Feminism; Fundamentalism

Feminist practices, 12, 15, 341–42, 358; academic, 352–53, 355; transnational, 349, 357

Fitzhugh, George, 124–25

Flores, Francisca, 23

Forrester, John, 113

Foucault, Michel, 8, 48, 59

Frager, Ruth, 200

Franco, Jean, 77

Fraser, Nancy, 75–77

Fregoso, Rosa Linda, 9, 45–46 n.25

"French Feminism Revisited" (Spivak), 359

Friedman, Susan, 195–96

Frost, Robert, 250–51, 260 n.16

Fuentes, Carlos, 268

Fundamentalism: and modernity, 323; representation in the West, 322; Shi'a Islam in Iran, 321–22, 329–36; and *ummat* (Islamic community), 332–36. *See also* Feminisms and fundamentalisms

Gafari, Hadi, 331, 335

Galindo, Hermila, 228–37

Gamboa, Ignacio, 219, 224

García Ortiz, Francisca, 231–32, 236–37

George v. State, 112, 134

"Gift Outright, The" (Frost), 250

Gilroy, Paul, 275, 292 n.9

Globalization, 3, 5, 15, 245, 248, 352, 356–57

González, Sylvia Alicia, 26–27

Gonzales-Berry, Erlinda, 276

Gordon, Avery, 249, 347 n.42

Goto, Shinpei, 310–11

Grewal, Inderpal, 13, 16, 348 n.49

"Guadalupe Series, The" (López), 29

Guillaumin, Collete, 145, 159 n.2, 343 n.5

Habermas, Jürgen, 76–77

Hall, Stuart, 282, 292–93 n.9

Hartman, Saidiya, 10

Harvey, David, 2
Hegel, G. W. F., 67
Hélie-Lucas, Marie-Aimée, 359
Hernández, Ester, 28–31, 34–38
Higginbotham, A. Leon, 120
History of Sexuality (Foucault), 8
Hobsbawn, Eric J., 245–46
Hollander, Anne, 298
Horne, Donald, 49
Humphrey v. Utz, 115, 135
Huxley, Thomas, 243

Identity: crisis of, 2, 320–21, 325, 340
Indian Act (Canada, 1951), 202–3
Inquiry into the Law of Negro Slavery, (Cobb), 132
In Theory: Classes, Nations, Literatures (Ahmad), 354–55
Irigaray, Luce, 1

Jameson, Fredric, 2, 51, 352
Jardine, Alice, 2
Jefferson, Thomas, 113
Joseph, Gilbert M., 221
Joseph, Suad, 12
Juteau, Danielle, 11

Kaplan, Caren, 16, 348 n.51
Kant, Immanuel, 233
Katei Gaho, 301, 311
Kawabata, Yasunari, 311–13
Kawakubo, Rei, 298–99
Kemble, Fanny, 122
Kennedy presidential inauguration (1961), 250–51
Khomeini, Sayyid Ruhullah Musavi (Ayatollah), 333–35
Kishi, Keiko, 311–13
Kondo, Dorinne, 15
Kristeva, Julia, 42 n.7
Kroker, Arthur, 51

La doctrina Carranza (Galindo), 234, 236
La Mujer Moderna (Galindo), 228–29
La Mujer Moderna (Gamboa), 219, 228–29
Landry, Bernard, 188
La Ofrenda/The Offering (Hernández), 35, 37–38
La Virgen de Guadalupe Defendiendo los Derechos de los Xicanos/The Virgin of Guadalupe Defending the Rights of the Xicanos (Hernández), 28, 30
Layoun, Mary, 9, 341
Lebanon: citizenship/citizenry, 162, 166–69, 173–75; civil society, 175; as compulsory model, 164, 179; and identity formation, 168–69, 173–77, 275; local and state elites, 163–65, 175, 180; multiethnic/national relations, 166–67, 176–80; nation-state building, 162–64, 180; and women, 164–66, 172–73, 177–80; and (patriarchal) kinship relations, 171–73, 177–78; religion, 170–73. See also Nationalism; Nation-state
Les filles de Caleb (Beaudoin), 56–58
Levesque, Rene, 57
Libertad/Liberty (Hernández), 29, 31, 35
Linnaeus, Carl, 243–44
Longeaux y Vásquez, Evangelina, 26, 44 n.15
López, Yolanda, 28–29, 32–36, 45 n.23
Lorde, Audre, 71
"Love and Revolution" (Castrellón), 27
Lubiano, Wahneema, 2
Lyotard, Jean-François, 69–70

Mallón, Florencia, 221
Manero, Antonio, 224
Mani, Lata, 314

"Maravilla" (del Fuego), 79–81

Margaret F. Stewart: Our Lady of Guadalupe (López), 34

Martí, José, 266

Martínez, Maria, 230

Marxism, 355, 361. *See also* Feminism

Masculinities. *See* Fashion; Femininities and masculinities

Masiello, Francine, 8

Mattelart, Armand, 15

Mbembe, Achille, 59

Mercer, Kobena, 279

Mestizaje. *See* Chicano

Migration, 264–65

Miles, Robert, 194

Miller, Peter, 59

Miséricorde (Tremblay and Larouche), 58

Mi Vida Loca (Anders), 85–90

Miyake, Issey, 298–99

Moallem, Minoo, 14–15

Mohanty, Chandra Talpade, 12–13, 195

Molina de Pick, Garcia, 24

Monroe Doctrine, 222, 234

Montreal P. Q., 58

Moraga, Cherríe, 28

Morris, Meaghan, 48

Multiculturalism (U.S.), 274–75, 286–87; and American national imaginary and identity, 245–49, 253; discourses of, 248–49, 256; and Eurocentrism, 244; multicultural nationalism, 245, 254; and nationalism, 251–54; and pluralism, 254–57; and politics of inclusion, 253–54; and politics of recognition, 257–59. *See also* Nationalism

Muramatsu, Yugen, 307

Murdock, Rupert, 47

"Nací Mujer" (Chacón), 27

Najmabadi, Afsaneh, 330

Nation, 6–12, 29, 35, 38–39, 40–41 n.3; and classification, 244; as collection of fragments in Lebanon, 168–69, 176–80. *See also* Chicana; Lebanon; Nation-state; Nationalism; Québec

National Action Committee on the Status of Women (NAC, Canada), 203–8

National Chicano Youth Liberation Conference, 23

Nationalism, 14–15; Australian, 49; and desire, 92, 96–97, 106; as discourse, 252–53; literature of, 251; as narrative, 93–94, 106–7; and national citizen and national territory, 95–97; and sexual possession, 96–97; and racism, 194. *See also* Chicana; Lebanon; Multiculturalism; Nation-state; Québec

Nation-state, 3–6, 162–80; and citizenry/citizenship, 10–12; and doubleness (boundary subjects), 5–6, 9; and postmodernity, 2; and power/knowledge, 8; regulatory practices of, 10–11; sexual and racial difference, 1–2; women and, 1–2; woman as signifier of, 6, 10. *See also* Canada; Chicana; Lebanon; Nation; Nationalism; Québec; Transnational linkages

Native Women's Association of Canada (NWAC), 203

Newsome, Robert, 114, 116, 119

"Oka Crisis," 203

Okigbo, Christopher, 106

Olmos, James Edward, 81, 85

"On the Pulse of Morning" (Angelou), 246–47, 252

Outside in the Teaching Machine (Spivak), 359–60

Pacheco de Torres, Clarisa, 229
Pachuca/o, 72–73, 90; and Chicano
     society, 75; and female solidarity,
     74; in film, 81, 83; subjectivity and
     agency, 79. See also *Chicana*
Paletitas de Guayaba, Guayaba Pop-
     sicles (Gonzales-Berry), 276–79
Parizeau, Jacques (Premier), 57, 156,
     188, 210
Parmar, Pratibha, 351
Paz, Octavio, 268
Pérez, Emma, 11
Pérez, Laura Elisa, 8
Perry, Commodore, 305
Portrait of the Artist as the Virgen de
     Guadalupe (López), 29, 34
Pour changer le monde (To change the
     world), 209–10
Prakash, Gyan, 3
Probyn, Elspeth, 6
Public Culture, 354
Public sphere: public/private, 76–78,
     83, 89–90
Puerto Rican identity, 266–67

Québec: and Canada, 51; Catholic
     Church, 58, 146, 188, 201–2, 159 n.9;
     citizenship, 185, 192; and female
     workers, 149–56, 160 n.12; femi-
     nist and women's politics, 154,
     184–212; and First Nations, 51, 54,
     184–212; gendered and sexualized
     metaphors of the nation, 48–53,
     57–61; globalization, 192–93; in-
     digenous/settler schism, 184–212;
     linguistic ethnicity, 190–92; and
     local television, 51–54; mothers and
     housewives, 147–53, 156; national-
     ism and gender, 50, 54–56, 60–61,
     147–49, 153–58, 184–212; and nuns,
     147–58; and ordinariness, 48–51,
     59–61; racial minorities, immi-

grants, and pluralism, 184–212; rela-
     tional positionalities of racisms and
     ethnicities, 194–200; and sexuality,
     57–61; sovereignist movement, 62
     n.2, 187–94. See also Canada

Radhakrishnan, Rajagopalan, 5, 237
     n.5
Rahnavard, Zahra, 332
Ranger, Terrence, 245
Rape. *See* Slave law and rape
Reconstruction of Mexico, The (Alva-
     rado), 224
Regeneración, 23
Riddell Sosa, Ada, 25
Rincón, Bernice, 26, 44 n.15
Rivera y Sanromán, Agustín, 226–27
Rocco, Raymond, 293 n.14
Rose, Nikolas, 59
Rushdie, Salman, 322

Said, Edward, 163
Salee, Daniel, 193
Salt Eaters, The (Bambara), 16
Salt of the Earth (Biberman), 85
Sánchez, Rosaura, 268, 274, 290 n.5,
     292–93 n.9
Sandoval, Blanca R., 27–28
Satanic Verses, The (Rushdie), 322
Schwartzwald, Robert, 57
Shame (Rushdie), 354
Sharara, Yolla, 170
Shehaweh (Beaudion), 53–55
Shohat, Ella, 195–96, 262 n.35
Slave law and rape, 113–37; antimisce-
     genation statutes, 117; and black
     humanity, 111–12, 132; and common
     law, 111–12; discourse of seduction,
     121–25, 128, 138 n.5; patriarchal
     model of social order, 124–25, 136;
     person and property, 122, 126, 130,
     135–36; public good, 129–30; rights

of ownership, 127; sexuality, 116, 118, 120–21; submission, consent, and coercion, 113–16, 119–29

Smith, Anthony D., 159 n.6

Snow Country (Kawabata), 312–13

Solís, Javier, 280

Sommer, Doris, 251

Sophy (slave), 122

Soseki, Natsume, 303

Spillers, Hortense, 119, 141 n.31

Spivak, Gayatri Chakravorty, 8–9, 15, 16, 69, 70, 220, 249, 350, 353–61, 362 n.8; crisis, 356; culture and capital, 357; methodology, 356–57, 359

Stam, Robert, 195–96, 263 n.35

Stasiulis, Daiva, 11

State: and multiple nations, 12; and identity, 282

State of Missouri v. Celia, a slave, 112–16

State v. Mann, 126–27, 137

State v. Tackett, 115

Study of American Intelligence, A (Brigham), 243

Systema Naturae (Linnaeus), 243

Tafolla, Carmen, 78–79

Third World Women and the Politics of Feminism (Mohanty), 351

This Bridge Called My Back (Moraga and Anzaldúa), 38, 70

Transnational feminism. *See* Feminism

Transnational linkages, 265, 276, 278, 290 n.4, 359–60

Tremblay, Michel, 52

Trinh T. Minh-ha, 65

Un Presidenciable (Galindo), 235

Valdez, Luis, 81

Virgin of Guadalupe: as image for social justice, 28–38

Visweswaren, Kamala, 317

Wallerstein, Immanuel, 4

Watkins, Carleton, 250

Wedding in Galilee (Khleife), 94–106

West, Cornel, 251

"Woman to Woman" (González), 26–27

Women: as category, 136–37, 183

Women's Christian Temperance Union, 200

Wong, Sau-ling, 14

Workers: in maquiladoras, 68–69; and migrant camps in U.S., 69

Worley v. State, 135

Yamamoto, Yohji, 298–99, 301

Ybarra-Frausto, Tomás, 20, 41 n.6

Yucatán: education and teaching in, 224–28, 330; gendered nation building in, 221, 224–27, 236; Mexican neocolonialism, 221–22, 234; Mexican Revolution, 219–24, 226, 234; property rights and civil code reforms, 232–33; women/feminism in, 221–37; women's suffrage, 228–30, 234; Yucatán Feminist Congresses (1916), 219–20, 230, 232–37

Yuval-Davis, Nira, 142, 158 n.1

Zavala, Consuelo, 232–33

Zoot Suit (Valdez), 81, 83–84

Zubaida, Sami, 162–63, 165

Contributors

Norma Alarcón is Professor of Ethnic Studies, Women's Studies, and Spanish and Portuguese at the University of California at Berkeley. She is the author of a book on the Mexican writer Rosario Castellanos, NINFOMANIA: *El Discurso de la diferencia en la obra poetica de Rosario Castellanos,* and author of numerous essays on Chicana writers and on critical theory. She is the editor and publisher of Third Woman Press.

Iain A. Boal teaches in the Geography Department at the University of California at Berkeley. He is coeditor, with James Brook, of *Resisting the Virtual Life: The Culture and Politics of Information.*

Angie Chabram-Dernersesian is Associate Professor of Chicana/o Studies at the University of California at Davis, where she teaches courses in culture, poetry, narrative, and theater. She is coeditor of "Chicana/o Cultural Representations" (*Cultural Studies* 4, no. 3, 1990) and editor of "Chicana/o Latina/o Cultural Studies" (*Cultural Studies,* forthcoming). She has published in the areas of Chicana/o representations (identity, ethnography, whiteness, and feminism) and is currently doing a retrospective on Chicana/o cultural studies.

Rosa Linda Fregoso is Associate Professor of Women's Studies at the University of California at Davis. She is the author of *The Bronze Screen: Chicana and Chicano Film Culture,* the coeditor with Norma Iglesias of *Miradas de Mujer,* and the editor of *The Devil Never Sleeps and other Films by Lourdes Portillo.*

Inderpal Grewal is Professor of Women Studies at San Francisco State University. She is the author of *Home and Harem: Nation, Gender, Empire, and the Cultures of Travel* (also published by Duke, 1996) and coeditor (with Caren Kaplan) of *Scattered Hegemonies: Postmodernity and Transnational Feminist Practices* (1994). She is working on a book entitled *Transnational America: South Asians, Immigration, and Diaspora* (forthcoming from Duke) and on a textbook (with Caren Kaplan) to serve as an introduction to international women's studies.

Saidiya Hartman is Associate Professor of English at the University of California at Berkeley. She is the author of *Scenes of Subjection: Terror, Slavery, and Self-Making in Nineteenth Century America* (1997).

Ester Hernández is a San Francisco visual artist whose work in printmaking and pastels depicts the dignity, strength, experience, and dreams of Latina women.

Suad Joseph is Professor of Anthropology and Women's Studies, University of California at Davis. Her research focuses on her native Lebanon on questions of family systems, community/state, gender, and constructions of self and personhood. Her edited book, *Intimate Selving: Self, Gender and Identity Among Arab Families* is in press (Syracuse University Press). She is currently editing a book on *Gender and Citizenship in the Middle East.*

Danielle Juteau is Professor of Sociology at the Université de Montréal where she holds a Chair in Ethnic Relations. She is coauthor of two books on nuns as women and workers, and author of articles on ethnic social relations, including "Theorising Ethnicity and Ethnic Communalisations at the Margins: From Quebec to the World System" which appeared in *Nations and Nationalisms* (1996).

Caren Kaplan is Associate Professor in the Department of Women's Studies at the University of California at Berkeley. She is coeditor (with Inderpal Grewal) of *Scattered Hegemonies: Postmodernity and Transnational Feminist Practices* (1994) and the author of *Questions of Travel: Postmodern Discourses of Displacement* (also published by Duke, 1996).

Dorinne Kondo is Professor of Anthropology and American Studies and Ethnicity and Director of Asian American Studies at the University of Southern California. She is the author of *Crafting Selves: Power, Gender, and Discourses of Identity In a Japanese Workingplace* (1990), and *About Face: Performing Race in Fashion and Theater* (1997).

Mary N. Layoun is Professor in the Department of Comparative Literature at the University of Wisconsin at Madison. She has recently completed "Boundary Fixation? National Cultures in Crisis" and is currently working on "Occupying the National Family," a book manuscript on gendered citizenship in the early postwar period in Japan and the United States.

Yolanda M. Lopez is a visual artist interested in how images impact consciousness and consensus. Many of her works explore media images. She lives and works in San Francisco with her teenage son.

Minoo Moallem is Assistant Professor of Women's Studies at San Francisco State University. She teaches and writes on the intersection of race, gender, class, religion, and culture in the context of transnational migrations, globalization, citizenship, and fundamentalism. She is currently working on a book manuscript titled "Between Warrior Brother and Veiled Sister: Islamic Fundamentalism and the Cultural Politics of Patriarchy."

Emma Pérez is Associate Professor of History at the University of Texas at El Paso. She is author of the novel *Gulf Dreams* (1996) and a historical monograph *The Decolonial Imaginary: Writing Chicanas into History* (1999).

Laura Elisa Pérez is Assistant Professor in the departments of Ethnic Studies and Spanish and Portuguese at the University of California at Berkeley. She has published essays in the collection *Race, Identity, and Representation* as well as in the *Canadian Review of Comparative Literature, Paragraph, Revista de Critica Literaria Latinoamericana*, and *Modern Fiction Studies*, where her most recent article, "Spirit Glyphs: Reimagining Art and Artist in the Work of Chicana *Tlamatinime*," appears. She is now working on a book on alternative art and spiritual practices in the work of contemporary Chicana and Latin(a)merican women.

Elspeth Probyn is Associate Professor of Gender Studies at the University of Sydney. Her latest book is *Outside Belongings* (1996).

Daiva K. Stasiulis is Professor of Sociology at Carleton University, where she has taught since 1983. She has published extensively on racism, immigration, citizenship, and feminist debates on racialized and ethnic difference. She is the coeditor of *Not One of the Family: Foreign Domestic Workers in Canada* and *Unsettling Settler Societies: Articulations of Gender, Race, Ethnicity and Class*. Her most recent research examines the sexualization of children in film and other popular culture.

Library of Congress Cataloging-in-Publication Data
Between woman and nation : nationalisms, transnational feminisms,
and the state / edited by Caren Kaplan, Norma Alarcón, and Minoo Moallem.
p.   cm.
Includes bibliographical references and index.
ISBN 0-8223-2302-8 (cloth : alk. paper).
ISBN 0-8223-2322-2 (pbk. : alk. paper)
1. Women—Government policy.   2. Feminism.   3. Sex role.   I. Kaplan, Caren,
1955– .   II. Alarcón, Norma.   III. Moallem, Minoo.
HQ1236.B45   1999   305.4—dc21   98-32018CIP